Birdwatching In Britain
A SITE BY SITE GUIDE

Nigel Redman and Simon Harrap

CHRISTOPHER HELM
London

Dedicated to the memory of my father for enthusiastically encouraging my interest in birds. — NR

© 1987 Nigel Redman and Simon Harrap
Christopher Helm (Publishers) Ltd, Imperial House,
21–25 North Street, Bromley, Kent BR1 1SD

Maps by Robert Thorn
Line drawings by Craig Robson

Redman, Nigel
    Birdwatching in Britain.
    1. Bird watching — Great Britain
    I. Title II. Harrap, Simon
    598'.07'23441   QL677.5
ISBN 0–7470–2800–1

Typeset by Opus, Oxford
Printed and bound in Great Britain by Butler & Tanner Ltd, Frome

Contents

Acknowledgements

It is impossible for two people to have a comprehensive and up-to-date knowledge of a large number of birdwatching sites throughout Britain. In compiling this book we have drawn widely on the available literature, from national and regional guides to county bird reports and information leaflets produced for individual reserves. Major sources are listed in the bibliography (p.371) or at the end of the relevant site accounts.

In addition, a great number of people have provided specific information or have read and commented on sections of the draft: E. J. Abraham, Ian Andrews, Mark Andrews, Tim Appleton, Tony Baker, Mark Beaman, Dr Graham Bell, John Belsey, Dave Britton, Alan Brown, Bob Bullock, Dick Burness, Paul M. Burnham, Ewen J. F. Cameron, David Carstairs, Graham Catley, Tony Clarke, Tim Clifford, Mark Cocker, Tim Collins, Martin J. H. Cook, Simon Cox, Peter Cunningham, Martin Curry, Alan Davies, John Davis, J. J. Day, Alan Dean, Tim Dean, John Dickinson, Douglas Dickson, Mrs Rita Dunnett, Dr M. Elliott, Pete Ellis, Richard Fairbank, Dick Filby, Tom Francis, Ron Freethy, Steve Gantlett, John C. Gittins, Bob Gomes, Andy Goodwin, Peter R. Gordon, H. E. Grenfell, Richard Grimmett, Jean-Claude Harris, David Hawker, Chris Heard, Clive Hurford, Steve James, J. Jewell, J. Laughton Johnston, Bill Low, Steve Madge, A. R. Mainwood, Sinclair A. M. Manson, Pete Marsh, John Martin, Rod Martins, Eric Meek, Steve Moon, B. Moore, Derek Moore, W. Morton, Dr M. A. Ogilvie, Alan Parker, Brian Pawson, S. Phillips, Tony Pickup, Dave Pitman, Richard Porter, Nick Riddiford, Iain Robertson, Steve Rooke, Malcolm Rush, John Ryan, David Saunders, Richard Schofield, W. Simpson, B. R. Spence, Ray Turley, Keith Turner, Chris Tyas, Cliff Waller, Steve Whitehouse, John Wilson, James Wolstencroft, Kevin F. Woodbridge, Bernard Zonfrillo. We thank them all and apologise for any unintended omissions.

The following organisations have also given us welcome assistance: Bardsey Bird and Field Observatory, Cheshire Conservation Trust, Cleveland Nature Conservation Trust, Cumbria Trust for Nature Conservation, Deeside Naturalists Society, Dungeness Bird Observatory, East Lothian District Council, Fair Isle Bird Observatory Trust, Greenland White-fronted Goose Study, Isle of May Bird Observatory and Field Station, Lincolnshire and South Humberside Trust for Nature Conservation, Metropolitan Borough of Wirral, National Trust, National Trust for Scotland, Nature Conservancy Council, Portland Bird Observatory and Field Centre, Royal Society for the Protection of Birds, Sandwich Bay Bird Observatory Trust, Scottish Wildlife Trust, West Wales Trust for Nature Conservation, The Wildfowl Trust, Worcestershire Nature Conservation Trust, Yorkshire Wildlife Trust. Weather maps are reproduced with permission of the Controller of Her Majesty's Stationery Office.

We are also very grateful to Richard Porter and Graham Elliott of the RSPB for reading the manuscript, making comments, and satisfying us that the information on rarer breeding birds would not threaten any species or site.

We particularly wish to thank Craig Robson for his stylish line drawings, Robert Thorn for the maps, and Jenny Bates for cheerfully typing a large portion of the manuscript. A special debt of gratitude is extended to Mark Beaman who originally conceived the idea and without whom this book would not have been written. He also provided particular assistance with the Scottish sites. Duncan Brooks expertly exercised his considerable editorial skills on the entire text and we thank him for this. Finally we wish to thank the staff at Christopher Helm Ltd, and especially Jo Hemmings, Melanie Crook, and Ann Doolan for their tolerance and help throughout the preparation of this book.

Where does the birdwatcher go to watch birds? For most, the place to start is close to home — the garden, local park, or nearest area of countryside. Birds can and do occur everwhere, and you can watch them anywhere. Indeed, this is one of birdwatching's great attractions. Many birdwatchers have a 'local patch' that even after many years is still the place they go to most, its attraction being that it is convenient and can be visited and enjoyed whenever there are a few hours to spare. If you are not sure where to go locally, contact (and join) your local bird club or RSPB members' group, who will have many suggestions.

A guide to all the places where you could go birdwatching in Britain would run into several volumes — there are nearly as many as there are birdwatchers. However, except for the fortunate few, the birds that can be seen regularly on one local patch are similar to those on many others. You would not travel hundreds of miles, or plan a holiday, to visit an area where you would see the same birds that occur close to home. The assumption behind *Birdwatching in Britain* is that you would travel to see a particular species, or range of species, which you cannot see locally. With that in mind, we have chosen the very best sites or areas (described in the Site Accounts, pp. 17–326), on the following basis:

1. Does the area provide good birdwatching, whether for a few hours or several days?
2. Can you see some of the more localised and uncommon species? A few sites have been included which have just one or two of these, but most will have a range of interesting birds, be they regional specialities, important concentrations at certain seasons, or passage migrants.
3. Accessibility. Is it possible to visit the area without making special arrangements? For some this can take weeks, and rules out a casual trip. We have made an exception in the case of offshore islands, which usually require advance planning, because their attractions often easily outweigh any inconvenience.

Our choices have been made irrespective of scenic considerations or the possibility of good walking, and there is inevitably a bias towards coastal areas. Most birdwatchers live inland, and the coast offers the most interesting variety of habitats and birds, as well as being the best area to see migrants. There is also a bias towards certain regions, for example East Anglia. This is, quite simply, because they are so good. We have not tried to give equal weight to each region or county, and if any part of the country has few sites with the necessary qualifications, then there are few entries in this book. This does not mean that there are no good places for birds, but that they may be inaccessible to the casual visitor or of a local, rather than national, interest. In the end, however, the final selection has been a personal one, based on our own experience.

A danger of a guide to 'good' places for birdwatching is that all the birdwatchers cram into a few areas. To an extent, this has already happened. The better-known sites already attract many people, and in October hordes of birdwatchers go the the Isles of Scilly, leaving the east coast deserted. However, many of the other sites we have detailed are also excellent, yet attract few people. There is still plenty of scope for you to try somewhere that is both new and exciting.

In the second major section of the book (the Species List, pp. 327–61) we deal with the 283 species of bird which occur regularly in Britain. Brief details of status, distribution, and habitat are given, sufficient to give a clear picture of whether or not you could see the bird locally, and if not, where to go to find it. For the more localised species, an indication is given of which sites they can be seen at and, if appropriate, how to go about finding them once you get there.

Timing is often an important consideration, and as an introduction to this, the Calendar (pp. 7–15) gives a month-by-month outline of the avian world, as well as ideas on where to go and what to look for at any particular time.

To use this book, you have a choice of two approaches. If you are interested in birdwatching in a particular region or area, you can refer to the endpaper maps or list of sites in the Contents and select the relevant entry. Reference to the detailed site account should provide all the information you need for a successful visit. If, on the other hand, you are interested in a particular uncommon, local, or difficult-to-see species, you can refer to the Species List, which will be your guide to how, when, and where to find it. All in all, *Birdwatching in Britain* is intended to provide an efficient guide for today's mobile birdwatcher who wants to visit Britain's best birding areas. This is a book for every birdwatcher, but primarily those not in the comparatively small circle 'in the know' about all those special places for birds.

Site Accounts

115 sites or groups of sites are arranged in seven regions for convenience and described in detail. A further 88 are treated more briefly. Sites show considerable variation and defy precise definition: while most are distinct units, others are conglomerates of several adjacent areas. These may be two or three spots which, on their own, would not merit an entry, but which when combined provide a convenient and varied range of habitats within a discrete area. In other cases, several areas have been combined in a single site because they are ornithologically very similar. Such 'super-sites' include vast tracts of land with ill-defined boundaries, such as the Cairngorms or Sutherland, as well as groups of islands. The total number of localities treated is thus actually close to 400. The accounts themselves vary in length and to some extent format, depending on the amount of information considered necessary to enable you to get the best value out of a visit. Each is usually arranged as follows:

The *name* of the site is followed by the county (or counties) in which it is situated, using the post-1974 boundaries.

An *introductory paragraph* gives the general location, main ornithological interest, and the most profitable period(s) for a visit. The existence of reserves is also indicated, together with their extent.

The *Habitat* section briefly outlines the habitats represented and the general lay-out of the area.

The *Access* section is particulary important. For those sites where the use of the text in conjunction with any of the standard road atlases is sufficient, no map is provided (we recommend the *Ordnance Survey Motoring Atlas of Great Britain*). For the majority however, a specially drawn map accompanies the text to illustrate the features described. The exceptions are very large sites, such as the Cairngorms and Speyside, Sutherland, and the New Forest, where access away from roads and main tracks in such extensive and complicated areas is impossible for us to depict adequately. Reference to larger-scale Ordnance Survey maps is recommended in these cases.

At the beginning of the section is the relevant OS 1:50,000 Landranger sheet number(s). Directions from the nearest town or main road are given to the point(s) where you park and exploration on foot begins. (Distances and other measurements are in imperial units to conform with current road signs and atlases.) Take care to park in designated areas wherever possible, and if there are none use common sense and do not obstruct farm gates or private roads. From here, details of the best trails, vantage points, and hides are given, together with brief notes on any specialities. Any restrictions on access and permit arrangements are also specified. Prices have generally been included and refer to adults, although many reserves allow concessions to children and OAPs. Most are correct for 1986.

Visiting arrangements for reserves vary a great deal and are subject to frequent changes. We have specified the most vital information but a few points apply to most reserves and have not been constantly repeated. You should assume that all reserves are closed on Christmas and Boxing Days, and that dogs are not allowed onto any reserve. Larger groups are normally required to make special arrangements with the warden prior to a visit. Where members of various organisations are allowed free entry or reductions on permit prices, they should expect to produce their membership card (if issued). Remember also that information/visitor centres often have more restricted times of opening than the reserve itself. As a number of the sites are RSPB reserves it is worth noting that an annual summary of access arrangements is issued free to members.

For offshore islands, brief details of ferries and flights are given. Accommodation is outside the scope of this book (though fuller information is provided for bird observatories), but its availability on islands is indicated. Full details can be obtained from the relevant tourist office.

Birding may take you into unfamiliar situations where there is an element of risk for the inexperienced. We hardly need to point out the dangers presented by cliffs, but saltmarshes and tidal flats are also potentially lethal. In some places the tide can advance extremely quickly and unless you have expert local knowledge it is best to leave these well before high water or to avoid them altogether.

In the *Birds* section, we have tried to highlight the more interesting species you may see, as well as mentioning some of the commoner ones; very common species are generally omitted. It should be stressed that you will not see all the birds on a single visit or even after several. At migration sites particularly, many days can be quite birdless if the weather conditions are wrong, and good 'falls' should be regarded as unusual. Scarce migrants are frequently specified where their occurrence is reasonably regular, although some may only be recorded once or twice a year, but as a rule rarities have only been mentioned if they have occurred in a more-or-less predictable pattern. This section has been roughly divided into seasons, but the treatment has been kept flexible. Rather than give a bald list of species which may be found, we have attempted to provide more detail which will assist in locating particular birds, such as an indication of a species' abundance, as well as any specific locations within the site and, in some cases, tactics helpful in tracking down the bird. Where relevant, general weather considerations are also mentioned.

Many of the accounts include a section entitled *Other Sites in the Area*. Here, other places in the general area which may be usefully combined with a visit to the main site are treated more briefly. In most cases, a site in this category would not normally justify a specific visit (unless it was being worked as a local patch).

The final section of the site accounts is *Information*. For reserves, the address of the warden is given but names have been omitted because they are subject to frequent changes. In many instances telephone numbers have also been included, but we stress that these should not be abused. Do have consideration for the warden and always write if possible. Sources of further information or permits may also be quoted. (However, with the exception of reservoirs, most permits are nowadays available on site.) Books or checklists devoted entirely to the site are mentioned but county avifaunas and local bird reports, both essential sources for anyone particularly interested in an area, are not. Finally, because many bird reports still use the pre-1974 boundaries for their recording areas, the recorder to whom records should be sent is specified. A list of the relevant recorders' names and addresses appears in Appendix A (pp. 362–5). We urge everyone to send details of their observations to the appropriate recorder, because many interesting and valuable records are otherwise lost to posterity.

Species List

A list of all regular breeding species, winter visitors, and migrants follows the site accounts. This is designed to give you a rapid means of finding out which areas or individual sites are good for a particular species, and any other relevant information which will enable you to find the bird. Each species account includes a concise statement of the bird's British status, range, and pattern of occurrence and its preferred habitat. In some cases, an indication of the size of the British population will be given. The majority of British birds are reasonably common within their ranges at the appropriate time of year, and for these the accounts are generally brief. For scarcer species, a number of sites may be listed by number or a general comment given. This list is not intended to be comprehensive and does not act as an index to each mention of the bird in the site accounts. Its purpose is to detail a few places where there is a real chance of finding that particular species. However, some are scarce migrants for which there are no guaranteed sites, and which may elude even the most ardent birder for years. Others are rare breeding birds for which no sites can be given.

Many of the most sought-after species are rare breeders in Britain (e.g. Honey Buzzard, Golden Oriole). Naturally, many people would like to know where to go to see these, but publication could result in increased disturbance to the birds or their habitat by well-meaning birdwatchers (or other, less well-meaning people). Information is often passed on only by word of mouth, but the number of interested people is now so great that even a supposedly secret pair of Montagu's Harriers recently attracted 3,000 people in a single season. It is obviously necessary to give careful thought to the question before any site is published, and we have been guided by the following principles:

Rare Breeding Birds

1. Necessity. A bird may be a rare breeder, but easy enough to see at other times of the year (e.g. Brambling).
2. Practicality. Many breeding records are just one-offs, the birds occupying an area for only a year or two. Publication of any current site is therefore pointless (e.g. Montagu's Harrier).
3. Is the information already widely published? We have felt free to mention any birds that are already included in books, leaflets, and other publicity material that is widely distributed.
4. Access. Is it possible to see the birds from a public right of way?
5. Vulnerability. Can the birds be seen, possibly by large numbers of people, without disturbing them or their habitat? Is the site wardened, so that visitors can be adequately controlled?

After considering these issues we are left with a surprisingly small number of candidates for disclosure. We have rejected some — for example, Golden Oriole: although widely known, access to the main breeding site is difficult without trespassing, and the birds are vulnerable to disturbance. Others we have accepted, and these will be found in the site accounts. In the case of any particularly delicate species we have consulted the opinions of the relevant conservation body before deciding to go ahead. There will always be some people who believe that any information is too much information, and that all rare breeding birds should be kept totally secret, but we believe that the ordinary birdwatcher's desire to see them is perfectly legitimate, and that there has to be a good reason not to reveal them. Our attitude involves a small element of risk to the birds, but in our opinion this is outweighed by the benefits greater public awareness and interest bring. The onus is on you, the bird-watcher, to behave responsibly. The basic ground-rules are found in *The Code of Conduct for Birdwatchers* (Appendix D, pp. 369–70) but additional suggestions are that you carefully consider whether you really need to visit the site at all, and, if so, that you should avoid multiple visits. The full list of specially protected rare breeding species is found in Appendix C (p. 368).

Twitching, that is travelling to a specific spot to see a specific rare bird in order to add it to your life-list, is now widely accepted as an enjoyable and legitimate part of birdwatching. Many rarities have received media coverage, even meriting a spot on the Nine O'Clock News, and this has helped to project the idea that all birdwatchers are twitchers, or that twitching is the major part of birdwatching. *Birdwatching in Britain* is not, however, a twitch-

Rarities

er's manual. Most rarities only stay a few days and many are found on local patches which, after their brief moment of glory, return to their former status. It is usually not possible to identify sites for specific rarities, though certain areas regularly attract rare birds in general, and indeed most of the sites in this book have recorded at least one or two. We have not listed rarities that have turned up in the past, or, in most cases, mentioned that rarities have occurred at all; for most sites that should be obvious. Some site accounts are, however, much more rarity-orientated than others. No birdwatcher visiting Fair Isle or Scilly could claim not to be interested in seeing them.

At most sites, the chances of your visit accidentally coinciding with a rare bird are slim, and unless rarities are specifically twitched you will see few. The usual source of information for a twitch is the 'grapevine', an informal network of telephone contacts largely based on personal acquaintances, and so the only way to hear about many rarities is to go out birdwatching and make friends. Some information is available publicly (see Ceefax, BBC 2, page 262, updated every Friday evening), but should you become a twitcher, it is best to remember from the outset that it is regular local birdwatching that is likely to provide the most solid foundation for a lifetime's enjoyment, and that rare birds are only the icing on a very rich cake.

While every effort has been made to make the site accounts as accurate and up-to-date as possible, there will inevitably be errors. We would welcome any corrections or extra information for incorporation in further editions of the book. Please write to the authors c/o Christopher Helm Ltd.

The ornithologist's seasons differ significantly from those of non-birdwatchers. An example is the autumn wader passage, which begins in July (or even mid-June in some cases) at a time when many people are preparing to go on their summer holidays. Even so, the seasons in the avian world still cannot be easily defined; both the spring and autumn migrations extend for several months and breeding seasons vary considerably. Crossbills may nest in January, Marsh Warblers in June, and Rock Doves the whole year round. While most species have regular patterns of occurrence, precise timings are often determined by the weather and geographical location.

The key to finding birds is knowing where and when to look. In this section, we give a brief summary to the ornithological year, together with some ideas on good areas or specific sites to visit. Many species are most easily found at certain times, and this is also highlighted.

By the turn of the year all the winter visitors have arrived and settled in. Although this can be a quiet time of year with little movement, there is plenty to see for those willing to brave the elements. Perhaps more than at any other season, the weather determines the fortunes of British birds. Is it going to be a normal, severe, or mild winter?

January

The most productive birdwatching in January is generally to be found at reservoirs, gravel pits, and the coast. On inland waters Mute Swan, Canada Goose, Wigeon, Teal, Pochard, and Tufted Duck are all widespread and standard fare. Inland, there are few waders apart from Golden Plover, Lapwing, and Snipe, but on the coast there will be a good variety, especially on estuaries. Oystercatcher, Ringed Plover, Grey Plover (except parts of Scotland), Dunlin, Knot, Bar-tailed Godwit, Curlew, Redshank, and Turnstone are all widespread. Small numbers of Spotted Redshank, Greenshank, and Common Sandpiper, usually thought of only as migrants, winter in the south and west. Coastal habitats also offer a variety of divers, grebes, wildfowl, and raptors. On saltmarshes Twite and Snow Bunting are quite widespread (the latter also on dunes), especially on the east coast. Much more locally there are small numbers of Shore Lark and Lapland Bunting. Communal roosts are a feature of winter. Hen Harriers use reedbeds and heathland, often the same sites for many years, and are occasionally joined by Merlins. Reservoirs and estuaries often have large gull roosts, the latter also spectacular numbers of waders. Various passerines — wagtails, thrushes, Starlings, finches, and buntings — use thickets or reedbeds, and attract hunting raptors, especially Sparrowhawks.

The onset of hard weather usually marks a rapid change of pace. Freezing conditions, especially with overnight snow, may prompt localised *hard-weather movements*. Lapwing, Golden Plover, Skylark, Meadow Pipit, thrushes, Starling, finches, and buntings are typical species to respond to ground frost by moving south and west. A prolonged freeze, either here or on the

7

continent (especially the Baltic and Low Countries) will produce a more widespread displacement, the spectrum of birds involved depending on the areas affected. Coastal species — divers, the rarer grebes, and seaduck — may occur on inland waters and, when these freeze, on rivers. Various species of geese and Smew are often more widespread and in greater numbers in these conditions. There is also a distinct chance of something more unusual — Bean Geese or perhaps a Lapland Bunting caught up with a flock of Skylarks. If the hard weather lasts, it can spell disaster for some resident birds, including Kingfisher, Wren, Stonechat, Cetti's and Dartford Warblers, Goldcrest, and Long-tailed Tit. These suffer because they do not move to warmer climes. Fieldfares and Redwings regularly seek food in urban gardens, and in exceptionally severe weather Bitterns will be forced out of their reedbeds and may be found in more open situations. By contrast, in mild winters, wildfowl numbers may be well below normal, and individuals of several species of summer migrant may winter.

Many birdwatchers like to start the year with a *big day list*, and with effort and good planning it is possible to tally 100 species in some areas. The North Norfolk coast offers one of the best opportunities for a big total. Throughout the month, in addition to the numerous reservoirs, estuaries, and other coastal localities, the following are worth a visit: Buckenham (for regular Bean Geese: p. 121), Slimbridge (for wild geese and swans: p. 172), and Tregaron (for Red Kites: p. 188). A weekend in the south-west is also recommended, offering a wide variety of coastal birds, several species of raptor, and a good chance of the rarer gulls. Small numbers of wintering Black Redstart, Blackcap, Chiffchaff, and Firecrest can also be found.

February

February is similar to January, the main interest being wintering birds. This is a good month to check gull flocks, at roosts, rubbish tips, and fishing harbours, for less common species such as Glaucous and Iceland Gulls. Already some resident birds are thinking about breeding: Long-eared and Tawny Owls are very vocal in February while crossbills may actually be nesting. Some seabirds start returning to their colonies, although breeding will not commence until April. Any of the sites mentioned for January are equally rewarding in February. Additionally, try the Solway Firth (for wildfowl and raptors: p. 323), the Ouse Washes (for peak numbers of wild swans: p. 146), and Walberswick (for raptors, etc: p. 115).

March

Generally an unspectacular month. A number of resident species are busy establishing territories and many winter visitors begin to slip away — there may be movements of diurnal migrants such as Lapwing, Starling, and various finches heading back to their continental breeding grounds from wintering areas in Britain and Ireland. By mid-month summer migrants begin to arrive in small numbers. Sandwich Tern, Sand Martin, Wheatear, Ring Ouzel, and Chiffchaff are always amongst the first, and several scarcer species are also early migrants, including Garganey, Black Redstart, and Firecrest, and Stone Curlews are often back on their breeding grounds by the end of the month. The Scandinavian race of Rock Pipit occurs on passage in small numbers and some will have assumed summer plumage, assisting in identification. This is a good time of year to see the common resident woodland species, many of which have begun to sing. Scarcer species to look for include small, unobtrusive flocks of Hawfinches, especially in hornbeams, and optimists can try for Goshawks, which when displaying are more prominent than usual. March is the peak month for Ring-billed Gulls, and also a good time to look for Cetti's Warbler, thus a visit to Blackpill (p. 177) or Radipole (p. 56) could be fruitful.

April

The departure of winter visitors is an inconspicuous affair — they just seem to disappear. There is, however, often a notable passage of Jack Snipe, and it is worth looking for them in locations which have not held wintering birds. In contrast, the arrival in strength of summer visitors is dramatic, but cold weather, especially north or north-east winds, may delay mass arrivals, and the recent run of late springs, often featuring snowfalls in late April or early May, means that birdwatchers (and birds) may have a thin time. Normally south coast localities are the most productive, especially for early migrants — the east coast and East Anglia can still be struggling in April. A feature of spring migration is that birds may overshoot their normal breeding areas and be found well to the north. This is especially likely in clear, anticyclonic conditions, and a typical example is Hoopoe, for which April is the peak month. Naturally, birds which have overshot are most frequent on the south coast, but they occur as far north as Shetland. Apart from the pioneers, most migrants overfly the south coast (unless they run into bad weather) and big arrivals may be prominent inland. At any inland locality, passerine migration can be notable; species like Tree Pipit, White Wagtail, and Wheatear are widespead. In the north, the numbers of seaduck reach a peak, especially Long-tailed Duck, and can be seen to advantage at Golspie (p. 277) or Spey Bay (p. 273). Ospreys will have arrived and it is a good time for lekking Black Grouse, crossbills, and most other specialities, though Dotterel will not yet be in.

May

A dynamic month. Other than a few stragglers, wintering birds will have gone and the arrival of summer visitors continues in force, with most having reached us by the end of the month. Late migrants, such as Swifts and Spotted Flycatchers, are rarely seen before May. As usual, coastal sites are likely to provide the most interest.

East or south-east winds and even foul weather are welcomed by birdwatchers because they increase the chances of some of the scarcer migrants. Birds destined for continental, especially Fenno-Scandian, breeding grounds may be disorientated by cloud and rain and then drifted to Britain by easterly winds. This may produce large falls on the east coast, and there was a notable example of this, a huge fall of Bluethroats, in May 1985. Red-backed Shrike, Ortolan Bunting, and Scarlet Rosefinch are other scarce migrants which may be caught up in these movements.

The eastern fringe of Britain lies just on the edge of some migrants' normal route, particularly several species of wader. In these conditions East Anglia comes into its own. Small numbers of Kentish Plover and Temminck's Stint are annual in May (and in fact traditional at Cley). There is also a chance of rarities, notably Broad-billed Sandpiper. Dotterel (headed for Scotland?) have traditional stop-over sites in otherwise barren prairie-like fields in the early part of the month and Whimbrel are widespread and conspicuous migrants on all coasts. In north-west England, particularly Morecambe Bay, there is a marked passage of Ringed Plover, Dunlin, and Sanderling, usually peaking 10–20 May, and on the south coast in late April and early May there is a strong passage of Bar-tailed Godwits. Inland waters can also be interesting: there is a small but regular passage of Sanderlings and Turnstones, and sometimes marked movements of Arctic Terns. Throughout the country, spring passage can produce a good diversity of waders, but they usually only stay for short periods, and occur in much smaller numbers than the autumn. Most of the spring passage of Black Terns is concentrated into May, and another notable feature is the small but regular passage of Pomarine Skuas along the south coast, especially conspicuous at Dungeness (p. 86). Most are seen in the first two weeks of the month, and this species can also be found off the Uists (p. 310), sometimes together with large numbers of Long-tailed Skuas. Scilly (p. 17) is well worth trying in May, offering a good chance of a migrant Golden Oriole or something rarer, as well as breeding seabirds. Fair Isle too (p. 290) can be exciting, especially later in the month. There may be relatively large numbers of Marsh and Icterine Warblers and Red-backed Shrikes, and Thrush Nightingale is something of a speciality at this time.

June

In June, though there is little migration, there is a distinct possibility of an outstanding rarity in the early part of the month. Most birds are now breeding and flocks of tame juvenile Starlings are notable in urban areas. It is a good time to visit a seabird colony, preferably a large one, which can be an unforgettable experience. Species to look for in the early part of the month are Marsh Warbler and Honey Buzzard. The New Forest (p. 69) is one of the sites for the latter and most of its other specialities can be found at this time. Quail arrive in variable numbers, and are usually found calling from cereal fields, but are always devilishly hard to see. Trips to the Scottish Highlands will be well rewarded, and the Western and Northern Isles are excellent places for a short holiday. Mid-June marks the beginning of autumn with the return of the first Green Sandpipers.

July

Generally quiet. Breeding birds have largely stopped singing and can be difficult to locate, although some species rearing their second or third broods may sing again briefly. Nightjar and Grasshopper Warbler are two species which regularly sing in July. Things are not helped by the abundance of recently fledged juveniles which make a bewildering variety of noises. Many seabirds begin to leave their cliffs, ducks moult into eclipse plumage, and there are large congregations of moulting Lapwings. The autumn wader passage started in a small way in June, and now begins to gather strength. The first to return south are immatures, non-breeding and failed adults, and females which may have left their mates still tending unfledged young. Often still in partial breeding dress, Curlew Sandpiper and Spotted Redshank are particularly notable. Males follow a few weeks later and by the end of the month over 20 species may be present at prime wetland sites, especially in East Anglia. If there is going to be a Crossbill invasion, it usually begins in July. There are also occasional influxes of Cory's Shearwaters into the south-west later in the month, and one rarity for which July is *the* month is Caspian Tern.

August

Seawatching can be profitable, especially on the east and south-west coasts. Arctic Skuas are widespread and at many sites Greats are also regular in small numbers. Pomarine Skuas are scarce and are only at all regular at a handful of east-coast sites, notably Flamborough Head (p. 232), and Long-tailed Skua is rare everywhere. Large movements of Manx Shearwater, Gannet, and Kittiwake may well include numbers of Balearic and, especially towards the end of the month, Sooty Shearwaters.

There are large influxes of waders to Britain's major estuaries, especially Knot, which will stay for two or three months to moult. The Ribble (p. 211), Wash (pp. 140, 153) and Morecambe Bay (p. 215) are especially important. Waders feature at inland localities as well. Ringed and Little Ringed Plovers, Dunlin, Ruff, Green-shank, Redshank, and Green and Common Sandpipers are standard, and on the coast Whimbrel and Spotted Redshank are also both regular at many sites, but Wood Sandpiper is usually scarce everywhere, even on the east coast. Around the last week of August the first juveniles appear, fresh from their Arctic breeding grounds, and are often tame. A variety of terns begin to move, often congregating off estuary mouths, for example the Dee (p. 205) or the Tees (p. 237). Common and Sandwich are the most numerous, but Little, Arctic, and Black are also widespread. These congregations attract Arctic Skuas and, in the north, Greats too. It is a good time to look for vagrant White-winged Black Tern, Chew (p. 52) and Dungeness (p. 86) being particularly regular localities.

Passerine migration also gets underway in August, both for day and night migrants. Intially a trickle, by the end of the month it may be a flood. Willow Warblers are particularly prominent, and other typical species are Redstart, Whinchat, Wheatear, Garden Warbler, and Pied Flycatcher. The right conditions may produce a substantial 'fall' of migrants — the sudden arrival of large numbers. High pressure and clear weather over Scandinavia will encourage birds to start out on their southward journey and if they meet bad weather and easterly winds further south, this can disorientate and drift them westwards towards Britain. August Bank Holiday is a traditional time to visit the east coast. Small falls of commoner migrants may include scarcer species such as Wryneck, Bluethroat, Icterine and Barred Warblers, Red-backed Shrike, and Ortolan Bunting. South coast localities also receive their fair share of good birds, and one of late August's specialities is the elusive Aquatic Warbler.

September

September is the key month for migration and there is usually plenty to see almost anywhere. It is the best month for seawatching, on both the east coast (north-west to north-east winds) and in the south-west — if there are strong north-west winds, St Ives (p. 29) is the place to be. Sabine's Gull and Leach's Petrel are specialities, and the latter is sometimes also found in

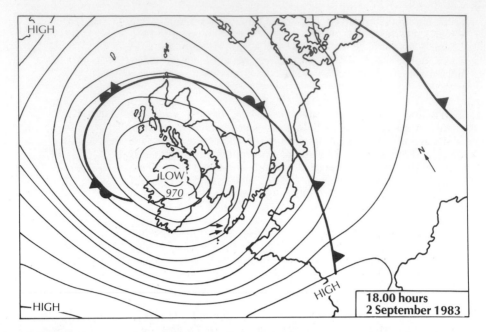

18.00 hours
2 September 1983

2 September 1983 (map Crown copyright)

3 September 1983 produced the best seawatching ever at St Ives (and other stations in the south-west). Highlights included Cory's Shearwater (1), Great Shearwater (50), Wilson's Petrel (1), Storm Petrel (10,000), Leach's Petrel (10), Pomarine Skua (20), Long-tailed Skua (2), and Sabine's Gull (100). This chart, for 18.00 the previous day, shows the classic condition of a severe NW gale affecting SW England, and the sight of this on the Six O'Clock News would send keen seawatchers speeding SW for dawn the next day.

large numbers off the Wirral (p. 205) and at other sites in north-west England after north-west gales.

Passage waders are still very much in evidence. Ruff, Spotted Redshank, and Greenshank peak, and variable numbers of Little Stint and Curlew Sandpiper appear both on the east coast and inland, their numbers falling off as you move west. American waders are annual in small numbers, especially in the south-west. Pectoral and Buff-breasted Sandpipers are the most frequent.

Passerines are prominent and the chances of big falls on the east coast are good in the right weather conditions. The commoner species such as Wheatear, Whinchat, and Redstart can also be seen inland, but it is on the coast that there is a real chance of scarcer migrants. As well as those listed under August, Tawny Pipit and Melodious Warbler are specialities on the south coast. Another species to look for is Hobby: migrants are widespread in southern England but sightings are unpredictable; they are, however, often seen chasing hirundines and large autumn roosts of the latter offer the best chance. Bearded Tits are generally more conspicuous now, their numbers swelled by juveniles, and if you are desperate to see a Spotted Crake this is the month to try. The last half of September is the best time to visit Fair Isle (p. 290): Richard's Pipit, Barred and Yellow-browed Warblers, and Scarlet Rosefinch are found annually amongst a host of other migrants, but it is Fair Isle's extraordinary ability to turn up outstanding rarities that is its greatest attraction.

This is *the* month for rarities. As the departure of summer visitors tails off, so the chance of vagrants increases. Weather plays an important part in determining what the flavour of the month is — American or Asiatic, or maybe both. Westerly vectors favour the Americans, while the development of an intense anti-cyclone over Siberia is the classic precursor to the drift of Siberian birds into Europe. The best birdwatching is naturally at coastal migration sites: on the east and south coasts, the Irish Sea observatories, Orkney, Shetland, and, most outstanding of all, Scilly (p. 17). The mass migration of birdwatchers to Scilly in October undoubtedly results in other good localities being underwatched, but the supremacy of these tiny islands is unquestioned. A number of Scilly's regular specialities, such as Richard's Pipit, Yellow-browed Warbler, Firecrest, and Red-breasted Flycatcher can be found elsewhere, but there is nowhere better for vagrant American passerines. Fair Isle (p. 290) should not be forgotten however, and has, on occasion, managed to outshine even Scilly (see weather map below).

October

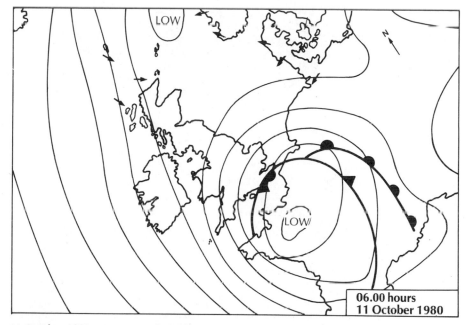

11 October 1980 (map Crown copyright)
A small low over the coast of Scandinavia slowly filled, producing a NE airstream, while other lows to the south gave E–SE winds over the Baltic. Siberian passerines which had previously *moved NW from southern Asia into the Baltic States and Finland were pushed in these conditions onwards to Fair Isle. On 12 October there were three Siberian Stonechats, a Rustic Bunting, and, top of the list, Britain's first Yellow-browed Bunting.*

06.00 hours
11 October 1980

As the month progresses there are likely to be large diurnal passages of migrants such as larks, pipits, and finches. These tend to follow leading lines such as the coast or a river or escarpment, and a carefully chosen spot can, in the first few hours after dawn, produce exciting movements, even inland. There are also sizeable arrivals of wintering wildfowl and waders and there may be massive falls of thrushes, Robins, and Goldcrests on the coast (see weather map overleaf). On the east coast, look out for small influxes of immigrant Woodcock, Long- and Short-eared Owls, and Water Pipit. A few Great Grey Shrikes are usually associated with these movements, as, more irregularly, are Rough-legged Buzzard and Waxwing. Late Chiffchaffs are seen in many places and may winter, and at the end of the month, especially in the south-west, they are joined by numbers of Siberian Chiffchaffs.

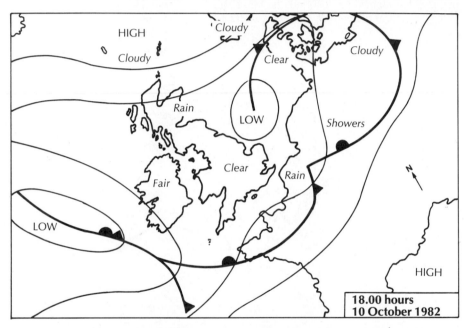

**18.00 hours
10 October 1982**

10 October 1982 (map Crown copyright)
On 10 October, rain and cloud cover over NE England, the North Sea, and southern Baltic created conditions where migrants departing Scandinavia in clear weather were disorientated and drifted westwards by light E–NE winds. Spectacular 'falls' occurred the next day, from Norfolk northwards, especially on the Isle of May, where there were 4,000 Robins, 4,000 Fieldfares and 15,000 Goldcrests. Earlier in the month a sequence of weather patterns had been ideal for drifting Pallas's Warblers from Siberia into Europe, and these now joined the common species. 36 were found on 11 October alone, and the autumn's total of 127 smashed the previous record of 33 in 1981.

November

Very few summer migrants are left at the beginning of November, but late Swallows, House Martins, Black Redstarts, Blackcaps, Chiffchaffs, and Firecrests can be found in sheltered corners, both inland and on the coast. The month is however dominated by the continuing arrival of winter visitors and it is a good time to look for Water Pipits. East Anglia is as good as anywhere at this time: there may be movements of adult Little Gulls offshore and north-east to north-west winds sometimes result in wrecks of Little Auks here and all along the east coast, especially Yorkshire (Spurn, p. 227, or Filey, p. 236). Occasionally there are also Grey Phalaropes with them.

December is relatively quiet. Most of the winter birds will have arrived and settled down although some species continue to build up in numbers until January. Hard-weather movements are unlikely until the end of the month. Smew are typically late in reaching Britain and Iceland Gulls are not usually seen before mid-December. As in January, estuaries and reservoirs provide the best birdwatching — wader numbers will have peaked and usually remain stable until February. Inland, look for Siskins and Redpolls, especially in waterside alders, and for Long-eared Owls, which often form communal roosts and are quite wide-spread.

December

Key to Maps

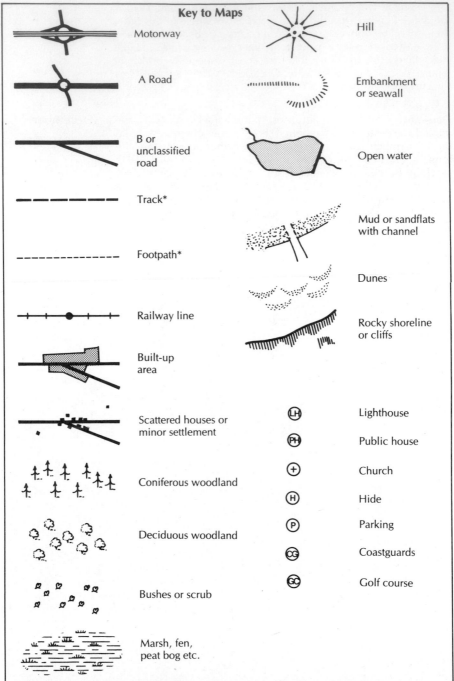

Motorway

A Road

B or unclassified road

Track*

Footpath*

Railway line

Built-up area

Scattered houses or minor settlement

Coniferous woodland

Deciduous woodland

Bushes or scrub

Marsh, fen, peat bog etc.

Hill

Embankment or seawall

Open water

Mud or sandflats with channel

Dunes

Rocky shoreline or cliffs

LH Lighthouse

PH Public house

+ Church

H Hide

P Parking

CG Coastguards

GC Golf course

*Does not necessarily indicate a right of way. While every effort has been made to locate legitimate routes, this has not always been possible to guarantee (notably in Scotland, where they are not marked on OS maps). If in doubt, always ask first. You should also note that paths and tracks within reserves may be restricted to permit holders, or only be available at certain times.

SOUTH-WEST ENGLAND

About 150 islands, of which only the five largest are inhabited, make up the picturesque archipelago of Scilly. The entire group is only 10 miles across and lies 28 miles off Land's End. The geographical position of Scilly ensures a wide variety of migrants in spring and autumn, and many seabirds breed in summer. The best times for migrants are mid-March to May and August–October; breeding seabirds are best seen May–July.

Over the last few years the Isles of Scilly have established themselves as the premier site in Britain for rarities, even overtaking the legendary Fair Isle. Although American species predominate and are now an annual feature, almost anything can and does turn up. October is the key month but late September and early November can also be outstanding. In addition to true vagrants, some of Britain's scarcer migrants, which occur only irregularly on the mainland, can almost be guaranteed on Scilly.

Weather has a major influence and is best described as unpredictable. The conditions bringing vagrants to Scilly are complex and only partially understood. Light southerlies favour falls of migrants in spring. In autumn SW winds prevail, and fast-moving wave depressions originating off America are sometimes responsible for small falls of American landbirds, chiefly late September to late October. American waders are less affected by these depressions and tend to arrive somewhat earlier. SE winds in autumn may bring Asiatic birds but sometimes rarities appear in apparently unsuitable weather conditions. Strong SW–NW winds can be good for seawatching but this pursuit is rarely well rewarded on Scilly.

Scilly is exceedingly popular with holidaymakers during summer but by October they are replaced by legions of birdwatchers. Strangely, the islands are comparatively neglected by birders in spring.

Habitat

The smaller islands tend to be rocky and sparsely vegetated, while the larger ones, particularly those inhabited, have a range of habitats. Around the coast are granite cliffs, rocky shores, and sandy beaches. Exposed areas with poor soil remain as heathland or grassy downs, and on St Mary's the golf course and airfield have created an important habitat. The few freshwater pools and associated marshland with dense clumps of sallows are especially attractive but there is little natural woodland. Cornish elms grow in the more sheltered areas and stands of introduced pines occur in places. The Tresco Abbey Gardens hold a wide variety of exotic trees and shrubs but are not very exciting ornithologically.

Large areas of the inhabited islands are farmed. This includes grazing land, but the dominant industry on Scilly, other than tourism, is flower farming. The tiny bulb fields are surrounded by tall hedges of introduced shrubs to protect them from the winds.

Access
OS Sheet No. 203
OS Outdoor
Leisure Map
1:25,000 OLM 25

Scilly can be reached by air or sea. A British Airways helicopter service operates between Penzance and St Mary's daily except Sundays; the journey takes 20 min and the number of flights per day is considerably reduced November–March. Early booking (through any BA booking office or agent) is essential, especially for October. Penzance Heliport is situated 1 mile E of Penzance beside the A30. Open air car parking is available at the heliport (fee). Fixed-wing air transport is offered by Brymon Airways who operate 8-seat Islanders from Plymouth, Exeter, and Newquay; an aircraft may be chartered at short notice for those urgent twitches to the islands. The Isles of Scilly Steamship Company operates a daily service (except Sundays) between Penzance and St Mary's on the MV *Scillonian*. The crossing takes 2½ hrs and can be very rough, especially in autumn. There is a reduced service in winter and an open car park is available at Penzance (fee). Once on the islands it is easy enough to walk almost anywhere but there are taxis and buses on St Mary's. Inter-island boat trips are mainly operated from St Mary's, usually leaving the quay at 10.00 and 14.15 each day; full details are posted on a blackboard beside the Atlantic Hotel in the main street and on the quay. It is possible to charter boats for trips at other times subject to availability and weather and 'seabird special' cruises are offered regularly. A variety of accommodation is available on all inhabited islands: cottages and flats for hire, guest houses, hotels, and camp sites. However, most birders stay on St Mary's: there is considerably more accommodation, the widest range of evening entertainment, and the best boat services for getting to the other islands. It is advisable to book accommodation as early as possible. Lists and prices are available from the Isles of Scilly Council. A good network of roads, footpaths, and nature trails exists on all main islands enabling access to most areas. Birders should avoid trespassing at all costs and most of the fields can easily be viewed from the edges. The islanders are naturally apprehensive of the hordes of invading birders in October and irresponsible behaviour can cause bad relations. The airport is restricted at all times but can be viewed from the perimeter and the golf course should not be traversed when play is in progress.

St Mary's
(see map)

This is the largest island and contains a wide variety of habitats. In addition to the sites detailed, it is worth checking all sheltered bushes and trees for migrants and the ploughed and grassy fields for larks, pipits, and buntings.

The Garrison A choice of trails leads around this headland. Access is from Hugh Town, up a steep hill past Tregarthen's Hotel. There is a stand of pine trees next to the playing field (camp site nearby) and plenty of sheltered spots for migrant passerines amidst the more open areas. The Lower Walk, accessible via Sally Port, has attractive belts of elms.

Peninnis Head The fields and bushes are well worth checking on the way down. Certain migrant species favour the short turf around the headland and the Head itself is one of the best

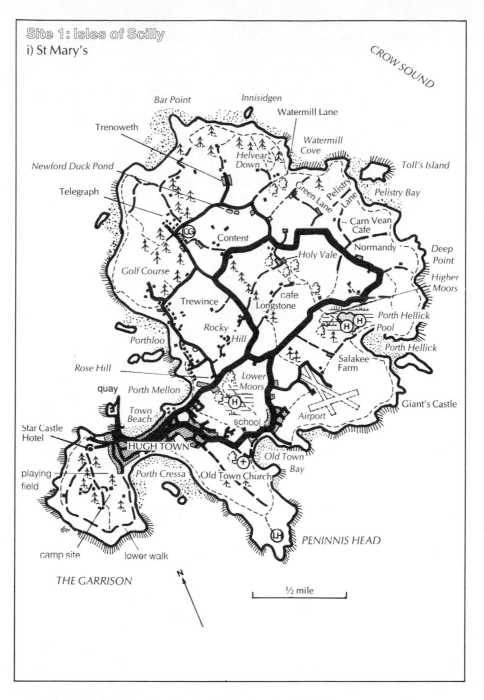

Site 1: Isles of Scilly
i) St Mary's

CROW SOUND

Bar Point
Innisidgen
Watermill Lane
Trenoweth
Watermill Cove
Newford Duck Pond
Helvear Down
Toll's Island
Telegraph
Green Lane
Pelistry Lane
Pelistry Bay
Content
Carn Vean Cafe
Holy Vale
Normandy
Deep Point
Golf Course
Higher Moors
cafe
Trewince
Longstone
Rocky Hill
Porth Hellick Pool
Porthloo
Porth Hellick
Rose Hill
Salakee Farm
quay
Porth Mellon
Lower Moors
Star Castle Hotel
Town Beach
school
Airport
Giant's Castle
HUGH TOWN
playing field
Porth Cressa
Old Town Church
Old Town Bay
camp site
lower walk
PENINNIS HEAD
THE GARRISON
N
½ mile

seawatching points on St Mary's. The elms in Old Town
churchyard regularly attract migrants.
Lower Moors A nature trail (Rose Hill to Old Town Bay) crosses
the marshes and reedbeds and there is a hide and small scrape.
Check the dense sallows carefully.

Airport Waders (including occasional Dotterel and Buff-breasted Sandpiper), pipits, and buntings occur from time to time. Check from the edges only.

Salakee A track leads from the airport to Salakee Farm. From here continue straight on to Porth Hellick or turn left to the road. The fields around the farm have turned up some outstanding rarities.

Porth Hellick Pool and Higher Moors A nature trail skirts the W side of the pool and continues through the marshland of Higher Moors. Two hides overlook the pool and reedbeds, which attract wildfowl and a few waders; migrant passerines favour the sallows.

Holy Vale Formerly known at the Holy Grail after an outstanding spate of rarities! It is one of the best areas and receives considerable attention. The trail from Higher Moors crosses the road and continues through sallows, brambles, and marshland into a narrow trail through tall elms with dense undergrowth — a jungle by Scilly standards. The trail continues to Holy Vale Farm and the main road.

Watermill Lane and Cove Newford Duck Pond, the elms alongside Watermill Lane, and the bushes near the cove are worth checking. From the cove, a coastal path heads south to Pelistry and north to Bar Point, passing through bracken-covered slopes and scattered clumps of pines.

Golf Course Dotterel and Buff-breasted Sandpiper are almost annual, and pipits and buntings turn up regularly. The surrounding fields may also hold the same species.

St Agnes
(see map)

The most south-westerly of the inhabited islands, facing directly into the Atlantic and therefore the first landfall for American vagrants. It is a little more than a mile in length with a very small population. The islet of Gugh is joined to St Agnes at low tide by a sand bar.

The Parsonage This secluded garden, a small orchard surrounded by elms, hedges, and dense vegetation is undoubtedly the best spot for migrant passerines and rarities on St Agnes. Birders are allowed through the gate into the garden but not into the orchard. The house next to it is strictly private. The trees of the Parsonage can also be viewed from the lane outside.

Big Pool This pool, surrounded by sedges, usually appears devoid of birds but a number of unexpected species have turned up here over the years.

Periglis and Porth Killier The best bays for waders on St Agnes.

Chapel Fields and Troy Town Fields These small bulb fields, surrounded by brambles and hedges, are always worth checking in autumn.

Barnaby Lane A tree-lined lane favoured by warblers and Firecrests.

Covean A track leads to this sheltered cove from Covean Cottage in Higher Town. Tamarisks, brambles, and hedges surround the bulb fields.

Wingletang Down This area of moorland with gorse bushes and granite boulders is often disappointing for birds but Lapland Buntings are fairly regular and some rarities have been found. Horse Point is the best seawatching site on St Agnes.

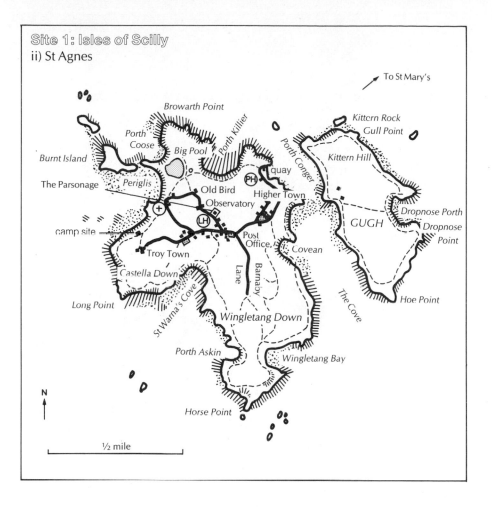

Site 1: Isles of Scilly
ii) St Agnes

The island, dominated by Tresco Abbey and its gardens of exotic trees and plants, is a privately leased estate and a landing charge is payable in summer. Depending on the tides, boats land either at Carn Near or New Grimsby. Although private, access is generally unrestricted along footpaths and roads. Areas of woodland occur in many places but most are unproductive pine plantations. Tresco is a large island with a great potential for rarities. Most birders only make brief visits and to the same few areas — greater coverage would undoubtedly produce more.

Tresco (see map)

Abbey Pool A small pool with sandy edges easily checked for waders.

Great Pool The largest area of fresh water on Scilly, surrounded by reedbeds and sallows. Not all of the pool can be viewed easily; in particular try at each end and from certain points along the N

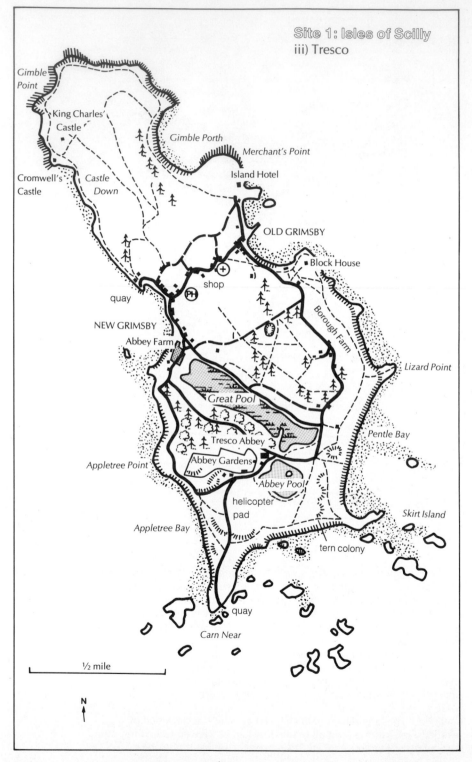

Site 1: Isles of Scilly
iii) Tresco

Gimble Point

King Charles' Castle

Gimble Porth

Merchant's Point

Island Hotel

Cromwell's Castle

Castle Down

OLD GRIMSBY

⊕

shop

Block House

quay

PH

Borough Farm

NEW GRIMSBY

Abbey Farm

Lizard Point

Great Pool

Tresco Abbey

Pentle Bay

Appletree Point

Abbey Gardens

Abbey Pool

helicopter pad

Skirt Island

Appletree Bay

tern colony

quay

Carn Near

½ mile

N

side. Wildfowl are a notable feature and rarer species are found quite regularly. An American Black Duck was resident from 1976 to 1983, leaving a number of Mallard × Black Duck hybrids as its legacy. The sallows around the edges should be checked, and the fields on the N side often hold finches and buntings.

Borough Farm The fields and hedges around the farm have attracted several rarities in recent years. Access is limited to the main tracks through the farm.

Bryher

Lying immediately W of Tresco, Bryher is surprisingly little visited by birders. The weedy fields in the centre of the island attract finches and buntings and any area of bushes should be checked. The pool on the W side has turned up some unusual waders though the commoner species prefer the coastal bays and Stinking Porth is one of the best.

St Martin's

This large island lies N of St Mary's. There are two widely separated landing points: Lower Town at low tide, Higher Town at other times. Much of the island is cultivated and the top is rather open. The most sheltered areas are the fields and hedges on the S side. One of the best areas is E of Higher Town: from the quay, walk towards Higher Town and bear right around the coast, checking the bushes and trees on the left; after ½ mile turn left up a track to a farm where a short nature trail runs through fields; there are some mature elms here.

Unihabited Islands

The main interest is breeding seabirds. Several of the best islands have restricted access during the breeding season, but they can be easily viewed from the boats.

Birds

374 species of birds have been recorded on Scilly including a remarkable number of rarities and numerous firsts for Britain.

Spring passage gets underway in March, and the main passage continues into April–May, but numbers are rarely impressive. Spring overshoots are annual, the most frequent species being Hoopoe in March–April. A Woodchat Shrike or something rarer is a distinct possibility and small numbers of Golden Oriole are regular in May.

Summer is essentially for breeding seabirds. Most are present April–July, although some species may be seen around the islands all year. Shags and Kittiwakes are common but Fulmars are still scarce. Razorbills are the most numerous auks but only c 200 pairs breed. Guillemots are surprisingly uncommon. Most of the Puffins breed on Annet which is also the home of Manx Shearwaters and c 2,000 pairs of Storm Petrels. The latter two species, however, are rarely seen around the islands during the day and are best seen from the *Scillonian*. A colony of Common Terns breeds on Tresco and a few pairs of the declining Roseate Tern breed alongside them.

Autumn wader passage is July–October with a peak in September, but numbers are generally small. The commoner waders include Little Stint and Curlew Sandpiper. American vagrants (18 species recorded) are annual, mainly in September. Lesser Golden Plover and Pectoral Sandpiper are two of the more frequent but the most predictable is Buff-breasted Sandpiper, a grassland wader uncommon on the E coast of America but an annual visitor to the golf course and airfield in September, sometimes in small flocks. One or two Dotterel quite often share this habitat, occurring late August to October.

American Robin

Seabird passage is rarely impressive and is usually best during or after SW or NW gales. The best seawatching points are Peninnis Head and Deep Point (St Mary's), Horse Point (St Agnes), and the N tip of Tresco. Seabirds are often better observed from the *Scillonian*. Manx and Sooty Shearwaters and Great and Arctic Skuas are quite regular in September, but Great Shearwaters are rather rare. Later in the autumn, gales may bring in Storm and Leach's Petrels or Grey Phalaropes.

Passerine migration is most evident in September and includes Redstart, Ring Ouzel, Whinchat, and Pied Flycatcher. Many of the scarcer migrants are annual on Scilly and sometimes outnumber their more familiar counterparts. Amongst the earlier arrivals are Icterine and Melodious Warblers and Red-backed and Woodchat Shrikes, which occur from late August to October. Other species recorded annually in variable numbers, mainly September–October, are Wryneck, Richard's and Tawny Pipits, Bluethroat, Barred Warbler, Scarlet Rosefinch, and Lapland, Snow, and Ortolan Buntings. Yellow-browed Warbler, Firecrest, and Red-breasted Flycatcher are regular between late September and early November, sometimes in comparatively large numbers,

Firecrest

and can almost be guaranteed in October. A number of rarities are now annual, or almost so, on Scilly. These include Short-toed Lark, Rose-coloured Starling, and Rustic and Little Buntings. Late September to the end of October is the best time for American landbirds; one of the most frequent is Blackpoll Warbler, but Gray-cheeked Thrush, Red-eyed Vireo, Rose-breasted Grosbeak, and Bobolink have all put in a number of appearances. Asiatic visitors tend to arrive slightly later, mostly early October to early November: the most regular in recent years have included Olive-backed Pipit and Booted, Radde's, Dusky, and Pallas's Warblers. Rarities from closer to home also occur: Red-throated Pipit and Subalpine, Greenish, Arctic, and Bonelli's Warblers have each been recorded a number of times.

Raptors are not infrequent in autumn, with Merlin and Peregrine seen almost daily from October. Rarer visitors include occasional Osprey, Honey Buzzard, harriers, and Red Kite. Late September and October usually produces a few Spotted Crakes and Corncrakes but their retiring habits cause them to be easily overlooked. By November, things have quietened down considerably, migrant passerines largely comprising Blackcaps, Chiffchaffs, and a few Firecrests, some of which will stay all winter. New arrivals include Woodcock, one or two Short-eared Owls, and perhaps a Long-eared Owl. Black Redstarts sometimes arrive in considerable numbers at this time, frequenting the rocky coasts and bulb fields.

Winter is bleak and few birders visit the islands. Severe gales are frequent, though freezing conditions are rare. One or two Great Northern Divers are usually present in the channels between the islands, Crow Sound being particularly favoured. Gannets and Kittiwakes can usually be seen offshore and there are numbers of Purple Sandpipers around the coasts. Geese are occasional visitors in very small numbers and a variety of duck winters on the Great Pool on Tresco. Visiting Water Rails greatly outnumber the few residents and a wintering Merlin could be seen anywhere.

Information

Accommodation: Isles of Scilly Council, St Mary's, Isles of Scilly.
British Airways, Penzance: Tel. 0736-63871/2.
British Airways, St Mary's: Tel. 0720-22646.
Brymon Airways: Roborough Airport, Plymouth, Devon: Tel. 0752-705151.
Brymon Airways, St Mary's: Tel. 0720-22709.
Land's End aerodrome: Tel. 0736-788771/788601.
Isles of Scilly Steamship Co, Penzance: Tel. 0736-62009/64013.
Isles of Scilly Steamship Co, St Mary's: Tel. 0720-22357/8.
Porthcressa Cafe: In October, the basement of this cafe in Hugh Town becomes the nerve-centre of evening activity for the birders on St Mary's. Various entertainments are provided and the daily log is called here. Outside, a blackboard is regularly updated with bird news as it comes in. Longstone Cafe, between Rocky Hill and Holy Vale, also has such a notice-board, as does Carn Vean Cafe.

References: *A Guide to Bird-watching in the Isles of Scilly* by David Hunt (1978)
A Check-list of the Birds of the Isles of Scilly by S.J.M. Gantlett (1985)
Recorder: Isles of Scilly.

Site No. 2 Porthgwarra — St Just (Cornwall)

The Land's End area is famed for attracting migrants in spring and autumn and, in particular, rarities. Although overshadowed by Scilly, it has produced some outstanding rarities and is worthy of more extensive coverage, especially in late autumn. Seawatching off Porthgwarra can be rewarding.

Habitat

The exposed peninsula of Land's End comprises moorland and rough grazing fields surrounded by impressive granite cliffs. Trees and bushes only gain a foothold in the more sheltered valleys and hollows and these are important refuges for migrants.

Access
OS Sheet No. 203

All sites in this area are close together and several may be combined in a single visit.

**Porthgwarra
(see map)**

The most famous valley of W Cornwall. Its position at the SW tip of the peninsula ensures a regular trickle of American landbirds. Leave Penzance W on the A30. At Catchall, turn left onto the B3283 to St Buryan. After St Buryan, join the B3315 and continue towards Land's End for 2 miles. At Polgigga, turn left to Porthgwarra. There is a car park in the village, just beyond the final hairpin at the end of the valley. Migrant passerines can turn up in any suitable cover. In particular, check the dense bushes in

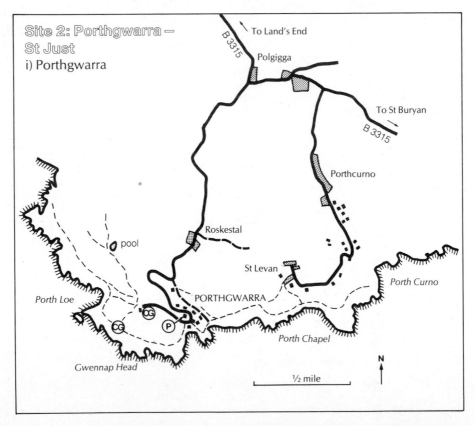

Site 2: Porthgwarra — St Just
i) Porthgwarra

To Land's End
B 3315
Polgigga
To St Buryan
B 3315
Porthcurno
pool
Roskestal
Porth Loe
St Levan
Porth Curno
PORTHGWARRA
P
Porth Chapel
Gwennap Head
N
½ mile

the valley itself as well as the gardens in the village. From the car park the road continues to the coastguard cottages and several paths lead to the clifftops and across the moorland to a small pool at the head of the valley. Seawatching is best from Gwennap Head, close to the coastguard lookout. From Porthgwarra village a coastal footpath heads E to St Levan where there are more gardens and trees.

Sennen Cove

The village of Sennen Cove lies at the S end of Whitesand Bay, 1 mile N of Land's End. Divers, grebes, and various seabirds may be seen offshore in season. From Land's End, turn left off the A30 after Sennen onto a minor road to Sennen Cove. There is a car park overlooking the bay. Walk along the beach or seawatch from the coastguard lookout W of the village.

St Just Airfield (see map)

This small airfield 3 miles NE of Land's End is not heavily used and attracts waders (see below). From Land's End, turn left (N) onto the B3306 towards St Just. The airfield is on the left after 1½ miles. The best views are from the minor road to Nanquidno along its N side.

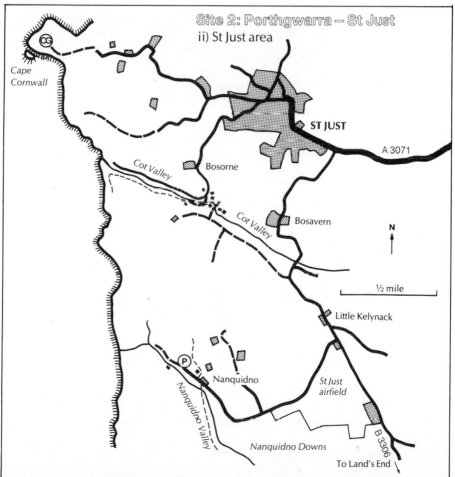

Site 2: Porthgwarra – St Just
ii) St Just area

Cape Cornwall

ST JUST

A 3071

Cot Valley

Bosorne

Cot Valley

Bosavern

N

½ mile

Little Kelynack

Nanquidno

St Just airfield

Nanquidno Valley

Nanquidno Downs

B 3306

To Land's End

Nanquidno
(see map)

This sheltered, well-vegetated valley E of St Just airfield is another excellent area for migrant passerines, and several American rarities have turned up. Park at the end of the road and explore the dense bushes and trees along the valley bottom.

Cot Valley
(see map)

This valley lies N of Nanquidno and is also good for migrants. Leave St Just village on the road to Cape Cornwall and almost immediately turn left onto a minor road signed Cot Valley. Parking is limited along the road. Check the gardens at the head of the valley and other areas of cover. The road, and also a footpath, continues alongside the valley to the coast.

Birds

Spring migration begins early, in March, and a wide variety of migrants pass through in April–May, though generally in small numbers. Typical species include Turtle Dove, Cuckoo, Redstart, Whinchat, Ring Ouzel, Grasshopper Warbler, and Spotted and Pied Flycatchers. An unusual migrant or a rarity is most likely in May.

Seabird passage in spring is light, peaking April–May. All three divers may be seen as well as small numbers of Manx Shearwaters, Common Scoter, Whimbrel, Sandwich and Common Terns, and the occasional skua. Numbers and diversity of seabirds increase again from July. Balearic Shearwaters and Great and Arctic Skuas are seen regularly in small numbers. Much less frequent, and generally later in the autumn, are Great and Sooty Shearwaters and Pomarine Skua. The best winds are usually SE–SW and not too strong. In recent years, Cory's Shearwaters have appeared off Porthgwarra July – August, sometimes in large numbers.

Passerine migrants reappear from August, and one or two scarce migrants, such as Melodious Warbler or Woodchat Shrike, are found annually. Later, light easterlies may bring Wryneck, Barred Warbler, Yellow-browed Warbler, or Red-breasted Flycatcher. October–November sees movements of Skylarks, pipits, Robins, Goldcrests, and finches, and a few Black Redstarts, Ring Ouzels, and Firecrests. A sprinkling of raptors arrives at this time including Hen Harrier, Merlin, Peregrine, and Short-eared Owl, but late autumn is most notable for rarities, including occasional American landbirds, especially after strong SW winds.

The short turf of St Just airfield attracts Golden Plovers and Lapwings in autumn, and species such as Ruff and Whimbrel may accompany them. Very small numbers of Dotterel are regular in autumn and occasionally also Buff-breasted Sandpiper. Richard's and Tawny Pipits and Lapland and Snow Buntings occur infrequently. Some of the fields and grassy clifftops offer a similar habitat.

Winter is fairly quiet. A few seabirds such as Gannets can be seen and divers are sometimes offshore. Small numbers of Hen Harriers and other raptors winter on the moorlands and Chiffchaffs and Firecrests in the sheltered valleys. Resident species are usually in evidence, including Buzzard, Sparrowhawk, Peregrine, Little Owl, Green Woodpecker, Rock Pipit, and Raven.

Information

Recorder: Cornwall.

Site No. 3 St Ives (Cornwall)

St Ives is known as one of Britain's best seawatching points — if not *the* best. In appropriate weather in autumn the seabird passage can be truly spectacular (see p. 12), but if the winds are wrong you could see nothing. In addition to large numbers, good days offer a chance of seeing species rarely seen from land. The main attractions in winter are divers and perhaps one of the rarer gulls.

Habitat

St Ives lies on the W side of St Ives Bay, and N of the town is The Island — actually a rocky headland.

Access
OS Sheet No. 203

Drive to the N end of the town following signs to the car park on The Island and walk to the top of the headland. Seawatching is best from the perimeter of the coastguard lookout. For gulls, check the harbour and (from the car park) the sewage outfall. Other parts of the bay can be seen from various points in the town and you can walk E along the shore to look for terns on Porth Kidney Sands.

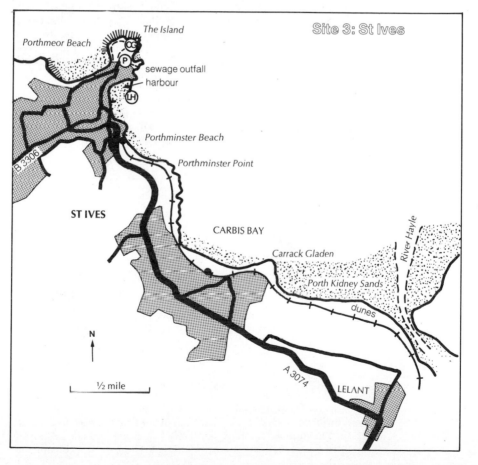

Birds

Weather is critical for big movements of seabirds. The ideal winds are WNW–N, preferably preceded by a SW gale. Such conditions may only occur a few times a year, and rather than visit on the off-chance you should ideally wait until the correct conditions are forecast. Good winds can produce seabirds at any time of year but the greatest number and diversity occur late August–November. In W winds seawatching can be better at Pendeen Watch, c 10 miles W of St Ives, though the birds are generally more distant.

A few Great Northern Divers and Slavonian Grebes are regularly seen in St Ives Bay in winter. Black-throated Divers are less common and are more likely in late winter or early spring. Seaduck (mainly Eider and Common Scoter) are not numerous. Gannets, Cormorants, and Shags may be seen offshore at any time. A few Purple Sandpipers winter on the headland. Gull flocks should always be checked; Glaucous is the most regular of the scarcer species and late winter is the best time for one. Iceland Gull is also frequent at this time.

In spring, Mediterranean and Little Gulls are occasional. There is a small passage of Sandwich Terns, with a few Common and Arctic. In appropriate weather there may be a movement of Manx Shearwaters and Kittiwakes and perhaps the odd Storm Petrel.

The early part of the autumn passage is dominated by Fulmars, Manx Shearwaters, Arctic Skuas, and Common and Sandwich Terns. Smaller numbers of Sooty and Balearic Shearwaters, Great Skuas, Little Gulls, and Roseate, Little, and Black Terns are seen regularly. Storm Petrels occur but in very variable numbers. NW winds in September are likely to bring in thousands of Gannets and Kittiwakes. Leach's Petrels and Sabine's Gulls are two of St Ives' specialities and sometimes occur in quite large numbers, though a few of each is more normal (beware of misidentifying young Kittiwakes as Sabine's Gulls — it happens a lot). Pomarine Skuas are occasional and Long-tailed Skuas are rare. Auk passage is almost exclusively Razorbills and Guillemots, in tremendous numbers in late autumn.

Leach's Petrels and Sabine's Gull

Seabird numbers drop-off by November though Great Skuas, Kittiwakes, and auks are still much in evidence. Two late species, seen in variable numbers, are Grey Phalarope and Little Auk. All three divers may be found, including Red-throated, normally the scarcest species in Cornwall. Rock Pipits occur around the coast and one or two Black Redstarts or Snow Buntings may visit The Island.

Recorder: Cornwall.

Information

Site No. 4 Hayle Estuary (Cornwall)

The Hayle estuary's compact size and easy access allow close views of a good variety of wildfowl, waders, and gulls. It is best visited in autumn and winter, and American vagrants are a regular feature.

The estuary is surrounded by urban development and is effectively divided into two sections, the main bay and Copperhouse Creek; the latter lies within the town of Hayle itself. At low tide, most of the estuary is mudflats with an area of saltmarsh in the SW corner. Carnsew Pool is separated from the main part of the estuary by a narrow embankment; it is tidal but retains some open water even at low tide.

Habitat

The B3301 (formerly the A30) runs alongside the estuary offering good views from the roadside. However, one of the best viewing points is the RSPB hide which overlooks the main channel at the SW corner. This is sited next to the Old Quay House Inn near the junction of the A30 and the A3074 to St Ives. Birders are allowed to use the inn's car park. Access to the hide is unrestricted and there is also an information hut here. Waders are best seen within 2 hrs of high tide. Carnsew Pool can be viewed from a public footpath which runs along the embankment on three sides of the pool and also gives good views of the mudflats. Access is from the B3301 W of Hayle or from the town itself — through a small industrial area W of the viaduct. It may also be worth walking along the spit towards the mouth of the estuary. Small numbers of waders roost on the spit and the Pool's embankments. Copperhouse Creek can be watched from the B3301 and the footpaths surrounding it.

Access (see map)
OS Sheet No. 203

In winter Black-throated and Great Northern Divers and Slavonian Grebes are occasionally present on Carnsew Pool. A few Goldeneye and Red-breasted Merganser are regular. The majority of ducks on the estuary in winter are Teal and Wigeon with smaller numbers of Gadwall. A few Knot, Spotted Redshank, Greenshank, and Common Sandpiper usually winter among the commoner waders. Large numbers of gulls are present; small numbers of Mediterranean, Little, and Glaucous are regularly seen, especially in late winter, and one or two Ring-billed and Iceland Gulls are found annually. A Peregrine can be seen irregularly through the winter.

Birds

Spring passage brings small flocks of Whimbrels, and a few Little Ringed Plovers and Wood Sandpipers are seen annually. Small numbers of terns pass through, and Roseate, Little, and Black Terns may feature in these movements.

A greater variety of waders occurs in autumn and although the numbers of each are usually small, they may include Little Stint or Curlew Sandpiper. An American rarity is found almost annually, the most frequent being White-rumped and Pectoral Sandpipers and Long-billed Dowitcher. Dedicated gull-watchers are likely to find Mediterranean and Little Gulls and small numbers of terns are regularly seen.

Information   Recorder: Cornwall.

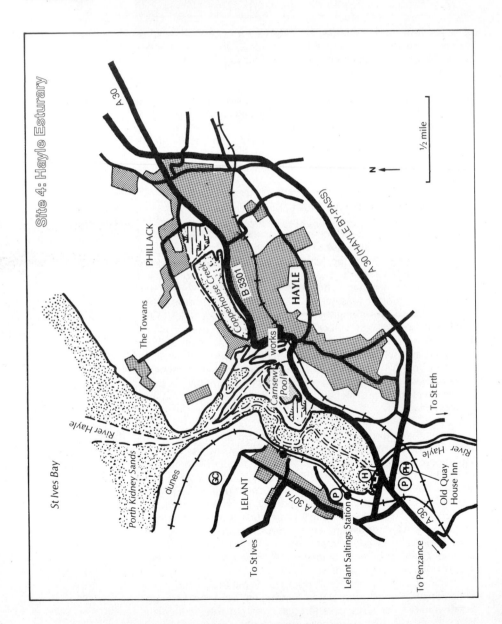

Site 4: Hayle Esturary

Site No. 5 Marazion (Cornwall)

Marazion Marsh covers 85 acres and lies on the coast E of Penzance. It attracts a number of interesting species, including rarities, in spring and autumn.

Most of the marsh is dense reeds and sedges with scattered clumps of bushes. A few open pools with muddy margins attract waders. A road runs along the seaward side, a railway crosses the marsh, and housing flanks another side, but despite this the area remains relatively undisturbed.

Habitat

Leaving Penzance on the A30 to Hayle, fork right at Longrock to follow the coast road to Marazion. The marsh is easily viewed from the road. There is a car park just beyond the railway bridge and another at the E end from which a footpath leads across the marsh.

Access
(see map)
OS Sheet No. 203

Cetti's Warblers are resident and with patience may be seen at any time. Wintering birds include small numbers of the commoner ducks, Water Rail (mostly heard), and occasionally Jack Snipe.

Birds

Spring sees a sprinkling of early passerine migrants and passage waders, and Garganey are regular in early spring. Later on a scarce migrant or a rarity is almost inevitable; some of the more likely candidates are Little Egret, Spoonbill, Marsh Harrier, and Hoopoe. Water Pipits are occasionally found on the drier edges.

Autumn waders include Little Stint, Curlew Sandpiper, and Wood Sandpiper, and an American wader such as Pectoral Sandpiper or Long-billed Dowitcher is found most years. Spotted Crakes are fairly regular but rarely seen. The passage of hirundines often attracts a Hobby in autumn and Little Gulls and Black Terns are seen occasionally. A few Aquatic Warblers are seen each year, usually in mid – late August, and although this species is renowned for skulking in reedbeds Marazion probably offers the best chance of seeing one in Britain — but beware of young Sedge Warblers with crown-stripes.

Part of this huge bay can be viewed from the beach at Marazion. There is unrestricted access to other areas from the coast road but much of it is disturbed.

Other Sites in the Area
5.1 Mount's Bay
(see map)

Great Northern Divers are regular in winter and Black-throated Divers are frequent but less common. Slavonian Grebes are also usually to be found. Sanderling are common on the sandy beaches while Purple Sandpipers prefer the rocky areas. Large numbers of gulls collect on the shore or at the freshwater outflows when the tide is out. Scarce species such as Glaucous, Iceland, Mediterranean, and Little Gulls are regularly found and rarities such as Ring-billed have been seen a number of times. A small passage of terns occurs in spring and Kentish Plover is almost annual.

This 90-acre reservoir lies just W of Penzance. Areas of mud are exposed around its edges when the water is low, usually in autumn. The surrounding area is largely fields. Leave Penzance

5.2 Drift
Reservoir

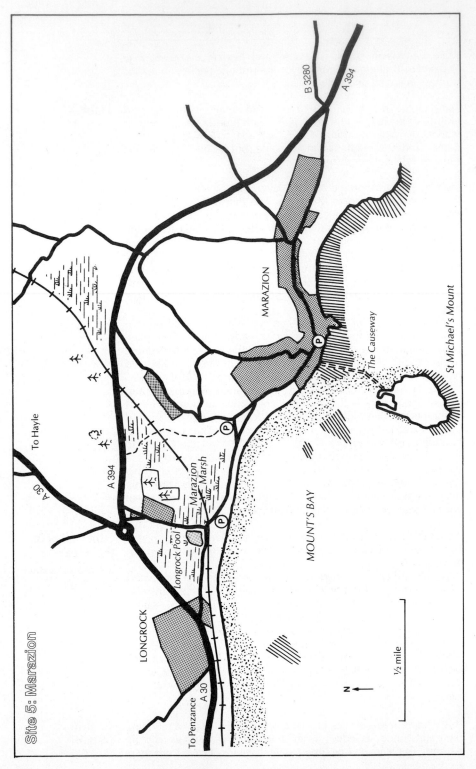

Site 5: Marazion

SOUTH-WEST ENGLAND

LONGROCK

To Penzance
A 30

A 30

To Hayle

A 394

Longrock Pool

Marazion Marsh

MOUNT'S BAY

N

½ mile

MARAZION

B 3280

A 394

The Causeway

St Michael's Mount

SW on the A30 and at Lower Drift turn right on a minor road to
Sancreed. After a few hundred yards the road passes close to the S
end of the reservoir. Part can be viewed from here and you can
walk around the sides (no permit required). For views of the N
end, continue along the road and fork right towards Sellan. Drift's
main interest is waders and gulls in autumn and winter. An
American wader is almost annual in autumn.

Recorder: Cornwall.   **Information**

Site No. 6 Stithians Reservoir (Cornwall)

This 273-acre reservoir lies S of Redruth and is best in autumn and
winter for wildfowl and waders. Indeed, it holds an American
wader almost every autumn.

Much of the reservoir is shallow with natural banks and mud is   **Habitat**
frequently exposed when the water level drops, while marshy
areas at either end provide variety. The surrounding area is largely
open moorland. There is some disturbance by windsurfers at
weekends.

Leave Helston on the A394 towards Penryn. After 4½ miles turn   **Access**
left (N) onto a minor road signed Stithians. After Carnkie the road   **(see map)**
crosses the S tip of the reservoir. Waders can be seen well from   OS Sheet No. 203
the road here and there is a marshy area S of the road. Two hides
are available (keys and permits from South West Water Authority)
though they are not really necessary on a casual visit. Continue
along the road to the N of the reservoir. After the Golden Lion
pub, the road again crosses an arm of the reservoir giving views
over exposed mud and open water. From here you can also walk
along the W edge.

Waders are the prime interest. Spring passage is poor but autumn   **Birds**
can be excellent. The most frequent species from July onwards
may include numbers of Little Stint, Curlew Sandpiper, and Wood
Sandpiper, and occasional Little Ringed Plover. Later in the
autumn, numbers of Golden Plover and Lapwing reach several
thousand. The Golden Plover flock attracts one or two vagrant
Lesser Golden Plovers almost every year, but they can be hard to

Lesser Golden Plover and Golden Plovers

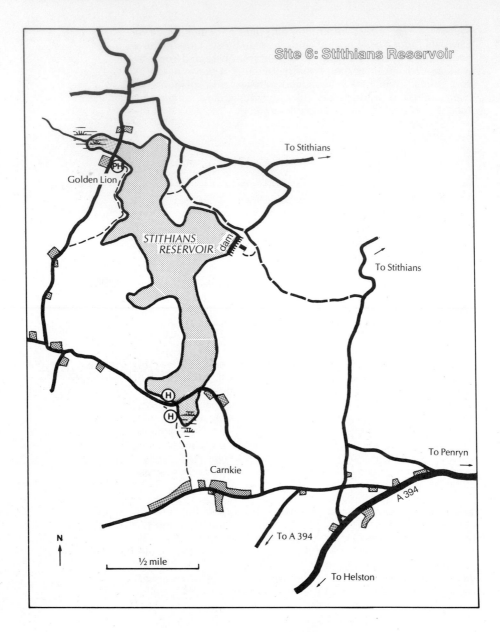

pick out on the ground. Another American rarity of incredible regularity is Pectoral Sandpiper — sometimes several together. Other vagrants which have been recorded a number of times are Long-billed Dowitcher and Lesser Yellowlegs. A variety of raptors has been seen, and in autumn Peregrines are not infrequent. A few Little Gulls and Black Terns occur each autumn.

Most of the wildfowl arrive in November; a few Goldeneye winter and Scaup are occasional. Few of the waders, other than Golden Plover and Lapwing, remain during the winter, though there are usually a few Ruff.

Gerrans Bay lies on the S Cornish coast E of the Fal estuary and is bounded by Portscatho and Nare Head. It is the best place in the SW to see Black-throated Divers. Viewing is best from Pendower Beach at the innermost part of the bay. Access is from the A3078 S of Tregony along a minor road signed Pendower Beach and Hotel. Park by the road close to the hotel and view from the cliff-top. Alternatively, look out from the point of Pednavadan (N of Portscatho) on the W of the bay. Black-throated Divers normally occur November–April, peaking in early April, and late-staying individuals may attain summer plumage before departing. A few Great Northern Divers and Slavonian Grebes are usually present and small numbers of seaduck and auks may also be seen.

Other Sites in the Area
6.1 Gerrans Bay
OS Sheet No. 204

South West Water Authority (permits and keys to hides): Fisheries and Recreation Officer, 3–5 Barnfield Road, Exeter, Devon. Tel. 0392-31666. Recorder: Cornwall.

Information

Site No. 7 Davidstow, Crowdy, Siblyback, and Colliford (Cornwall)

These four sites are on the perimeter of Bodmin Moor. None is particularly outstanding but all have the potential for rarities in autumn.

A disused airfield on the N edge of Bodmin Moor, with the ruined control tower and runways still present. The short turf is grazed by sheep, and shallow pools occur after rain.

7.1 Davidstow Airfield

Leave Camelford NE on the A39. After 2 miles turn right onto a minor road running through the airfield. Pull off to the left and drive along the old runways scanning for birds. Stay in your vehicle: this does not scare the birds and enables more ground to be covered. The control tower area is often best for waders.

Access (see map)
OS Sheet No. 201

Large flocks of Golden Plover and Lapwing occur in autumn and winter and occasionally a Lesser Golden Plover is with them. A few Ruff are usually present and Buff-breasted Sandpipers now turn up annually. Very small numbers of Dotterel are reasonably regular in spring and autumn. Hen Harrier, Merlin, and Peregrine are sometimes encountered in autumn and winter, and Goshawks have been claimed on a number of occasions.

Birds

This 115-acre reservoir is very close to Davidstow Airfield. Mud is exposed when the water is low and there are marshy areas on its E side.

7.2 Crowdy Reservoir

A signed road from the airfield leads to the reservoir. Alternatively it can be reached directly from Camelford: turn right (SE) off the A39 at the N edge of the town and after 1 mile turn left to the airfield. The reservoir can be viewed from the road but for close views follow a track to the water's edge. A hide is sited at the N end (key and permit from South West Water Authority).

Access (see map)
OS Sheet No. 201

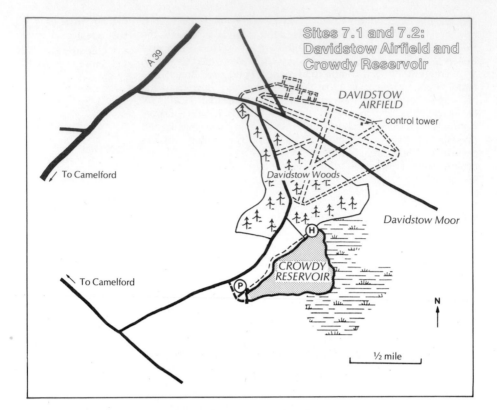

Sites 7.1 and 7.2:
Davidstow Airfield and
Crowdy Reservoir

DAVIDSTOW
AIRFIELD

control tower

To Camelford

Davidstow Woods

Davidstow Moor

CROWDY
RESERVOIR

To Camelford

N

½ mile

Birds	There are reasonable numbers of the commoner ducks in winter, usually including a few Goldeneye. Raptors may also be seen (similar to Davidstow). A variety of waders frequents the muddy margins in autumn and occasionally includes a rarity. Very small numbers of Black Terns are recorded annually in spring and autumn.
7.3 Siblyback Reservoir	This 140-acre reservoir lies on the SE edge of Bodmin Moor, N of Liskeard, surrounded by moorland and grassland. Areas of mud are exposed on the N shore when the water is low.
Access (see map) OS Sheet No. 201	Leave Liskeard N on the B3254. After 1 mile fork left onto a minor road to St Cleer. Turn right immediately after the village and continue past the crossroads to the reservoir and car park overlooking it. You can walk in either direction but the N end is generally best and there is a hide here (permit from South West Water Authority).
Birds	There is a variety of ducks in winter, and a few Goosander and Smew are annual visitors. Jack Snipe can sometimes be found in the marshy edges and Golden Plovers and Lapwings are common in the fields. Hen Harrier, Merlin, and Peregrine are seen occasionally in winter. The autumn wader passage includes most of the usual species and a rarity is found most years. Small numbers of Little Gulls and Black Terns occur each autumn.

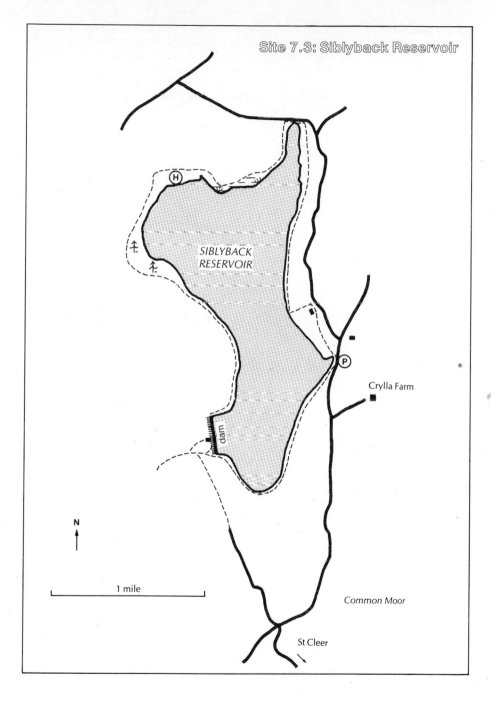

Site 7.3: Siblyback Reservoir

SIBLYBACK
RESERVOIR

Crylla Farm

dam

N

1 mile

Common Moor

St Cleer

At *c* 600 acres, this new reservoir a few miles W of Siblyback is the largest in the county and well worth visiting, especially in autumn and winter, for ducks and waders. The NE part is relatively shallow and has grassy islands. At present disturbance is minimal, unlike Siblyback.

7.4 Colliford Lake

Access (see map)
OS Sheet No. 201

Turn S off the A30 at Bolventor onto a road signed 'Dozmary Pool'. Follow this road for c 2 miles, passing Dozmary Pool to the left, and reasonable views may be had of the reservoir's NE arm from the roadside. Continue S, turning W by the china-clay works, and pass below the dam (the dam area is poor for birds due to the deep water). Another road follows the reservoir's W side affording reasonable views of the NW arm.

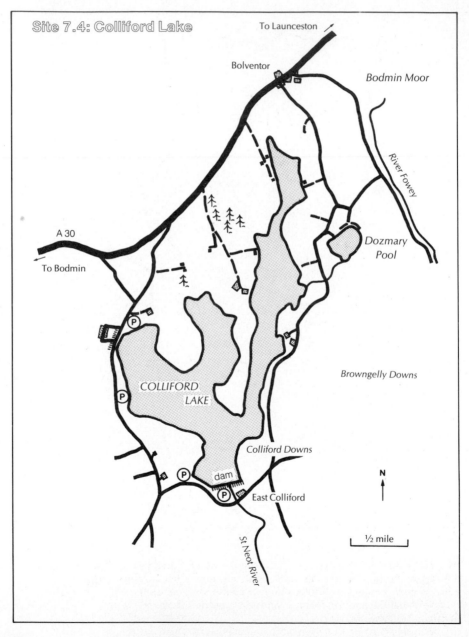

Site 7.4: Colliford Lake

To Launceston

Bolventor

Bodmin Moor

River Fowey

A 30

Dozmary Pool

To Bodmin

Browngelly Downs

COLLIFORD LAKE

Colliford Downs

dam

East Colliford

St Neot River

N

½ mile

There is a good autumn build-up of ducks, with a chance of **Birds**
Garganey, and the shallow margins have produced Pectoral
Sandpiper and Spotted Crake as well as the commoner waders. In
winter Smew and Goosander seem to be regular in very small
numbers, and look out for the odd Scaup and Ruddy Duck.
Towards dusk both Hen Harriers and Merlins come in to roost
about the reservoir, and Short-eared Owls winter in small
numbers. Particularly good vantage points for these are at the NW
and NE corners of the reservoir. Dippers inhabit the nearby Fowey
Valley.

South West Water Authority (permits and keys to hides): Fisheries and **Information**
Recreation Officer, 3–5 Barnfield Road, Exeter, Devon. Tel. 0392-31666.
Recorder: Cornwall.

Site No. 8 Prawle Point (Devon)

This outstanding migration watchpoint is the most southerly point
on the S Devon coast, and lies S of Kingsbridge. Although best in
spring and autumn there is usually something to see at any time of
year. Prawle is also one of the most reliable places in Britain to
see Cirl Buntings.

The cliffs along this coast are quite spectacular. The tops are **Habitat**
covered with grass, bracken, gorse, and boulders, and behind lie
fields surrounded by stone walls and hedges. Sheltered hollows
and valleys contain dense vegetation and bushes attractive to
migrants. There is a small wood near East Prawle.

Leave Kingsbridge E on the A379. Turn right at Frogmore or **Access**
Chillington onto minor roads S to East Prawle. Continue through **(see map)**
the village, down the 'no through road', to the National Trust car OS Sheet No. 202
park at the end in a sheltered hollow surrounded by bushes. These
bushes often harbour migrants and, indeed, are one of the best
places to look. Several places should be checked:

Continue to the point from the car park, past the coastguard **Prawle Point**
cottages, checking for migrants on the way. Seawatching is best
from the memorial seat below the W side of the point.

From the car park walk E along the coastal path, checking bushes **Eastern Fields**
and gullies. Beyond Langerstone Point a small wood lies on the
left. After checking the wood you can return to the car park along
the lane, via the top fields.

This deep, lush valley lies about a mile W of the point. It can be **Pig's Nose Valley**
reached either by walking NW along the coastal path via
Gammon Head or from East Prawle village.

Early mornings are generally best for seeing migrant passerines. If
a fall has occurred, all suitable cover should be checked
thoroughly, especially in sheltered areas. There is disturbance by
non-birders at weekends. Seawatching is often best in hazy
conditions or after strong onshore gales.

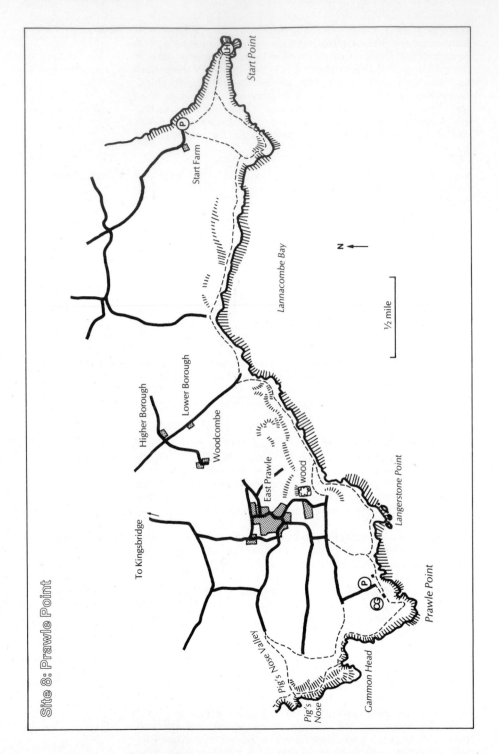

Site 8: Prawle Point

Start Point

Start Farm

Lannacombe Bay

½ mile

N

Higher Borough

Lower Borough

Woodcombe

East Prawle

wood

Langerstone Point

To Kingsbridge

Prawle Point

Pig's Nose Valley

Pig's Nose

Cammon Head

Amongst the residents, Cirl Bunting is Prawle's speciality. Several **Birds** pairs breed in hedgerows around Prawle and in winter small flocks may be found in the bushes around the car park. Little Owls are frequently seen and other residents include Buzzard, Sparrowhawk, Rock Pipit, and Raven.

Cirl Bunting

In winter, a few divers occur offshore — Great Northern is the most frequent. Small numbers of Shags and Common Scoter are usually to be seen as well as many Gannets, gulls, and auks. Flocks of Golden Plover favour the short grassy fields and a few Purple Sandpipers winter below the cliffs. The bushes may hold the odd wintering Chiffchaff or Firecrest and more open areas should be checked for the occasional Black Redstart.

The first spring arrivals include Wheatears and Goldcrests, and a few migrant Black Redstarts and Firecrests may be found from mid-March and Hoopoe is seen most years. A wide variety of migrant passerines occur, mostly in April–May, and a few raptors also pass through. Seawatching can be productive in spring: regular species include all three divers, Manx Shearwater, Fulmar, Eider, Common Scoter, Red-breasted Merganser, Whimbrel, Bar-tailed Godwit, skuas, and terns; late April to early May is probably best. Scarce migrants and rarities are occasionally found, mostly in late spring.

Small numbers of Balearic Shearwaters tend to replace the Manx subspecies from mid-July. They are sometimes accompanied by a Sooty Shearwater but this species is more frequent in September. Arctic and Great Skuas are regular in autumn. Passerine migrants are mainly present August–September; the main species are Yellow Wagtail, Tree Pipit, Wheatear, Whinchat, Redstart, warblers, and flycatchers. Late September and October brings big movements of hirundines, pipits, and wagtails, usually also a few Ring Ouzels. A Merlin or Hobby is also often present at this time. Late autumn is the time for the most exciting species. A few Firecrests are usually present from late September into November, and Melodious, Icterine, and Yellow-browed Warblers and Red-breasted Flycatcher are all found most years, but only in very small numbers. An American passerine is a possibility after W gales and an Asian vagrant such as Pallas's Warbler may turn up as late as November. Late autumn also brings a few Black Redstarts.

Other Sites in the Area
8.1 Start Point
(see map)

This is another good migration watchpoint E of Prawle. However, cover is limited and passerine migrants tend to move away quite quickly. Cirl Buntings are equally prominent here. Leave the A379 at Stokenham and follow minor roads to the car park on the point. Walk ½ mile to reach the point itself and seawatch from the lighthouse compound. Check all cover and sheltered areas for migrants.

Information

Recorder: Devon.

Site No. 9 Slapton Ley (Devon)

Slapton Ley is a nature reserve managed by the Field Studies Council. Its reedbeds and bushes attract a variety of migrants and some interesting breeding species but the area is best known for wildfowl in winter.

Habitat

A series of freshwater pools lies behind a long shingle bank on the coast of Start Bay. The largest of these is Slapton Ley itself; 1½ miles long and fringed with reeds, especially in Ireland Bay. Wintering ducks occur on the open water, often favouring the Lower Ley. Dense bushes along the seaward edge provide habitat for migrant passerines. Immediately N of Slapton Ley, and separated from it by a narrow strip of land, is Higher Ley. This is now mainly an extensive reedbed with encroaching scrub. S of Torcross, the much smaller Beesands Ley consists of open water fringed with reeds. Further S still, Hallsands Ley is a semi-dry reedbed.

Access
(see map)
OS Sheet No. 202

Slapton is c 6 miles S of Dartmouth on the coastal A379. The road runs along the seaward side of the lake and there are 3 car parks. Slapton Ley can be easily viewed from these, and the sea is worth checking at various points along the beach. Further exploration may well be profitable. A ringing hut maintained by the Devon Birdwatching and Preservation Society is sited between Slapton and Higher Leys and a logbook is kept in a tin under the left side for reporting sightings when the hut is unmanned. Opposite the hut a trail leads through a gate and gives good views over Ireland Bay. Continue until a gated track leading to France Wood appears on the left (permit required): dense bushes and an overgrown quarry are worth checking for wintering Chiffchaff and Firecrest. Higher Ley may be viewed from the coast road (e.g. at Strete Gate) or along a path which leads N from the ringing hut. Beesands Ley can be reached by walking S along the coast from

Torcross or by driving S from Stokenham (on A379) on minor roads to Beesands village; the Ley lies immediately N of the village.

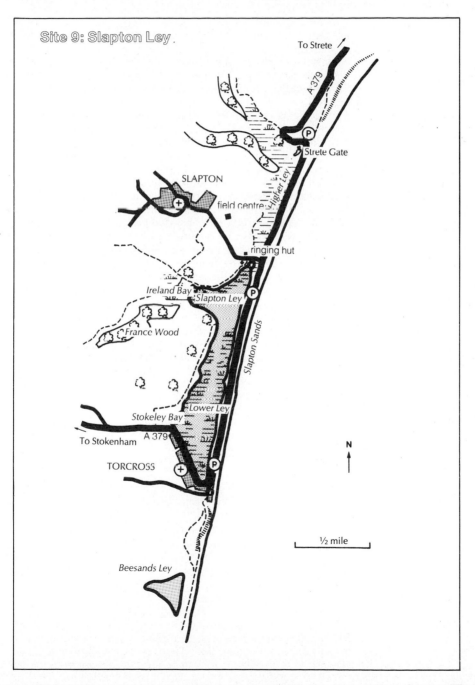

Site 9: Slapton Ley.

To Strete

A379

Strete Gate

Higher Ley

SLAPTON

field centre

ringing hut

Ireland Bay

Slapton Ley

Slapton Sands

France Wood

Lower Ley

Stokeley Bay

To Stokenham

A379

TORCROSS

N

½ mile

Beesands Ley

Birds
Divers and grebes occur on the sea in winter — Great Northern Diver and Slavonian Grebe being the most likely. Shag, Eider, and Common Scoter are also regular offshore. Slapton is particularly attractive to diving duck, and there are usually a few Gadwall. Small numbers of Ruddy Duck occasionally winter, and Long-tailed Duck turns up most years. In hard weather, Goosander and Smew may visit. There have been a number of records of Ring-necked and Ferruginous Ducks in recent years. Gull flocks on the beach in winter should be checked for rarer species such as Mediterranean or Glaucous Gulls. A number of Water Rails inhabit the reedbeds, and in hard weather Bittern and Bearded Tits may visit. A few Chiffchaffs and Firecrests usually winter in the surrounding bushes and a Black Redstart may be found on the beach.

In spring all three divers occur offshore and passage terns are noted in small numbers. Garganey is a regular visitor to the Ley in early spring. A variety of migrant passerines may be found in the bushes and Wheatears favour the shingle bank. Scarcer migrants include the occasional Marsh Harrier or Hoopoe.

In summer a few pairs of Great Crested Grebes breed and Sedge and Reed Warblers are common. Resident Buzzards, Sparrowhawk, and Raven are all seen frequently, and the explosive song of Cetti's Warblers is a familiar sound all year from the dense scrub and reedbeds. Cirl Buntings occur in the sheltered valley leading inland; they often sing from high trees in summer, but in winter move nearer the coast and favour hedgerows and low bushes. In late summer, light S winds can produce feeding flocks of Manx Shearwaters at sea as well as the more usual Gannets and Kittiwakes. Occasionally a Sooty Shearwater is seen.

In autumn large numbers of Swifts and hirundines collect over the lake and are sometimes chased by a Hobby. Black Terns are regular and ringing has shown that the elusive Aquatic Warbler turns up most years in small numbers after E winds, though they are unlikely to be seen. At sea Arctic Skuas chase the Sandwich Terns and after severe gales in late autumn oddities such as Grey Phalarope may shelter on the Ley.

Information
Slapton Ley Field Centre, Slapton, Kingsbridge, Devon TQ7 2QP. Recorder: Devon.

Site No. 10 Exe Estuary (Devon)

The Exe, containing 6 miles of extensive tidal mudflats between Exeter and the sea, is the most important estuary for wildfowl and waders in the SW. A variety of habitats ensures a good diversity of birds all year although it is best during migration seasons and in winter. It is noted in particular for wintering Brent Geese, Avocets, and Black-tailed Godwits.

Habitat
The estuary is tidal as far as Countess Wear on the outskirts of Exeter and is over a mile wide in places, with considerable areas of mud and sand at low tide. Two sand spits lie at its mouth: Dawlish Warren extends for a mile into the estuary from the W

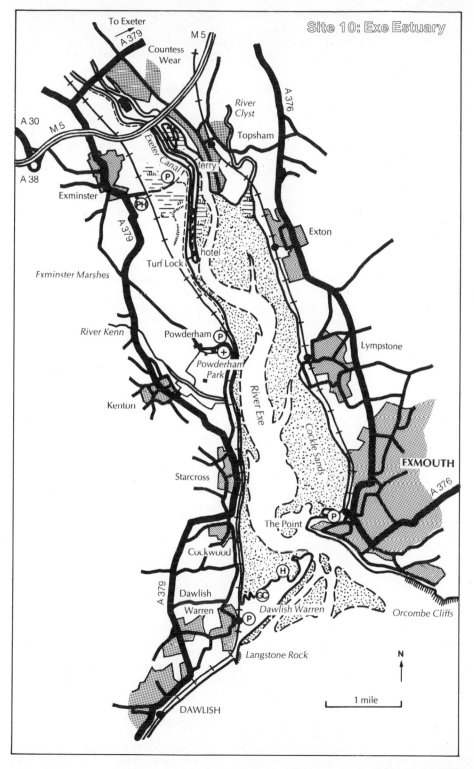

Site 10: Exe Estuary

To Exeter
A 379
Countess Wear
M 5
River Clyst
A 376
A 30
M 5
Exeter Canal
Topsham
ferry
A 38
Exminster
PH
Exton
hotel
Turf Lock
Fxminster Marshes
Lympstone
River Kenn
Powderham
Powderham Park
Kenton
River Exe
Cockle Sands
Starcross
FXMOUTH
A 376
The Point
Cockwood
H
Dawlish
GC
Warren
Dawlish Warren
Orcombe Cliffs
A 379
Langstone Rock
N
1 mile
DAWLISH

and contains a series of dunes, a golf course, and a small reedbed. Behind it lies an area of saltmarsh; on the E the spit at Exmouth is much smaller and there are high cliffs E of the town. Between Exminster Marshes and Topsham is a tidal reedbed in the estuary's narrower inner section.

**Access
(see map)**
OS Sheet No. 192

The estuary can be observed from many points but the W side tends to be most profitable due to less development and restriction of shooting — though the light is inevitably unfavourable in the early morning. The waders can be very distant at low tide and are best seen 2–3 hrs before high water. Alternatively, they may be observed at their high tide roosts, notably at Dawlish Warren or on the Exminster Marshes. The sea is best watched from Langstone Rock (SW of Dawlish Warren) or from Exmouth. Exmouth and Dawlish Warren suffer from considerable tourist activity particularly in summer; weekdays or early mornings are best. The area can be conveniently worked from four places:

**Exminster
Marshes**

These fresh marshes comprise rough grazing dissected by ditches and subject to occasional flooding. They are situated on the estuary's upper W bank, separated from it by the disused Exeter Canal.

S of Exminster on the A379 turn left to the Swan's Nest Inn and park after ½ mile. A footpath to the left leads across the marshes to the estuary (where there is a passenger ferry to Topsham). Continue S along the canal to Turf (about 1¼ miles). This track gives good views over the marshes, the tidal reedbed, and the estuary. At Turf you can cross over the lock and walk a short way upstream to get a better view of the estuary. Continuing S from Turf, an embankment follows the edge of the estuary.

Powderham

The wooded parkland of Powderham Park lies on the estuary's W bank immediately S of Exminster marshes. A small river runs through the park, occasionally flooding certain areas. The park and adjacent meadows to the N are used by roosting waders at high tide.

Continue S on the A379 from Exminster, turn left at the first crossroads to Powderham, and park by the church. A track N leads to the embankment which gives good views of the estuary and reaches Turf Lock after c 1½ miles. S from the church the road follows the edge of the estuary, and the park and its meres can be seen from various points along here.

Dawlish Warren

Dawlish Warren is a Local Nature Reserve managed by Teignbridge District Council. The central area comprises dunes, bushes, and a reedbed. A golf course lies on the N side and the beach is popular with tourists. A public hide overlooks the estuary and gives close views of roosting waders at high tide. Access is unrestricted except for the golf course, which is private.

S of Starcross turn left onto a minor road leading to Dawlish Warren. Cross the railway under the bridge and walk NE across the dunes, past the reedbed. The estuary can be viewed from the N side of the Warren and the hide is on this shore beyond the golf course. From Dawlish Warren station walk S to reach the coast and Langstone Rock.

The seafront gives good views of the sea and the mudflats. Head E **Exmouth** along the seafront to reach Orcombe Cliffs. A sheltered bay N of the spit is favoured by Brent Geese; this can be viewed from the Imperial Road car park W of the station.

Red-throated Divers and Slavonian Grebes are regular in winter, **Birds** usually off Dawlish Warren or Langstone Rock but sometimes also off Exmouth. Small parties of Eider and Common Scoter are often on the sea and the latter may include the odd Velvet Scoter. The regular wintering flock of Brent Geese numbers over 2,000 birds; their preferred feeding area is the bay N of Exmouth, though they are also seen off Dawlish Warren at high tide. Bewick's Swan and White-fronted Goose are only irregular on Exminster Marshes. Several thousand Wigeon winter, favouring the saltings behind Dawlish Warren or Exmouth. Other dabbling ducks include small numbers of Gadwall and Pintail. Goldeneye and Red-breasted Merganser prefer the deeper channels and a Long-tailed Duck is found most winters. Scaup are irregular, off Turf or on the sea. Peregrines are seen fairly regularly in winter while the resident Buzzards and Sparrowhawks are more frequent. Thousands of waders winter, including Grey Plover and Turnstone and a few Knot and Sanderling. Over 600 wintering Black-tailed Godwits are of national importance; they may be seen on the E shore or off Powderham and usually roost on Exminster Marshes, which also hold Golden Plover and a few Ruff. Redshanks roost in Powderham Park at high tide and should be checked for Spotted Redshank and Greenshank. The wintering Avocets form the third largest flock in Britain and are usually found off Turf. On the coast a few Purple Sandpipers inhabit the rocks below Orcombe Cliffs and less frequently at Langstone Rock. The large gull roost on the marshes is mainly Black-headed Gulls but should be checked for the occasional Mediterranean Gull. Short-eared Owls are often seen over Exminster Marshes or at the E end of Dawlish Warren and a Kingfisher may be found along the canal. A few Chiffchaffs winter in the bushes on Dawlish Warren, occasionally accompanied by a Firecrest. Cirl Buntings should be looked for in low vegetation on the seafront at Dawlish and Black Redstarts occasionally winter.

Spring is heralded by the arrival of Wheatears and sometimes a Garganey on Exminster Marshes. Terns are regularly seen offshore and roost on the Warren; Sandwich are the commonest with smaller numbers of Common and Little and a few Arctic, while one or two Roseates are regular in May. Passage waders include Whimbrel and Green Sandpipers.

In summer a few Shelduck and Lapwing breed on Exminster Marshes and the reedbeds hold Sedge and Reed Warblers and Reed Buntings. There is a small heronry in Powderham Park. Cirl Buntings breed in hedges near Langstone and around Exminster; they are present all year.

The autumn wader passage begins in July and occasionally a Little Stint or Curlew Sandpiper may be found amongst the commoner species. Small numbers of Black Terns are regularly noted over the canal and Little Gulls may also be seen. Osprey is almost annual in autumn and occasionally one stays for a week or two. Hobbies sometimes chase the hirundines in the late afternoon, particularly as they go to roost in the reedbeds. Gales in late autumn are likely to bring seabirds inshore. Gannets and Great and Arctic Skuas are often seen but seawatching is much better off more prominent points such as Prawle. Scarce migrant passerines are found regularly at Dawlish Warren in autumn.

Information

Dawlish Warren, warden: c/o Teignbridge District Council, 32 Courtenay Street, Newton Abbot, Devon TQ12 2QR. Tel. 0626-66951.
Recorder: Devon.

Site No. 11 Lundy (Devon)

The island of Lundy, c 3½ miles long, lies in the Bristol Channel 12 miles N of Hartland Point. The cliffs hold good numbers of breeding seabirds but the island is best known as a migration watch-point; a bird observatory operated from the Old Lighthouse from 1947 to 1973.

Habitat

The cliffs rise to over 300 feet and are most impressive on the W and N sides. Much of the island top is barren moorland which is damp in places, with a few small areas of standing water, notably at Pondsbury. The sole habitation on the island is a small village at the S end where there are some fields. The Eastern Sidelands and sheltered valleys such as Millcombe Valley contain bushes and a few small areas of woodland.

**Access
(see map)**
OS Sheet No. 180

A regular supply ship operates from Ilfracombe and a steamer runs day trips in the summer (but these do not allow much time on the island). A variety of accommodation is available on Lundy but space is limited. For information on transport and accommodation contact the Island Administrator.

The gardens and bushes of Millcombe Valley are perhaps the best area for migrants in spring and autumn. Other suitable areas for warblers and flycatchers are largely confined to the Eastern Sidelands and a walk up the E coast checking the bushes and disused quarries may be profitable. The main seabird colonies are at North Light and Battery Point. A track from the village leads N across the moorland to North Light. Immediately E of the lighthouse, a series of steps descends into Kittiwake Gulley offering good views of the breeding seabirds.

Birds

Spring migration begins in March and then usually includes a few Black Redstarts and Firecrests. A steady stream of the commoner summer visitors passes through in April–May. E or SE winds are generally best for falls of migrants. Small numbers of Redstarts, Ring Ouzels, and Pied Flycatchers are recorded annually, and scarce migrants are a regular feature, especially after light S winds. Hoopoe is generally one of the first, in late March or April, and a few Dotterel are seen each year in late April or May. Both species favour short turf. Late spring often brings a Golden Oriole or two, and migrant raptors may include Merlin and Short-eared Owl.

Although many of the seabirds, such as Gannet, are visible offshore all year, the breeding species mostly return to their ledges

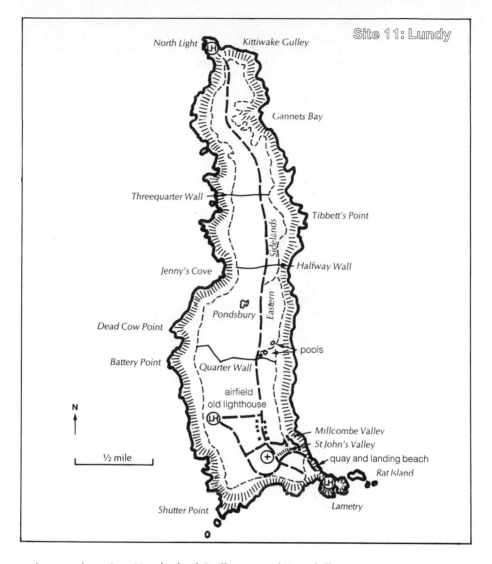

or burrows in spring. Hundreds of Guillemots and Razorbills nest alongside over 1,000 pairs of Kittiwakes and smaller numbers of Fulmars and Shags. Up to 100 pairs of Puffins breed, mostly at Battery Point. Gulls (mostly Herring) are also numerous. Manx Shearwater and Storm Petrel breed in small numbers, largely on the W side, but they only return to their burrows at night and the best chance of seeing them is on the boat crossing. Rock Pipit and Raven are resident.

Autumn wader passage is fairly insignificant due to scarcity of habitat, but several American waders have been seen, usually after W gales; Pectoral Sandpiper is almost annual. A few returning Dotterel are seen each year. Passerine migrants filter through in August–September, sometimes accompanied by something scarcer such as Melodious or Barred Warbler. Ortolan Buntings are annual from late August and a few Lapland Buntings usually turn up later. In late autumn there are large movements of larks, pipits, finches, and buntings. Rarities can be found at any time but are most likely from late September to early November. Lundy has an astonishingly long list of goodies and has been sadly neglected by rarity-hunters. No less than seven firsts for Britain have been found here.

Puffins

Information

Island Administrator (Woolacombe): Tel. 0271-870870.
Lundy Field Society, Hon. Secretary: 2 Beaufort Close, Reigate, Surrey RH2 9DG. Tel. 07372-45031.
Accommodation bookings: Landmark Trust, Shottesbrooke, Maidenhead, Berks SL6 3SW. Tel. 062 882-5925.
Reference: *The Birds of Lundy* by J.N. Dymond (1980).
Recorder: Devon.

Site No. 12 Chew Valley Lake (Avon)

This reservoir S of Bristol covers c 1,200 acres. Formed in 1953, it has become one of the most important in Britain, noted for wintering wildfowl but also attracting an impressive passage of waders and other migrants. It is worth a visit at any time of year but is least productive in mid-summer.

Habitat

Most of the lake is open water, part of which is set aside as a sailing area. The natural banks are attractive to waders, and in addition to exposed mud there are reedbeds, bushes, and trees around the edge. A nature reserve has been established at Herriott's Bridge.

The surrounding roads offer good views at the dam E of Chew Stoke, at Villice and Heron's Green Bays, and at Herriott's Bridge; the latter two are generally best. From Chew Magna on the B3130, take the B3114 to Chew Stoke. Continue on this road through the village and after 1 mile it runs alongside Villice Bay. Heron's Green is a little further on. Continue to West Harptree and join the A368 towards Bath. Herriott's Bridge is on this road c 1 mile NE of the village. At Bishop Sutton turn left onto a minor road which completes the circuit back to Chew Stoke via the dam.

**Access
(see map)**
OS Sheet Nos.
172 and 182

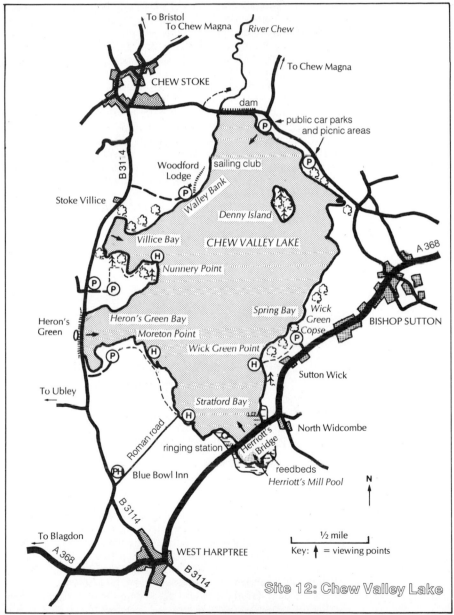

Site 12: Chew Valley Lake

For a more thorough investigation four hides are sited around the edge with car parks off the roads. The hide at Nunnery Point is the best place for viewing gulls in the evening. A permit is required for the hides and access along the shore is not allowed. Permits cost £4.00 per annum or 50p per day by post or personal application from Woodford Lodge which is N of Villice Bay (open 08.45 – 16.45 on weekdays, also at weekends from early April to mid-October).

Birds

Bewick's Swans are regular in winter as well as a variety of ducks including Gadwall and Pintail. Small numbers of Goldeneye, Smew, and Goosander are regular but the lake is perhaps best known for its Ruddy Ducks — this was their first breeding site in Britain. They are most numerous at the S end of the lake. Divers and the rarer grebes are not infrequent and many Dunlin remain through the winter. Water Rail and Bearded Tit are occasionally seen in the reedbeds and Golden Plover are found on the surrounding fields. There is a big gull roost in winter, mainly Common and Black-headed but a rarity such as Ring-billed is noted occasionally. A few Water Pipits are regular in winter.

A wide variety of waders turn up on passage, mainly in autumn, likely species including Curlew Sandpiper, Black-tailed Godwit, Spotted Redshank, and Wood Sandpiper. There is a small passage of Black Terns in spring and autumn and a vagrant White-winged Black Tern is almost annual.

Summer is quiet. Garganey breed but are only infrequently seen. Other breeding species include Gadwall, Ruddy Duck, and Reed and Sedge Warblers.

Ruddy Ducks

Other Sites in the Area
12.1 Blagdon Lake (see map)

This 440-acre reservoir lies to the W of Chew and although generally less productive it can turn up some interesting birds. The S and E sides of the lake are generally the best parts of it. You can view from the road at the dam and at Rugmoor Bay, while along the S shore there are two hides (permits from Bristol Waterworks Company at Woodford Lodge by Chew Valley Lake) and a footpath. From the N end of the dam there is public access to the reservoir's wooded N arm.

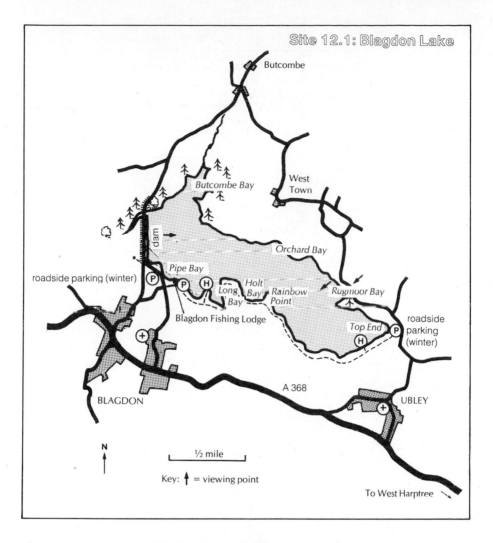

Site 12.1: Blagdon Lake

Butcombe

West Town

Butcombe Bay

dam

Orchard Bay

roadside parking (winter)

Pipe Bay

P   P   H

Long Bay   *Holt Bay*   *Rainbow Point*   *Rugmoor Bay*

Blagdon Fishing Lodge

Top End   P   roadside parking (winter)

H

BLAGDON

A 368

UBLEY

N

½ mile

Key: ↑ = viewing point

To West Harptree

This reservoir, between Cheddar and Axbridge, has man-made banks but nevertheless holds a number of wildfowl in winter which can include unusual species such as Smew. In autumn exposed mud attracts waders and there is a good passage of terns. Several rarities have been found in recent years. Access is by permit from Bristol Waterworks Company at Woodford Lodge (by Chew Valley Lake).

12.2 Cheddar Reservoir

Permits: Bristol Waterworks Company, Fisheries and Recreations Dept., Woodford Lodge, Chew Stoke, Bristol BS18 8XH. Tel. 0272-332339. Recorder: Avon.

Information

Site No. 13 Radipole Lake and Lodmoor (Dorset)

Radipole Lake is an RSPB reserve of 192 acres in the centre of Weymouth. Lodmoor is another RSPB reserve of 150 acres on the coast just E of the town. Both reserves are excellent and worth a visit at any time of year. Residents include Cetti's Warbler and Bearded Tit and both areas attract a wide variety of migrants and wintering birds as well as regular rarities.

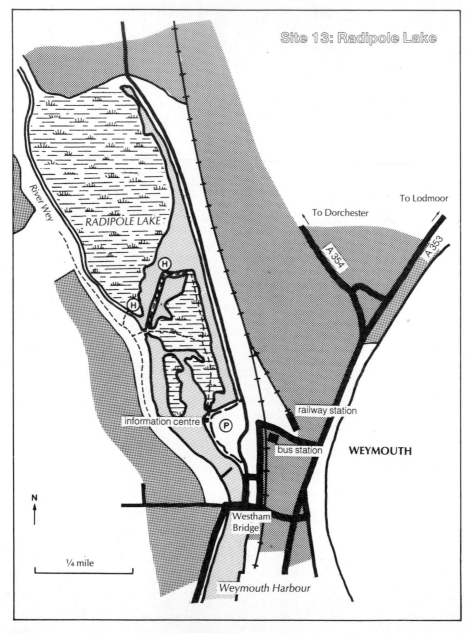

Radipole Lake was formerly the estuary of the River Wey but since the building of the Westham Bridge in 1924 has slowly become a freshwater lake. Extensive reedbeds cover much of the area but the remaining open water includes both shallow areas and deep channels. Dense scrub borders the trails and the perimeter while at the N end there are some water meadows. Lodmoor has pasture, shallow water, reedbeds, and dykes, and is separated from Weymouth Bay by a seawall.

Habitat

The reserve lies close to Weymouth bus and railway stations. A large car park is available beside the S end of the lake. An Information Centre sited here is open at weekends all year and weekdays 10.00 – 17.00 April–September. Several raised trails transect the reedbeds and two hides give good views over the lagoons and reedbeds. The reserve is open at all times.

Access
OS Sheet No. 194
**Radipole Lake
(see map)**

Leave Weymouth N along the coastal A353. The entrance to the reserve is at the public car park by the Sea Life Centre along this road. The reserve is open at all times and three hides are provided off the perimeter footpath.

Lodmoor

Cetti's Warblers and Bearded Tits are resident at both sites, as are Kingfishers and a few Water Rails. In the summer months many Reed and Sedge Warblers breed as well as a few pairs of Grasshopper Warblers and Lesser Whitethroats in the areas of scrub.

Birds

Water Rail

A wide variety of migrants may be seen in spring and autumn and there is always a chance of something unusual. Garganey are regular in spring and are one of the earliest-returning migrants. Waders are generally present in small numbers depending on water levels, and possibilities include Little Stint, Black-tailed Godwit, and Wood Sandpiper. Little Gulls and Black Terns occur but cannot be guaranteed. Thousands of hirundines, hundreds of Pied Wagtails, and up to 3,000 Yellow Wagtails use the reedbeds for roosting during passage. Spotted Crakes are found most years but this species is easily overlooked. Ringing at Radipole has shown that small numbers of Aquatic Warblers pass through annually but this denizen of dense reedbeds is rarely seen. 1–2 are found each year by the lucky few, usually in August or early September.

Winter sees the arrival of relatively small numbers of ducks which include some Gadwall, Scaup, and Goldeneye. Generally Lodmoor is more attractive to wildfowl than Radipole. A few Jack Snipe winter, and an influx of continental Water Rails increases the chances of seeing one. Cetti's Warblers are usually easier to see in winter and a few Water Pipits are regularly present at Lodmoor, often remaining until April by which time some will be in summer plumage. Gulls are prominent at both sites and an impressive list of rare species has been recorded; Mediterranean and Ring-billed Gulls are noted regularly November–May and Glaucous and Iceland are occasionally found in winter. The gulls are best seen at roost in the evening, close to the Information Centre at Radipole.

Information

Warden (Radipole and Lodmoor): 52 Goldcroft Avenue, Weymouth, Dorset DT4 OES.
Recorder: Dorset.

Site No. 14 Portland Harbour, Ferrybridge, and The Fleet (Dorset)

These areas are best in autumn and winter for a variety of waterfowl, waders, and gulls, and can be conveniently combined with a visit to Radipole Lake and Portland Bill.

Habitat

Portland Harbour is a large artificially enclosed harbour lying between Weymouth and the Isle of Portland — not actually an island but joined to the mainland by the unique Chesil Beach, a great 18-mile-long wall of shingle. Between the Beach and the coast is a narrow strip of tidal water known as The Fleet which enters Portland Harbour at Ferrybridge.

**Access
(see maps)**
OS Sheet No. 194

1. The Harbour is best seen from Weymouth at the ruins of Sandsfoot Castle which lies on Old Castle Road. It can also be viewed from Ferrybridge but this area is often much disturbed by windsurfers.
2. The mudflats at the SE end of The Fleet can be checked from Ferrybridge and there is a car park nearby which overlooks it. N of Ferrybridge a footpath follows the NE edge of The Fleet as far as Langton Herring before turning inland.
3. The Fleet near Langton Herring is another good area for waders and wildfowl and can be reached by leaving Weymouth NW on the B3157: turn left at a mini-roundabout near Chickerell, park at a gate c 100 yards before the Moonfleet Hotel, and follow the footpath down to The Fleet. The bay N of Herbury Gore sometimes holds a good variety of waders, and Rodden Hive can also be rewarding.

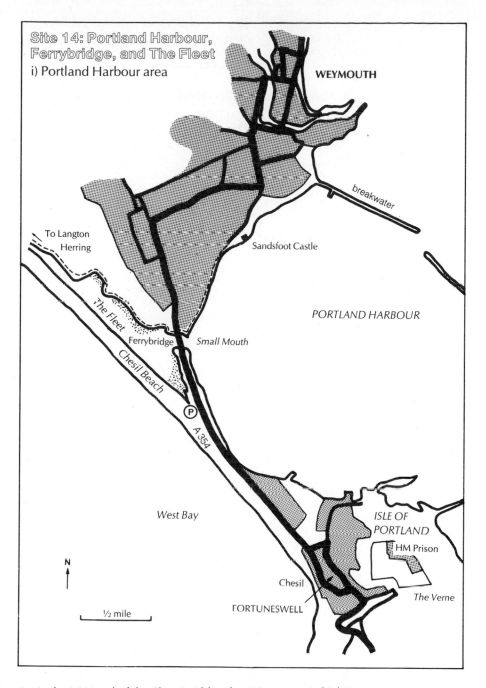

Site 14: Portland Harbour, Ferrybridge, and The Fleet
i) Portland Harbour area

WEYMOUTH

breakwater

To Langton Herring

Sandsfoot Castle

PORTLAND HARBOUR

The Fleet

Ferrybridge   Small Mouth

Chesil Beach

P A 354

West Bay

ISLE OF PORTLAND

HM Prison

N

½ mile

Chesil

FORTUNESWELL

The Verne

4. At the NW end of the Fleet is Abbotsbury Swannery which is excellent for a wide variety of wildfowl besides Mute Swans. The Swannery itself lies ½ mile S of Abbotsbury village but is only open May–September. Outside these months the area can be viewed from Chesil Beach by taking a turning off the B3157 signed 'Subtropical Gardens' 100 yards W of Abbots-

bury village. From the end of this road you can walk left along the beach to view the reedbeds and lagoons.

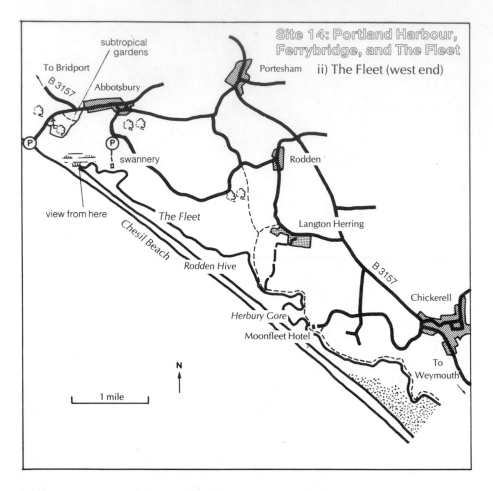

Site 14: Portland Harbour, Ferrybridge, and The Fleet

ii) The Fleet (west end)

subtropical gardens

To Bridport

B 3157

Abbotsbury

Portesham

P

P

swannery

Rodden

view from here

The Fleet

Chesil Beach

Langton Herring

Rodden Hive

B 3157

Chickerell

Herbury Gore

Moonfleet Hotel

To Weymouth

N

1 mile

Birds

The harbour is best in calm weather November–March. All three divers are regular in small numbers, Red-throated being least frequent. Black-necked Grebes haunt the vicinity of Sandsfoot Castle while Slavonian are more widespread. A variety of seaduck occur including Red-breasted Merganser and Goldeneye (both common) and a few Eider, Long-tailed Duck, and Common and Velvet Scoter. The bushes and gardens around Sandsfoot Castle usually hold small numbers of wintering Chiffchaffs, Blackcaps, and Firecrests. Brent Geese are frequent at Ferrybridge, but the bulk of the flock winters further up the Fleet. A good selection of waders can be seen on the Fleet in autumn and winter including the occasional rarity. Gulls and terns should always be checked as several of the rarer species have turned up and Mediterranean and Little Gulls are regular.

In spring and autumn the Subtropical Gardens and the bushes and reedbeds along the beach at Abbotsbury hold a good selection of migrants. In winter the lagoon here is a haven for large numbers of wildfowl and Bearded Tits can frequently be seen in the reedbeds.

Recorder: Dorset.

Information

Site No. 15 Portland Bill (Dorset)

The Isle of Portland protrudes c 6 miles into the English Channel from the Dorset coast, the S tip being known as Portland Bill. An active bird observatory is maintained at the Bill in recognition of its importance as a migration watch-point for both landbirds and seabirds. The best times for a visit are March–May and August–October.

At first sight Portland appears uninviting being virtually treeless and heavily scarred with limestone quarries. Much of the N part of the island is settled or quarried but the S third is largely rural. This is the observatory's recording area, with the village of Southwell forming the N boundary. The various habitats include dry-stone-walled fields, clumps of bushes, hedgerows, grassy commons, and disused quarries which have now become overgrown with a rich variety of plants; all are attractive to migrants. The West Cliffs rise to over 200 feet and are used by breeding seabirds but the East Cliffs are low and of little interest. There is virtually no wader habitat.

Habitat

Leave Weymouth S on the A354 signed to Portland and continue through Fortuneswell and Easton to Southwell. Turn left in Southwell to Portland Bill. The observatory is sited in the Old Lower Lighthouse beside the road c ½ mile before the Bill. There is parking at the observatory for residents but casual visitors should use the large car park N of the new lighthouse.

Access (see map) OS Sheet No. 194

Generally, the most productive birding areas are within the observatory's recording area but much of this is commonland and has become very popular with non-birders at weekends; on bank holidays it can be positively crowded. The best time to look for migrants is early morning and late afternoon when there is least human activity. Cover is fairly limited and any patch of bushes may hold migrants, but several areas deserve specific mention:
1. Observatory garden, containing a variety of cover and a small pond. Trapping and mist-netting are carried out here.
2. The bushes around the Coastguard Cottages.
3. Culverwell, a dense area of bramble and elder.
4. Any of the overgrown quarries, especially the one behind the Eight Kings pub in Southwell.

The Top Fields are noted for attracting migrants, especially finches and buntings. Certain species, such as pipits and Wheatears, favour the short turf of the commons. Seawatching is best at the Bill tip beside the obelisk which gives some protection to this spartan pursuit. In the spring and summer the West Cliffs hold one of the S coast's few seabird colonies; a footpath runs along the clifftop. If time permits, the Verne, at the N end of Portland, is worth checking for migrants. This scrub-covered plateau is situated above the dockyard and below Verne Prison (see Portland Harbour map, p.59).

Portland Bird Observatory is open March–November and at other times by special arrangement with the warden. It has comfortable self-catering accommodation for up to 20 in 6 bedrooms and for another 4 in a small self-contained flat. Charges are £2.00 per person per night (dormitory), £2.30 (double room), and £10.00 per night (flat). Members of Portland Bird Observatory and Field Centre pay reduced charges. Further details from the warden.

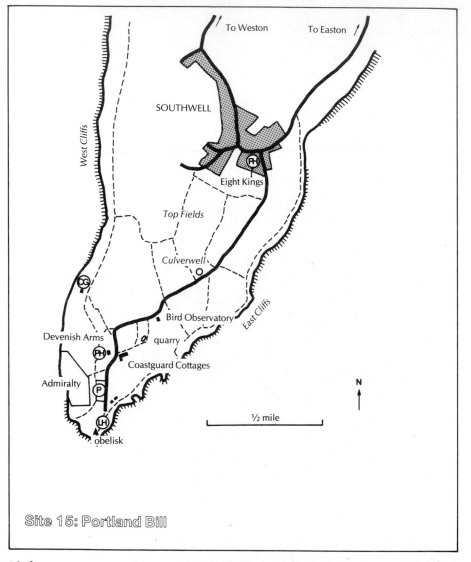

Site 15: Portland Bill

Birds

Winter can be bleak but a variety of divers, seaducks, and auks may be seen offshore. Gannets sometimes appear in large numbers in January and Purple Sandpipers winter on the rocks around the Bill. A few Black Redstarts may be present.

The spring seabird passage begins in March with divers, Gannets, and Common Scoter heading E up the Channel. It continues through April into early May when Manx Shearwaters, skuas, and terns add to the variety. Many of the shearwaters are seen in the evenings. A small concentrated passage of Pomarine Skuas occurs in early May. Passerine migration also begins in March, and summer visitors arrive in force in April—May, frequently including a 'spring overshoot' such as Hoopoe; small numbers of Ring Ouzels and Firecrests are regular (as in autumn).

Summer is fairly quiet but small numbers of Guillemots, Razorbills, and Puffins breed alongside Fulmars, Kittiwakes, and a few Shags. Rock Pipits are resident and Little Owls inhabit the quarries.

Autumn seabird passage is less predictable than spring, and the more pelagic species are only noted occasionally, usually when onshore winds prevail. The Balearic race of Manx Shearwater is annual between July and October but numbers vary. Sooty Shearwaters, Grey Phalaropes, and Little Gulls are recorded irregularly at this time but Great and Arctic Skuas are more frequent. The bulk of the landbird passage is August—September when chats, warblers and flycatchers may be much in evidence. Migrants also include Turtle Dove, Swallow, House Martin, Yellow Wagtail, Whinchat, and Pied Flycatcher. The chance of finding one of the scarcer migrants adds spice to Portland at this time of year. Melodious Warbler and Woodchat Shrike may turn up after S winds and a Tawny Pipit or two is annual in September. Ortolan Buntings are regularly found in the Top Fields, and anti-cyclonic conditions may bring one of the eastern drift migrants such as Wryneck, Bluethroat, Icterine Warbler, Barred Warbler, or Red-breasted Flycatcher. A few of each are recorded most years and Portland's list includes many outstanding rarities.

In late autumn Portland witnesses large-scale movements of partial migrants such as Skylark, Meadow Pipit, Starling, Chaffinch, Goldfinch, and Linnet. Spells of cold weather at the onset of winter frequently result in hard-weather movements of birds heading out to sea to the W or S. These typically comprise Lapwing, Redwing, and Fieldfare, but Golden Plover and Skylark may also move on. Small numbers of some finches migrate throughout the winter.

Tawny Pipit

Warden: Bird Observatory, Old Lower Light, Portland Bill, Dorset DT5 2JT. Tel. 0305-820553
Recorder: Dorset.

Information

Site No. 16 Poole Harbour and Isle of Purbeck (Dorset)

Poole Harbour is the largest estuary in Dorset. Its N and E shores have suffered considerable urbanisation at Poole and Bournemouth but the other sides are largely undeveloped. The harbour is good for wildfowl and waders in autumn and winter, and divers and grebes are often found in the coastal bays. To the S is the Isle of Purbeck (not actually an island), much of this being heathland and a stronghold for Dartford Warbler. Several areas are protected by nature reserves.

Habitat

Tidal mudflats and saltings surround the harbour, with the richest areas on the W and S shores. The open, dry heathlands of the Isle of Purbeck are mainly heather and gorse with some bracken. There are small areas of both deciduous and coniferous woodland, carr, and fresh marsh with reedbeds and small pools. The heaths have a particularly rich flora and fauna with many rare plants, all the British reptiles, and a host of insects.

Access
OS Sheet No. 195
OS Outdoor
Leisure Map
1:25,000 OLM15
**Poole Harbour
(see maps)**

The harbour itself can be viewed from Arne and also at South Haven Point on Studland where, with the changing tides, duck, waders, and grebes fly in and out of the harbour. Brand's Bay, which can also be seen from Studland Heath, is probably the best area for wildfowl and waders. Gulls, waders, and ducks frequent the NE shore and the B3369 between Poole and Sandbanks can be excellent at low tide but it is very disturbed in summer.

**Studland Heath
(see map)**

Much of this heath is a National Nature Reserve managed by the NCC. The habitats are essentially as at Arne. Leave Wareham on the A351 and turn left onto the B3351 at Corfe Castle. On reaching Studland, Ferry Road heads N to South Haven Point. A toll is payable on this road but there is a car park before it on the seaward side. The road continues through prime heathland which is good Dartford Warbler country. The reserve lies on either side of the road and access is unrestricted but visitors should read the notices at the reserve entrances. There are two nature trails: the Dune Trail is open all year and the Woodland Trail operates April–September. A large freshwater pool (Little Sea) E of the road is attractive to ducks in winter. There is an Information Centre and an observation hut which gives a good view over the pool but these are only open on Sundays, 11.00 – 17.00. A hide at the N end is always open. Alternatively, you can travel from Bournemouth and Poole by taking the B3369 to Sandbanks and catching the ferry to South Haven Point.

**Shell and
Studland
Bays (see map)**

Both these bays, N and E of Studland peninsula, are a favourite haunt of divers, grebes, and seaduck in winter. Shell Bay can be easily reached from the car park at South Haven Point. Studland Bay can be approached via the Knoll car park or through Studland village; a minor road leads to the seafront where there is a car park. A bridleway from Studland village follows the clifftops to the Foreland. This gives good views over the bay and the two clumps of trees beside the path can harbour migrant passerines.

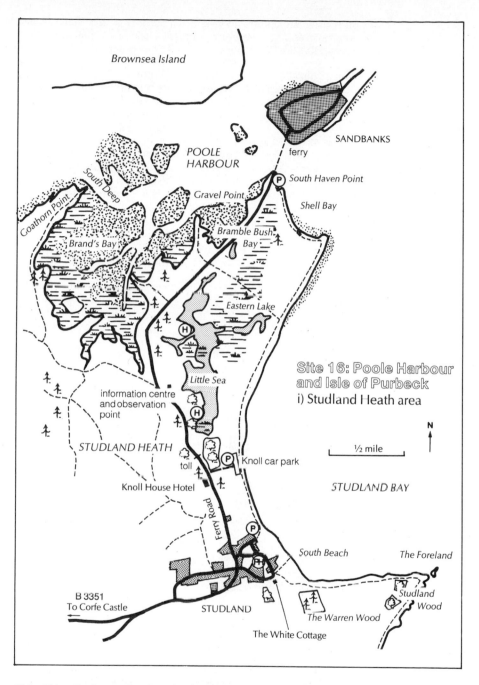

Site 16: Poole Harbour and Isle of Purbeck
i) Studland Heath area

½ mile

N

This 1½-mile long island is the largest in Poole Harbour. It is owned by the National Trust, and the N part is managed as a reserve by the Dorset Naturalists Trust. Its habitats include woodland, heath, and freshwater pools and marshes. A hide overlooks the lagoon and marsh and is a good place to view wildfowl, waders, and terns. A number of waders roost on

Brownsea Island

Brownsea at high tide and there is a heronry on the island. Boats to Brownsea Island go from Sandbanks (taking 10 min) and Poole Quay (30 min). The island is closed September–March.

Arne (see map)

This peninsula protrudes into the SW corner of Poole Harbour. The RSPB reserve of 1,307 acres consists mainly of heathland but with some woodland and freshwater reedbeds and marsh. Leave Wareham S on the A351 and after 1 mile turn left at Stoborough; in c 2 miles the Reception Centre and car park are on the right. The reserve is open at all times but visitors must keep to the footpaths. The ¾-mile Shipstal nature trail is open from the end of May to early September and takes in all the representative habitats as well as giving fine views over the saltings and harbour; two hides are provided. To reach the nature trail continue beyond the Reception Centre to Arne village and park in the car park; the trail begins opposite Arne church. Arne is one of the best places to see Dartford Warbler. It is present all year but often keeps hidden in the gorse, particularly when windy.

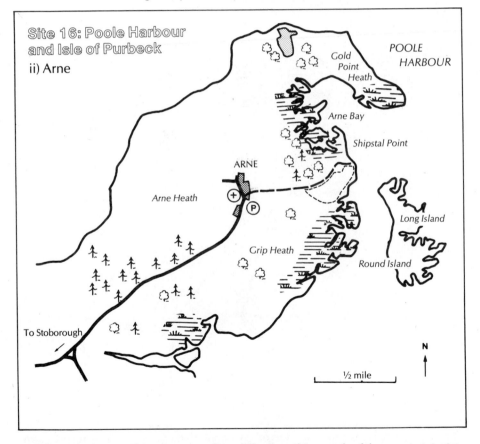

Site 16: Poole Harbour and Isle of Purbeck

ii) Arne

POOLE HARBOUR

Gold Point Heath

Arne Bay

Shipstal Point

ARNE

Arne Heath

Long Island

Grip Heath

Round Island

To Stoborough

N

½ mile

Durlston Head – St Aldhelm's Head (see map)

There are some fine cliffs along this stretch of the coast. A variety of seabirds breed in summer (March–July is best) and passerines occur on migration, especially in the sheltered valleys. The Heads themselves are sometimes good for seawatching. A minor road from Swanage leads S to Durlston Head where there is an

Information Centre. Durlston Head, where a few rarities have been found, is heavily vegetated with large stands of trees and bushy valleys. From here you can walk W along the cliff path towards St Aldhelm's head (c 5 miles), the main interest of the walk being breeding seabirds including Puffin. Alternatively, St Aldhelm's Head may be reached on foot from Worth Matravers. The well-vegetated valley running between Worth Matravers and Winspit can be very good for migrants.

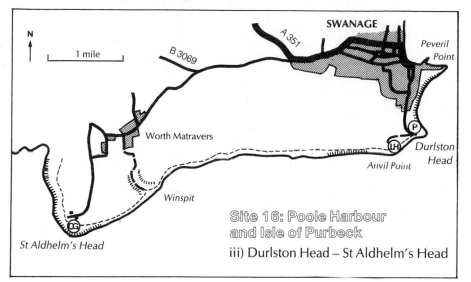

Site 16: Poole Harbour and Isle of Purbeck

iii) Durlston Head – St Aldhelm's Head

Birds

Winter is a good time to visit, and with luck you can see three species of diver and five species of grebe. Black-necked and Slavonian Grebes are regularly present, sometimes in the harbour but more frequently in the coastal bays. Seaduck also winter, mainly Red-breasted Merganser and Common Scoter. Cormorant, Shag, and a few solitary auks are also usually present on the sea. Wildfowl in the harbour include Brent Geese, Pintail, and, in the channels, Goldeneye. A few Avocets, Black-tailed Godwits, and Spotted Redshanks winter and Sanderlings can be found on the shores of Studland Bay. Hen Harriers are occasional and Water Rails and Bearded Tits may be seen in the reedbeds at Arne or around Little Sea. Dartford Warblers are often silent and unobtrusive in winter. Black Redstarts sometimes winter, usually on the coast, and in milder years one or two Firecrests and Chiffchaffs.

Autumn and spring bring a greater variety of waders to the harbour. Seawatching can be productive from the headlands, especially in spring, and the coastal bushes attract passerine migrants.

In summer Grey Herons and Sandwich Terns nest on Brownsea Island. Breeding birds of the cliffs include Fulmar, Shag, Kittiwake, Guillemot, Razorbill, and Puffin. Dartford Warblers are more in evidence on the heathland and Nightjars may be looked for at dusk. The small areas of woodland hold Sparrowhawk, Green and Great Spotted Woodpeckers, and Marsh Tit.

Dartford Warbler

Information   Arne, warden: Syldata, Arne, Wareham, Dorset BH20 5BJ.
Studland Heath, warden: Coronella, 33 Priest's Road, Swanage, Dorset BH19 2RQ.
Brownsea Island, warden: The Old Manor, Brownsea Island, Dorset.
Recorder: Dorset.

SOUTH-EAST ENGLAND

Site No. 17 New Forest (Hampshire)

This outstanding area of mixed woodland and heathland, lying between Southampton and Bournemouth, is managed by the Forestry Commission and is popular with tourists in summer. A number of scarce species breed (although most are difficult to locate) and a fine variety of common woodland and heathland birds can be seen. May–June is the best time to visit, with early mornings being the most profitable.

Habitat

The extensive woods are a mixture of mature oak and beech with conifer plantations. The conifers are generally less interesting ornithologically but can hold some unusual species, especially the younger plantations. The heathland comprises heather, gorse, and bracken with areas of rough grassland and scrub; parts are waterlogged. Although much of the area is commonland, some areas are enclosed and access forbidden.

Access
OS Sheet Nos.
195 and 196.
OS Outdoor
Leisure Map
1:25,000 OLM22

Birds can be found almost anywhere, the secret being to search out the less disturbed areas. Good areas include Beaulieu Heath (Hatchet Moor), Denny Lodge, Rhinefield, and Eyeworth Walk. More specifically, three areas deserve mention.

Hampton Ridge

This is situated in the NW of the forest. Leave Fordingbridge E on the B3078. After 1 mile turn right to Blissford. The Ridge is reached by tracks E from Blissford, or from Abbots Well to the S. The main track across the Ridge passes through excellent heathland with gorse and there is a good possibility of Dartford Warbler. It also offers fine views over the distant forest with a chance of raptors. After almost 2 miles the track reaches woodland (Pitts Wood Inclosure and Amberwood Inclosure). The elusive Woodlark may be found here as well as Crossbill and Siskin.

Beaulieu Road

Leave Lyndhurst E on the A35. At the end of the town turn right on the B3056 to Beaulieu. After 3 miles pull off to the right just before the road crosses the railway line at Beaulieu Road station. The small patch of pines beside the road is a picnic site and sometimes holds Crossbills. A track leads through the trees and across the heath towards Bishop's Dyke and Denny Wood. From the heath, looking towards the woods, look out for Hobby in the late afternoon. Honey Buzzard soar over the woods on occasion and Woodlarks are sometimes present in the area.

Acres Down

Take the A35 W from Lyndhurst. After c 1 mile turn right onto a minor road to Emery Down and continue NW towards Stoney Cross. 2 miles beyond Emery Down, where there is a right turn to Newtown, turn left onto a small road. Shortly after this road turns to gravel there is a small car park on the left, and from here walk up a small hillock for views over a large tract of woodland to the E. Buzzards and Sparrowhawks are regularly seen, and Honey Buzzard, Goshawk, and Hobby are possible.

Birds

Buzzard, Sparrowhawk, and Hobby are widespread and frequently seen. Honey Buzzard is a New Forest speciality but needs a great deal of luck. Localised breeders with a marked preference for conifers are Siskin and Crossbill. Firecrests also favour them, but not exclusively. They were first discovered as a British breeding species in the New Forest, but remain very elusive and numbers fluctuate widely. Recently planted conifers or woodland edges are favoured by the very localised Woodlark and the much commoner Tree Pipit; Woodcock and Nightjar are sometimes found here as well as on the heaths and dusk is the best time to look for them. Deciduous woodland harbours all three woodpeckers, Redstart, Wood Warbler, Marsh and Willow Tits, Nuthatch, and Treecreeper. Hawfinches are much less widespread and unlikely to be seen. The star bird of the heath is the Dartford Warbler for which the New Forest is a major stronghold; other heathland birds include Curlew, Wheatear, Stonechat, and Whinchat, but the chances of finding a Red-backed Shrike are now slim.

In winter, Hen Harrier and Great Grey Shrike may be encountered on some of the less disturbed heaths.

Nightjars

Other Sites in the Area

To the S there are several interesting coastal spots on the Solent although they are best in autumn or winter and thus not easily combined with a visit to the New Forest.

17.1 Keyhaven and Pennington Marshes

Extensive areas of saltings on the coast are separated from the fresh marshes and lagoons by a seawall. South of Lymington, leave the A337 in Pennington onto a minor road S to Lower Pennington and continue to the coast. The marshes and saltings can be viewed from the seawall. The area is notable for waders in autumn and Merlin and Short-eared Owl are regular in winter.

17.2 Stanpit Marsh

This local nature reserve lies on the N side of Christchurch Harbour and comprises tidal mudflats, saltings, and fresh marsh.

There is an Information Centre, a nature trail, and free public access. The reserve is reached from the car park in Stanpit Lane on the SW side of Christchurch. The main ornithological interest is wildfowl and waders in autumn and winter. S of the harbour, Hengistbury Head is a local migration watchpoint.

Stanpit Marsh, warden: 67 Thornbury Road, Southbourne, Bournemouth. **Information**
Recorder: Hampshire.

Site No. 18 Langstone and Chichester Harbours (Hampshire, West Sussex)

This massive complex of tidal mudflats and saltings forms one of the most important estuaries on the S coast and is of both national and international significance for wintering waders and wildfowl. Several areas are Local Nature Reserves and 1,370 acres of Langstone Harbour are an RSPB reserve. The best time to visit is autumn and winter.

Habitat

The estuary itself is largely tidal mudflats and saltings. Much of the surrounding area is built up, especially at the W end, but the shoreline of Chichester Harbour is mostly undeveloped. There is some farmland on Hayling Island and around the E end of the complex. Farlington has some fresh marsh and lagoons.

Access (see map)
OS Sheet Nos. 196 and 197

The harbours can be reached from many points although certain areas have restricted access, particularly much of Chichester Harbour. The major wader roosts are on Farlington Marshes and its offshore islands, W Hayling Island, and Thorney Island. The mouths of the estuary can be viewed from East Head (W of West Wittering) and from both sides of Hayling Island. Views inside the estuary can be had from Hayling and Thorney Islands and the N shore can be seen from a coastal footpath. The following four routes are among the best.

Farlington Marshes

Leave the A27 Chichester–Fareham road at the intersection with the A2030 immediately N of Portsmouth. A track leads off the roundabout between the A27 (E) and A2030 (S) exits and runs E below and parallel to the A27 towards Farlington Marshes. Follow the coastline on foot around the W side of the marshes. A freshwater lagoon and associated marshland are worth checking on the way round. Continue around the peninsula. Areas of scrub at the N end attract migrants.

Thorney Island

Leave the A27 at Southbourne onto a minor road S to Prinsted. Park and walk S along the E shore of Thorney Island. Alternatively, from the A27 at Hermitage take the minor road to West Thorney and explore the E coast from here. Pilsea Island off the S tip is good for roosting waders at high tide.

Hayling Island

Take the A3023 S from Havant, cross Langstone Bridge onto Hayling Island, and walk around the W side of the island. The flock of

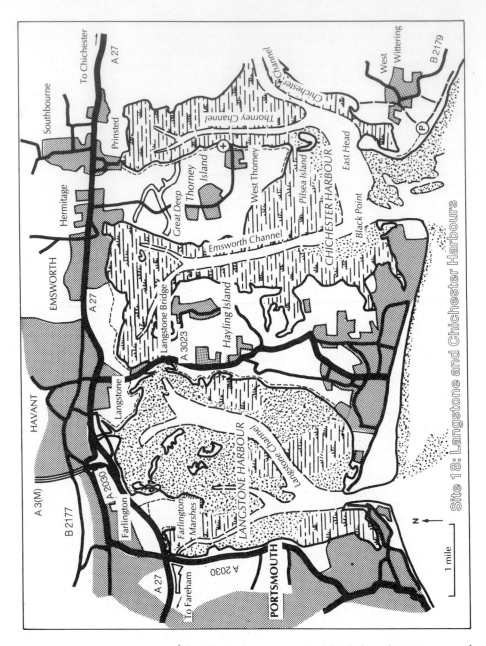

Site 18: Langstone and Chichester Harbours

Black-necked Grebes is best seen at high tide from the NW corner of Hayling Island.

North Shore

From the N side of Langstone Bridge walk E along the coastal footpath towards Emsworth.

Birds

Up to 90,000 waders (mostly Dunlin) and 15,000 wildfowl winter in the huge complex of mudflats. The numbers of Grey Plover and Black-tailed Godwit are of national importance, and the largest flocks of Knot on the S coast are found here. Small numbers of Ruff, Spotted Redshank, and Greenshank winter in the area. Brent Goose numbers have increased dramatically over the last few years to peak at 10,000; they can be seen in many places and are quite approachable at Farlington. The numbers of Shelduck, Wigeon, Teal, and Pintail are important, and Goldeneye and Red-breasted Merganser frequent the channels. Up to 30 Black-necked Grebes may be seen — the largest regular wintering flock in Britain; they favour the NE part of Langstone Harbour. A few Slavonian Grebes may also be present. As many as 20,000 gulls roost in the harbour, mostly Black-headed. Sparrowhawks and Short-eared Owls are occasionally seen hunting over the marshes.

Brent Geese

A wider variety of waders occurs in spring and autumn, which may include Little Stint and Wood Sandpiper.

There is less of interest in summer, but Sandwich, Common, and Little Terns breed as well as Oystercatcher, Ringed Plover, and Redshank.

Information

RSPB Reserve, summer warden: c/o Reserves Division, RSPB, The Lodge, Sandy, Bedfordshire SG19 2DL.
Recorders: Hampshire, Sussex.

Site No. 19 Pagham Harbour (West Sussex)

This site, S of Chichester, is one of the best on the S coast. 1,100 acres are a Local Nature Reserve managed by West Sussex County Council. Although primarily a major wintering area for wildfowl and waders it is also noted for migrants and is an important breeding site for several species.

Habitat

800 acres consist of relatively undisturbed tidal mudflats intersected by numerous channels while shingle beaches flank

either side of the harbour mouth. Patches of gorse and scrub occur around the perimeter alongside the harbour banks and seawalls and are attractive to migrant passerines. Small areas of reeds grow around the non-tidal pools. The only woodland of note is at Church Norton and this is good for migrants. The harbour is surrounded by fields on which waders frequently roost at high tide.

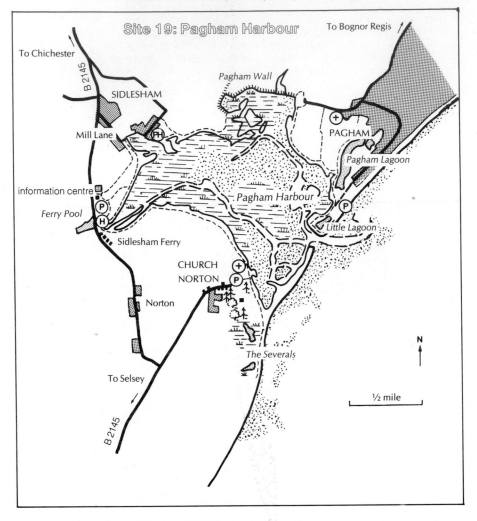

Access (see map)
OS Sheet No. 197

There is a public footpath around the entire embankment enclosing the harbour as well as a few other paths. Visitors should keep to these paths. Parts of the shingle are closed off from April to July to assist the breeding birds. It is not practical to walk around the entire harbour but there are four good access points.

Sidlesham Ferry

The B2145 from Chichester crosses the W arm of the harbour here. An information centre, manned mainly at weekends, and a small hide are sited beside the road on the N side. A nature trail starts from here following the seawall NE towards Sidlesham village. Ferry Pool, W of the road and easily viewed from it, attracts many interesting waders in autumn and winter and a number of rarities have been found. From Sidlesham Ferry, the walk along the seawall around the S edge of the harbour to Church Norton is recommended. This stretch offers some of the best views over the harbour although at low tide the waders tend to be well scattered and distant.

Church Norton

Continue S from Sidlesham Ferry on the B2145, turn left to Church Norton after 1¼ miles, and park at the end of the road beside the church. A short track leads to the harbour. The woodland and hedges are worth checking for migrants and the harbour mouth can be seen well from here. Turn right to reach the shingle shore. Seaducks and grebes are regularly seen offshore in winter. Just inland of the beach to the S there are some small freshwater pools and reedbeds (the Severals) which can hold interesting birds.

Sidlesham Village

The Crab and Lobster pub is at the edge of the harbour and from here you can walk E around the seawall towards Pagham village.

Pagham Lagoon

From Chichester take the B2145 S. After 1½ miles turn left onto the B2166 and in 2½ miles turn right to Pagham village. The road W out of the village past the church leads to the harbour's NE corner. Walking round to the right eventually leads to Sidlesham and left takes you to the coast past the end of Pagham Lagoon. Alternatively, a road follows the coast past the lagoon to a car park on the spit. The end of the spit is a good place from which to see waders and duck at the mouth of the harbour, especially at high tide. Pagham Lagoon itself can be quickly checked and is best in winter. The scrub and gardens near the lagoon can hold migrants.

Birds

In winter Red-throated Diver, Slavonian Grebe, Eider, Common Scoter, and Red-breasted Merganser are regular offshore and best viewed from Church Norton. Guillemot and Razorbill are less frequent. In the harbour several hundred Brent Geese winter as well as many dabbling duck, including Pintail. Goldeneye favour the deeper channels and Smew are occasionally seen on Pagham Lagoon. Large numbers of waders use the harbour and a few Avocet, Ruff, and Black-tailed Godwit are often to be seen on the Ferry Pool. Water Rail, Kingfisher, and Bearded Tit frequent the Severals in small numbers in winter. Short-eared Owls sometimes hunt over the saltings, which attract Rock Pipit and Twite.

In spring and (especially) autumn waders are more varied and regularly include Little Stint and Curlew Sandpiper, while Black-tailed Godwits sometimes occur in large numbers. Sandwich and Common Terns are often present but Arctic and Black Terns are less frequent and Little Gulls are only occasional. Red-necked Grebe is a rare autumn visitor, usually on the sea. Passerine migration is sometimes prominent, and typical species include Yellow Wagtail, Redstart, Whinchat, Wheatear, Spotted Flycatcher and a variety of warblers. Black Redstart and Pied Flycatcher are annual but in small numbers. Firecrests are quite scarce, occurring mainly in spring, and Hoopoe is recorded most years. Wryneck and Melodious Warbler occur in autumn but are only occasional.

In summer up to 70 pairs of Little Terns, plus Oystercatchers and Ringed Plovers, breed on the shingle beaches and on the shingle island inside the harbour. Shelduck nest in the adjoining fields and

Little Terns

Reed and Sedge Warblers occupy the reedbeds. Barn Owls are often seen hunting in the Sidlesham Ferry area and breed nearby. Although they may hunt by day, dawn and dusk offer the best chances of seeing one. Little Owls can sometimes be seen round Church Norton, and Ring-necked Parakeets are not infrequent there.

Other Sites in the Area
19.1 Selsey Bill

Although not in the same league as Dungeness or Portland, Selsey is one of the most important seawatching sites on the S coast. To reach the Bill, continue S from Sidlesham Ferry on the B2145 and at Selsey turn left down East Street and right just before the Fisherman's Joy pub; continue to the sea. The best place to seawatch is a short distance E of the Bill.

Peak seabird movements occur in spring, especially between late April and early May, the most favourable winds being light SE. Large numbers of Common Scoter migrate E, with the majority in late April, but Velvet Scoter are much less frequent. Other birds which are seen regularly with peak numbers in spring are divers, Eider, Red-breasted Merganser, Bar-tailed Godwit, terns, and auks. A few Pomarine Skuas are recorded in early May each year, while Arctic Skuas are not uncommon in both spring and autumn. Shearwaters are infrequent, mostly occurring in autumn, but Gannets and Kittiwakes are seen all year. Black Redstarts are recorded regularly, mainly in spring or late autumn, and one or two occasionally winter on the Bill.

19.2 Chichester Gravel Pits (see map)

These pits are by the A27 Chichester by-pass E of the town. Leave the A27 at Westhampnett onto a minor road S. Park after ¼ mile and walk along a path to the right; the pits right of the path are generally the best for waders. Continue S on the road and on reaching the B2144 turn right. Another good pit can be seen on the right from the road. Continue to rejoin the A27, turn left (S), and at the next roundabout take a minor road to Runcton. Some more pits can be seen on the right and a footpath runs along their W side. Another pit can be seen from the B2145 immediately S of the A27.

In winter a few Scaup and Ruddy Duck are often to be found but the pits are best in hard weather when Goosander, Smew, and the occasional diver may occur. In autumn, waders frequent the muddy margins, small numbers of Little Gulls and Black Terns are regular, and large numbers of hirundines roost.

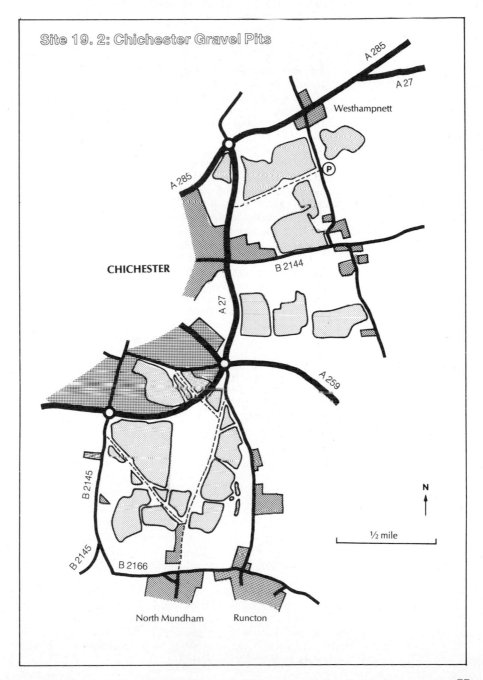

Site 19. 2: Chichester Gravel Pits

19.3 Amberley Wild Brooks

These marshes in the valley of the River Arun are situated immediately N of Amberley, c 8 miles N of Littlehampton. From Arundel take the A284 N and after 2½ miles turn right onto the B2139. Continue for 2½ miles and turn left into Amberley. A track leads N across the marshes from the village and it is possible to walk all the way to Greatham Bridge, 2 miles away. Alternatively, drive to Greatham Bridge on minor roads around the E side of Amberley Wild Brooks via Rackham and Greatham. Waltham Brooks lie S of Greatham Bridge and can be viewed from the car park.

Wintering wildfowl are Amberley's main attraction: good numbers of the commoner ducks can be seen, plus up to 100 Bewick's Swans, mainly at Waltham Brooks. Geese, usually White-fronts are only occasional, but Hen Harriers and Short-eared Owls are often present. Garganey are regular in spring and Waltham Brooks attracts passage waders. The woodland between Rackham and Greatham holds all three woodpeckers and Marsh and Willow Tits.

19.4 West Beach, Littlehampton

West Beach lies on the coast between Littlehampton and Climping. Leave Littlehampton W on the A259 and ½ mile after crossing the river turn sharp left to backtrack on the old road to Littlehampton. Continue for ¾ mile and just before the footbridge turn right towards the mouth of the Arun. Park after ¼ mile and walk SW towards the coast alongside the N edge of the golf course, looking for migrants on the way. At the coast turn right and work the coastal bushes. Alternatively, a minor road leads to the coast from Climping, past the Black Horse pub. Check the trees and bushes in this area and continue E along the coast towards the golf course.

A good variety of migrants occurs in spring and autumn including small numbers of Redstart, Black Redstart, Ring Ouzel, Firecrest, and Pied Flycatcher. Hobby and Short-eared Owl are occasional and several rarities have been found in recent years. In winter Purple Sandpipers occur at the river mouth at high tide.

Information

Pagham Harbour Local Nature Reserve: Selsey Rd, Sidlesham, Chichester PO20 7NE   Tel. 0243-56508.
Reference: *The Natural History of Pagham Harbour Part 1* by W. W. A. Phillips and I. Kraunsoe. This checklist of the birds of Pagham is available from the Information Centre.
Recorder: Sussex.

Site No. 20 Thursley Common (Surrey)

This National Nature Reserve of 893 acres is an important part of the West Surrey heathlands. Several specialities breed, notably Hobby, Woodlark, and Dartford Warbler.

Habitat

The principal habitats are wet and dry heath, woodland, and bog. The dry heath is dominated by heather with some gorse, and invading birch scrub is cleared to maintain this habitat. Fire is a great hazard but controlled burning is carried out to assist the regeneration of heather. In addition, water levels are regulated to prevent the bogs and pools drying out.

The common is adjacent to the A3 c 8 miles SW of Guildford. **Access (see map)**
Access is from Thursley village, the road along the common's S   OS Sheet No. 186
edge, or the Churt–Elstead road on the W side. There is a car park
on the latter road. The common is open to the public free of charge
but you should keep to the paths.

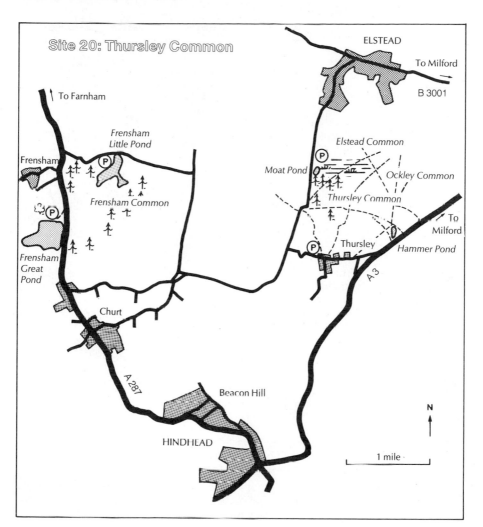

This is one of the best places to see Hobby. A good time to look is   **Birds**
late afternoon during summer as they hawk for insects or chase
hirundines; find a good vantage point to watch from. Sparrowhawk also breeds and is regularly seen. A few pairs of Curlew nest, a
scarce breeding bird in S England. The small fluctuating population
of Dartford Warblers favours areas of gorse but can be hard to find.
Woodlark is another speciality and may be found in the scrubby
heathland or woodland edge. Although resident they are often
easiest to see when performing song-flights in early spring. Commoner breeding species include all three woodpeckers, Tree Pipit,

Redstart, and Stonechat. Nightingale may also be seen but requires a little more effort.

In winter, Hen Harrier and Great Grey Shrike are occasionally seen.

Hobby

Other Sites in the area
20.1 Frensham Common
(see map)

This area of heath and woodland lies a few miles W of Thursley, straddling the A287. There is a car park on the left just beyond Frensham Great Pond, *c* 2 miles N of Churt. The area is crossed by many paths but a walk through the woods and across the common to the Little Pond is probably the most profitable. Breeding birds include Buzzard, Hobby, all three woodpeckers, Woodlark, Tree Pipit, Nightingale, Redstart, Stonechat, and Dartford Warbler.

Information

Thursley Common, warden: 8 Homefield Cottages, Highfield Lane, Thursley, Godalming, Surrey.
Recorder: Surrey.

Site No. 21 Staines Reservoir (Surrey)

Of the many reservoirs in the London area, Staines is undoubtedly the best known and most accessible. It provides a sanctuary for many wintering waterfowl and attracts a variety of migrants.

Habitat

The reservoir's 420 acres are divided by a narrow causeway. The edges are of sloping concrete but nevertheless attract a few waders during the migration seasons. Recently the two sections have been drained (separately) for many months at a time, and the resulting mudflats and pools have formed a haven for waders, including several rarities.

Access
(see map)
OS Sheet No. 176

The A3044 runs N between King George VI and Staines Reservoirs and almost halfway along there is a building on the lefthand side. Park here on the grass verge and on the opposite side go through a kissing gate up to the causeway bisecting the reservoir. The iron railings on each side are useful for resting telescopes if you have no tripod — a telescope is usually essential. There is no restriction on access to the causeway, and at weekends it can become almost crowded, mainly with birders and dog-walkers. There is no facility for walking around the reservoir and King George VI Reservoir opposite is totally restricted.

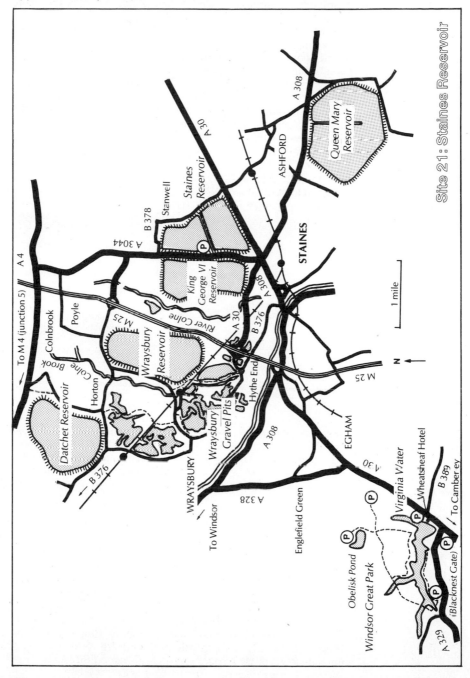

Site 21: Staines Reservoir

Birds

Large concentrations of waterfowl are present in winter. Black-necked Grebes are regular in small numbers and can be seen at almost any time of year, though peak counts are usually August–October. Although almost annual, Slavonian and Red-necked Grebes should be regarded as unusual. The majority of duck are Tufted Duck and Pochard, but small numbers of Goldeneye and Goosander are present in winter. Smew are nowadays seen only infrequently.

A wide variety of migrants can be seen in spring and autumn. Common, Arctic, and Black Terns are regular as are Little Gulls. Black Terns in autumn should be checked for a vagrant White-winged Black Tern (now almost annual somewhere in the London area). A sprinkling of waders can be found on the concrete edges, though the number and variety increases dramatically when the reservoir is drained. Migrant passerines often occur along the causeway, and include Wheatear, Yellow Wagtail, and Whinchat. Hobbies are not infrequently seen in spring and autumn, usually at dusk chasing hirundines.

Summer is usually quiet but some outstanding rarities have turned up in June and July, while Black-necked Grebes usually reappear from mid-July.

Black-necked Grebes

Other Sites in the Area
21.1 Queen Mary Reservoir
(see map)

This is another good reservoir situated near Sunbury and conveniently close to Staines. It is possible to walk around the perimeter but a permit (from Thames Water, in advance) is required to visit it. The E part of the reservoir is free from sailing activities. The entrance to the reservoir is at the NE corner off a minor road running SE from the A308.

21.2 Wraysbury Gravel Pits
(see map)

These lie W of Staines Reservoir in the Colnbrook valley and are a regular haunt of Smew in winter as well as a variety of other wildfowl. Leave the A30 NW of Staines onto the B376 to Hythe End and Wraysbury. After ¼ mile there is a stile on the right just before the bridge over the Coln Brook, and this leads onto a footpath which runs parallel to the river. The pits on the right are a favoured haunt of Smew, particularly the end pit. A few wintering Chiffchaffs are usually present in the bushes. Another pit can be easily viewed from the B376 between Hythe End and Wraysbury. Ring-necked Parakeets are regularly seen in this area and are resident. The pit immediately S of Wraysbury station is also good for Smew: leave

Wraysbury towards the station and turn right to the station before reaching the hump-back bridge; a pit on the right can be viewed from the roadside. Wraysbury Reservoir lies E of the gravel pits but there is no access to it. To the N, Datchet Reservoir (Queen Mother Reservoir) attracts grebes and the occasional diver: access is limited to a small section of its NE corner which can be reached from the Colnbrook–Horton road.

Lying at the S end of Windsor Great Park, a few miles SW of Staines, this is a well-known haunt of Mandarins and Hawfinches throughout the year. Leave Staines on the A30 and after the Wheatsheaf Hotel turn right onto the A329, parking after 1 mile in the public car park on the right. Walk towards Virginia Water bearing left to cross an arm of the lake over a small stone bridge. There are some hornbeams in this area which are favoured by Hawfinches though it is best to look for them in the early morning before the area is disturbed. Mandarins can be found anywhere on the lake: the best areas are N of the car park and at the E end; in autumn flocks congregate on the Obelisk Pond.

21.3 Virginia Water (Surrey, Berkshire) (see map)

Thames Water (free annual birdwatching permits for Queen Mary and other reservoirs): New River Head, Rosebery Avenue, London EC1R 4TP. Tel. 01-837 3300 ext. 2273.
Recorder: Greater London (covers the area within 20 miles of St Paul's Cathedral). Virginia Water records to Surrey and Berkshire recorders.

Information

Site No. 22 Beachy Head (East Sussex)

The cliffs of Beachy Head, immediately SW of Eastbourne, jut S into the English Channel and this prominent position has produced one of the best migration watchpoints on the S coast, both for seabirds and landbirds. Generally, it is only worth visiting in spring and autumn, and even then can be very quiet indeed if the winds are unfavourable.

A narrow belt of coastal downland extends for about 4 miles between Eastbourne and Birling Gap, lying S of the minor road which connects the two. Areas of gorse and scrub occur on the downland and there is a small wood at Belle Tout. N of the road is farmland (mainly crops). The chalk cliffs vary from 50 feet at Birling Gap to over 500 feet opposite Beachy Head Hotel and are constantly being eroded.

Habitat

There are three main areas to check, all connected by the minor road which runs around the headland. The more energetic may wish to walk along the clifftops between each site in order to cover as much of the habitat as possible, particularly if it is a good day for migrants. Due to disturbance from non-birders, early mornings are always best.

Access (see map) OS Sheet No. 199

From the car park walk a short distance to the coast and turn towards some beach huts. This is the best place to seawatch from. The area of bushes E of Birling is often good for migrants.

Birling Gap

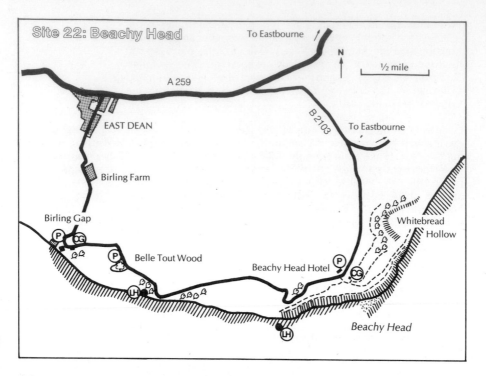

Belle Tout Wood

There is a small car park on the W side of the wood. Belle Tout is worth checking for passerine migrants, especially in autumn. Despite its small size, birds are often very hard to find. The gorse and scrub on the slopes E of Belle Tout should also be explored for migrants.

Whitebread Hollow

Park just E of the Beachy Head Hotel and walk along the cliff path to the top of the hollow, a large SE-facing basin of scrub and woodland; the dense cover makes it a difficult area to work. Mist-netting is carried out here by the Beachy Head Ringing Group (mainly at weekends, August–November). The cliff path and the area between the hollow and the sea can also be rewarding.

Birds

Seabird passage is best in spring, between mid-March and mid-May. Light SE winds are most favourable. Good numbers of both Red-throated and Black-throated Divers migrate E in early spring together with many Common Scoter. Brent Geese and a few Velvet Scoter can also be seen. From April, terns and Bar-tailed Godwits move in large numbers and skuas occur most days in the first half of May. Pomarine Skuas are regularly seen in small groups, especially after SE winds. A few Manx Shearwaters, Mediterranean Gulls, Roseate Terns, and Puffins are seen each year and Little Gulls and Black Terns are regular, sometimes in impressive numbers. Black Redstarts and Firecrests can be found from mid-March at Belle Tout and Birling Gap. The commoner migrants pass through in April – May and regularly include Nightingale, Redstart, and Ring Ouzel. Grasshopper and Wood

Warblers and Pied Flycatchers are seen most years and scarce migrants such as Hoopoe and Serin are occasionally found.

In summer a few pairs of Fulmar nest and breeding passerines include Nightingale. Dartford Warblers used to breed and are still occasionally seen in autumn.

Pomarine Skuas

There is little seabird passage in autumn. Migrant passerines, on the other hand, are usually present in good numbers, especially warblers and chats. Black Redstart, Ring Ouzel, and Firecrest are regular in late autumn. Scarce migrants are found most years; some of the more likely candidates are Dotterel, Wryneck, Tawny Pipit, Icterine, Melodious, and Yellow-browed Warblers, Red-backed Shrike, and Ortolan Bunting. Perhaps the most regular is Tawny Pipit — check the stubble fields in the second half of September for this species. A number of rarities have occurred, one of the most frequent being Pallas's Warbler, which has been found several times in Belle Tout Wood in late October or early November.

There is little to see in winter. Movements of Gannets, auks, or divers are always a possibility and occasionally a Peregrine visits the cliffs. There is often a Little Owl in Belle Tout and Stonechats and Corn Buntings may be seen on the headland.

Other Sites in the Area

22.1 Cuckmere Haven

The valley of the Cuckmere River lies 3 miles W of East Dean, crossed by the A259. From here footpaths lead either side of the river to the Haven. A small scrape E of the river mouth often has a few waders and sometimes wintering Twite. Kingfishers are regular (except summer) on the N oxbow and ditches W of the river.

Recorder: Sussex.

Information

Site No. 23 Dungeness (Kent)

This unique peninsula, situated between Hastings and Folkestone, is famed for migrants in spring and autumn and has an active bird observatory. In addition, the RSPB maintains a bird reserve which holds important gull and tern colonies on the flooded gravel pits.

Habitat

The area is a flat expanse of shingle with ridges and hollows. The flora is generally sparse, though in the deeper hollows and other sheltered areas a denser vegetation including gorse and broom has developed. The only natural fresh water on Dungeness is the Open Pits and these are surrounded by dense reeds, sedges, brambles, and sallows. Recently, gravel workings have created more open water with islands, considerably improving the diversity of birds.

**Access
(see map)**
OS Sheet No. 189

From New Romney, turn left on to the B2075 to Lydd about a mile W of the town centre (also signed Dungeness 6½). On entering Lydd, fork left after the airport and on reaching a roundabout take the first exit. A long road leads directly to Dungeness. Lydd can also be reached by a minor road from Rye via Camber. Dungeness can be conveniently worked from two points.

RSPB Reserve

About 1½ miles after the roundabout you reach the ARC pits on the left. Dungeness Reserve (RSPB) is signed on the right along a track with the warden's house on the corner. Follow the track to the Information Centre and park there. The centre is sited at the edge of Burrowes Pit and there are 3 hides nearby giving good views over the pit and its islands. Most of the reserve's specialities can be seen from the hides although there is a trail of 1½ miles for the more energetic. The nearby ARC pits are always worth a look and can be viewed easily from the road. The RSPB reserve, covering 1,962 acres, is open every day except Tuesdays, 09.00–21.00 (or sunset when earlier). Entrance is £2, or free to RSPB and YOC members.

**Bird Observatory
Recording Area**

Continuing along the Lydd–Dungeness road, fork right about ½ mile after the ARC Pits and again shortly after (do not take the first right fork which leads to the power station). Continue around the headland to Dungeness itself. Shortly after the Britannia pub the road reaches the old (black) lighthouse. Park on the right opposite the lighthouse (if visiting the observatory you can drive along the private road to it around the seaward side of the old lighthouse). Dungeness Bird Observatory is the end one of a row of coastguard cottages and is surrounded by a moat filled with bushes. This, and the various clumps of bushes scattered across the shingle attract migrants in spring and autumn. Access is largely unrestricted, and from the observatory you can walk to both the Open Pits and Long Pits.

Dungeness is famed for seawatching and the best point to watch from is opposite 'The Patch'. This disturbed area of water, caused by the power station outflow, regularly attracts large numbers of gulls and terns, often including some uncommon species. There is a seawatching hide on the shingle for observatory residents and Friends of Dungeness Bird Observatory.

Hostel-type self-catering accommodation is available at the observatory for up to 10 people throughout the year at £2 per night. Bookings should be made in advance to the warden.

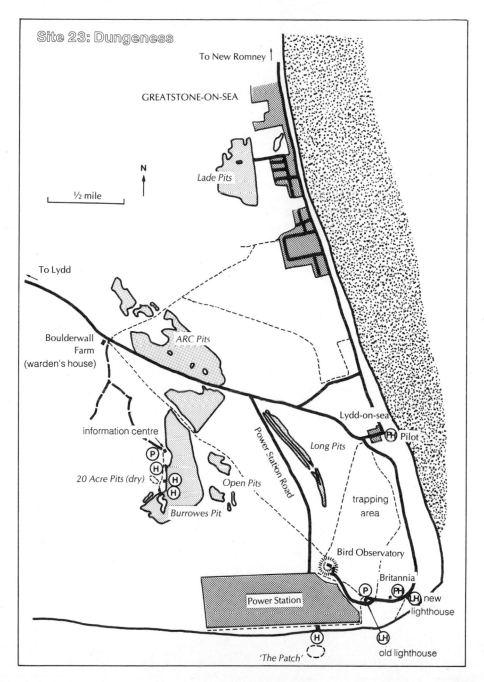

Birds

Spring migration gets underway in mid-March and the main passage commences in April and continues to mid-May. Most of the common migrants are well represented, while Ring Ouzel and Firecrest are regularly seen. S or SE winds in late May and June are likely to bring a rarity; Hoopoe is one of the more likely, and Wryneck, Icterine Warbler, Red-backed Shrike, and Serin are almost annual at this time. Seabird passage is particularly good in spring with the peak occurring April to mid-May. The bulk comprises Common Scoters, Bar-tailed Godwits, and Common Terns, together with a wide variety of divers, grebes, ducks, waders, skuas, gulls, and terns. A concentrated passage of Pomarine Skuas is noted each spring, usually in the first half of May. Little Gulls are sometimes numerous on the Patch, while Mediterranean Gull and Roseate Tern are regular in very small numbers.

In summer the islands in Burrowes and the ARC Pits hold impressive colonies of terns and gulls: mainly Common and Sandwich Terns and Black-headed and Herring Gulls, but a few pairs of Common Gulls also nest (the only regular breeding site in southern England). Recently, one or two pairs of Mediterranean Gulls have attempted to breed and also a single pair of Roseate Terns, but a great deal of patience is usually required to find them. A few pairs of Little Terns breed on the coastal shingle and also on a specially created island on the Burrowes Pit. Unfortunately, Kentish Plover and Stone Curlew no longer breed at Dungeness. Up to six pairs of Black Redstart breed around the power station and can be seen along the perimeter fence.

The volume of autumn passerine migration is impressive, and, from late August, E winds may bring Wrynecks, Redstarts, and Pied Flycatchers. By September there is a chance of scarcer migrants from the continent. Tawny Pipit, Bluethroat, Icterine and Barred Warblers, Red-breasted Flycatcher, Red-backed Shrike, and Ortolan Bunting are all seen most years but usually very few of each. October is the most likely time for a major rarity. Good days are dependent on suitable weather such as E winds and early morning precipitation; consequently, birdless days are not

White-winged Black Tern and Black Terns

infrequent. By late September the bulk of migrants will be birds arriving from the continent to winter, including Skylarks, Meadow Pipits, Robins, thrushes, finches, and even tits, and these movements will continue into November.

In August, Gannets, Common Scoter, and Sandwich Terns are likely to be the most obvious seabirds moving W, while Great Skuas and Manx Shearwaters (of the Balearic race) are occasionally seen. The Patch is probably now at its best; a few Arctic Terns and Little Gulls are usually among the commoner species, whilst Black Tern numbers peak from the end of August to early September and a vagrant White-winged Black Tern is usually found among them. Although the Patch is the most likely place to look for one, all the pits in the area should be checked. The return wader migration begins in July and the commoner species may include small numbers of Little Stints and Curlew and Wood Sandpipers. A good variety of waders can be seen from the hides on the RSPB reserve.

Winter is quiet, although large numbers of duck use the areas of open water. Amongst the commoner dabbling and diving ducks a few Goldeneye, Smew, and Goosander may be found. Offshore, a variety of divers, grebes, and seaduck occur.

Other Sites in the Area

23.1 Lade Pits (see map)

These are W of the coast road between Dungeness and Greatstone-on-Sea. Turn left off the coast road 2 miles N of the Pilot pub in Lydd-on-Sea and, after crossing the railway, turn right through the houses. After bending left the road reaches a bridge and the pits, which attract a variety of waders in spring and autumn.

23.2 Pett Level (East Sussex)

This series of pools surrounded by damp meadows lies alongside the coast road between Winchelsea Beach and Fairlight. The pools are easily viewed from the road and are drained in mid-July to attract a variety of waders.

23.3 Rye Harbour (East Sussex)

This Local Nature Reserve of 950 acres comprises shingle, saltings, and gravel pits as well as arable land and scrub. A minor road immediately S of Rye on the Winchelsea road follows the S side of the River Rother to Rye Harbour, with a car park and information centre at its end. Continue on foot but keep strictly to the footpaths. The reed-fringed pits are overlooked by two hides and attract a wide variety of wildfowl, waders, and terns, particularly in spring and autumn. Flocks of Common Scoter are seen regularly in Rye Bay and sometimes include Velvet Scoter.

Information

RSPB Reserve, warden: Boulderwall Farm, Dungeness Rd, Lydd, Kent TN29 9PN.
DBO, warden: Dungeness Bird Observatory, Romney Marsh, Kent TN29 9NA. Tel. 0679-21309.
Rye Harbour, warden: 1 Coastguard Cottages, Rye Harbour, E. Sussex.
Pett Level, warden: 23 Saltings Way, Upper Beeding, W. Sussex.
Recorder: Kent (Dungeness and Lade Pits), Sussex (Pett Level and Rye Harbour).

Site No. 24 Sandwich Bay (Kent)

On the E coast of Kent S of Ramsgate, this area is noted for migrants, including a sprinkling of scarce species and rarities. A bird observatory operates over c 3,200 acres of privately-owned dunes and marshland. The peak seasons are March–June and August–November. Pegwell Bay to the N and Sandwich Bay itself attract waders and wildfowl, especially in winter. Large areas of the mudflats, saltings, and dunes around the mouth of the Stour estuary are protected as reserves and are maintained by the National Trust and Kent Trust for Nature Conservation.

Habitat

The coast is dominated by a series of sand-dunes, many of which have been converted into golf links. Inland, a good proportion of the area is farmland, and waders roost on these fields at high tide. Small areas of freshwater marsh, reedbeds, bushes, and trees add diversity. To the N the River Stour enters the sea at Pegwell Bay and extensive mud and sandflats and saltings surround the estuary.

**Access
(see map)**
OS Sheet No. 179

Leave Sandwich E along Sandown Road towards Sandwich Bay Estate. The observatory, at Old Downs Farm, is on the right shortly after the toll gate (cost £2). Access to the main areas of interest is as follows.

Sandwich Bay Estate

Passerine migrants are mainly attracted to the bushes and gardens in the vicinity of the Estate. Access is from the toll road via the gate opposite the track to the observatory. Cross the field to the stile and check the bushes around the Heligoland traps. There are no restrictions on visiting the observatory but birders should not enter the enclosed trapping areas and should respect residents' privacy when watching birds in gardens.

Worth Marshes

From the observatory, continue S beyond the Estate on the Ancient Highway towards the Chequers pub. Footpaths cross Worth Marshes to North Stream and back to Old Downs Farm.

NT and KTNC Reserves

From the observatory, continue through the Estate to the coast and drive N beside the beach to Prince's Golf Club car park. Walk N along the beach to the reserves. Access is largely unrestricted except for certain areas during the breeding season. You can either return via the riverside footpath to New Downs Farm or across the New Downs Farmland, checking the conifers at the N end of Prince's Golf Course on the way.

The entire area is privately owned and you should keep to the roads and public footpaths at all times. Sandwich Bay Bird Observatory is open all year and provides hostel-type self-catering accommodation for up to 12 people at £2 per night (£1.25 for members of SBBO Trust). Further details are available from the honorary warden.

Birds

The first arrivals of the spring are in March and include Garganey, Black Redstart, and Firecrest, and by the end of the month Sandwich Terns begin to arrive. The bulk of the passage is April–May, when a number of scarce migrants are regularly recorded, including Kentish Plover and Golden Oriole.

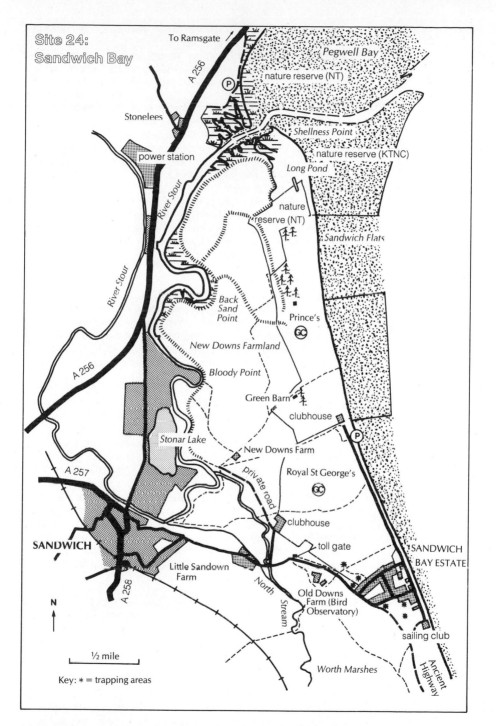

To Ramsgate

A 256

P

Pegwell Bay

nature reserve (NT)

Stonelees

Shellness Point

power station

nature reserve (KTNC)

Long Pond

River Stour

nature
reserve (NT)

Sandwich Flats

River Stour

*Back
Sand
Point*

Prince's
GC

New Downs Farmland

Bloody Point

Green Barn

clubhouse

A 256

P

Stonar Lake

New Downs Farm

private road

Royal St George's
GC

A 257

clubhouse

SANDWICH

toll gate

SANDWICH
BAY ESTATE

A 258

Little Sandown
Farm

North Stream

Old Downs
Farm (Bird
Observatory)

N

sailing club

Ancient
Highway

½ mile

Key: * = trapping areas

Worth Marshes

The summer months are quiet but up to 30 pairs of Little Terns breed in the area, and Kittiwakes, from their breeding cliffs at Dover, are seen frequently.

The autumn wader passage begins in mid-July and continues into September. Typical species include Curlew Sandpiper, Black-tailed Godwit, and Wood Sandpiper. August brings the return of the passerine migrants, mainly chats, warblers, and flycatchers. E winds encourage the occasional fall, which inevitably includes a scarce species or two. By late autumn the bulk consists of Goldcrests, Robins, thrushes, Starlings, and finches arriving from the continent to winter in Britain. Rarities can turn up at any time but late spring and particularly late autumn are the most likely periods. Sandwich Bay has recorded a number of outstanding species, and recently Pallas's Warblers have been almost annual in late October or early November, sometimes several at once.

Divers, grebes, and seaduck may be seen offshore in winter and Hen Harriers and Short-eared Owls hunt over the marshes. Golden Plovers and Lapwings take up residence in the fields and a variety of the commoner waders inhabit the mudflats. Snow Buntings are regular on the shore and Twite can be found around the estuary.

Other Sites in the Area
24.1 Folkestone

The sewage outfall at Copt Point, N of Folkestone harbour, is a particularly good spot for Mediterranean Gull. Several are seen regularly throughout the winter, from September onwards. Either view from the clifftops or descend (with great care) to the base of the cliffs. At high tide many gulls roost in Folkestone harbour and Purple Sandpipers roost on the harbour walls.

24.2 St Margaret's Bay

The coastline here is the closest point to France and consequently can be an excellent place to observe visible passerine migration. Big falls of common migrants are not infrequent in autumn, especially October, and scarcer species are occasionally found. Weather conditions appear to be irrelevant and falls can even occur in SW winds when other migration watchpoints are struggling. Unfortunately the birds rarely linger and an early morning visit is essential. Leave Dover on the A258 to Deal and after c 2 miles turn right onto the B2058 to St Margaret's at Cliffe. On entering the town, turn right onto an unclassified road leading to the lighthouse and park before reaching it. The lighthouse is situated at the head of a small valley and a footpath leads from it to a pillbox on the clifftops. This is the best place to observe migration in the first few hours after dawn. Afterwards, the valley can be checked for migrants filtering up it.

Information

Sandwich Bay Bird Observatory, hon. warden: 2 Old Downs Farm, Guilford Rd, Sandwich Bay, Kent CT13 9PF. Tel. 0304-617341.
KTNC and NT Reserves: c/o SBBO.
Recorder: Kent.

Site No. 25 Stodmarsh (Kent)

Stodmarsh is a National Nature Reserve lying in the Stour valley 5 miles NE of Canterbury. One of the finest wetlands in S England, it is notable for breeding Cetti's and Savi's Warblers. It is also well worth a visit during the spring migration and regularly turns up uncommon birds. 402 acres are managed by the Nature Conservancy Council.

The large shallow lagoons, extensive reedbeds, and partially flooded riverside meadows have been created by a gradual subsidence of underground coal workings. Patches of woodland and scrub have developed in the drier areas. Water levels are carefully controlled and grazing is allowed on the damp meadows to produce suitable habitats; parts of the reedbed are cut annually to improve growth.

Habitat

Leave Canterbury on the A257 towards Sandwich. After c 1½ miles, just past the golf course, take an inconspicuous left turn onto an unsigned minor road. This leads to the village of Stodmarsh, c 4 miles away. In the village, turn left immediately after the Red Lion pub down a narrow, unmetalled lane for a short distance to the reserve car park on the right. Various leaflets are on sale here from a small hut. The only access to the NNR is along the Lampen Wall (a flood protection barrier), which provides an excellent vantage point. From the car park continue on foot to the end of the lane, turning sharp right over a stile and onto the Lampen Wall. The path runs alongside woodland and scrub, then past open water and reedbeds into a drier, scrubby area, and finally after c 1 mile reaches the River Stour. It continues along the S bank of the river with reeds, wet meadows, and pasture to the right. You can walk all the way to Grove Ferry (c 2 miles), where there is a pub, picnic site, and cafe. However, if time is limited it is best to cover only a short stretch of the riverside path and then return to the car park.
Several other areas of the Stour Valley may be worthy of exploration. These are best reached from the A28 Canterbury–Margate road.

Access
(see map)
OS Map No. 179

Leave the A28 W into the village of Westbere. Park at the W end of the village and cross the railway line. A footpath leads across the marshes to the river, which it then follows in both directions, alongside reedbeds and open water.

Westbere
Marshes

2½ miles NE of Canterbury, at Sturry, a minor road leads S to Fordwich village. Park in the village and walk E alongside the river.

Fordwich

3½ miles after Sturry on the A28 a right turn leads to Grove Ferry down Grove Ferry Hill. The riverside path to Stodmarsh can be worked from here and the marshes and fields beside the road between Grove Ferry and Wickhambreaux may also be worth checking.

Grove Ferry

Stodmarsh's position, in a major river valley only a few miles from the coast, ensures an impressive passage of migrants, especially in spring. It is one of the best places to see early arrivals, before the main influx into Britain. A pair or two of Garganey may breed on or near the reserve, but the best chance of one is an early migrant. The wet meadows S of the riverside path are a favoured area. Osprey and Marsh Harrier are uncommon but regular migrants and others include any of the sea terns as well as Black Tern.

Birds

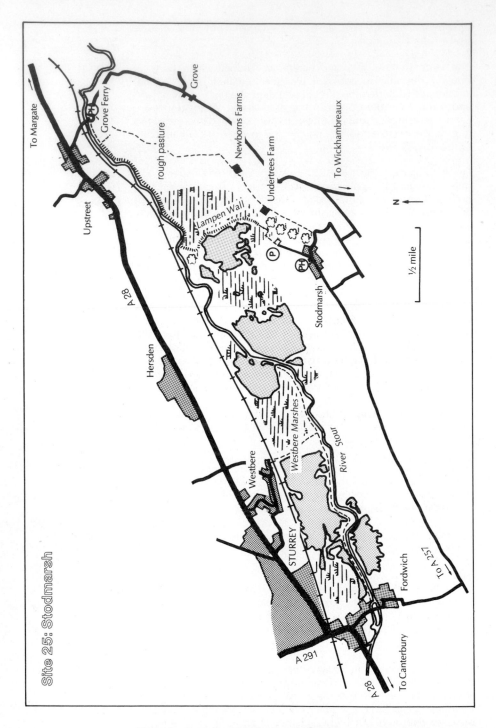

Site 25: Stodmarsh

Whimbrel, Ruff, and Black-tailed Godwit are also regular.
Although one or two pairs of Bittern probably nest, they are
difficult to see. In spring and early summer one is more likely to

hear the male's characteristic booming. Savi's Warbler is another speciality; one or two pairs breed annually and can usually be heard and, with perseverance, seen in the reedbeds E of the Lampen Wall, from mid-April onwards. Savi's are usually most vocal around dawn and dusk, but may sing briefly during the middle of the day. Stodmarsh's other warbler speciality, Cetti's Warbler, is commoner, more vocal, and resident. Before the hard winter of 1985/6 it was not unusual to hear up to 8 birds singing explosively from the dense thickets and scrub between the car park and the river. With patience they can be seen but are often reluctant to leave cover. Bearded Tits are not uncommon and small parties can usually be found in the reedbeds, particularly on still days. A few pairs of Grasshopper Warblers breed in the drier areas while Reed and Sedge Warblers and Reed Buntings are very common. Lapwing, Redshank, and Snipe breed on the wet meadows as well as Shoveler and Teal.

Cetti's Warbler

Large numbers of wildfowl winter on the reserve, mainly the commoner dabbling and diving ducks. Hen Harriers are frequently seen and Golden Plover can be found in the surrounding fields. A few Water Pipits favour the riverside meadows and a Great Grey Shrike is occasionally present, while Cetti's Warblers are often easiest to see in winter. As a bonus, two Glossy Ibises have wintered in the area since 1975 and 1979. They are usually present September–April, summering on the Isle of Sheppey. During the day they are inconspicuous as they feed in ditches in the rough pasture, but can sometimes be seen from the riverside path or even the road between Stodmarsh and Grove Ferry. They are easiest to see shortly before dusk as they go to roost, frequently flying over the Lampen Wall. At least one bird was still present in 1986.

Warden: 4 Sandpit Cottages, Wickhambreaux, Canterbury, Kent.   **Information**
Recorder: Kent.

Site No. 26 Isle of Sheppey (Kent)

The Isle of Sheppey lies on the S side of the Thames estuary, flanked by the Swale and Medway estuaries and connected to the mainland by the Kingsferry Bridge. It is particularly productive in winter, harbouring significant numbers of wildfowl and waders in addition to several unusual species. A greater variety of waders, and sometimes impressive movements of seabirds, can be seen in autumn.

Habitat

The S half of the island is the most productive for birds. Much of this area comprises rough grazing and marshes intersected by dykes and creeks, as well as some arable land, all protected from exceptionally high tides by long seawalls. At low tide, extensive mudflats are exposed on the Swale, bordered by saltings.

**Access
(see map)**
OS Sheet No. 178

Although interesting birds can be found in many places, three areas in particular are worthy of investigation.

Shell Ness

This hamlet lies at the E tip of Sheppey. Take the B2231 to Leysdown-on-Sea and continue along the seafront towards Shell Ness. Park just before the hamlet and walk along the seawall to the coast. It is worth checking the sea as well as the marshes and mudflats. Continuing along the beach, the bay beyond the pill box holds considerable numbers of wintering waders at high tide. After checking this area return along the seawall a few hundred yards and turn left along the seawall which runs approximately parallel to the coast. It may be worth walking up to 2 miles before returning.

Harty Ferry

From Leysdown, return W along the B2231 for c 2 miles. Before reaching Eastchurch turn left on a minor road signed 'Ferry Inn' towards the Isle of Harty. This crosses Capel Fleet (often worth a look) and eventually ends at the Swale, beyond the inn. In winter this is a good area for geese, swans, and raptors.

Elmley Marshes

Elmley Marshes are an RSPB reserve of 3,364 acres. Part (the Spitend Marshes) has been successfully managed to become an important area for both breeding and wintering waterbirds. Three hides overlook the lagoons and marshes and two overlook the Swale.

After crossing the Kingsferry bridge, continue on the A249 for c 1 mile. Turn right, following the RSPB signs, onto a rough track to reach the car park at Kingshill Farm after 2 miles. A walk of 1 mile is necessary to reach the hides. Keep to the main footpaths and walk below the seawall to avoid disturbing the birds. The reserve is open every day (except Tuesdays) from 09.00 to 21.00 (or sunset if earlier). Entrance is free.

Birds

Unless specifically mentioned for a site, the birds detailed below can be seen at any of the areas.

Sheppey is particularly good in winter although often cold and windswept. Divers and grebes are regular off Shell Ness, the most frequent being Red-throated Diver and Great Crested Grebe; other species are occasional. Hen Harriers are a winter speciality,

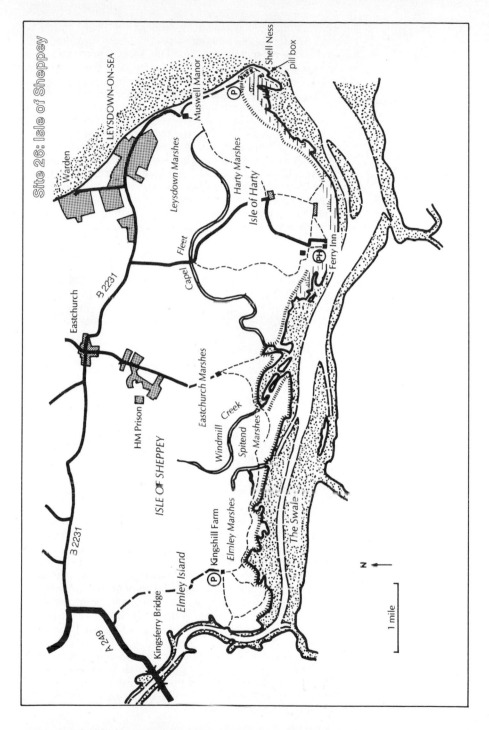

quartering the fields and marshes almost anywhere. Rough-legged Buzzards are only rare visitors but Merlin and Peregrine are more frequent, though not often seen on a casual visit. White-fronted

Goose is another winter speciality and all the fields should be checked. The Capel Fleet–Harty Ferry area is often favoured, and they sometimes roost at Elmley. Small numbers of Bewick's Swans and the occasional Whooper sometimes frequent the Harty Ferry area while Brent Geese may be seen anywhere around the coast. Very large numbers of duck winter, the commonest being Wigeon, Teal, Mallard, Pintail, and Shoveler. Large rafts of duck are often present offshore at Shell Ness and should be checked for Eider, Common Scoter, Goldeneye, and Red-breasted Merganser. Velvet Scoter are less frequent. At low tide waders can be seen anywhere on the extensive mudflats and at high tide they roost at Shell Ness and Elmley. Knot and Dunlin are the commonest, and other species include Sanderling. Short-eared Owls are present all year, though more numerous and most easily seen in winter. Twite and Lapland and Snow Buntings are sometimes seen on the beach at Shell Ness but Shore Larks are less frequent.

Short-eared Owls

The diversity of species increases in spring and autumn although the huge numbers of wildfowl and waders are missing. Marsh Harriers are more frequent at these seasons but can be seen throughout the year, and Garganey are sometimes found at Elmley in spring. The wide variety of waders may include Curlew Sandpiper and Black-tailed Godwit, in addition to the wintering and breeding species, and rare waders are seen annually. Seawatching off Shell Ness can be productive in autumn, particularly after strong N winds. Gannet, Great and Arctic Skuas, Kittiwake, and Common, Little, and Sandwich Terns are the most frequent species. Migrant passerines are not a feature but include Wheatear and Whinchat.

In summer a variety of the commoner ducks breed, occasionally including Garganey. Lapwing and Redshank are common and Common Terns nest on some of the saltmarsh islands at Elmley. Yellow Wagtail and Meadow Pipit are common breeding birds throughout.

Information

Elmley, warden: Kingshill Farm, Elmley, Sheerness, Isle of Sheppey, Kent ME12 3RW.
Recorder: Kent.

Site No. 27 North Kent Marshes (Kent)

These extensive marshes lie in the Thames estuary immediately W of the Isle of Sheppey, bordered by the Rivers Thames and Medway. Similar to Sheppey, they are best in winter or during the migration seasons.

Habitat

Mainly grassland and saltmarsh dissected by dykes and seawalls, and surrounded by mudflats at low tide, much of the area has been drained for growing wheat. Flooded pits at Cliffe are the result of clay extraction. An area of deciduous woodland and scrub near High Halstow is the RSPB reserve of Northward Hill.

Access
(see map)
OS Sheet No. 178
Cliffe

At the W end of the marshes, these pits are perhaps the most interesting area, attracting a variety of duck in winter and a wealth of waders on passage. The water level determines the best pits for waders. Turn left off the B2000 at the N end of Cliffe village and on reaching the first pool turn right. This road passes around the perimeter of the pools (several of which can be seen well) and continues to the Coastguard Cottages. A short walk beyond these leads to the seawall. Going N to Lower Hope Point may be profitable or alternatively walk S back around the pits via Cliffe Creek. It is a long walk all the way round but if time is short much of the area can be viewed from the roads. In addition to the Coastguard Cottages road, the road to the Works passes other pools and a track runs through the pits to Cliffe Creek.

Northward Hill

This 134-acre reserve lies immediately N of High Halstow. The oakwoods hold Britain's largest heronry; over 200 pairs are present February–July and a good range of woodland species can also be seen. High Halstow is N of the A228 in the centre of the North Kent Marshes. Parking is available by the village hall and the entrance to the reserve is N of Northwood Avenue. There is free acess at all times but the heronry may only be visited escorted (charge £1); apply in writing to the warden.

Halstow Marshes

In the centre of the North Kent Marshes these are excellent for wildfowl and waders, especially at the coast. Egypt and St Mary's Bays are particularly notable for waders at high tide. From High Halstow continue E towards the A228. After ½ mile turn left (N) to Decoy Farm and park at Swigshole. Fork right from here across the marshes to St Mary's Bay. Continue along the seawall W to Egypt Bay where another track leads back to Swigshole.

Birds

Bewick's Swans and White-fronted Geese regularly winter on the marshes and large numbers of dabbling duck can be seen including Pintail. The deeper pools attract diving duck, sometimes including Smew and Scaup. Waders are abundant and the typical wintering species include a few Avocets on Cliffe pools. Hen Harriers and Short-eared Owls can usually be seen hunting over the marshes and Merlins are regular. Snow Buntings can be rather elusive but Lapland Buntings are more frequent.
    Garganey may turn up in small numbers in spring and Black Terns are regular in both spring and autumn but the main interest is the passage of waders. Species which may be found include

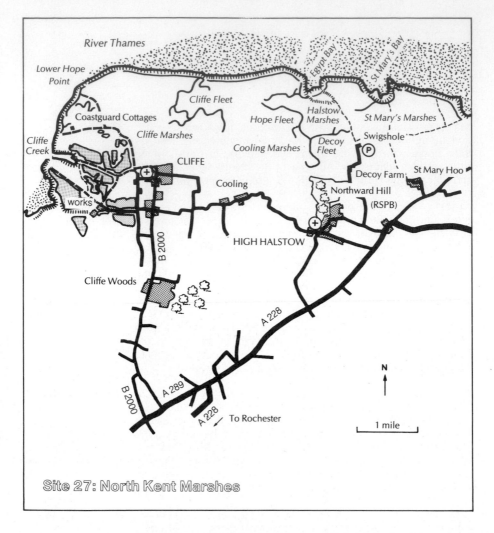

Site 27: North Kent Marshes

Little Stint, Curlew Sandpiper, and Wood Sandpiper, and something more unusual is a distinct possibility.

Garganey with Teal

Summer is quiet. Shelduck, Lapwing, and Redshank breed on the marshes and at Northward Hill the heronry and woodland species are the main attraction (although the reserve is best visited April–June when it can be combined with passage waders at Cliffe). Little Owls are common in the area and quite easy to see, but though Long-eared Owls breed at Northward Hill they are rarely seen. Other species on the reserve include all three woodpeckers and Nightingale.

Information

Northward Hill, warden: Swigshole Cottage, High Halstow, Rochester, Kent ME3 8SR.
Recorder: Kent.

EAST ANGLIA

Site No. 28 Old Hall Marshes (Essex)

Old Hall Marshes lie on the N shore of the Blackwater estuary 8 miles S of Colchester. They comprise the largest area of coastal marsh in Essex and the fourth largest in England. 1,134 acres are an RSPB reserve, which includes Great and Little Cob Islands. A variety of wildfowl breed, but the primary interest is in the winter and migration seasons when significant populations of wildfowl and waders are present.

Habitat

Three-quarters of the reserve is unimproved grazing marsh, the rest is improved grassland, arable fields, and saltmarsh. Much of the marsh has become drier in recent years but the management aim is to raise water levels for the benefit of breeding and wintering wildfowl, waders, and Bearded Tits.

Access (see map)
OS Sheet No. 168

From Maldon, take the B1026 to Tolleshunt D'Arcy. At the N end of the village turn right onto a minor road E. After 1¼ miles, the road bends sharp right and immediately after the bend turn left onto the track to Old Hall Farm and the warden's house. Park here and continue on foot. The seawall extends around the perimeter of the marshes and there is also a central path (which saves the lengthy walk around the seawall). It is only possible to leave the public footpaths by written application to the warden, but most of the birds can be seen without this.

Birds

Several thousand Brent Geese winter in the area and are often quite approachable. Duck are numerous and there is a regular herd of Bewick's Swans. Eider, Goldeneye, Red-breasted Merganser, and occasionally Long-tailed Duck frequent the various tidal waters. Red-throated and Great Northern Divers and Great Crested, Little, and Slavonian Grebes are all worth looking out for and Hen Harriers, Merlins, and Short-eared Owls are quite frequent. The usual waders are numerous while Twite are the most interesting passerines to occur regularly.

During migration seasons, waders likely to be encountered include Little Stint, Curlew Sandpiper, and godwits, and rarer species have been identified on a number of occasions. Breeding species include Shelduck, Pochard, Lapwing, Redshank, Yellow Wagtail, and Reed Bunting, and Common Terns may be viewed flying to and from Great Cob Island. Marsh Harriers are not infrequently seen in summer.

Other Sites in the Area

The whole of the N shore of the 10 mile long Blackwater estuary is an excellent birdwatching area in winter and Slavonian Grebes are a speciality of this river.

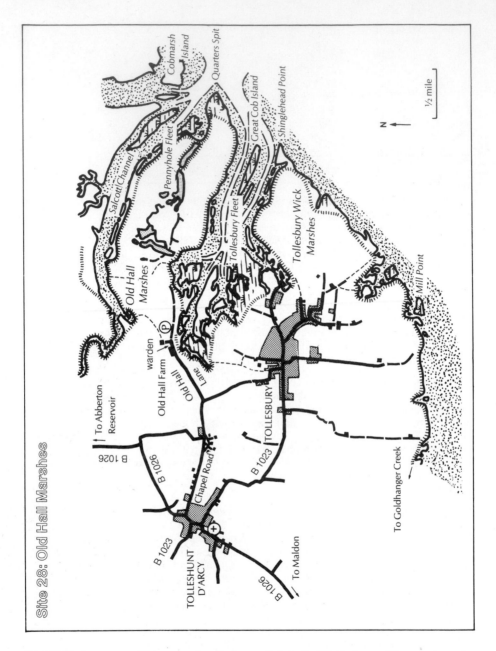

Site 28: Old Hall Marshes

28.1 Tollesbury Wick Marshes (see map)

These marshes lie immediately E of Tollesbury village and can be viewed from the surrounding seawall which is continuous with that of Old Hall Marshes — and the birdlife is essentially the same. It is possible for the energetic walker to continue to Goldhanger or even Heybridge Basin and there are several public footpaths from the seawall back to the B1023 near Tollesbury village. It is not permitted to take cars down through the various farms and the OS map should be consulted to locate legitimate rights of way and to assess distances.

Bradwell is on the S shore near the mouth of the Blackwater estuary. To visit Bradwell Bird Observatory turn E off the B1021 ½ mile N of the junction with the Steeple road (2 miles N of Tillingham). Turn right by the church and continue to the end of the road, then walk ½ mile to St Peter's chapel. The observatory is 100 yards S of this and from here it is worth walking S along the Dengie coastline (there are large high tide roosts of waders only a short distance from the observatory) or N and then E round to Bradwell Waterside. Alternatively, continue along the B1021 direct to Bradwell Waterside and follow the seawall in either direction (W leads to St Lawrence Bay and Ramsey Marsh). Bradwell Bird Observatory has dormitory accommodation for 8.

28.2 Bradwell

Old Hall Marshes, warden: 1 Old Hall Lane, Tollesbury, Maldon, Essex. Bradwell Bird Observatory: G. Smith, 48 The Meads, Ingatestone, Essex. Recorder: Essex.

Information

Site No. 29 Abberton Reservoir (Essex)

Abberton is the best-known reservoir in East Anglia. Noted for wildfowl, its proximity to the coast also ensures a good variety of waders. A visit can be rewarding at any time of year.

Covering 1,210 acres and 4 miles long, the reservoir is fed by Layer Brook at the W end and the Roman River passes close to the dam at the N end. Most of the perimeter has concrete banks, but the W end has natural margins with lush vegetation and some bushes.

Habitat

It is not possible to walk around the reservoir's perimeter but most birds can be seen from the two roads which cross the W end. Leave Colchester S on the B1026 and after 4½ miles there is a parking area beside the road. A turnstile (cost 20p) on the left leads to a hide overlooking a large bay. Half a mile further on the road crosses the reservoir. Continue for 1¼ miles to a T-junction and turn right onto a minor road N towards Layer Breton and Birch. After ½ mile the road crosses the reservoir again. It is worth checking both crossings and the hide.

Access
(see map)
OS Sheet No. 168

Numbers of Tufted Duck, Pochard, and Coot peak in late summer during moult, whilst Gadwall, Shoveler, and Pintail are commonest in autumn and Teal and Wigeon most numerous in winter. Goldeneye often number several hundred and Abberton is the most important inland site for this species in Britain. Goosander and usually a few Smew are also present. Red-crested Pochard may occur at any season (although some are probably escapes). Large numbers of Canada and Greylag Geese are now regular and Bewick's Swans and White-fronted Geese occur, especially in hard weather, grazing in the surrounding fields.
    Many migrant waders pass through in spring and autumn, notably Turnstone (mainly spring) and Little Stint (mainly autumn). The scarcer grebes, Garganey, Little Gull, and Black

Birds

Tern are recorded annually and there are sometimes huge flocks of Swifts and hirundines.

Red-crested Pochard with Pochards and Tufted Duck

Site 29: Abberton Reservoir

To Colchester

B 1026

Roman River

Birch

Birch Green

Layer Breton

Abberton Reservoir

Layer Brook

B 1026

N

1 mile

Since 1981 Cormorants have nested in willows between the two causeways, easily viewable from both; this is the only tree-nesting colony in Britain. Great Crested Grebes and sometimes a pair or two of Ruddy Ducks nest at the W end and Common Terns nest on a raft in front of the hide.

Warden: The Gorse, Layer Breton, Colchester, Essex CO2 0PN.   **Information**
Recorder: Essex.

Site No. 30 Walton-on-the-Naze (Essex)

The Naze forms the easternmost point of the large complex of marshes of Hamford Water. Between Harwich and Clacton, the area forms an ideal habitat for wintering wildfowl and waders as well as migrants. It is best in autumn or winter.

The area is mainly tidal flats and saltings with some rough   **Habitat**
grassland and pools, while bushes along the cliff path attract migrant passerines. Part is an Essex Naturalists' Trust reserve.

Drive to the extreme N end of Walton-on-the-Naze and park in   **Access**
the car park on the clifftop. Walk N along the cliff path. At low   **(see map)**
tide it is possible (and worthwhile) to continue, crossing various   OS Sheet No. 169
creeks as necessary, as far as Stone Point. Return by the same
route and allow enough time to avoid being cut off by the tide;
visitors unfamiliar with the area are advised to return to the
seawall 2–3 hrs before high water. On reaching the seawall
continue W towards Walton Channel. The seawall follows the
channel S and eventually back to the town; there is then a ½-mile
walk back to the car park.

Several thousand Brent Geese winter in Hamford Water and there   **Birds**
is also a good chance of seeing Eider offshore and Goldeneye and
Red-breasted Merganser off Stone Point or in Walton Channel.
Sanderling and the odd Purple Sandpiper frequent the shore and
the common waders are well represented. Hen Harriers and
Short-eared Owls hunt the saltmarshes and Twite and Snow
Buntings are also usually present.
   In spring and autumn a variety of waders are regular, including
Curlew Sandpipers (mostly in autumn). Passing Gannets and
Arctic Skuas are a possibility and the bushes on the clifftops are
excellent for passerine migrants. E winds during August–October
are especially favourable. Redstart, Black Redstart, Ring Ouzel,
Firecrest, and Pied Flycatcher are recorded most years plus the
occasional Wryneck.
   Oystercatchers, Ringed Plovers, and Little Terns nest along the
beach towards Stone Point and visitors should keep below the
highwater mark during the breeding season.

Recorder: Essex.   **Information**

107

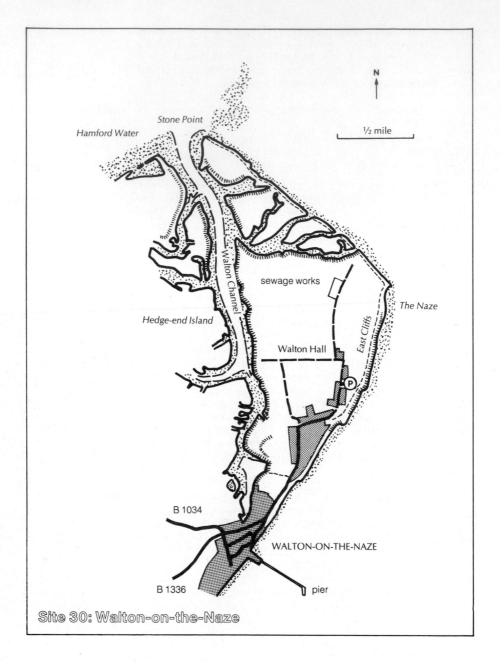

N

½ mile

Hamford Water

Stone Point

Walton Channel

sewage works

The Naze

Hedge-end Island

East Cliffs

Walton Hall

P

B 1034

WALTON-ON-THE-NAZE

B 1336

pier

Site 30: Walton-on-the-Naze

Site No. 31 Landguard Point (Suffolk)

Landguard is Britain's newest bird observatory, set up as recently as 1983. Adjacent to and part of Landguard Nature Reserve (managed by the Suffolk Trust for Nature Conservation), it has already proved an important site for migrant passerines, including several rarities.

Habitat

Landguard Point is a shingle spit immediately S of Felixstowe at the mouth of the River Orwell. The tangled vegetation and bushes are attractive to migrants and other habitats include gravel workings, a common, and a small freshwater pool. All around is the dockland sprawl of Felixstowe and Harwich.

Access
OS Sheet No. 169

A minor road S of Felixstowe leads to the reserve. One of the old gun emplacements has been converted into the observatory's HQ but there is no accommodation. The reserve is open at all times, though the ringing area is not open to the public.

Birds

The Point is most active in spring and autumn when hundreds of the commoner thrushes, warblers, and finches pass through. Over 100 Pied Flycatchers were ringed in 1984 and some of the scarcer migrants recorded annually include Wryneck, Ring Ouzel, Bluethroat, Black Redstart, and Firecrest, while Icterine Warbler is almost annual. Sea passage off Landguard is not usually notable but a few shearwaters and skuas are recorded each autumn.

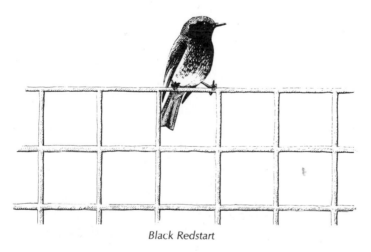

Black Redstart

In summer, Ringed Plovers and Little Terns breed on the shingle and Black Redstarts nest around the docks and the fort area.

Other Sites in the Area
31.1 Felixstoweferry

From Felixstowe drive N through Old Felixstowe on the coast road to Felixstoweferry. The estuary of the River Deben is good for waders in winter and the marshes of Kings Fleet are attractive to geese and ducks as well as Short-eared Owls and other raptors. Access across the marshes is along the seawall. Gulls are worth checking in the area — several of the scarcer species have been recorded recently.

Information   For further information about Landguard contact: Rex Beecroft (Chairman), Alcedo, Hall Lane, Witnesham, Ipswich, Suffolk, or Alan Paine (Recorder), 22 Spriteshall Lane, Felixstowe, Suffolk IP11 9QY. Recorder: Suffolk.

Site No. 32 Alton Water (Suffolk)

Just 5 miles south of Ipswich and close to the Stour estuary, Alton Water has become established as an important area for waterbirds, best in winter or during passage.

Habitat   This reservoir has largely natural edges and the marshy fringes are attractive to waders. The surrounding area is farmed with some woodland.

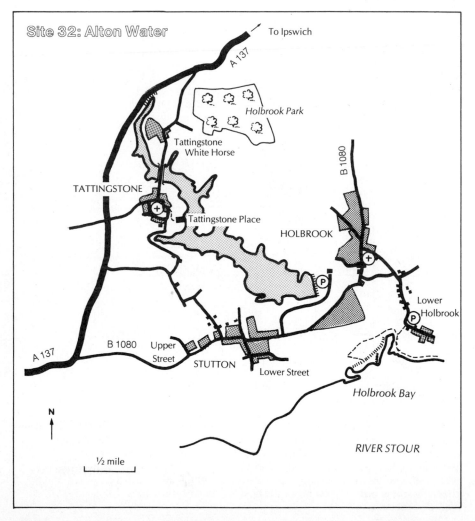

Site 32: Alton Water

Leave Ipswich S on the A137. After 4 miles the road runs along the N tip of the reservoir, probably the best area and easily viewed from the road. About 1 mile further S on the A137 a minor road to the left leads to Tattingstone. A left turn in the village, opposite the church, runs across the reservoir giving further views. Continuing S from Tattingstone towards Stutton, the minor road passes alongside another part of the reservoir. There is also access between Stutton and Holbrook: leave the B1080 at the official gate and continue to the dam where there are toilets and a car park.

**Access
(see map)**
OS Sheet No. 169

The commoner ducks reach several hundred in winter, with smaller numbers of Gadwall, Shoveler, and Goldeneye. Scaup, Long-tailed Duck, Smew, and Goosander are regularly recorded. Feral Greylag and Canada Geese are often present in the surrounding fields and Jack Snipe are sometimes found in the lakeside vegetation. Passage brings a sprinkling of waders and terns of the more usual inland species, while in summer Alton Water is an important breeding site for Great Crested Grebe (c 65 pairs).

Birds

This large bay lies on the N shore of the Stour estuary, SE of Alton Water. Leave the B1080 at Holbrook onto a minor road heading SE to Harkstead. After 1 mile a track at the beginning of Lower Holbrook leads to the innermost part of the bay. Walk in either direction along the seawall. In winter Brent Geese regularly congregate in the bay and there is a large wader roost at high tide.

**Other Sites in
the Area
32.1 Holbrook
Bay (see map)**

Wolves Wood is a 92-acre RSPB reserve of mixed broad-leaved woodland with an area of coppiced scrub, N of the A1071 between Ipswich and Hadleigh, 3 miles E of Hadleigh. Access is signed from the main road. The reserve is open at all times and there are several trails. Breeding birds include Woodcock, Lesser Spotted Woodpecker, Nightingale, a variety of warblers, six species of tit, and Hawfinch.

**32.2 Wolves
Wood**

Wolves Wood, warden: 34 Orchard Close, Great Oakley, Harwich CO12 5AX.
Recorder: Suffolk.

Information

Site No. 33 Minsmere (Suffolk)

Minsmere is one of Britain's finest reserves. Situated on the Suffolk coast between Southwold and Aldeburgh, it is owned by the RSPB. The diversity of habitats within its 1,560 acres ensures a wide variety of birds at all seasons, although it is perhaps best in May when over 100 species can be seen in a day. There are several rare breeding birds and many interesting migrants can be seen in spring and autumn.

460 acres of marshland include a large reedbed with several open meres. An area of rough grazing lies just S of the reserve, drained by the New Cut, but Minsmere's most famous habitat is the Scrape, an area of shallow, brackish water and mud, sprinkled

Habitat

111

with small islands which attract breeding birds. Water levels and salinity are controlled by sluices to maintain the optimum condition at any given season, but the Scrape is best April–September. 600 acres of the reserve are mixed woodland; the most accessible area is the South Belt, a narrow strip bordering the reedbeds. The 400 acres of heathland, comprising heather with gorse and birch scrub, are somewhat less accessible. A small area of dunes on the coast is rather disturbed, but the bushes by the main sluice are attractive to migrant passerines.

Access
(see map)
OS Sheet No. 156
The Reserve

Two routes are available:
1. Via Eastbridge (cars only). From Leiston take the B1122 N and turn right to Eastbridge. After Eastbridge cross over the New Cut; from here the reserve is signed.
2. Via Westleton. At the N end of Westleton leave the B1125 onto a minor road to Dunwich. After ½ mile turn right and follow signs to the reserve.

Both routes lead to the Reserve Centre where permits are obtained. The number of visitors (per day) is limited and you are advised to arrive early. The reserve is open every day except

Site 33: Minsmere

N

½ mile

Key to hides:
1. Centre   5. South
2. North   6. West
3. East   7. Tree
4. Public   8. Island Mere

Tuesday, 09.00–21.00 or sunset when earlier. Only members of the RSPB or YOC are admitted on Sundays and bank holiday weekends. Members are admitted free, non-members £2. There are eight trails each c 2 miles long, and eight hides; six around the Scrape and two (Tree and Island Mere hides) overlooking reedbeds and meres.

The Beach and Public Hide

From Westleton take a minor road E towards Dunwich. After 1¾ miles turn right, signed Dunwich Heath and Minsmere. There is a car park (fee) at the end, on the top of Minsmere Cliffs overlooking the reserve. A footpath leads down the cliffs to the beach. Continue S towards the sluice bushes and a track to the right goes to the Reserve Centre. There is a public hide on the seawall giving excellent views over the Scrape.

Birds

A large number of birds of c 20 species breed on the Scrape. Many Common Terns nest on the islands alongside Black-headed Gulls, and Sandwich Terns are also regularly present but no longer breed. Little Terns nest on specially created shingle islands on the Scrape. The best-known inhabitant of the Scrape, however, is the Avocet: many breed annually and are mainly present from mid-March to September. Several of Minsmere's other specialities occur in the reedbeds. A few pairs of Bitterns breed but are difficult to see; April–June is the best time for a sighting. On the other hand, Marsh Harriers are hard to miss in the summer months and are best seen from the Island Mere hide. Bearded Tits are now common, and in autumn may number over 1,000. Water Rails also breed but this is another shy species which is heard more than seen. Sedge and Reed Warblers are both common. Savi's Warbler has bred on a number of occasions, and the songs of Cetti's and Grasshopper Warblers are a familiar sound of the drier edges of the reedbeds. A few pairs of Grey Herons nest in the reeds (despite there being no shortage of trees) and Kingfishers are present throughout the year around the meres. The woodlands hold a selection of species including all three

Bearded Tits

woodpeckers, Nightingale, and Redstart. The common birds of the heathlands are Tree Pipit, Stonechat, and Yellowhammer, and at dusk you should look for Woodcock and Nightjar — both are seen regularly but in small numbers. Sadly, Stone Curlew, Woodlark, and Red-backed Shrike are no longer found.

A wide variety of migrants may be seen in spring and autumn. Large numbers of waders visit the Scrape, the peak periods being May and July–August. Species regularly present include Knot, Little Stint, Curlew Sandpiper, Ruff, Black-tailed and Bar-tailed Godwits, Whimbrel, Spotted Redshank, Greenshank, and Green, Wood, and Common Sandpipers. Temminck's Stints are recorded annually, usually in spring, and rarities can turn up at any time. Over 20 species are regularly present in autumn. Spoonbill is a speciality of Minsmere and individuals may stay for many weeks. Purple Heron is less frequent but is one of Minsmere's most regular rarities. A few Little Gulls often remain through the summer but Black Terns are more frequent in autumn. Falls of migrant passerines can occur and it is worth checking any patch of cover along the coast.

In the winter, the Scrape is quieter. A few waders remain but wildfowl are more in evidence with good numbers of the commoner species. Goosander and Goldeneye are regular on Island Mere. Offshore, small parties of Common Scoter and Eider are not unusual and Red-throated Divers are frequent. Small numbers of Bewick's Swans and wild geese sometimes graze in the meadows adjacent to the New Cut. Greylag and White-fronted Geese are the most likely but Bean and Barnacle Geese have also occurred. Marsh Harriers occasionally overwinter, but Hen Harriers are more likely. Shore Larks and Twite favour the drier parts of the Scrape and Siskins are partial to the alders of the South Belt. Scarcer visitors include Buzzard and Rough-legged Buzzard, Jack Snipe, Great Grey Shrike, and Water Pipit.

Other Sites in the Area
33.1 Sizewell Power Station

This is a site for Black Redstarts which should be looked for in spring or summer around the perimeter fence. The warm water outflow offshore regularly attracts gulls and terns. A minor road E from Leiston leads directly to the power station. From the seafront car park walk a short way N along the beach. Alternatively, you can walk c 2 miles S along the beach from the sluice at Minsmere; this is most profitable in spring and autumn when passerine migrants may be present in the coastal bushes. Scarcer species which turn up from time to time include Wryneck, Barred Warbler, and Red-backed Shrike.

Information

Warden: Minsmere Reserve, Westleton, Saxmundham, Suffolk IP17 2BY. Tel. 072873-281.
Reference: *Minsmere: Portrait of a Bird Reserve* by Herbert Axell and Eric Hosking (1977). A comprehensive account of the reserve and its wildlife.
Recorder: Suffolk.

Site No. 34 Walberswick (Suffolk)

Walberswick National Nature Reserve covers 1,500 acres on the coast S of Southwold. It includes Westwood Marshes, which extend inland for c 2½ miles, and the mudflats and saltings of the S edge of the Blyth estuary. The variety of habitats guarantees an impressive list of breeding species and the coastal location ensures a good variety of migrants. However, Walberswick is probably best in winter, particularly for raptors.

Habitat

The coast S of Walberswick village is bordered by shingle banks and a series of brackish pools. Further inland Westwood Marshes probably form the largest continuous area of freshwater reedbeds in the country. Invading scrub of sallow, alder and birch is controlled to protect the reedbeds while the reeds themselves have to be checked to prevent encroachment into the open pools. The higher ground surrounding the marshes is dominated by heathland and areas of woodland, mainly oak, birch, and Scots pine. The River Blyth forms the N boundary of the reserve; 2 miles inland the river opens out into a large tidal estuary, important for wildfowl and waders.

Access
(see map)
OS Sheet No. 156

The area can be conveniently worked from 3 points:
1. Drive into Walberswick village on the B1387. Towards the end of the village turn right at the sharp bend and immediately bear left to the beach car park. From here walk S along the beach, looking for birds on the sea as well as inland on the Corporation Marshes. There are two banks close together on the right after about 1¼ miles. Take the second one to the derelict wind pump; this trail gives good views over the reedbeds and lagoons, and the bushy slopes of Dingle Hills on the left are good for migrant passerines. Bearing right at the wind pump will eventually bring you back to the car park. There are other tracks across the marshes for the energetic but it is essential to keep to the paths.
2. Return to Walberswick village and take the B1387 westwards. Shortly before leaving the village fork left onto a minor road and follow it for 2 miles to Westwood Lodge. Park nearby. From here there is a magnificent view over the marshes. This is the best place to see raptors in winter — late afternoon is the best time to look.
3. The A12 crosses the W end of the Blyth estuary just N of Blythburgh. There is a lay-by on the W side of the road and the estuary can be viewed from the embankment opposite. In Blythburgh itself, the White Hart pub lies at the junction of the A12 and B1125. A footpath from here leads along the S edge of the estuary and an observation hide is available for public use. The estuary is best viewed on a rising tide — at low tide the waders may be distant but at high tide they will have departed.

Birds

Walberswick attracts many of the species found at Minsmere and therefore the list of species below is far from exhaustive. The main differences are that Walberswick lacks the Scrape and is considerably less watched.

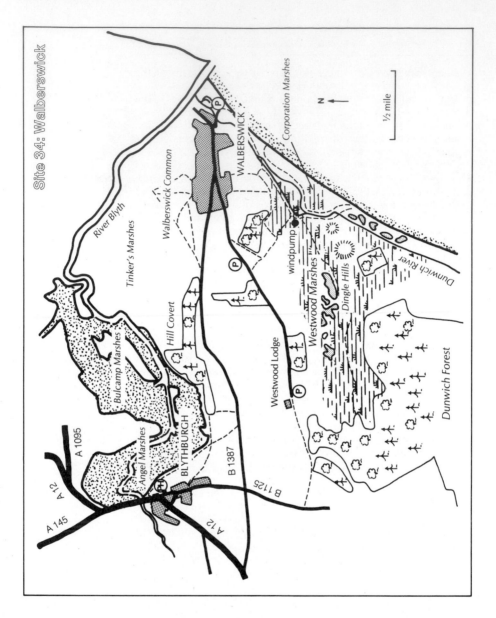

The reedbeds hold breeding Bitterns, Marsh Harriers, Water Rails, and Bearded Tits. Nightingales and Grasshopper Warblers are not uncommon in summer but, sadly, Stone Curlews are declining and Red-backed Shrikes have vanished.

Waders are much in evidence in spring and autumn with the greatest concentration on the Blyth estuary. Species may include Grey Plover, Black-tailed and Bar-tailed Godwits, Whimbrel, Spotted Redshank, and Greenshank. Migrant passerines can be interesting.

In winter, Hen Harriers and Sparrowhawks are regularly seen, especially from Westwood Lodge. A Marsh Harrier usually

Grasshopper Warbler

overwinters and Rough-legged Buzzard and Merlin are not infrequent in some years. At dusk Barn Owls may be seen around Westwood Lodge, while wintering Short-eared Owls prefer the shore area. Red-throated Divers and small flocks of Common Scoter are regular offshore, sometimes together with a few Velvet Scoter. Twite and Snow Bunting usually winter and should be looked for on the beach or in the drier areas around the Corporation Marshes. Shore Larks are also very occasionally seen.

Information

Warden: Angel Cottage, Blythburgh, Halesworth, Suffolk.
Recorder: Suffolk.

Site No. 35 Benacre and Covehithe (Suffolk)

Benacre Broad is a fine wetland on the coast between Lowestoft and Southwold and is a National Nature Reserve. Although less extensive than Minsmere or Walberswick the area offers some outstanding birding, particularly in autumn or winter.

Habitat

The broad is separated from the sea by a narrow shingle beach and bordered by mature mixed woodland and farmland. To the N there are some flooded gravel pits immediately inland of the beach which are partly fringed with reeds and sallow bushes. Covehithe Cliffs to the S are being constantly eroded by the sea. Covehithe and Easton Broads are smaller than Benacre and have deteriorated considerably, partly as a result of drainage.

**Access
(see map)**
OS Sheet No. 156

1. Leave the A12 at Wrentham on a minor road E to Covehithe. Beyond the village the road ends at the sea. Park and walk N along the top of the cliffs. After ¼ mile the path descends to the beach and, after passing a small wood, Benacre Broad lies to the left. Much of the broad can be seen from the beach and a

track along the S side leads to a hide (access unrestricted) which gives good views of the broad.

2. Continuing along the beach N for about ¾ mile you reach the gravel pits and Benacre Ness. The latter is a potentially good place from which to seawatch in favourable weather conditions. The flooded pits attract a variety of waterbirds and the bushes here and in the vicinity of Beach Farm are the best area to look for passerine migrants. The marshes of Kessingland Level may be worthy of exploration if time permits. Alternative

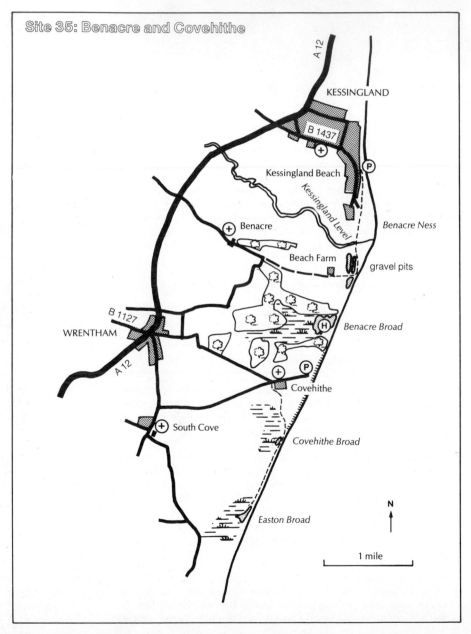

Site 35: Benacre and Covehithe

access to the area is from Beach Farm via Benacre village and from Kessingland Beach: in Kessingland village take the B1437 to the coast, park, and walk S along the beach.

3. Covehithe and Easton Broads lie c 1 and 2 miles S of Covehithe respectively. A footpath leads S from Covehithe village to Covehithe Broad. Easton Broad can then be reached along the beach.

Birds

A variety of waterbirds breed including seven species of duck and Water Rail. Bittern and Marsh Harrier occur in some summers but Bearded Tits nest regularly. Little Terns nest on the shingle beach and the woodlands hold most of the typical species including Nightingale and Redstart.

Waders are a feature of Benacre Broad in autumn and several rarities have been found. Seabirds may be conspicuous offshore at this time and frequently include skuas and auks. A wide variety of migrant passerines may be seen.

Winter is usually the best season at Benacre. Red-throated Divers are frequent offshore and seaducks typically include Scaup, Eider, Common Scoter, and Red-breasted Merganser; Long-tailed Duck and Velvet Scoter are less frequent. Goldeneye are usually present on the broad and Smew and Goosander are regular in small numbers. Hen Harriers regularly hunt over the reedbeds, a Marsh Harrier occasionally winters, and Sparrowhawks are frequent. Several of the rarer raptors have been seen here, the most likely being Rough-legged Buzzard. Bewick's Swans and wild geese are sometimes to be found in the area, particularly on Kessingland Level, and Short-eared Owls may also be seen here. With luck, Shore Larks and Lapland and Snow Buntings may be encountered on the beach, and gulls occasionally include Glaucous or Mediterranean.

Other Sites in the Area
35.1 Lowestoft
OS Sheet No. 134

The fishing industry inevitably attracts large numbers of gulls in winter: Glaucous is regular and Iceland and Mediterranean are sometimes found. The area between the harbour and Lowestoft Ness is generally best. Purple Sandpipers are regular, favouring rocks or man-made structures. A few Shags and Sanderlings are also usually to be found in winter. Kittiwakes breed regularly in Lowestoft; South Pier is a favoured site and some remain throughout the winter. A few pairs of Black Redstart also regularly breed. North Denes is a grassy area N of the cricket ground. It is a camping site in summer but at migration times attracts gulls, waders, pipits, and wagtails. The scrub and woodland on the cliff edge is worth checking for warblers, flycatchers, and chats, as are the gardens of Belle Vue Park and Sparrows Nest Theatre. Look out for Ring Ouzels on the cricket ground itself. Kensington Gardens, a small park and bowling green S of Clairmont Pier, are worth checking in autumn when the wind is NE. Scarce migrants have been found here on a number of occasions.

Recorder: Suffolk.

Information

Site No. 36 Breydon Water (Norfolk)

These extensive tidal mudflats form the estuary of the Rivers Waveney and Yare. Immediately W of Great Yarmouth, the estuary is an important wintering area for waders and wildfowl and the variety increases during the migration seasons.

Habitat

Grazing marshes lie on either side of the estuary's mudflats.

**Access
(see map)**
OS Sheet No. 134

The NE corner of Breydon Water is the most productive. It is the last to be covered by the rising tide and most of the waders on the estuary can be seen here an hour before high tide. A telescope is usually essential. There are two public hides for which keys may be borrowed from Great Yarmouth Public Library. However, the birds can be just as easily seen from outside the hides. Drive to Great Yarmouth railway station and park on the left; a footpath on the river bank leads to the hides. Part of the NE corner can also be seen from the A47 c 1 mile W of the town. For the more energetic, a footpath follows the S side of the estuary for c 3 miles to Burgh

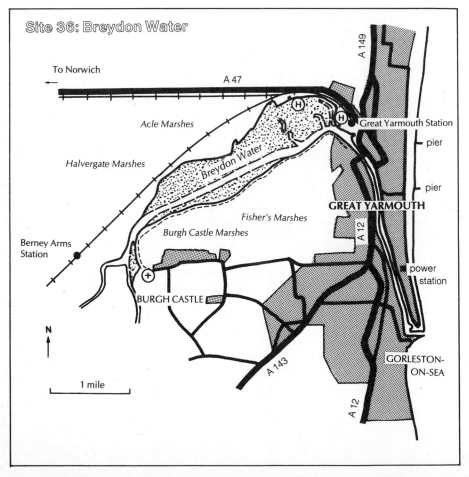

Site 36: Breydon Water

To Norwich

A 47

A 149

Acle Marshes

Great Yarmouth Station

pier

Halvergate Marshes

Breydon Water

pier

GREAT YARMOUTH

Fisher's Marshes

A 12

Burgh Castle Marshes

Berney Arms
Station

power
station

BURGH CASTLE

N

A 143

GORLESTON-
ON-SEA

A 12

1 mile

Castle. This can be quite productive in winter, particularly for wild swans and Hen Harrier. It is best to begin from Burgh Castle; a footpath leads N to the estuary from the village. The river mouth itself, at Gorleston-on-Sea, is a regular haunt of gulls in winter.

Birds

Good numbers of waders and wildfowl are present throughout the winter; these include Brent Goose and Pintail, while Scaup and Goldeneye are sometimes seen in the main channel. Bewick's and Whooper Swans frequent the fields and marshes S of the estuary and Hen Harrier and Short-eared Owl are also regularly seen. Twite and Snow Bunting are not infrequent in winter, and a small flock of Lapland Buntings is annual in the area between Great Yarmouth and Burgh Castle, but can be difficult to find. At Gorleston-on-Sea or Yarmouth harbour the flocks of gulls should be checked for occasional Glaucous and Mediterranean Gulls.

More wader species occur during migration, the more regular species including Avocet and Black-tailed Godwit, and in the last few years Broad-billed Sandpiper has been almost annual. Spoonbill and Black Tern are regular visitors in spring and autumn. Black Redstarts breed in the vicinity of the power station.

Recorder: Norfolk.

Information

Site No. 37 Strumpshaw Fen and Buckenham (Norfolk)

The marshes of the Yare valley, E of Norwich, are important for wildfowl in winter as well as supporting some unusual breeding birds. The RSPB reserve of Strumpshaw Fen is one of the best areas and the nearby Buckenham Marshes are the site for Britain's only regular wintering flock of Bean Geese.

Habitat

Strumpshaw Fen, covering 602 acres, has reedbeds, alder and willow carr, damp woodland, open water, and grazing marshes. Buckenham Marshes are well-drained rough grazing adjacent to the River Yare.

Access (see map)
OS Sheet No. 134

Strumpshaw Fen

Leave Norwich E on the A47 and after 5 miles turn right towards Brundall. Shortly after the railway bridge at the end of Brundall village turn right signed Hassingham and Cantley, and right again into Low Road immediately after. This leads to the reserve car park. Cross the railway line on foot to reach the reserve and information centre. Several trails and hides are provided for visitors. The reserve is open daily 09.00–21.00 (or sunset when earlier), without charge. Most of the reserve is N of the Yare, but an area of carr on the S side reaches as far as Rockland Broad. A public footpath starts opposite the New Inn in Rockland St Mary and runs to the river, giving good views over the reedbeds and Rockland Broad.

Buckenham

Continuing along Low Road from the Strumpshaw car park, turn right at the T-junction and cross over the level crossing. You have to toot your horn and may have to wait a few minutes for the gates to be opened. The road continues along the S side of the railway line. Turn right opposite Buckenham station and park at the corner where the road reaches the river. Continue on foot to a hide, provided by the RSPB, just beyond the old windmill. The Bean Geese often feed here but a telescope may be necessary to see them well. Alternatively, drive direct to Buckenham station: after Brundall, take the Hassingham and Cantley road; the third turning on the right is signed to Buckenham and after c 1 mile turn right to Buckenham station.

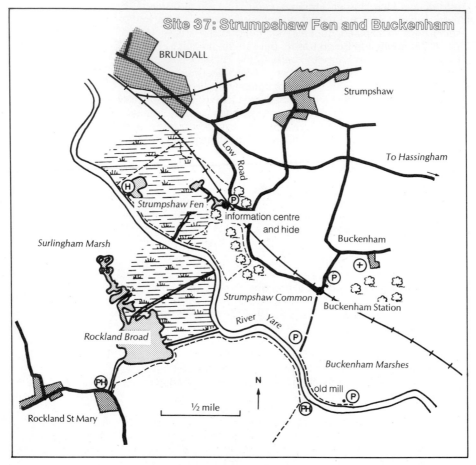

Birds
Strumpshaw

In the carr, Cetti's and Grasshopper Warblers are quite common as well as a good variety of the commoner warblers. Savi's Warbler has bred once. Marsh Harriers and Bearded Tits nest regularly but Garganey are only occasional and Bittern is now only an irregular visitor. Other breeding species include Water Rail, Woodcock, and Kingfisher. The common birds of the grazing marshes are Lapwing, Snipe, Redshank, and Yellow Wagtail, and a good variety of woodland species include all three woodpeckers and Willow Tit.

A Great Grey Shrike has frequently wintered on the reserve and Hen Harriers and Bearded Tits are often seen.

The flock of Bean Geese, numbering up to 300, is present
between late November and March and a smaller flock of
White-fronted Geese is also often found. Other birds in winter
include many Wigeon, Golden Plover, Fieldfare, and Redwing.
Hen Harriers and Short-eared Owls are not infrequent and
occasionally a Merlin may visit the area.

Buckenham

Bean Geese

Warden: Staithe Cottage, Low Rd, Strumpshaw, Norwich, Norfolk NR13
4HS.
Recorder: Norfolk.

Information

Site No. 38 Hickling Broad (Norfolk)

The largest of the Norfolk Broads, Hickling lies just N of Potter
Heigham, only a few miles from the coast. 1,361 acres is a
National Nature Reserve and the NE section is a reserve owned by
the Norfolk Naturalists' Trust. A wide variety of species breeds,
augmented in spring and autumn by migrants. Winter is the
quietest season.

Much of the broad is open water surrounded by extensive areas of
reedbed, but part of the NNT reserve is a series of muddy scrapes
for waders and ducks. Bushes and woodland girdle the broad's
perimeter. Hickling is one of the few places where swallowtail
butterflies still occur; they are on the wing June–August.

Habitat

A public footpath along the S edge of Hickling encompasses all
the major habitats and will enable most of the specialities to be
seen. Leave Potter Heigham NW on the A149 towards Catfield.
After c 1½ miles turn right over a level crossing towards Rookery
Farm and Decoy Lane. There is a crossroads after ½ mile, and ½
mile further on a gate with a stile on the right. Park here and
continue over the stile and along the raised bank. The path runs
alongside the broad for c 3 miles. A footpath N from Potter
Heigham church also leads to the broad and the parking is easier
here. The NNT reserve is open daily (except Tuesdays) April–

**Access
(see map)**
OS Sheet No. 134

October, 09.30–18.00. Permits are required and should be obtained from the warden's office 09.00–10.00 or 13.00–14.00 each day (09.00–14.30 from Spring Bank Holiday to mid-September); cost £1.85 or (half day) £1.25. The office is just off Stubb Road near the Greyhound Inn in Hickling. A variety of trails and hides is provided for permit holders and boat trips can be arranged. The hides give good views of passage waders and reedbed specialities. The reserve can only be visited November–March by special arrangement.

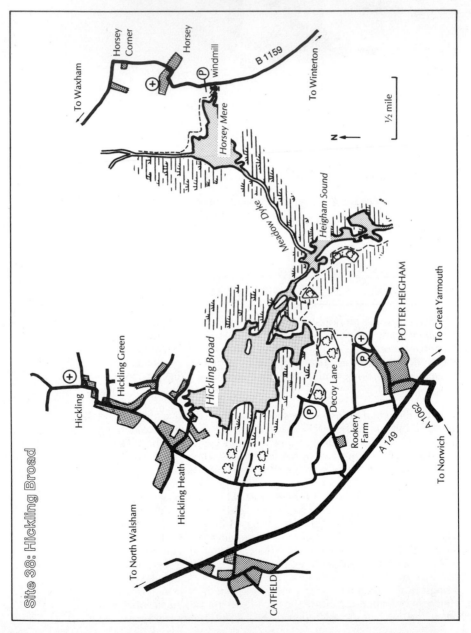

Birds

Bittern and Bearded Tit both breed, but the former is rarely seen. Warblers include Reed, Sedge, and Grasshopper, and Savi's Warblers often nest and are visible from the embankment. Cuckoos are commonly seen over the reedbeds and other breeding birds include Great Crested Grebe, Common Tern, Yellow Wagtail, and Reed Bunting. A variety of woodland species can be seen including Turtle Dove, Redpoll, and Marsh Tit.

Garganey are regular in spring, and Marsh Harrier, Little Gull, and Black Tern may be seen in spring or autumn. A wide variety of waders uses the broad on migration. One of the more frequent rarities is Purple Heron.

Many dabbling duck winter and Goldeneye are regular but Smew are only occasionally seen. Hen Harrier and Short-eared Owl are not infrequent.

Other Sites in the Area

38.1 Horsey Mere (see map)

This smaller broad E of Hickling is a National Trust reserve. Access is limited to a short track leading to the mere from the Horsey Windmill car park on the B1159. Birds here are similar to those of Hickling. A few Bewick's and Whooper Swans are sometimes present in the fields S of the mere, as well as occasional wintering Ruff and Black-tailed Godwit. Hen Harrier and Merlin are sometimes seen.

38.2 Waxham Dunes

The dunes and associated bushes on the coast E of Waxham village are attractive to migrant passerines in autumn. They can be reached along a track leading to the coast from close to Waxham church.

38.3 Winterton Dunes

The more extensive dunes of Winterton are a National Nature Reserve covering 59 acres. Lying on the coast N of Winterton village, access is unrestricted and the dunes are best approached by a footpath leading N along their inland side. They are often disturbed at weekends. The area is most notable for migrant passerines, but sometimes Woodcock and Long-eared and Short-eared Owls are also seen in late autumn, when Little Gulls can be found off the coast. Divers and seaduck may be seen in winter and raptors are regularly recorded in both winter and spring; the most frequent are Hen Harrier, Sparrowhawk, Rough-legged Buzzard, and Merlin.

Information

Hickling, warden: Warden's Office, Stubb Rd, Hickling, Norwich NR12 0BW. Tel. 069261–276.
Recorder: Norfolk.

Site No. 39 Cley—Salthouse (Norfolk)

Cley is probably the best-known mainland birding site in Britain and c 325 species have been recorded here including a host of rarities and several firsts for Britain. Cley Marsh itself covers 435 acres and is owned by the Norfolk Naturalists' Trust. The adjacent Arnold's Marsh is owned by the National Trust while the Salthouse Marshes are largely private. Birding at Cley is good at any time of year but the greatest diversity of species (and the most birders) occurs in spring and autumn.

Habitat

Cley Marsh comprises extensive reedbeds, pools, and grazing meadows. A series of scrapes have been excavated and Arnold's Marsh is also prime wader habitat — shallow pools and mud bordered by sand-dunes and grassland. The marshes at Salthouse are similar but have largely remained unmanaged. The entire area lies S of a shingle beach which protects it from the sea. South of the A149 heathland and woodland mix with arable land.

Access
(see map)
OS Sheet No. 132
Cley Marsh

The best sites at Cley and its surrounding areas are as follows:

The NNT reserve lies just E of Cley next the Sea. Bounded by the sea to the N, the East Bank to the E, the A149 to the S and the road to the coastguard station to the W, it is conveniently viewable from these and, if time permits, the complete circuit of 3 miles can be profitable. Alternatively, sections can be worked from any of the three car parks:
1. The NNT reserve car park is S of the A149 c ½ mile E of Cley village. The visitor centre is next to it and there are two public hides nearby on either side of the road.
2. The East Bank car park has limited space, but is convenient if you just wish to work the East Bank.
3. The Coastguards car park (fee in summer) is a convenient point from which to work the beach, the Eye Field, and the North Scrape hides. It is also the starting point for the walk to Blakeney Point. A small cafe is open in the summer and there are toilets here. You can seawatch from the shelter of beached fishing boats or the hide at the top of the old coastguard lookout (nominal fee).

There are 10 hides overlooking Cley Marsh but a permit is required for all except the roadside public hides. Permits are available from the NNT Centre, open daily except Monday (other than bank holiday Mondays), 10.00–17.00 April–October. Visiting November–March is by special arrangement with the warden. Permits cost £1.70 (85p for NNT members, who can buy a yearly pass for £5 which gives access to the hides at any time before 10.00 and after 17.00). The *North* and *Maynard's Hides* overlook the North Scrape. They give good views of waders, and Avocets favour this area. *Avocet, Dauke's* and *Teal Hides* give views of the other scrapes and are probably the best places to see waders. *Irene Hide* overlooks Pat's Pool and is usually good for waders and wildfowl. The *Bittern Hide* rarely produces Bitterns but is good for close views of waders and Bearded Tits. Water Rail, Spotted Crake, and Jack Snipe are regularly seen from here in autumn and Water Pipits occur in winter. The *Pool Hide* is usually disappointing. The Eye Pool regularly attracts interesting waders in autumn, while Brent Geese, Golden Plover, and occasionally Lapland Buntings frequent the Eye Field in winter.

Arnold's Marsh

This pool immediately E of Cley Marsh is favoured by waders, ducks, and resting terns and can be viewed from the East Bank. A walk along the N side, inland of the shingle bank, will give closer views of birds at the back of the pool.

Walsey Hills

This small hill covered in scrub is a migration watchpoint of the Norfolk Ornithologists' Association (NOA). It lies immediately S of the A149 c 200 yards E of the East Bank car park and overlooks

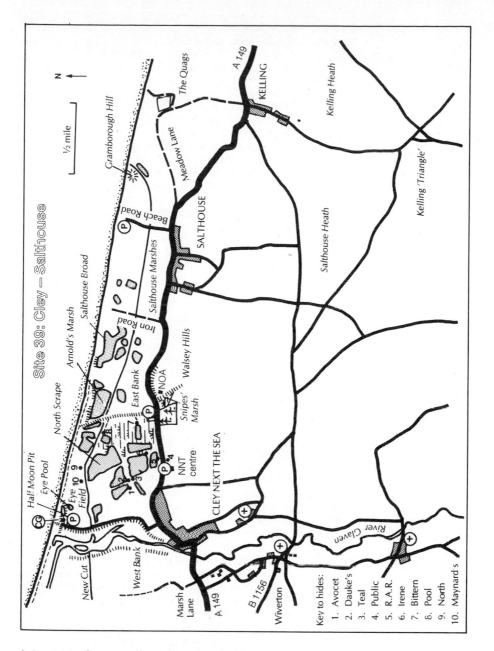

Site 39: Cley – Salthouse

Key to hides:
1. Avocet
2. Dauke's
3. Teal
4. Public
5. R.A.R.
6. Irene
7. Bittern
8. Pool
9. North
10. Maynard's

Snipes' Marsh, a small pool surrounded by reeds. The bushes attract migrants and the information centre has a book shop and provides bird news. It is open daily (except Mondays) during the summer and at weekends in winter.

Marsh Lane

This track leads N from the A149 c ½ mile W of Cley, opposite the first turning to Wiveton. Cars are not permitted down the lane. The mature trees along the first stretch attract passerine migrants. Further on, the track continues across the E side of Blakeney

Marshes. Although less interesting than Cley Marshes, some unusual birds have been found here.

Salthouse Marshes

These lie E of, and are continuous with, Cley Marshes. Being largely private, it is not possible to wander across them. Three access points are worthwhile:
1. The Iron Road is a track between the A149 and the coast, W of Salthouse village. It is good for seeing waders in spring and autumn, depending on water levels.
2. The Beach Road is a metalled road to the coast from the E side of Salthouse village. There is a small car park at the end. Shore Larks are regularly seen in winter on either side of the car park.
3. The Quags lie at the E end of Salthouse Marshes. About ½ mile E of Salthouse the A149 bends to the right heading inland and at this point a track forks left. Follow this, checking the pools and marshes on the left. After ¾ mile the track turns sharp right towards Kelling. At the bend there are more pools and damp grassy fields. A number of less common migrants such as Blue-headed Wagtails and several Red-throated Pipits have turned up in spring.

Birds

Bitterns breed but are only occasionally seen, usually in flight as they move to different parts of the reedbed. The booming of the male is often heard in spring. A colony of Avocets has recently been established and Bearded Tits breed throughout the reedbeds. Easily located by the 'pinging' calls, they are especially frequent along the East Bank and around the Bittern Hide. Sandwich, Common, and Little Terns visit, and a few non-breeding Little Gulls also sometimes summer. Reed and Sedge Warblers are common in the reedbeds and Yellow Wagtails favour the meadows. Wheatears can be seen along the beach, often in the vicinity of the North Hide.

The greatest diversity of waders occurs in spring or autumn. The autumn passage commences in July and typical species include Little Ringed Plover, Little Stint, Curlew Sandpiper, Ruff, Black-tailed Godwit, Whimbrel, Spotted Redshank, Greenshank, and Green, Wood, and Common Sandpipers. Spotted Crake and Jack Snipe are occasionally seen from the Bittern Hide in autumn while Water Rails are more frequent at this time. Garganey are regular, usually in spring, as are Spoonbill, Marsh Harrier, and Black Tern. A few Wrynecks and Barred Warblers are found each year, usually August–September; Walsey Hills is a favoured area, but any bushes in the area should be checked. N and NW gales can produce some reasonable movements of seabirds. Arctic and Great Skuas are regular August–September as well as small numbers of auks and seaduck. Manx is the most likely species of shearwater but Sooty is not infrequent. Long-tailed and Pomarine Skuas are rare but annual. Storms in October–November can produce small 'wrecks' of Leach's Petrels and Little Auks. Little Gulls are regular offshore, especially in late autumn, and occasionally Woodcock and Long-eared and Short-eared Owls can be seen flying in off the sea at this time.

In winter Brent Geese frequent the grassy fields alongside the flocks of feral Greylag and Canada Geese. Golden Plover, Lapwing, Redwing, and Fieldfare also favour the fields while Hen Harrier and Short-eared Owl regularly hunt over them. Many dabbling duck winter on the marsh, largely Wigeon, Gadwall, Teal, Pintail, and Shoveler. Goldeneye are frequent on Arnold's Marsh and Red-throated Diver and Red-breasted Merganser are regular offshore. Black-throated Diver and Red-necked and Slavonian Grebes are much less common. For many years an adult Glaucous Gull has patrolled the area between Blakeney and Weybourne between late August and March, sometimes roosting on Salthouse Marshes. The original individual, nicknamed 'George', was present 1963–81 and has been replaced by another, known as 'Boy George'. Shore Larks are present most years and Snow Buntings also inhabit the beach, anywhere between Cley coastguards and the Quags, while Lapland Buntings show a preference for the Eye Field.

Shore Larks

The disused RAF camp N of Weybourne is an area of grassland and scrub favoured by migrants, in particular Ring Ouzel and Black Redstart. Much of the area has recently been ploughed.

Other Sites in the Area
39.1 Weybourne Camp

This scrubby hillside N of the A149 between Weybourne and Kelling holds breeding Nightingales and various warblers. A network of small tracks gives easy access from the main road.

39.2 Muckleburgh Hill

These lie S of Salthouse and Kelling villages. Several minor roads cross the heaths giving easy access. The gorse and heather with scattered birches is a breeding area for Nightjar, Nightingale, and Redpoll. Long-eared Owls also breed and may be located by the calls of the young in late spring. In winter Hen Harriers come to roost and are sometimes seen during the day; Rough-legged Buzzard and Great Grey Shrike also occasionally winter.

39.3 Salthouse and Kelling Heaths (see map)

An area of mature oak woodland at the junction of the Kelling, Weybourne, and Holt roads, c 1½ miles S of Kelling. Most of the common woodland species can be seen as well as Lesser Spotted Woodpecker and Wood Warbler.

39.4 Kelling 'Triangle' (see map)

Information

Cley Marsh (NNT), warden: Watcher's Cottage, Cley, Holt, Norfolk.
Walsey Hills (NOA), warden: Tel. 0263–740094.
Nancy's Cafe: This excellent unpretentious cafe is open daily (except Mondays) 09.00–18.00 and is a source of local bird information as well as providing welcome nourishment. During the winter it is only open at weekends. Nancy's is situated in the main street of Cley opposite the George Hotel.
References:
Cley Marsh and its Birds by Billy Bishop (1983).
A Check-List of the Birds of Cley by S.J.M. Gantlett (1984). This comprehensive up-to-date checklist is available at Nancy's and Walsey Hills (price £2.80).
Recorder: Norfolk.

Site No. 40 Blakeney Point and Harbour (Norfolk)

The unique 3½ mile shingle spit of Blakeney Point is best known for its falls of migrant passerines and a large colony of terns. The point is owned by the National Trust and has been a nature reserve since 1912.

Habitat

Extensive sand dunes cover much of the point itself while the spit is largely shingle. Marram grass helps stabilise the dunes and areas of dense Suaeda bushes occur on the S edge of the spit particularly at Halfway House and the Hood. Patches of tree lupin occur on the point and both these and the Suaeda bushes are excellent for migrants. The tidal Blakeney Harbour lies to the S and contains extensive well-vegetated saltmarshes.

**Access
(see map)**
OS Sheet No. 132

In summer it is possible to get a boat from Morston or Blakeney quays to the point (at high tide) but ornithologically the point is best August–September and it is then more profitable to walk out from Cley coastguards. This is a long, tiring walk and, if the tide is not high, it is easier to walk along the beach. However, the bushy edge of Blakeney Harbour should be covered in at least one direction to look for migrant passerines. There is an information centre and a tea room at the point and hides from which you can view the terns. If walking out to the point, the best areas for migrants are Halfway House, the Hood, and Long Hills. The tiny rectangular plantation c 200 yards E of the tea room also regularly attracts birds. In summer visitors are requested to avoid disturbance to the tern colony, but access is otherwise unrestricted. Blakeney Harbour can also be viewed from Morston or Blakeney:
1. A muddy trail leads out to the harbour from Morston quay.
2. From the car park on the harbour's edge at Blakeney, a seawall leads out to the E of a deep channel. There are tidal saltmarshes on the left while the drier rough grassland of Blakeney Fresh Marshes lies on the right. At high tide, many waders roost on the saltings.

Birds

A large colony of terns breeds at the tip of Blakeney Point. The majority are Sandwich and Common, but Little also breed as well as one or two pairs of Arctic. Other breeding species include Shelduck, Oystercatcher, Ringed Plover, and Redshank.

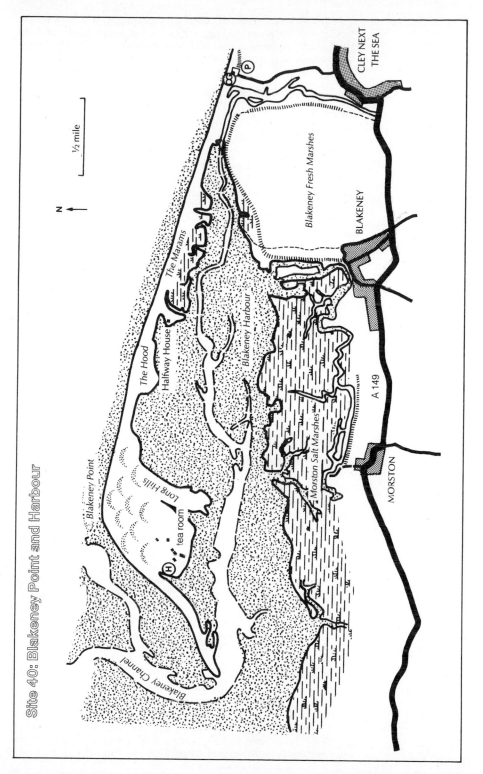

Site 40: Blakeney Point and Harbour

CLEY NEXT THE SEA

Blakeney Fresh Marshes

BLAKENEY

The Marams

The Hood

Halfway House

Blakeney Point

Long Hills

tea room

H

Blakeney Channel

Blakeney Harbour

Morston Salt Marshes

A 149

MORSTON

N

½ mile

Although migrants do occur in spring, autumn is by far the best time to visit the point. Falls can occur at any time of day; it should be quickly apparent as you walk out whether birds have arrived. The commonest species are Willow Warbler, Redstart, and Pied Flycatcher. Scarcer migrants found annually include Dotterel, Wryneck, Bluethroat, Icterine and Barred Warblers, Red-breasted Flycatcher, and Ortolan Bunting. N winds may well induce an impressive seabird passage, typically Gannets, Kittiwakes, and a variety of terns with a few Manx Shearwaters and Arctic and Great Skuas. Pomarine and Long-tailed Skuas, Sabine's Gull, and Sooty Shearwater are only occasionally seen.

In winter, Brent Geese feed in Blakeney Harbour alongside many Wigeon and the commoner wintering waders. Goldeneye and Red-breasted Merganser frequent the channels and divers and grebes are sometimes seen offshore. Short-eared Owls are regular over the marshes and Twite and Lapland Bunting are generally somewhere in the area but difficult to locate.

Information

Warden: 35 The Cornfields, Langham, Holt, Norfolk NR25 7DQ. Tel. 0263–740480 (summer), 023 875 401 (winter).
Recorder: Norfolk.

Site No. 41 Wells–Holkham (Norfolk)

This stretch of the N Norfolk coast is a National Nature Reserve. Good numbers of migrant passerines, including occasional rarities, can be found in autumn in the appropriate weather conditions. The fields immediately to the S regularly attract a variety of geese in winter.

Habitat

At low tide extensive sand and mudflats are exposed along the coast and bordering these is a long chain of sand dunes anchored by tough grasses. A narrow belt of pines (Holkham Meals) extends for c 3 miles along the dunes. The N exposed side of the pines does not support much ground vegetation but along the S edge dense areas of scrub and deciduous trees flourish. A particularly lush hollow near the E end is known as the Dell: mainly birches and sallows, it is usually wet underfoot. An area of fields lies between the pines and the A149. The extensive, walled grounds of Holkham Park are immediately S of the road — grassy parkland with mature deciduous woodland and a large artificial lake.

**Access
(see map)**
OS Sheet No. 132

The A149 passes through Overy Staithe and Holkham but by-passes Well-next-the-Sea. Several turnings lead to the town centre and the area can be conveniently approached from six places:
1. Holkham Meals: east end. From the quay in Wells take the road N for 1 mile. On the left beyond the caravan site is a public car park (fee in summer). From here walk around the N end of the boating lake and just beyond it through a kissing gate into an area of bramble scrub. This path follows the S edge of the pines to Holkham Gap, a distance of c 1½ miles. The Dell lies a few hundred yards along to the right of the path,

beyond the brambles, and is the best area for passerine migrants. Further along, the path skirts several more areas of scrub and brambles, and a long pit known as the 'drinking pool' is often worth a look — it is hidden from the path in a dense area of scrub on the right.

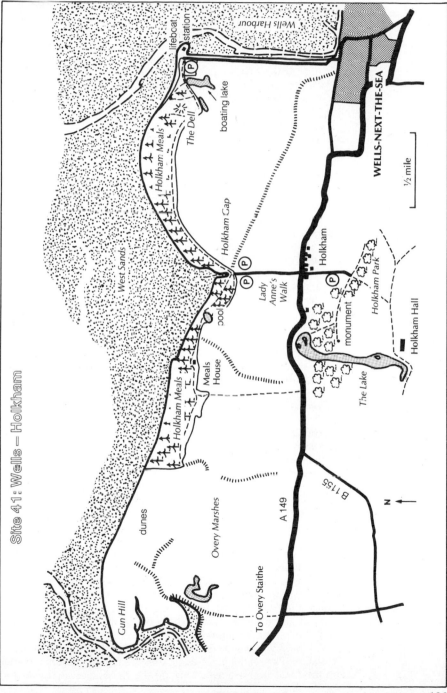

2. Holkham Meals: west end. From the village of Holkham on the A149 a small private road (Lady Anne's Drive) leads N to Holkham Gap. Park here (fee in summer). From the Gap, follow the path W along the S edge of the pines. The habitat is similar to the E end; the path passes a small pool on the left and a solitary private house. At the end of the trees you reach an area of sand dunes with scattered bushes, often favoured by migrants. Access is unrestricted in the pines and it is worth exploring away from the path. The area is popular with walkers and is best in early morning, both for the birds and lack of disturbance. As an alternative when working either end, you can return along the shore looking for waders, Brent Geese, and grebes and seaduck in winter. However, Holkham Meals is best for migrants in spring and autumn and generally the E end is more productive.

3. The fields between the A149 and Holkham Meals hold small flocks of geese in winter. Although a few paths cross the fields, they are best viewed from the road with a telescope.

4. ½ mile E of Overy Staithe a track N from the A149 leading to Gun Hill offers an opportunity to walk across the Overy Marshes to the dunes. Geese can sometimes be seen from this path in winter.

5. Holkham Park. At the village of Holkham turn S off the A149 (opposite Lady Anne's Drive) and after a few hundred yards park on the right. The road continues to the gates of the park and a small gate to the right of the main gates allows free access. Beyond the gates the road leads to Holkham Hall and the lake. To the right a track passes through mature woodland to a monument and to another part of the lake. Holkham Park is a good site for Hawfinch in winter.

6. Wells harbour can be viewed from the bank to the right of the road between Wells and the car park or from the lifeboat station at the point. Waders and Brent Geese frequent the marshes while grebes and seaduck are often offshore and occasionally penetrate the channel. The marshy area to the W of the road sometimes has Twite and Lapland Bunting.

Birds

Geese are the main attraction in winter. The fields S of the pines regularly hold a flock of White-fronted Geese. These do not mix with the resident Canada and Greylag Geese (most of which are to be found in Holkham Park around the lake). Numbers of Pink-footed Geese can also be seen. Egyptian Geese are resident and usually to be found here. They are seen in pairs and do not mix with other geese. Large flocks of Brent Geese can be seen almost anywhere in winter, from the shore and saltmarshes to the grassy fields near the road. In recent years vagrant Bean, Red-breasted, and Lesser White-fronted Geese have all been found in the fields. Small numbers of the commoner waders inhabit the coastal mudflats and offshore small flocks of Common Scoter, Eider, and Red-breasted Merganser are not unusual and sometimes Scaup, Long-tailed Duck, and Velvet Scoter can also be found. Red-necked and Slavonian Grebes can occasionally be seen and are best looked for at high tide.

All three woodpeckers and Nuthatch inhabit the woodland in Holkham Park and a few Hawfinches are regularly seen in winter in the large hornbeams just inside the main gate. Redpolls and

Crossbills can be found in the pines of Holkham Meals and from autumn 1983 to spring 1986 a few Parrot Crossbills were present near the car park at the Wells end of the pines. Remarkably, a pair bred in 1984 and 1985.

Migrants occur in Holkham Meals in both spring and autumn but the area is at its best August–October. Even then the pines can be very quiet indeed, but in appropriate weather (usually NE – SE winds) falls of passerines are often impressive. Early autumn (August–September) falls usually involve the commoner British warblers, Spotted and Pied Flycatchers, Redstarts, and Goldcrests. Wryneck, Icterine and Barred Warblers, and Red-backed Shrike are not infrequently seen at this time, but in small numbers. Red-breasted Flycatcher is much less common. Later (September–October), there may be a chance of seeing eastern vagrants such as Yellow-browed and Pallas's Warblers, both of which are almost annual here while Radde's and Dusky Warblers and Olive-backed Pipit have been recorded several times. October–November sees major influxes of wintering species, notably Fieldfares and Redwings, and it is possible that something unusual is also involved, such as Waxwing or Great Grey Shrike.

Red-backed Shrike

Warden: 7 Kelling Rd, Holt, Norfolk.
Recorder: Norfolk.

Information

Site No. 42 Titchwell (Norfolk)

Titchwell is now an RSPB reserve and as a result of effective management has become one of the best birding sites on the Norfolk coast. Interesting birds can be found at any time of year but the greatest diversity is in spring and autumn.

The 510-acre reserve contains brackish and freshwater marsh, aster and lavender saltmarsh, tidal and freshwater reedbeds, sand dunes, and shingle beach. Between the wetland habitats and the road there is a small area of scrub and drier vegetation with some trees.

Habitat

**Access
(see map)**
OS Sheet No. 132

About ⅓ mile W of the village of Titchwell on the A149 a small track (signed to the RSPB reserve) leads N towards the coast. The car park and the Reserve Centre are to the right after c 200 yards. Continue on foot along the track onto the seawall for views over the marshes. Two hides on the right are open throughout the year without permit or charge. The seawall eventually reaches the beach, and turning right a short track through the dunes after c 300 yards leads to a sunken hide overlooking the tern colony. This hide is only open April–July. Access to the reserve is limited to the seawall, the hides, and the beach.

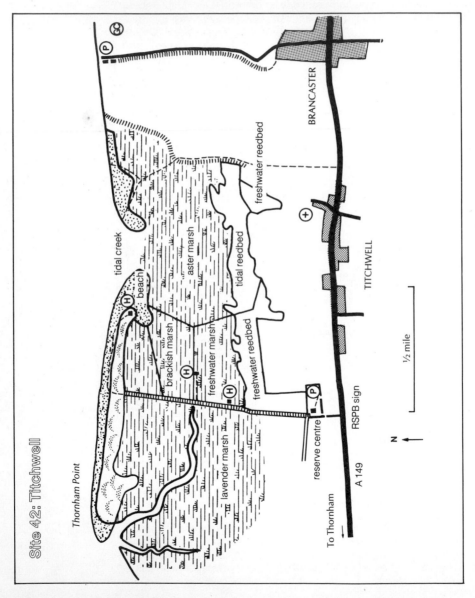

Site 42: Titchwell

Birds

Bittern and Marsh Harrier both breed on the reserve. While the latter is often conspicuous, Bitterns are notoriously secretive and views are likely to be of a bird briefly flying low over the reeds between feeding and roosting areas at dawn and dusk. Bearded Tits are common in the reedbeds as are Reed and Sedge Warblers and Reed Buntings. Water Rail usually breeds but this is another secretive bird, most easily seen in late summer or autumn when migrants augment the population. Little and Common Terns breed on the beach alongside Oystercatcher and Ringed Plover and recently a few pairs of Avocets have colonised Titchwell. Yellow Wagtails are common in the more vegetated marshes. The scrubby area near the car park is inhabited by a variety of warblers, notably Grasshopper.

Garganey are occasionally seen in spring and autumn and Spoonbill, Little Gull, and Black Tern are regular migrants; Spoonbills are sometimes also seen during the summer. In the autumn huge numbers of Swallows and martins roost in the reedbeds and the water levels are kept low on the marsh to attract waders. Titchwell is now the best place on the Norfolk coast for these and over 20 species are frequently present August–September, often including Little Stint, Curlew Sandpiper, and Black-tailed Godwit. Seabird movements can occur offshore after a strong N wind; Gannets and Kittiwakes form the bulk with a scattering of Great and Arctic Skuas and the occasional shearwater.

In winter, divers, grebes, and seaduck are frequently present offshore; Red-throated Diver, Eider, and Common Scoter are the most regular. The water on the marsh is deeper now, and Goldeneye and Red-breasted Merganser are often seen, together with large numbers of dabbling ducks. At high tides large flocks of waders, mainly Oystercatcher, Knot, and Bar-tailed Godwit, come in to roost on the beach. Hen Harriers roost in the reedbeds and are best seen in the last hour before dusk. Short-eared Owls occasionally hunt over the saltmarsh which is the home of wintering Twite, and Snow Buntings are regular on the beach.

Other Sites in the Area
42.1 Burnham Norton

Situated c 5 miles E of Titchwell, this is a regular wintering site for Lapland Buntings. From a small car park at the NE end of the village, a muddy track leads N across the marshes towards the seawall. Any of the grassy fields can hold Lapland Buntings which may be mixed with Yellowhammers and Corn and Reed Buntings.

42.2 Barrow Common

This lies S of Burnham Deepdale. Turn right (S) off the A149 E of Brancaster at the Jolly Sailors pub, before reaching Burnham Deepdale. This minor road leads across the Common where Woodcock and Long-eared Owls are occasionally seen, while the fields to the S are sometimes favoured by Pink-footed Geese.

Information

Titchwell, warden: Three Horseshoes Cottage, Titchwell, Kings Lynn PE31 8BB.
Recorder: Norfolk.

Site No. 43 Holme (Norfolk)

The reserves at Holme, owned by the Norfolk Naturalists' Trust and the Norfolk Ornithologists' Association, are an outstanding area of the N Norfolk coast. The best time to visit is in spring or autumn for the migrant passerines although some interesting birds can also be found in winter.

Habitat

A small area of saltmarsh lies to the W of Gore Point but the main habitat is the extensive area of sand dunes. Sea buckthorn scrub stabilises these in places and is particularly attractive to migrants. Immediately to the N of 'The Firs' (the NNT warden's house) is a small pine plantation, also attractive to migrants. Inland of the dunes, there is a large brackish pool (Broad Water) and some pools and scrapes favoured by waders. These are surrounded by reedbeds and rough grassland.

Access
(see map)
OS Sheet No. 132

At Holme next the Sea on the A149, three minor roads lead N towards the sea. Take the westernmost road and after c ¾ mile take the second right turn along a rough track with speed ramps (toll in summer). Continue for c ¾ mile. Shortly after a gate there is a small public parking area on the left from which you can explore the saltmarsh and W side of the dunes. (Further W along the coast, at the back of the houses, an area of rough pasture and bushes may be worth checking for migrants.) Continuing along the track you will reach the reserves car park. Holme Dunes (NNT), 600 acres, is open every day except Tuesday, 10.00–17.00. Holme Bird Observatory (NOA), 6 acres, is open to members every day, 09.00 to ½ hr before sunset; to non-members, 10.30–16.00. Permits are required for both reserves (available on site) with concessions for NNT or NOA members. Seven hides which overlook Broad Water and the surrounding areas are available to all permit holders, but a seawatching hide N of The Firs is for NOA members only. Members of either NNT or NOA need not pay the toll.

Birds

Holme is noted for migrant passerines but these are dependent on suitable weather, N or E winds being most favourable. Wheatear, Whinchat, Redstart, a variety of warblers, and Spotted and Pied Flycatchers are all frequent. In autumn, Barred and Icterine Warblers are regular in very small numbers and Yellow-browed Warbler and Red-breasted Flycatcher are recorded most years. Wryneck, Bluethroat, Ring Ouzel, Firecrest, Red-backed Shrike, and Ortolan Bunting may occur in spring or autumn but are scarce, while Hoopoe is occasional in spring. A good variety of waders occurs on passage and in autumn seawatching may be productive when the tide is high; both Great and Arctic Skuas are regular.

Holme is fairly quiet in summer but Avocet has recently nested, and Little Tern and Bearded Tit both breed in addition to commoner species such as Oystercatcher, Ringed Plover, and Reed Warbler.

In winter, Red-throated Diver, Slavonian Grebe, Eider, Long-tailed Duck, Common Scoter, and Red-breasted Merganser are regularly seen offshore. Large numbers of gulls congregate on the

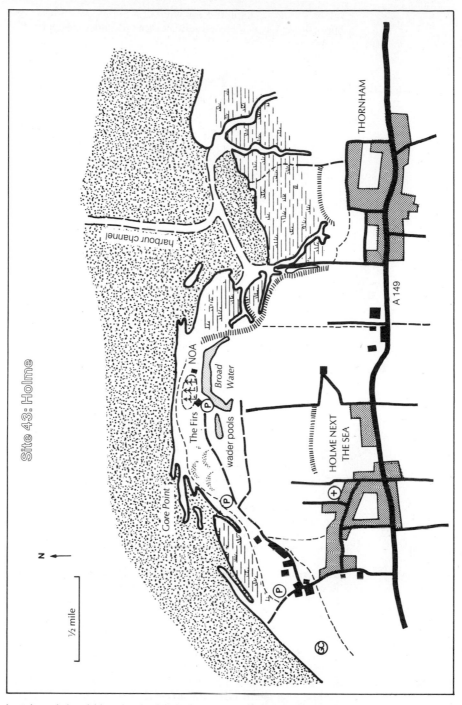

Site 43: Holme

THORNHAM

harbour channel

NOA

Broad Water

The Firs

wader pools

Gore Point

A 149

HOLME NEXT THE SEA

N

½ mile

beach and should be checked for Glaucous Gull. Brent Geese are
frequently present on the fields to the S. Hen Harriers and
Short-eared Owls are regularly seen but Rough-legged Buzzard
and Great Grey Shrike are much rarer. The beach, saltmarsh, and

dunes should be explored for wintering Shore Lark, Twite, and Snow Bunting which are usually present but sometimes difficult to locate.

Snow Buntings

Information

NNT warden: The Firs, Broadwater Road, Holme next the Sea, Hunstanton, Norfolk PE36 6LQ.
NOA warden: Aslack Way, Holme next the Sea, Hunstanton, Norfolk PE36 6LP.
Recorder: Norfolk.

Site No. 44 Snettisham (Norfolk)

The Wash is internationally recognised as a major site for wintering wildfowl and waders and the RSPB reserve at Snettisham, on the E side of the Wash c 8 miles N of King's Lynn, provides access to the wealth and diversity of its birds. Winter is the best time to visit.

Habitat

The reserve covers 3,250 acres, of which 2,880 acres are intertidal sand and mudflats and 300 acres are saltmarsh. Only a small strip of the coastline is included but a series of brackish, flooded lagoons (created by shingle extraction) and a shingle beach provide further habitats. The S pits have been managed to make them more attractive; islands have been created which provide roosting sites for waders and nesting sites for terns.

**Access
(see map)**
OS Sheet No. 132

Leave the A149 at the S end of Snettisham village W onto the beach road. This reaches the Wash at Snettisham Scalp after c 3 miles where there is a public car park. Cars are not permitted to park among the nearby caravans and chalets. From the car park walk S along the beach beside the pits. The southernmost (with four public hides) are the best and are c 1 mile S of the car park. To the N of the car park there is an area of dunes, gorse, and brambles with a small pool and reedbed which is good for migrants in spring. Alternative access is from Dersingham from which a public footpath leads directly to the S pits. The reserve is open at all times and a permit is not required.

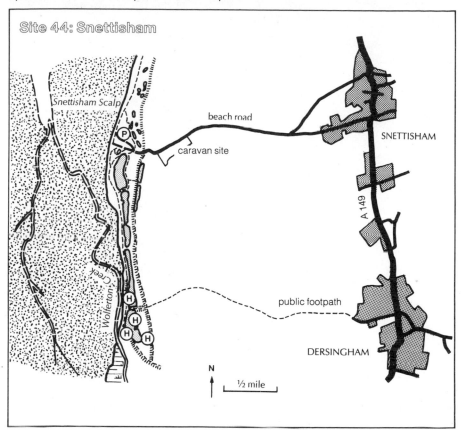

Birds

Waders peak during the winter and up to 70,000 have been counted. At low tide they are well scattered over the sand and mudflats and big numbers are best seen from Snettisham Scalp at or just before high tide. Oystercatcher, Knot, Dunlin, Bar-tailed Godwit, and Redshank are the commonest species. Wildfowl are also numerous. Up to 8,000 Pink-footed Geese roost on the mudflats November–February; by day they can frequently be seen feeding on the fields E of the pits and sometimes they are joined by small numbers of both Bewick's and Whooper Swans. Large numbers of Brent Geese are present offshore while occasionally small rafts of Common Scoter and Eider may be seen on the open water. Many ducks and waders use the pits in winter. Goldeneye and Red-breasted Merganser are invariably to be seen, together with the commoner dabbling and diving ducks. Scaup are also found quite regularly but Smew and Long-tailed Duck are only occasional. Sometimes one of the rarer grebes or a diver will also visit the pits. On the beach Snow Buntings are often present but Shore Lark and Lapland Bunting are less frequent.

The variety of waders increases during the migration seasons. Arctic Skuas are frequent offshore August–September. Passerine migrants should be looked for in the bushes along the shore. In particular, the area N of the car park is graced by the occasional Ring Ouzel.

Summer is quiet. A colony of Common Terns breeds on the pits together with large numbers of gulls and Oystercatcher, Ringed Plover, and Redshank.

Other Sites in the Area
44.1 Hunstanton

The road N out of Hunstanton passes close to the coast along the top of Hunstanton Cliffs before joining the A149. It is worth a stop here to look out to sea but a telescope is recommended. A few Fulmars inhabit the cliffs, and on the sea rafts of duck are present in winter. The majority are Common Scoter, but Eider, Long-tailed duck, Velvet Scoter, and Goldeneye are also regularly seen. Red-throated Divers and Slavonian Grebes are regular but other divers and Red-necked Grebe are much less frequent.

44.2 Roydon Common

This area of heathland lies NE of King's Lynn. Take the A148 exit to Fakenham from the roundabout at the E end of the King's Lynn by-pass and after 300 yards turn right onto a minor road which runs E to Roydon and Grimston. After ¾ mile turn right onto a sandy track and after 100 yards turn left into a small car park at the edge of the Common. Woodcock, Nightjar, Nightingale and Grasshopper Warbler all breed. In winter there is a roost of Hen Harriers and Merlins and also regularly the odd Hooded Crow. Great Grey Shrike is also occasionally seen.

44.3 Sandringham

Sandringham Country Park is part of the Sandringham Estate and is open to the public. Some areas of mature woodland hold Redstart, Nightingale, Wood Warbler, and Crossbill in summer. Golden Pheasants are regularly seen along the minor roads on either side of the A149, particularly at dawn; the road to Wolferton is one of the best.

Information

Snettisham, warden: 18 Cockle Rd, Snettisham, King's Lynn PE31 6HD. Recorder: Norfolk.

Site No. 45 Breckland (Norfolk, Suffolk)

Breckland is a unique area of sandy heathland and conifer plantations centred around Thetford. Famed for several scarce breeding species, it is best in spring or summer. Several areas are Local or National Nature Reserves.

Habitat

Originally the Brecks were mainly heathland but extensive plantations of conifers, mainly Corsican or Scots pines, have considerably reduced this habitat. Some good areas of heathland still remain and the plantations of varying ages have provided suitable habitat for certain species. The Little Ouse River bisects the Brecks but there is little standing water.

Access
OS Sheet No. 144

There are many interesting areas worthy of exploration but the following are particularly notable.

This is jointly managed by the NCC and Norfolk Naturalists' Trust **Weeting Heath**
and holds several pairs of Stone Curlews. Weeting is N of
Brandon on the B1106; from Weeting village take a minor road W
towards Hockwold cum Wilton. Park on the left, after c 1 mile, at
the end of a belt of pines. The summer warden's caravan is here
and permits are available for a small charge. Two hides overlook
the heath and are ideal for viewing the Stone Curlews. They are
often best seen in the late afternoon or evening and are in
residence between late March and August.

A good area to look for Woodlarks, and Golden Pheasants are **Santon Downham**
sometimes seen by the roadsides, usually at dawn or dusk. From
Brandon take the B1107 to Thetford. After 1 mile turn left to
Santon Downham. A left turn in the village leads N across the
Little Ouse River. A picnic site is signed on the right immediately
after the river. The area around the picnic site is worth looking at
for a variety of woodland species. A railway line runs N of and
parallel to the river and a walk alongside the line in either
direction may be profitable; the young plantations N of the
railway are a good place to look for Woodlarks.

This is another NNT reserve of 362 acres comprising woodland, **East Wretham
Heath**
scrub, heathland, and meres. A regular haunt of Hawfinches in
winter, which can usually be found in the mature hornbeams
around Ring Mere. Leaving Thetford N on the A11, turn left after 2
miles on the A1075 (signed to Watton and East Dereham). East
Wretham Heath is on the left after 2 miles. The reserve is open
daily (except Tuesdays) 10.00–17.00. Permits are required and
should be collected from the warden's house at 10.00 and 14.00
(cost 75p). The warden's house is the first on the left after the
railway crossing.

This area of woodland at the junction of the A11 and A1075 is **Hockham Belt**
good for Golden Pheasant. Early mornings are best, and although
shy, this introduced species can sometimes be detected by
listening for rustling leaf litter.

Several of the Breckland specialities have become so scarce that it **Birds**
would be inappropriate to publish precise details of their breeding
sites, but diligent searching will turn up most of the good birds.
The majority of the species detailed below are best seen in spring
or summer. Stone Curlews are not too uncommon but Red-
backed Shrikes have dwindled sharply; Breckland probably holds

Stone Curlew

a few of the last pairs in East Anglia. Both are summer visitors. Woodlarks are largely absent in winter, and fairly uncommon. They prefer recently planted areas of conifers and are easiest to see in early spring when in song-flight. Nightjars are late-arriving summer visitors and favour heathland and young plantations. Golden Pheasant, Long-eared Owl, and Crossbill are reasonably widespread, generally in the mature plantations. Hawfinches prefer hornbeams if available and although widespread and resident can be very unobtrusive. They are easiest to find in winter when they form loose flocks. Some of the other more interesting breeding species of Breckland are Sparrowhawk, Woodcock, Lesser Spotted Woodpecker, Tree Pipit, Nightingale, Redstart, Whinchat, Wheatear, Grasshopper Warbler, Wood Warbler, and Siskin.

In winter, Bramblings are widespread visitors but Great Grey Shrikes are scarce.

Information

East Wretham, warden: East Wretham Heath Nature Reserve, Thetford, Norfolk, IP24 1RU.
Recorder: Norfolk (N of Little Ouse River), Suffolk (S of Little Ouse River).

Site No. 46 Wicken Fen (Cambridgeshire)

11 miles NE of Cambridge, Wicken Fen is one of the few remaining examples of the once extensive fens of the Great Level. Its main interest is in winter for waterfowl and a Hen Harrier roost. Wicken Fen is probably the oldest nature reserve in the country, owned by the National Trust.

Habitat

The reserve covers 730 acres and has three distinct areas: the Sedge Fen, St Edmund's Fen, and Adventurers' Fen. The first two are original fen and have never been cultivated. In places the sedge is still cut in the traditional manner while elsewhere dense scrub including buckthorn has been allowed to develop. A sprinkling of mature trees adds further variety. Despite Adventurers' Fen's long history of drainage and flooding it holds much of the ornithological interest of Wicken. A large mere is surrounded by reedbeds and an area of marshland.

Access
(see map)
OS Sheet No. 154

Leave Cambridge N on the A10 and turn right onto the A1123 signed to Stretham. After 3½ miles, at the beginning of Wicken village, turn right onto a minor road signed Wicken Fen. Park in the large car park on the left a few hundred yards down the track. Continuing on foot you will reach the William Thorpe Building; permits and literature are on sale here and a list of recent bird sightings is displayed. The reserve is open daily and entry is free to NT members; permits for non-members cost £1. When the building is closed permits can be obtained from a machine outside. There is a choice of two routes:
1. An anticlockwise trail around the Sedge Fen taking in the Tower Hide, which gives a view over the entire reserve but is particularly good for watching the mere on Adventurers' Fen — a telescope is useful here. Various other paths cross the fen.

2. A walk alongside the S edge of Wicken Lode visiting the Mere Hide at the NE corner of the mere, giving closer views of this part of the mere and the reedbed. The key for the hide should be collected from the William Thorpe Building. There is no public access onto Adventurers' Fen.

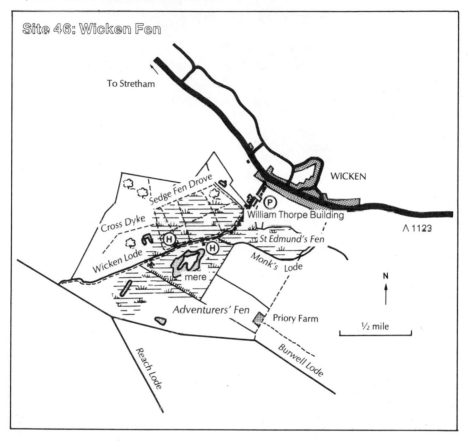

Site 46: Wicken Fen

In summer, typical wetland species such as Snipe, Redshank, **Birds** Reed Warbler, and Reed Bunting can be found easily. Much less so is Water Rail which almost certainly breeds on Adventurers' Fen. Sporadically, the rarer Spotted Crake has been heard calling at night and Garganey is an irregular summer visitor — look out for the latter from the Mere Hide in spring. Marsh Harriers are often present in summer as are Cetti's and Savi's Warblers and Bearded Tits. They all favour Adventurers' Fen and have occasionally bred. The carr of Sedge Fen holds a different variety of breeding species. There are several pairs of Lesser Spotted Woodpeckers and Willow Tits. Grasshopper Warblers breed and two other birds requiring a little more effort are Long-eared Owl and Woodcock. A few pairs of each nest but it is necessary to look for them at dusk. Woodcock are roding from early March and Long-eared Owls are calling frequently from mid-February to mid-March. Breeding sites vary from year to year but the area around Cross Dyke is a good place to look for both species.

Woodcock

In winter, the majority of waterfowl gather on or around the mere; mainly Wigeon and Mallard with smaller numbers of other species. Canada Geese are usually present on the drier parts of Adventurers' Fen and occasionally a few Greylag or White-fronted Geese may be seen. Bittern and Short-eared Owl are present most winters, usually just one or two of each, as well as variable numbers of Bearded Tits. All are best viewed from the Tower Hide. Great Grey Shrike may also winter on the reserve. The greatest spectacle of Wicken in winter is the Hen Harrier roost. Numbering up to 10 birds, males frequently predominate. They begin to arrive c 1 hr before dusk, usually from the W side of the Tower Hide, which provides an excellent vantage. Sometimes a Sparrowhawk is also present and often considerable numbers of Corn Buntings and Bramblings roost in bushes on the fen.

Information

Warden: Warden's House, Lode Lane, Wicken, Cambridgeshire CB7 5XP.
Reference: *The Birds of Wicken Fen* by C.J.R. Thorne and T.J. Bennett (1982). This useful booklet is on sale at the reserve (price 50p).
Recorder: Cambridgeshire.

Site No. 47 Ouse Washes (Cambridgeshire, Norfolk)

The unique wet meadowland of the Ouse Washes, in the heart of the East Anglian fens, is renowned as a refuge for wildfowl in winter and for several rare breeding species in summer. About 3,200 acres are protected in two separate reserves and a visit is profitable at any time of year.

Habitat

The Ouse Washes lie between two straight, almost parallel, artificial rivers (or drains), the Old and New Bedford Rivers.

Although little more than half a mile in width, they extend for over 20 miles between Earith in Cambridgeshire and Downham Market in Norfolk. The area is permanent pasture grazed in summer by cattle and sheep, and regularly flooded in winter; numerous ditches divide the flood plain into 'washes'. Apart from the high banks alongside the drains, the area is entirely flat and the few trees grow close to the banks.

This reserve is jointly owned by the RSPB (2,039 acres) and the Cambridgeshire and Isle of Ely Naturalists' Trust (380 acres). From Chatteris take the B1098 signed Upwell and Downham Market. The road turns sharp left after 2 miles and after a few hundred yards crosses Vermuyden's Drain. Immediately after crossing the drain turn right to Manea (signed 4 miles). At the beginning of the village a right turn is signed Purls Bridge, Welches Dam, and Nature Reserve. At Purls Bridge the road follows the Old Bedford River to Welches Dam, the headquarters of the reserve with a car park. The visitor centre is open on Saturdays and Sundays throughout the year. There are ten hides spread out along a 3-mile stretch of the Barrier Bank on the far side of the Old Bedford River. The river can be crossed at Welches Dam, or you can park at Purls Bridge and use the floating bridge a short distance NE of the point where the road from Manea reaches the river. Access is free at all times to the hides but it is not possible to leave the Barrier Bank. The hides on the N side of Purls Bridge are often the most productive but it is worth checking the notice board in the car park to find out what has been seen recently. Wildfowling takes place on adjacent washes September–January, but not on Sundays. On sunny days it is best to visit in the afternoons when the light is more favourable.

Access
(see maps)
OS Sheet No. 143
Ouse Washes Reserve

This reserve is owned by the Wildfowl Trust (800 acres). Leaving the A10 in Littleport, take the A1101 W. After 4 miles the road reaches the New Bedford River and runs alongside it for a further 1 mile. The main road then crosses the river over a suspension bridge to Welney village. Immediately before the bridge, continue straight on along a minor road (signed Wildfowl Trust Refuge and Ten Mile Bank) alongside the New Bedford River. After c 1½ miles is a car park on the right and the Reception and Information Centre for the Refuge . The entrance to the hides is over a footbridge opposite the car park. The Refuge is open daily 10.00–19.00 and permits cost £1.30. The observatory is a rather plush and spacious hide overlooking a large lagoon. A wide variety of wildfowl can be seen at close quarters from there in winter and it is the best place to see wild swans. Many other hides are situated along the bank. From May to August a 2-mile walk across the washes is available.

Welney Wildfowl Refuge

In winter the washes hold the largest inland concentration of wildfowl in Britain. The majority are Wigeon, averaging over 35,000 birds, with smaller numbers of Pintail, Shoveler, Pochard, Mallard, and Teal. Over 2,000 Bewick's Swans and up to 200 Whooper Swans also winter. Geese only occasionally visit the washes, mostly small parties of White-fronted. Small numbers of Hen Harriers and Short-eared Owls regularly winter but are not guaranteed. Rarer raptors include Merlin, Sparrowhawk, and

Birds

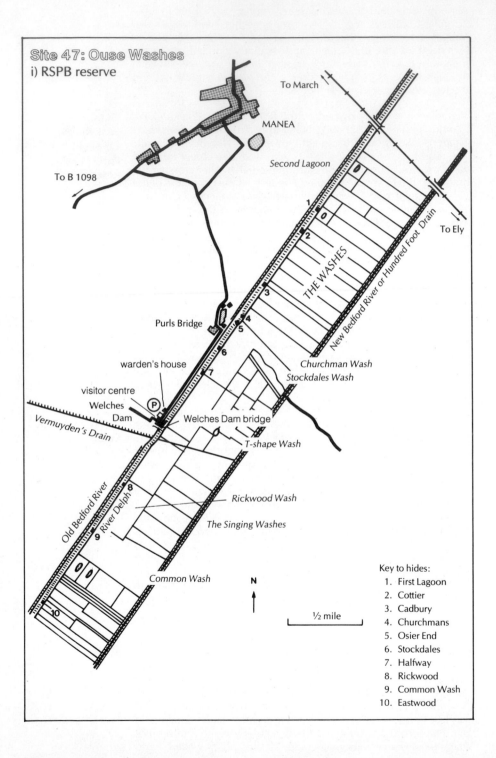

Site 47: Ouse Washes
i) RSPB reserve

To March

MANEA

To B 1098

Second Lagoon

THE WASHES

New Bedford River or Hundred Foot Drain

To Ely

1

0

2

3

Purls Bridge

4

5

6

Churchman Wash
Stockdales Wash

warden's house

7

visitor centre

Welches
Dam

P

Welches Dam bridge

Vermuyden's Drain

T-shape Wash

Old Bedford River

8

River Delph

Rickwood Wash

9

The Singing Washes

Common Wash

N

½ mile

10

Key to hides:
1. First Lagoon
2. Cottier
3. Cadbury
4. Churchmans
5. Osier End
6. Stockdales
7. Halfway
8. Rickwood
9. Common Wash
10. Eastwood

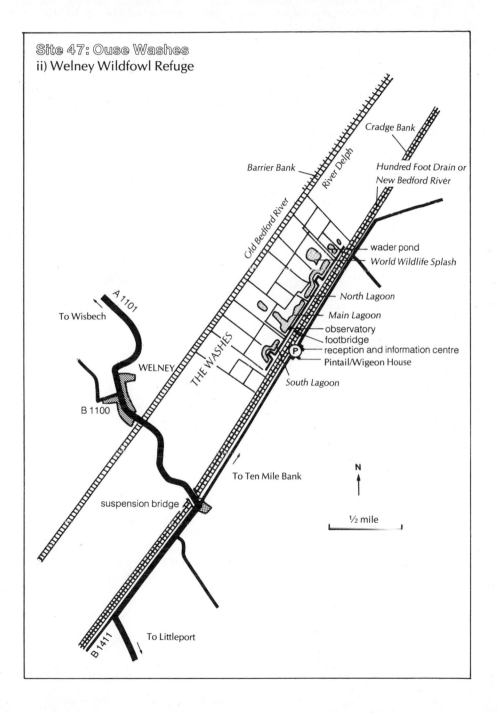

Site 47: Ouse Washes
ii) Welney Wildfowl Refuge

Cradge Bank

Barrier Bank

River Delph

Hundred Foot Drain or
New Bedford River

Old Bedford River

wader pond
World Wildlife Splash

North Lagoon

A 1101

To Wisbech

Main Lagoon
observatory
footbridge
reception and information centre
Pintail/Wigeon House

THE WASHES

WELNEY

B 1100

South Lagoon

To Ten Mile Bank

N

suspension bridge

½ mile

B 1411

To Littleport

Peregrine. Waders include Lapwing, Snipe, and Golden Plover, with smaller numbers of Ruff and Redshank. The flooded washes also provide a roosting site for thousands of gulls, largely Black-headed.

About 40 pairs of Black-tailed Godwits now breed, having re-colonised the area in 1952. Their spectacular display flights are best observed in spring and early summer. Ruff breed annually, but in variable numbers. Males lek for a brief period in early spring, the majority moving on to leave the females to raise their young. As the season advances, the females become quite inconspicuous. Lapwing, Snipe, and Redshank are common breeders and Garganey are among the nine species of breeding duck, but are unobtrusive in summer and best looked for in spring. Marsh Harriers are frequently present in summer and a pair or two of Short-eared Owls usually nest. Black Terns have occasionally bred and Little Gulls have attempted to do so once. Spotted Crakes have been heard at night and probably breed, but are unlikely to be seen. Reed Warblers and Yellow Wagtails breed in large numbers.

Black-tailed Godwits

Spring can be a particularly rewarding time to visit. Several of the breeding species may be easier to see; their numbers are augmented by passage birds (Garganey, Ruff, Black-tailed Godwit). Marsh Harriers and Black Terns are regular as well as a good variety of the commoner migrants. Waders are more in evidence in the autumn, and most of the common species are present from July. Rarities can turn up at any time and on a memorable occasion in June 1983 it was possible to see Purple Heron, Blue-winged Teal, Red-crested Pochard, Collared Pratincole, and Red-necked Phalarope in a single day.

Information

Ouse Washes Reserve, warden: Limosa, Welches Dam, Manea, March, Cambridgeshire PE15 0ND.
Welney Wildfowl Refuge: The Wildfowl Trust, Pintail House, Hundred Foot Bank, Welney, Wisbech, Cambridgeshire PE14 9TN. Tel. 0353–860711.
Recorder: Cambridgeshire (Ouse Washes Reserve), Norfolk (Welney).

Site No. 48 Grafham Water (Cambridgeshire)

Two arms of this 1,600-acre reservoir are a 370-acre reserve of the Bedfordshire and Huntingdonshire Wildlife Trust. Large numbers of grebes and wildfowl winter and passage brings a variety of waders and terns.

Habitat

The reservoir has a number of sheltered creeks and is surrounded by deciduous woodland, mixed plantations, rough grassland, and arable fields. Much of the open water is disturbed by sailing and fishing but the reserve at the W end provides a useful sanctuary.

**Access
(see map)**
OS Sheet No. 153

Leave the A1 at Buckden roundabout onto the B661 which passes the dam and then runs fairly close by the S shore to the village of Perry. The reservoir can be viewed from two car parks along this road: Plummers, E of Perry and probably the best, and Mander on the W side of the village. From Mander you can walk around the W shore of the reservoir to a hide (available on Sundays only, October–March, for a nominal charge), but there is no access to

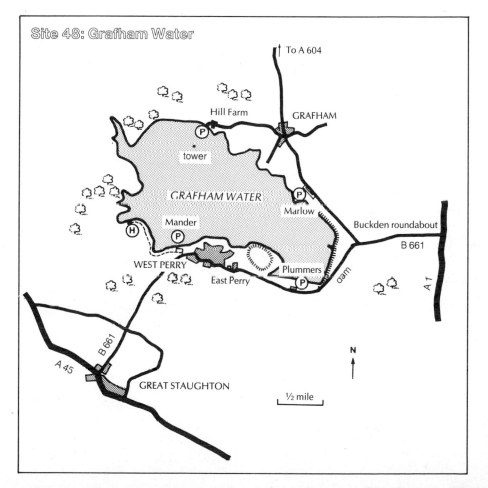

Site 48: Grafham Water

the reserve. The NE shore can be seen from a minor road which leaves the B661 before the dam and leads to Grafham village. There are two more car parks along this road: Marlow and the very small Hill Farm car park.

Birds

In winter up to 800 Great Crested Grebes are present but divers and the rarer grebes are only occasional. Bewick's Swans are regular in small numbers. Wintering duck include Teal, Gadwall, Wigeon, Shoveler, and Pochard. Up to 250 Goldeneye and up to 50 Goosander can also be seen but Scaup, Long-tailed Duck, Common Scoter, and Smew are only occasional visitors. A few Ruddy Ducks have become regular in recent years.

A variety of waders turns up in spring and autumn and Common and Black Terns are regular on passage. Arctic Terns are less frequent, occurring mainly in spring. Very small numbers of Little Gulls are also seen at these times.

Information

Bedfordshire and Huntingdonshire Wildlife Trust: Priory Country Park, Barkers Lane, Bedford. Tel. 0234-64213.
Recorder: Huntingdon and Peterborough.

CENTRAL ENGLAND

Site No. 49 Gibraltar Point (Lincolnshire)

To the south of Skegness, Gibraltar Point is where the Lincolnshire coast turns into the Wash. A bird observatory studies resultant concentrations of migrants, and the area also attracts numbers of wintering birds. It is worth visiting any time from August to early June. The National Nature Reserve covering 1,063 acres is managed by the Lincolnshire and South Humberside Trust for Nature Conservation.

Habitat

Two major ridges, the East and West Dunes, run roughly N–S parallel to the sea, supporting extensive sea buckthorn and some elder; between them are areas of both fresh and saltmarsh. An artificial pool, the Mere, in the N of the reserve attracts migrant ducks and waders. The Point is bordered by extensive mudflats and saltmarsh.

**Access
(see map)**
OS Sheet No. 122

Leave Skegness seafront S on a minor road to Gibraltar Point. Parking is available near the Mere and Visitor Centre (fee in summer). No permit is needed, but visitors should keep to the roads and paths, and keep out of the marked sanctuary areas. There is a public hide at the Mere. The Visitor Centre is open daily May–October and at weekends and bank holidays for the rest of the year. Basic accommodation is available at the Field Station for up to 28 people: late February to early November (full board) at £11 per day; the rest of the year (self-catering) £3 per day. A 6 bed annexe is available for the whole year (self-catering) at £3 per day.

Wildfowl and waders are best seen as they fly to roost at high tide on the Spit and sand ridges off the Point. The largest 'fly-pasts' are in spring and autumn, starting up to 2 hrs before high tide, and a NW–NE wind produces the biggest numbers. Seawatching can be a problem in the early morning because of bad light, and at low tide. The best place from which to watch is the base of the Spit, though in northward movements a position further N may be better. The extensive buckthorn, especially on the East Dunes, though difficult to work provides cover for migrants. The height of the dunes gives an overview in many places, and Mill Hill observation platform provides an all-round view and is ideal for watching movements of diurnal migrants in the early morning.

Birds

Once spring migration has started, E or SE winds combined with cloud, rain, or poor visibility may produce 'falls' of warblers, flycatchers, and chats, sometimes including scarcer species such as Nightingale, Ring Ouzel, Pied Flycatcher, and Firecrest. As at

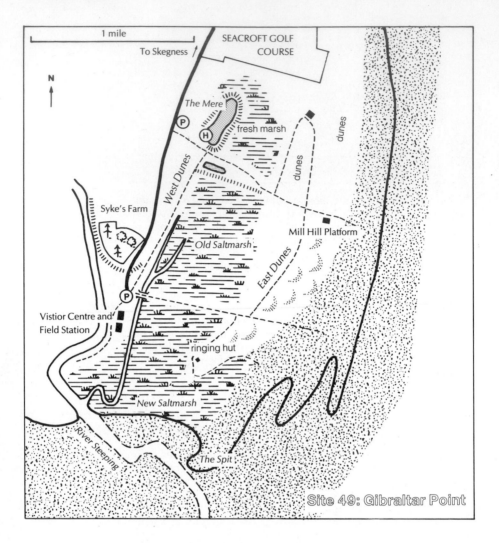

On the map:

1 mile

To Skegness

SEACROFT GOLF
COURSE

N

The Mere

P

H

fresh marsh

dunes

dunes

West Dunes

Syke's Farm

Mill Hill Platform

Old Saltmarsh

East Dunes

P

Vistior Centre and
Field Station

ringing hut

New Saltmarsh

River Steeping

The Spit

Site 49: Gibraltar Point

Spurn, the majority of diurnal migrants — pipits, wagtails, finches, and buntings — fly S in spring. Notable breeding birds include Shelduck, Ringed Plover, and Little Tern.

In autumn, wildfowl, waders, gulls, terns, and skuas can be seen on the sea and shore, and the Mere may attract Garganey, Little Ringed Plover, Little Stint, Curlew Sandpiper, Wood Sandpiper, and Spotted Redshank. Falls of night-migrants occur, and from late August these may be substantial, with a chance of Icterine or Barred Warbler, whilst Bluethroat, Red-breasted Flycatcher, and Red-backed Shrike are all annual in September. By October, large movements of thrushes, especially Blackbirds and Fieldfares, become prominent, as do Goldcrests, tits, finches, and buntings. In late autumn, look out for Great Grey Shrikes (which occasionally winter), but Waxwing, Rough-legged Buzzard, and Lapland Bunting occur much more erratically. Seawatching may be worthwhile during onshore winds; both Sooty Shearwater and Pomarine Skua are possible.

Winter brings Red-throated and possibly Great Northern Divers. Wildfowl include Brent Geese and sometimes a few Bewick's Swans and there are large numbers of the common open-shore waders. Occasionally a Glaucous Gull may be seen, but Sparrowhawk, Hen Harrier, Merlin, and Short-eared Owl are all regular. Rock Pipit, Redpoll, Twite, and Snow and Corn Buntings frequent the saltmarsh, dune-slacks, and beach, often in large numbers, whilst hard weather may bring movements of Lapwings, thrushes, and finches.

Information

Warden (including bookings for accommodation): Gibraltar Point Field Station, Skegness, Lincolnshire PE24 4SU. Tel. 0754-2677.
Recorder: Lincolnshire (records can be handed in at the Visitor Centre).

Site No. 50 Lincolnshire Coast

The coast N of Skegness has a fine range of habitats which are especially attractive in winter and passage periods. Despite this, observer coverage is low and it is therefore an ideal area for those who wish to find their own birds.

Habitat

The dune and beach system of the Humber estuary gradually narrows as it extends S to Theddlethorpe. Tidal sand and mud are backed by saltmarsh and two lines of dunes parallel the coast with wet slacks between them, often producing freshwater marshes dominated by rushes, sedges, and reeds, as well as areas of birch scrub. In places the dunes support sea buckthorn and other shrubs. S of this area the foreshore is fairly narrow and the coast is protected by seawalls, with a number of small pits behind.

Access
Chapel and Wolla Bank Pits
OS Sheet No. 122

Turn right off the A52 6 miles N of Skegness to Chapel St Leonards and drive through the village for 1½ miles to Chapel Point. Chapel Pit lies ½ mile N and Wolla Bank Pit a further ½ mile, both inland of the road. They are reserves of the Lincolnshire and South Humberside Trust for Nature Conservation (LSHTNC). Access is by permit only, but the casual visitor can view them from the road. Chapel Point is reasonable for seawatching, and the pits occasionally hold seaduck.

Anderby Creek
OS Sheet No. 122

Continue N for 1 mile from Wolla Bank Pit and then turn right to Anderby Creek. Park at the end of the road and either walk N on the track between the houses or along the dunes. The gardens hold migrants, but discretion is necessary when peering into them. The small pit among the houses, just inland of the track, attracts the odd seaduck.

Huttoft Bank and Pits
OS Sheet No. 122

Either continue N from Anderby Creek on the coast road to Huttoft, or leave Mablethorpe S on the A52, turning E after 3½ miles on a minor road to Sandilands. Follow this road for 2½

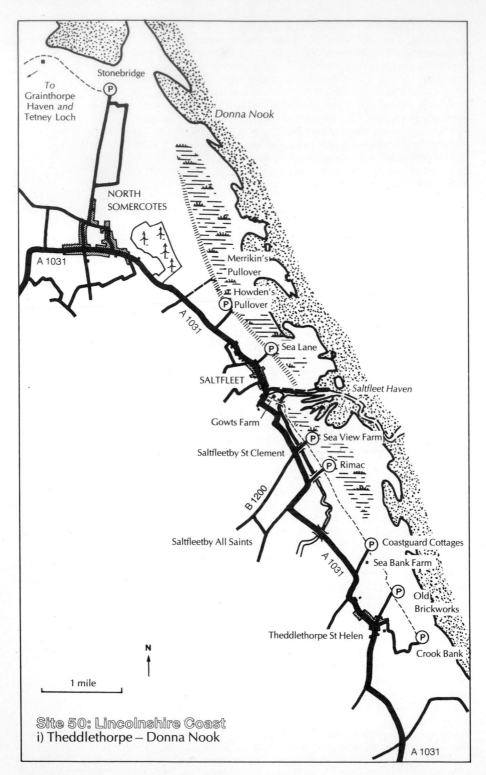

To
Grainthorpe
Haven *and*
Tetney Loch

Stonebridge

Donna Nook

NORTH
SOMERCOTES

A 1031

Merrikin's
Pullover

Howden's
Pullover

A 1031

Sea Lane

SALTFLEET

Saltfleet Haven

Gowts Farm

Sea View Farm

Saltfleetby St Clement

Rimac

B 1200

Saltfleetby All Saints

Coastguard Cottages

Sea Bank Farm

A 1031

Old
Brickworks

Theddlethorpe St Helen

Crook Bank

N

1 mile

Site 50: Lincolnshire Coast
i) Theddlethorpe – Donna Nook

A 1031

miles to Huttoft Bank, where there are tracks to the shore. It is possible to seawatch from the bank, and some pits inland of the road hold a good selection of duck. These pits are a reserve of the LSHTNC and cannot be seen from the road; access is by permit only.

4½ miles of coast from Theddlethorpe St Helen to Saltfleet Haven are a 1,090-acre National Nature Reserve, managed by the NCC (with an additional 95 acres run by the LSHTNC). Access is at six points off the A1031: Saltfleet Haven (where a footpath SE from Saltfleet passes Gowts Farm and crosses the main dyke), Sea View Farm, Rimac, Coastguard Cottages, Old Brickworks, and Crook Bank. Parking is available at all these points, and a footpath connects them. There is open access except to the *danger zone — visitors must comply with safety regulations displayed at the entrances.* The area is good for wildfowl, waders, and passerines on passage and in winter, and though a 1 1½ mile walk to the sea is necessary at Rimac in order to seawatch, it can be worthwhile.

Saltfleetby — Theddlethorpe Dunes NNR (see map) OS Sheet No. 113

This LSHTNC reserve covers 2,425 acres of foreshore and dunes along 6 miles of coast between Grainthorpe Haven and Saltfleet, abutting the NNR. Waders roost at Grainthorpe Haven and Donna Nook is excellent for migrants. There is open entry to the reserve, but *do not enter the danger area on the shore when the red flag is flying* (usually on weekdays). Access is from the A1031, and three points have parking facilities: Sea Lane at Saltfleet, Howden's Pullover (N of Saltfleet), and Stonebridge at Donna Nook. A public footpath runs NW from here along the seawall, with patches of cover for migrants. Access to the reserve is also possible along unmetalled roads at Merrikin's Pullover and Saltfleet Haven, but there are no parking facilities.

Saltfleet — Donna Nook (see map) OS Sheet No. 113

This RSPB reserve covers 3,111 acres of saltmarsh and dunes. Access is from Tetney Lock. Take the no-through road just N of the bridge over Louth Canal and park at the corner. Follow the footpath from here along the canal bank to the RSPB caravans. The reserve is open at all times, and is wardened in summer. The area is excellent for raptors in winter, and at high tide there are good views of wildfowl from the seawalls. The wader roost can be seen on the smaller tides from the end of the Haven track, but on spring tides only distant views are possible from the seawall. The MOD pools attract passage waders in spring, but tend to dry out over the summer. More consistent are the adjacent borrow pits and those nearer the Haven. Dotterel are annual on passage, frequenting the Reclaimed Fields, the fields on the road to Horse Shoe Point, or those near Low Farm. Breeding birds include Oystercatcher and up to 100 pairs of Little Terns. To protect the terns, the foreshore between the Haven and MOD pools is out of bounds in summer, as is the Haven track beyond the warden's caravan. Visitors should generally avoid tern nesting areas and heed warning notices.

Tetney Marshes (see map) OS Sheet No. 113

In winter there are Red-throated Divers and Great Crested Grebes offshore, but Black-throated Divers and Red-necked Grebes are much rarer. Seaduck can include Scaup, Eider, Common and

Birds

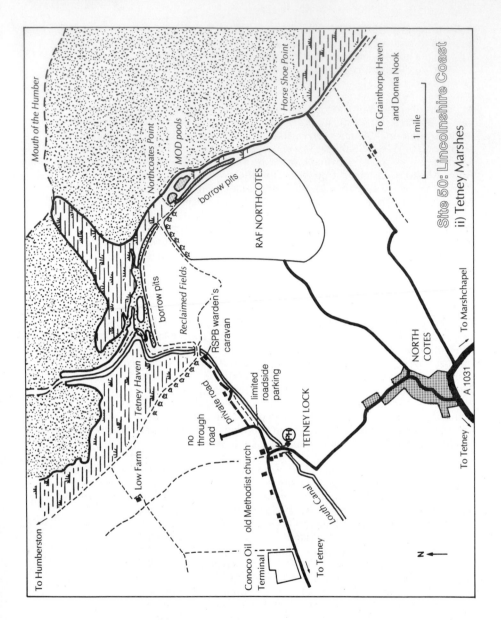

Site 50: Lincolnshire Coast
ii) Tetney Marshes

Velvet Scoter, Goldeneye, and Red-breasted Merganser, usually in small numbers, and sometimes also Long-tailed Duck; these are joined by Guillemots. Brent Geese are regular, as are Pintail, Shoveler, and large numbers of the commoner ducks. Short-eared Owls, Hen Harriers, and Merlins are quite frequent, and waders include Jack Snipe and Woodcock in the dune slacks as well as the usual coastal species. On the saltmarsh and tideline Twite, Snow Buntings, and Rock Pipits are reasonably common, but Shore Larks and Lapland Buntings are much more irregular. The buckthorn attracts large numbers of Fieldfares, Redwings, and Starlings.

On passage, Fulmars and Manx Shearwaters may be joined offshore by Sooty Shearwaters in a good onshore wind. Gannets and Cormorants are more regular, as are Arctic Skuas, but Great Skuas are quite scarce and Pomarines uncommon. Common, Arctic, Sandwich, Little, and Black Terns are joined in autumn by Little Gulls and Kittiwakes; Little Gulls are also regular May–June. Marsh Harriers may, with luck, be seen and there is a good variety of waders which, especially in autumn, may include Curlew Sandpiper, Little Stint, and sometimes Wood Sandpiper.

Landbird migrants can be excellent. As well as the usual chats, warblers, and flycatchers, Wryneck, Black Redstart, Icterine and Barred Warblers, Firecrest, and Red-backed and Great Grey Shrikes are all annual, usually in autumn, and Richard's Pipit, Bluethroat, Yellow-browed Warbler, and Red-breasted Flycatcher only slightly rarer. Late autumn can see arrival of Long and Short-eared Owls, Woodcock, and a few Bearded Tits. Something to look for on the saltmarshes in spring is the Scandinavian race of Rock Pipit.

Breeding species include Shelduck, the occasional Teal, Water Rail, Oystercatcher, Ringed Plover, and, notably, Little Tern in some numbers. The marshy areas have Grasshopper, Reed, and Sedge Warblers and occasionally Short-eared Owls, with Red polls in the birches.

Information

Lincolnshire and South Humberside Trust for Nature Conservation: The Manor House, Alford, Lincs LN13 9DL. Tel. 05212–3468.
NCC Saltfleetby/Theddlethorpe: 'Sandbanks', Saltfleetby St Clement, Louth, Lincs.
RSPB Tetney, summer warden: c/o The Post Office, Tetney, Grimsby, South Humberside DN36 5JT.
Recorder: Lincolnshire.

Site No. 51 Welbeck and Clumber Parks (Nottinghamshire)

Welbeck Park is a well-known site for Honey Buzzards which can be seen from the road with no risk of disturbance. At Clumber Park (National Trust) there is general access and a variety of woodland birds can be seen, including Hawfinches. Honey Buzzards are present most summers, and late May and early June is the best time to visit. For Hawfinches, winter is best, but with perseverance they can also be seen in summer.

Habitat

Ornamental lakes set in mixed woodland and farmland.

Access and Birds (see map)
OS Sheet No. 120
Great Lake, Welbeck

From the A616 bear N onto the B6005 towards Worksop, and after 1½ miles take a left at the first crossroads at a sign saying Carburton. Continue along this minor road for c 1 mile until you reach the beginning of the second section of the Great Lake. Park on the rough area by the fence on the right of the road (this is a narrow road and common sense should be exercised when parking). Looking N across the lake there is an isolated deciduous wood with a heronry. Honey Buzzards fly over this and/or the lake up to two or three times a day, giving the best views. About ¾ mile further on the gate just to the W of the Bentinck Monument is another spot to watch from, giving poorer, but more frequent views. This spot can only accommodate a handful of people. *Stay on the road at all times.* The whole of the area N of the road is private and well-keepered, with no public rights of way. In any event, the road is the best place to see the birds, being slightly elevated. The optimum time for Honey Buzzards is 10.00–15.00 on warm, slightly breezy days, as they soar on thermals. Normally there are 1–3 individuals, but up to 5 can be seen. Though present May–September, they become difficult to see in late August and early September. Sparrowhawks occur frequently and Osprey seems to be regular in spring and summer.

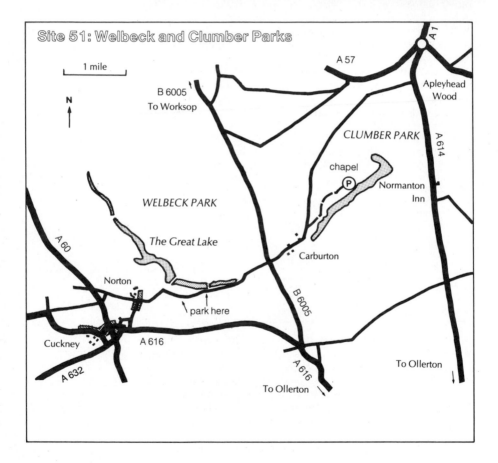

Site 51: Welbeck and Clumber Parks

Clumber Park

At the crossroads where you turn left for the Great Lake, turn right instead to Carburton and Clumber Park. Turning right after the first bridge, follow signs to the Chapel and park there (fee). The Park is also accessible from the A614 at Apleyhead Wood and Normanton Inn. Immediately behind the Chapel is an area of rhododendron, beech, yew, and other conifers. Hawfinches are present in greatest numbers (up to 30) in winter and are quite easy to see, usually in the tops of hornbeams beside the Chapel. Other birds to look for include Gadwall and Ruddy Duck on the lake, all three woodpeckers, Marsh and Willow Tits, and occasionally Crossbill or a wintering Firecrest. In summer there are Tree Pipits and Redstarts.

Hawfinches

Recorder: Nottinghamshire.

Information

Site No. 52 Blithfield Reservoir (Staffordshire)

Blithfield is an important reservoir for wildfowl and provides interesting birdwatching, especially in autumn and winter.

Blithfield covers 790 acres, has largely natural banks, and is surrounded by agricultural land. The E shore has been extensively planted with conifers and there is some deciduous woodland. There are areas of marsh along the inflows at the N end with willow scrub and, especially on the upper reaches of the River Blithe, alders. If the water level drops in autumn mudflats are exposed.

Habitat

The B5013 Rugeley–Uttoxeter road crosses the reservoir on a causeway, giving views of much of the open water, including the gull roost. Access is otherwise by permit (issued on behalf of the South Staffs. Water Co. by the West Midland Bird Club, £3.75 per year). There are seven hides and visitors can walk the entire shoreline (nearly 9 miles), though the N half is the best.

Access (see map)
OS Sheet No. 128

In winter Red-necked Grebes and divers (especially Great Northern) are occasional visitors. Bewick's Swans are regular and large numbers of duck occur: up to 1,000 Wigeon as well as Teal and a few Gadwall, Shoveler, and sometimes Pintail. There can be up to 60 Goosander and 50 Goldeneye, and a maximum of 630 Ruddy Ducks has been recorded. Smew and seaduck sometimes appear, especially during hard weather (though Common Scoter and Scaup may visit at any time of the year). The

Birds

gull roost often holds one or two Glaucous Gulls and sometimes Iceland as well, and there have been several records of Mediterranean Gull. The best time is from Christmas until March, especially for Iceland Gulls, and a telescope is essential to watch the roost. Siskins and Redpolls are regular visitors to the surrounding trees, notably the alders along the River Blithe.

Passage periods can be very good. Osprey and Peregrine have appeared in most recent autumns, and sometimes stay for long periods. Wader numbers are generally low in spring, but in autumn large numbers can be present, mostly Ringed Plover and Dunlin. As well as the usual species, Little Stint and Curlew Sandpiper occur regularly, especially in September. Sanderling,

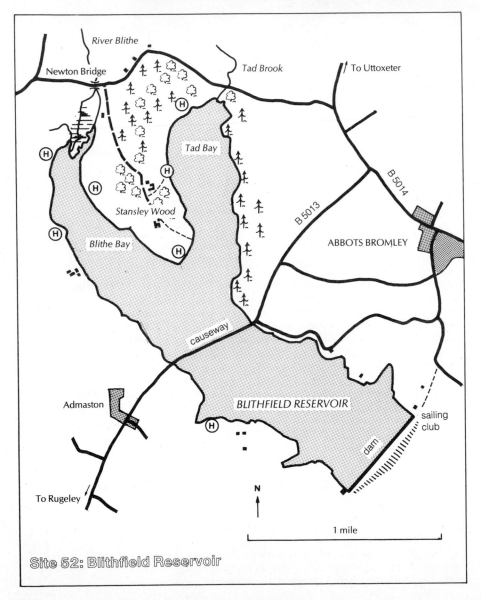

Site 52: Blithfield Reservoir

Jack Snipe, Spotted Redshank, Green Sandpiper, and Turnstone are also regular in small numbers and Common, Arctic, and Black Terns and Little Gull are quite often present. Breeding birds are unexceptional but include Great Crested Grebe, Sparrowhawk, and Lesser Spotted Woodpecker.

Used heavily for recreation, Chasewater holds only small numbers of wintering duck, notably Goldeneye. The casual visitor can expect to see little except the sizable winter gull roost, which is easy to work and often holds Glaucous Gull. Iceland Gulls are more erratic — there are good and bad years — but this is the most regular site in central England. The period Christmas–March is best. Access is off the A5 just W of Brownhills. A road leads past a large grandstand to the car park on the left by the dam. Views of the gulls are usually adequate from here, and the roost can be watched from the car, though a telescope is essential.

Other Sites in the Area
52.1 Chasewater
OS Sheet Nos.
128 and 139

Blithfield permits: Miss M. Surman, 6 Lloyd Square, 12 Niall Close, Edgbaston, Birmingham B15 3LX.
Recorder: Staffordshire.

Information

Site No. 53 Rutland Water (Leicestershire)

Rutland Water is huge. Since its construction in 1975 it has become one of the most important wildfowl sanctuaries in Britain, and is well worth visiting, especially during the winter and passage periods. Nine miles of shoreline along the W arms are a reserve of the Leicestershire and Rutland Trust for Nature Conservation (LRTNC), covering 350 acres.

As well as 3,000 acres of open water there are purpose-built islands, shingle banks, and three lagoons. There are areas of scrub woodland at Gibbet Gorse and Gorse Close, and mature deciduous woodland at Lax-Hill. Other interesting habitats include ancient meadows and reedbeds.

Habitat

1. View the SW tip of the reservoir from the A6003 at Manton Bridge — usually the best place for waders. There is no access off the road.
2. Lyndon Reserve. Leave the A6003 E at Manton, and take the first turning on the left after the village to the Interpretative Centre and shore. Access from the A1 is via the A606, following signs to Edith Weston and Manton. There are three hides and a nature trail through Gibbet Gorse. The reserve is open 10.00–16.00 daily (except Mondays and Fridays) May–October, and on Saturdays and Sundays November–April. Permits for non-members are 50p. Visitors must keep to the paths.
3. Egleton Reserve. From the A6003 take the minor road to Egleton. The entrance to the reserve is at the southernmost point of the village. Open on Saturdays, Sundays, Wednesdays, and bank holidays, 09.00–17.00, non-members of the

**Access
(see map)**
OS Sheet No. 141

LRTNC must obtain permits (£1.50 per day) from the Interpretative Centre in the car park. There are 10 hides and a trail through Lax-Hill and Gorse Close. Visitors must keep to the paths.

4. The dam area often has congregations of ducks in the winter, and may be the last place to freeze in hard weather; it is a good spot for divers. A car park near the N end is accessible from the A606.

5. Several signposted access points to the shore off the A606 and at Edith Weston give views of the reservoir for ducks, gulls, and terns.

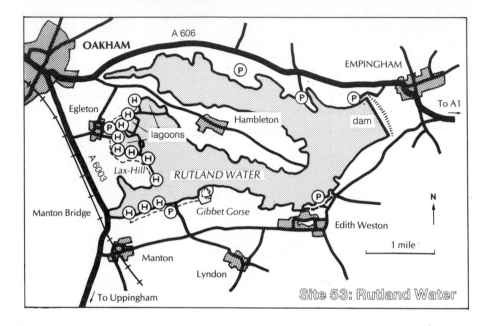

Smews and Tufted Ducks

Both Red-throated and Great Northern Divers are almost annual **Birds**
in winter, as are Red-necked and Slavonian Grebes. Wildfowl
include feral Greylag Geese, and peak counts of 1,000 Shoveler
and 1,550 Gadwall are outstanding. Ruddy Duck and Pintail are
also possible, as are Goosander (up to 120) and, notably,
Red-crested Pochard (up to seven have occurred, mainly in
autumn and winter). There are regularly small numbers of Smew,
and Scaup and other seaduck appear in ones and twos. Water
Rails and sometimes Jack Snipe winter in the marshy areas, and
the slopes of the dam often attract a large flock of Golden Plover.
Other waders include up to 20 Ruff and a few Green Sandpipers.
Short-eared Owls are regular, up to ten hunt over the rough
ground, and Long-eared Owls roost in Lax-Hill and Gibbet Gorse,
though they are difficult to find. Peregrines are a scarce but
increasing visitor and there are occasionally Bearded Tits.

Black-necked Grebes are quite frequently seen, especially in
spring, late summer, and autumn, while Garganey and Common
Scoter are also regular on passage. There are occasional records
of Osprey. Waders may include all the usual species as well as
Black-tailed Godwit, Whimbrel, and Spotted Redshank. Little
Stint and Curlew Sandpiper are annual, usually in autumn, and
Pectoral Sandpiper nearly so. Little Gull and Common, Arctic,
and Black Terns are regular, favouring the main water.

Ruddy Duck, Shoveler, and sometimes Garganey breed, as do
Oystercatcher, Little Ringed Plover, and Common Tern. The
woods have Long-eared Owls and Lesser Spotted Woodpeckers,
and Reed and Sedge Warblers breed in the waterside vegetation.
Hobbies often hunt over the area on summer evenings.

LRTNC warden: Fishponds Cottage, Stamford Rd, Oakham, Leicester- **Information**
shire.
An annual report is produced on the birds of Rutland Water.
Recorder: Leicestershire.

Site No. 54 Eyebrook Reservoir (Leicestershire)

N of Corby, Eyebrook Reservoir holds a good variety of winter
wildfowl and passage waders and in hard weather often attracts
interesting birds. It is managed as a reserve.

Open water covers 400 acres and there are natural, gently **Habitat**
shelving banks. There is an area of marsh at the N end, near the
inlet, and the E shore has been extensively planted with conifers.
The reservoir is used for trout fishing, but is otherwise undisturbed.

From the A6003 take the minor road W to Stoke Dry and carry on **Access**
through the village to the reservoir. The road runs around the N **(see map)**
end and then parallel to the W shore. The bridge over the Eye OS Sheet No. 141
Brook at the N tip and the W shore are best for passage waders.
Access off the road is only granted to members of the Leicestershire and Rutland Ornithological Society and there is a hide for
their use. However, the casual visitor can obtain good views from
the road.

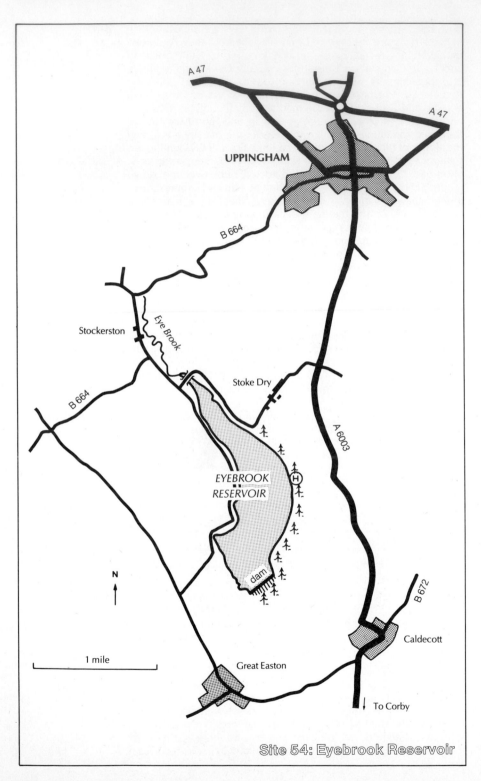

Site 54: Eyebrook Reservoir

Birds

Wintering wildfowl include Bewick's Swans, up to 80 of which can be present in mid-winter, together with feral Greylag and Snow Geese. Wigeon are numerous and small numbers of Goldeneye, Goosander, Ruddy Duck, Shoveler, and Pintail also occur, and sometimes Smew or Red-crested Pochard. Hard weather can bring seaduck, especially Scaup, Slavonian and Red-necked Grebes, and divers, particularly Great Northern. Peregrines are sometimes seen, and wintering waders include Golden Plover and the occasional Green Sandpiper or Jack Snipe. The large gull roost is comparatively easy to work, though a telescope is essential. It is best watched from the N half of the W shore of the reservoir. Glaucous and more rarely Iceland Gulls may be found but neither is regular.

Little Ringed Plovers

Common Scoter and Water Pipit sometimes occur in early spring and Hobbies are quite regular in spring and early summer. Black-necked Grebes are increasingly frequent on passage, especially in autumn, when an Osprey is recorded nearly annually. Autumn, when the water levels have dropped, is also the best time for waders. Little Stint and Curlew Sandpiper are annual, and other species may include Spotted Redshank. Common, Arctic, and Black Terns and Little Gulls are regular passage visitors. Breeding birds include Ruddy Duck and occasionally Gadwall or Teal.

Information

Recorder: Leicestershire.

Site No. 55 Pitsford Reservoir (Northamptonshire)

N of Northampton, Pitsford Reservoir has a good variety of duck in winter and waders on passage, and is worth a visit during these periods. 480 acres of the N shore are a reserve of the Northamptonshire Trust for Nature Conservation (NTNC).

Habitat

The reservoir covers 800 acres and has natural, gently shelving banks. The perimeter of the N half has been extensively planted with conifers, and there is also a mature oak copse; otherwise, the surrounding land is farmed.

**Access
(see map)**
OS Sheet Nos.
141 and 152

Access is from the following points:
1. The causeway, on the minor road to Holcot from the A508 at Brixworth. There is a car park at its W end.
2. Either end of the submerged road N of the causeway.
3. Pitsford. Leave the village on the road signed 'Reservoir Car Park' (fee).

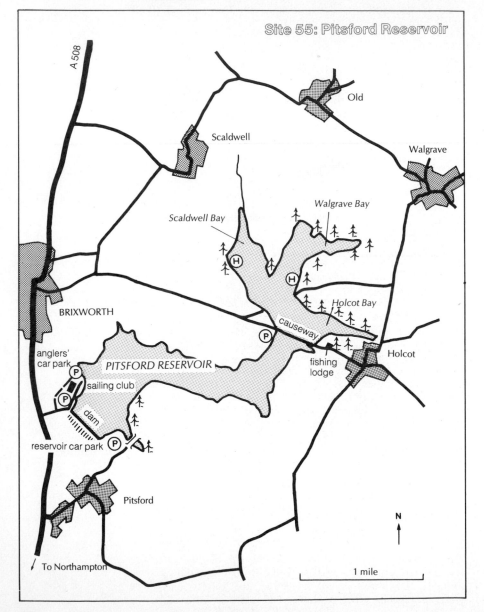

Site 55: Pitsford Reservoir

4. The anglers' car park, outside the reservoir perimeter fence, just N of the Sailing Club, is a good spot to watch the gull roost from.

Access to the N half of the reservoir is by permit. Yearly permits issued by the Anglian Water Authority are available at £6 from the Fishing Lodge by the causeway, but do not allow access to Walgrave Bay and hide. A permit for these is issued by the NTNC, and a day permit for the whole N section is available free on application to the warden (s.a.e. please). There is public access to the whole of the S half. Scaldwell and Walgrave Bays are best for waders, and the N half is also better for duck (though Wigeon prefer the more open vistas of the S half, and the dam area can be good, except when there are boats out).

Birds

Large numbers of Wigeon winter, as well as some Pintail, Gadwall, Shoveler, Goldeneye, Ruddy Duck, and usually about 40 Goosander. There is a large gull roost: Mediterranean, a few Glaucous, and sometimes Iceland Gulls are recorded most winters.

Ospreys are nearly annual on passage, and there can be a good variety of the usual waders, while Little Stint, Curlew Sandpiper, and Spotted Redshank are annual. In the late autumn and early winter, Bewick's Swans are regular and there are often 100–200 Dunlin. Tern passage is also good: Common, Arctic, and Black are regular, while Arctic Skuas too turn up surprisingly often.

Breeding birds include Great Crested Grebe, Shoveler, Gadwall, and occasionally Ruddy Duck. Nine species of warbler breed in the surrounding area, including Grasshopper, and Hobbies are quite frequent.

Information

Warden: c/o Northants TNC, Lings House, Billing Lings, Northampton NN3 4BE.
Recorder: Northamptonshire.

Site No. 56 Draycote Water (Warwickshire)

Draycote Water lies just SW of Rugby. Although heavily disturbed by sailing and fishing it attracts a good variety of duck in the winter, often including a few seaduck, as well as divers and grebes.

Habitat

The reservoir covers c 700 acres and the shoreline is partly natural and partly artificial embankments. There is a small marsh at the NE end, overlooked by a hide.

Access (see map)
OS Sheet Nos. 140 and 151

The entrance is off the A426 2 miles S of Dunchurch. A permit is required (£3.70 per year), available from the Severn Trent Water Authority or their agent. It is possible to drive clockwise around the entire perimeter, viewing from the car. Otherwise, a small section of the NE end is visible from the public footpath which leaves the A426 c ½ mile NE of the entrance, skirts the shore, and carries on to Thurlaston.

Birds

In winter divers are regularly seen, especially Great Northern, and often make long stays. A few hundred Wigeon occur, together with small numbers of Gadwall and Shoveler. Diving duck are more numerous and there are usually about·50 Goldeneye and smaller numbers of Goosander and Ruddy Duck. Common and Velvet Scoter, Red-breasted Merganser, Scaup, and Eider have all been recorded and two or three species of seaduck may be present at once, together with a Smew or two. There is a huge gull roost, mainly Common and Black-headed, but Glaucous are seen fairly frequently, sometimes together with Icelands. There are several winter records of Mediterranean and Little Gulls, but Kittiwakes are more frequent visitors at this season, especially after severe coastal gales. The surrounding pasture sometimes attracts Short-eared Owls.

Wader passage is poor, Common Sandpiper and Dunlin being the most frequent species. Black, Common, and Arctic Terns and sometimes Little Gulls also occur on passage.

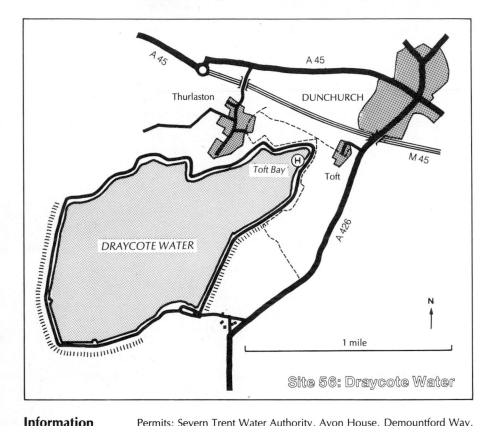

Site 56: Draycote Water

Information

Permits: Severn Trent Water Authority, Avon House, Demountford Way, Cannon Park, Coventry CV4 7EJ. Tel. 0203-416510. (Agent: Kites Hardwick Filling Station, on A426 500 yards S of reservoir entrance). Recorder: Warwickshire.

Site No. 57 Eckington Bridge (Worcestershire)

Marsh Warblers are one of Britain's rarest breeding birds, almost entirely confined to the valley of the River Avon. At Eckington Bridge, near Pershore, it is possible to see them without disturbing them or their habitat. The best time to visit is the first half of June. The area is a reserve of the Worcestershire Nature Conservation Trust.

A relatively small area of willows and nettles alongside the River Avon.

Habitat

Leave the A4104 S onto the B4080, which crosses the River Avon after 1 mile at Eckington Bridge. Park on the left just S of the bridge and walk W along the S shore of the river, coming to a

Access (see map) OS Sheet No. 150

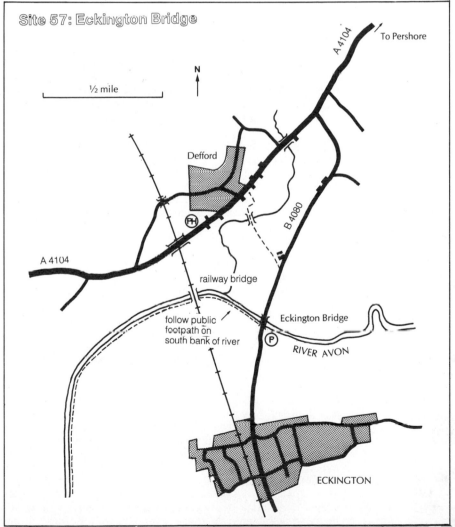

Site 57: Eckington Bridge

½ mile

N

To Pershore

A4104

Defford

B4080

A 4104

railway bridge

follow public footpath on south bank of river

Eckington Bridge

RIVER AVON

ECKINGTON

railway bridge after c 500 yards. Marsh Warblers frequent the rank vegetation on the opposite side of the river to where you are standing, both E and W of the railway bridge, and can often be seen in the willows along the riverbank. *On no account should you cross the river over the railway bridge.*

Birds

Marsh Warblers often arrive in the last week of May, but the best time to see them is when they are singing – most regularly in early morning and evening in the first two weeks of June; they sing infrequently, if at all, in July. Reed and Sedge Warblers also nest alongside the river in this area.

Information

Worcestershire Nature Conservation Trust: Hanbury Road, Droitwich, Worcestershire WR9 7DU. Tel. 0905-773031.
Recorder: Worcestershire.

Site No. 58 Slimbridge (Gloucestershire)

Slimbridge is the headquarters of the Wildfowl Trust, formed in 1946 by Peter Scott. The area was chosen because of the largest flock of wintering White-fronted Geese in Britain, and these remain the major attraction, together with a flock of Bewick's Swans. The Trust's refuge covers c 2,000 acres.

Habitat

Reclaimed meadows form an area of 1,000 acres known as the New Grounds, while 200 acres of grassy saltmarsh outside the seawall are known as the Dumbles. Beyond this, large areas of mud are exposed alongside the River Severn at low water. Some shallow pools have been created inside the seawall, attracting waders, and these are visible from the Trust's hides.

Access
OS Sheet No. 162

Leave the M5 at junction 14 and drive N along the A38, turning NW after 8 miles onto a minor road signed Slimbridge. The reserve is 2 miles from this turning. Coming from the N the turning is 4 miles from junction 13 on the M5.

Visitors can view the geese from three towers and nine hides, accessible through the Trust's collection. This is open daily, 09.30–17.00 (or dusk if earlier). Non-members pay £3. As well as the wild geese, the collection of captive waterfowl has grown into the world's largest — and best. There are also exhibitions, a restaurant, nature trail, and a hot-house with several species of tropical bird.

Birds

Some White-fronts arrive in early October, but numbers remain low until late November, when they begin to build up rapidly, peaking in the New Year — sometimes at over 7,000. Thereafter they decline steadily, and have usually all gone by early March. Lesser White-fronted Geese are found, on average, in four out of five winters. Up to three (occasionally up to six) arrive in late December or early January and stay till the begining of March. They usually require a good telescope and a great deal of patience to find. Individuals of several other species of geese can usually be found with the White-fronts. Several hundred Bewick's Swans winter; they feed on the fields and roost on the estuary, but also visit the Rushy Pen and can be seen at very close range. Nine species of duck are regularly present, including large numbers of Wigeon as well as Pintail, Gadwall, and Shoveler, and many come into the collection to feed. A Peregrine is almost always present in winter. Waders include several thousand Lapwings and Golden Plovers in the fields, as well as the common open-shore species.

Waders are more varied on passage, and can include Whimbrel, especially in spring, and Black-tailed Godwit in autumn.

Bewick's Swans

Views of the Severn estuary are possible from Frampton Breakwater and some nice flashes attract passage waders. Turn off the A38 3 miles N of the Slimbridge turning onto the B4071 to Frampton on Severn. Turn left into the village after 1½ miles and drive straight through to the bridge over the Gloucester and Sharpness Canal. Park and cross the bridge. The small reedbed by the bridge is worth a look for migrant warblers. From here you have two options:

Other Sites in the Area
58.1 Frampton

1. Walk S along the canal for 200 yards, where a gate on the right marks the start of a path to the seawall. Continue on S along the seawall, reaching Frampton Breakwater after 1 mile. There are two flashes by the seawall.
2. Go through the gate adjacent to the bridge and follow the seawall round N; there is a flash after c ½ mile.

Wildfowl and waders, as described under Slimbridge, may be seen in somewhat less artificial (and consequently less comfortable) conditions.

Enquiries to: The Wildfowl Trust, Slimbridge, Gloucester GL2 7BT. Tel. 045389-333 (Ansaphone information service outside office hours). Recorder: Gloucestershire.

Information

WALES

Site No. 59 Kenfig (Mid Glamorgan)

Kenfig, N of Porthcawl, has a variety of habitats attracting a range of wildfowl, raptors, and waders in winter and on passage. The area is a Local Nature Reserve covering 1,100 acres.

Habitat

Kenfig Pool is a natural 70-acre dune-slack lake, surrounded by areas of reeds and sallows and set in about 1,200 acres of dunes. The reserve is flanked on the seaward side by Kenfig Sands. At Sker Point there is a small area of rocky shore and the tiny Sker Pool attracts waders, especially after bad weather.

Access (see map) OS Sheet No. 170

Leave the M4 at junction 37 (Pyle) S on to the A4229. After ¼ mile take the B4283 through Cornelly past the Greenacre pub. Turn left on a minor road over the motorway, past the Angel, and straight on for ½ mile to the car park. The reserve centre is open Monday – Friday 08.30 – 16.30, weekends and bank holidays at least 14.00 – 17.00. The reserve is managed by Mid Glamorgan County Council, and there are no restrictions on access except to the pool's reedbeds during the breeding season. Otherwise it is possible to walk round the pool and there is a hide in the SW corner. This is usually open, but if not the key is available from the centre. Sker Point can be reached by walking through the dunes from the car park.

Birds

In winter, divers and the rarer grebes are irregular visitors to the pool, but small numbers of Whooper and, less often, Bewick's Swans are more frequent. Wildfowl also usually include Shoveler, Gadwall (up to 50) and Goldeneye. Around the pool there are often Water Rails, Jack Snipe, a few Chiffchaffs, and, much less often, Cetti's Warblers. Short-eared Owl, Merlin, Peregrine, and, less regularly, Hen Harrier are also visitors to the area. In the fields at Sker Farm there are usually several hundred Golden Plover and occasionally also a few Ruff, but the latter are often elusive. On the beach and the rocks at Sker Point there are Grey Plovers, Sanderlings, Purple Sandpipers, and Turnstones.

Breeding birds include Great Crested Grebe and Ringed Plover, with Stonechat and Grasshopper Warbler in rough vegetation in the dunes and Reed and Sedge Warblers around the pool.

Purple Heron has occurred several times in spring, and Bittern in late autumn — especially after E winds or hard weather. Passage also brings records of Garganey and Scaup on the pool. Waders can be found on both Kenfig and Sker Pools and the beach; this range of habitats means that a good variety is often present. Notable are relatively large numbers of Whimbrel in both spring and autumn. Common, Sandwich, and Black Terns are regular migrants, but Arctic and Little Terns and Little Gulls are less frequent. Seawatching from Sker Point can be worthwhile, though there is no shelter. From May to August on a rising tide in the early morning, Manx Shearwater, Fulmar, Gannet, and Common Scoter may be seen, the latter two mainly in late summer, when there are also occasionally Great or Arctic Skuas. A W wind is likely to push birds onshore and give the best views. In September, gales can produce the occasional Storm or even Leach's Petrel.

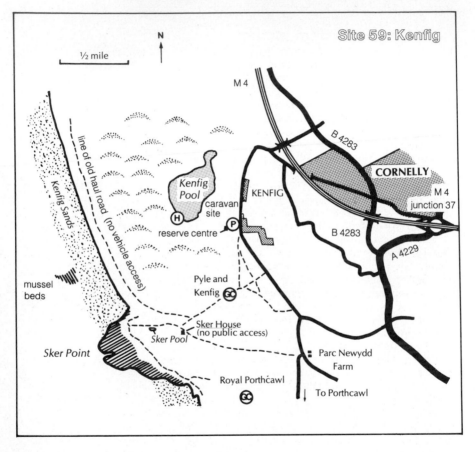

Other Sites in the Area
59.1 Eglwys Nunydd Reservoir

This concrete-banked water covers 200 acres and is managed as a reserve by the Glamorgan Trust for Nature Conservation. In winter the commoner duck are frequently joined by divers, grebes, Goosander, and seaduck. There are few waders on passage, but Common and Arctic Terns and Little Gulls are quite often seen. Leave the M4 at junction 38 and from the roundabout take the lane past the British Oxygen Company Works to the reservoir. Parking is not allowed inside the gates (your car may be locked in); entrance is on foot through a gate at the N end and is restricted to Trust members. For up-to-date information on access contact the Kenfig Reserve Centre.

Warden: Kenfig Nature Reserve Centre, Ton Kenfig, Pyle, Mid Glamorgan **Information**
CF33 4PT. Tel. 0656-743386
Recorder: Mid Glamorgan

Site No. 60 Blackpill (West Glamorgan)

Blackpill lies immediately W of Swansea. The beach is similar to hundreds of others, but, since Britain's first Ring-billed Gull was found here in 1973, they have occurred regularly, together with small numbers of Mediterranean Gulls. February–April is probably the best period to visit.

Habitat

Blackpill is the last part of the shore of Swansea Bay to be covered at high tide. The Clyne Stream runs out across the beach and provides birds with bathing facilities, whilst the sand bar, sea, and beach are used by roosting gulls.

Access
OS Sheet No. 159

Leave Swansea on the A4067. The road runs alongside the beach and the best place to watch from is the Boating Pool, between the Clyne and the B4436 turning. The period around high tide is usually the most productive on neap tides; an earlier arrival is desirable on spring tides.

Birds

The high tide gull roost, often of several thousand birds, is mainly Black-headed and Common Gulls, but each year four or five Ring-billed Gulls are recorded, most frequently February – April, and often stay for long periods. Mediterranean Gulls are commoner and may be found at any time, though from early spring to July is best. Iceland and Glaucous Gulls are sometimes seen in winter. The usual waders are present at Blackpill, which is used as a roost, including Grey Plover and Sanderling. On the sea there are occasionally divers or seaduck — Eider, Common and Velvet Scoters, Red-breasted Merganser, and Goldeneye — and a Peregrine is often present.

Little Terns occur in spring and late summer, and Little Gulls are also regular from March until June. Small numbers of Curlew Sandpipers are regular in autumn; other possibilities include Little Stint and Black-tailed Godwit and there is a notable concentration of up to 500 Sanderling. Offshore in late summer and autumn there are sometimes a few skuas and small numbers of terns; these may include Black.

Recorder: West Glamorgan.

Information

Site No. 61 The Gower Peninsula (West Glamorgan)

Gower has a wide variety of habitats and can provide an interesting day's birding at any time of the year. Three areas are particularly attractive: the Burry Inlet for wildfowl and waders,

Oxwich for marshland species, and Worms Head for breeding seabirds.

61.1 Burry Inlet

The S shore of the Inlet is largely owned by the National Trust, while Whiteford Burrows National Nature Reserve covers 1,977 acres of dune and foreshore. The Inlet's populations of Oyster-catcher, Knot, and Pintail are internationally important. Ideally a visit should be in winter, timed to coincide with the fortnightly spring tides, which usually occur in early morning and evening.

Habitat

The River Loughor forms a broad estuary, the Burry Inlet, into which flow four smaller rivers. Two-thirds of the Inlet are tidal flats and the remainder saltmarsh, concentrated on the S shore. Whiteford Burrows, a large dune system covering 540 acres, guards the S entrance to the Inlet and has been planted in places with Corsican pines.

Access
(see map)
OS Sheet No. 159

1. The B4295 gives views of the shore from Penclawdd to Crofty.
2. Llanrhidian Marsh is accessible from the minor road between Crofty and Llanrhidian which parallels the B4295. Old earth platforms at Wernffrwd and near Crofty make useful vantage points, especially at high tide. This area is good for duck, with Greenshanks on autumn passage as well as Green Sandpipers; both often winter.
3. The heavily grazed saltings below Weobley Castle are used by roosting waders on high spring tides. Large numbers of Golden Plover winter, and the area also attracts raptors. There are good views from the castle.
4. Continue on unclassified roads S of Landimore and on to Llanmadoc and Cwm Ivy. Follow the signposted footpath past the NCC information kiosk and pine plantations to the marsh. The reserve begins at the stile and permits are needed away from marked paths. The track winds through the dunes for c 2 miles to Whiteford Point, giving views of the Groose and Landimore Marsh from the stile before plunging back into the conifers. Just after the path re-emerges from the plantations, a hide overlooks the Inlet at Berges Island, a good spot for Brent Geese. Black-necked and Slavonian Grebes may be seen from the hide on a rising or falling tide. Further on, Whiteford Point is used by roosting waders on the lower tides, the sea holds grebes and divers. Cormorants roost on the abandoned lighthouse, and Eider and Brent Geese frequent the rocks and mud at its base. A suggested route would be to visit the hide on a rising tide, walk to the Point on the falling tide and finally back to Cwm Ivy along Whiteford Sands, a total of 5 miles.

Birds

In winter, Great Crested and Slavonian Grebes are regular in small numbers, but Black-necked Grebes are unfortunately no longer guaranteed. Wildfowl include up to 600 Brent Geese, large numbers of Pintail, and a few hundred Shoveler. Up to 200 Eider frequent the mussel beds around Whiteford Point, as well as small numbers of Red-breasted Merganser. Scaup, Long-tailed Duck, Common and Velvet Scoters, and Goldeneye also occur around the Point, and further up the estuary too, but irregularly and in very small numbers. Waders include Sanderling and a maximum of 19,000 Oystercatchers. Several hundred Turnstones

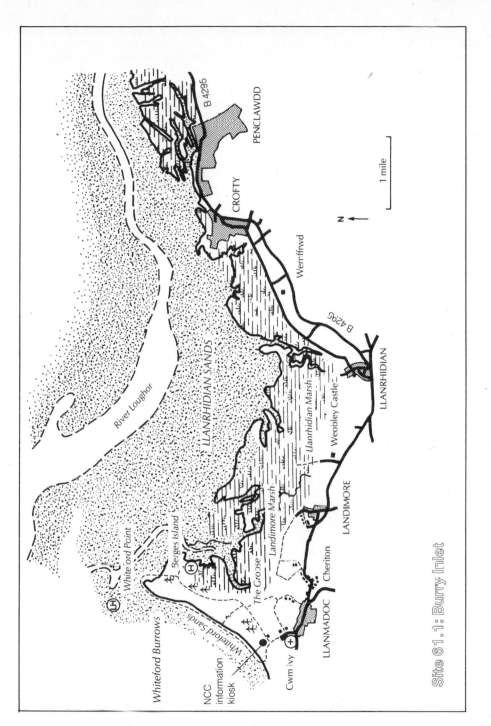

Site 61.1: Burry Inlet

frequent the mussel beds off the Point, together with a few Purple Sandpipers. Small numbers of Greenshanks and Spotted Redshanks winter, mainly at Whiteford, but also at Llanrhidian

Marsh, together with a few Green Sandpipers and Black-tailed Godwits. Buzzards and Sparrowhawks are resident and are regularly joined by Merlins and occasionally Peregrines, Hen Harriers, and Short-eared Owls.

In spring there can be large numbers of Whimbrel. Other migrants include terns, especially Common and Sandwich, but sometimes also Black.

In summer Eider are still present, as are numbers of non-breeding terns. Around Cwm Ivy you may find Raven or Grasshopper Warbler, but Whiteford is generally quiet at this season.

61. 2 Oxwich

Oxwich Bay, on the S shore of the Gower Peninsula, is a National Nature Reserve covering 720 acres. An excellent range of habitats attracts an appropriate diversity of birds, and a visit is worthwhile at any time, but especially in spring and summer.

Habitat

Two miles of sandy beach are backed by dunes and bordered to N and S by limestone cliffs. Nicholaston Pill flows across the beach attracting roosting gulls and waders. Behind the dunes are

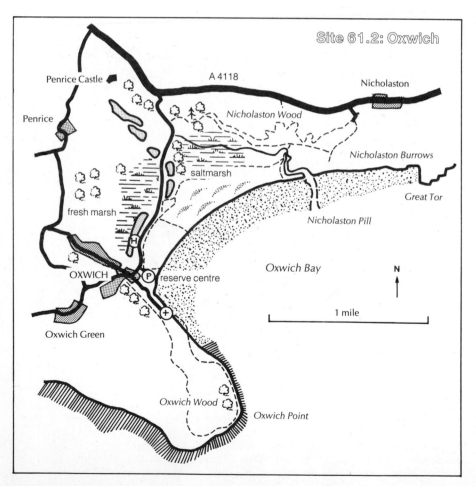

freshwater marshes with areas of open water, c 100 acres of reedbeds, and alder and willow carr. The small saltmarsh is rather dry and consequently unattractive. To the N and S, Nicholaston and Oxwich Woods are both largely deciduous.

Oxwich village is on a minor road S off the A4118; good views of the marsh are possible from this road. The Reserve Centre, on the seaward side of the village, is open 09.00 – 13.00 Monday – Friday all year; from April to mid-October also on Saturdays and Sundays 10.00 – 12.00. The reserve is managed by the NCC and there is open access to the dunes and beach (except for the enclosures) and the marked paths in Nicholaston and Oxwich Woods — the lower path in the former giving good views of the marsh. The freshwater marsh and carr are closed to casual visitors, though a permit to use the hide at the S end of the marsh can be obtained from the Reserve Centre. It is best early and late in the day, but is not open from mid-July to the end of August. A suggested route would be to park at the Centre, walk along the beach, over Nicholaston Pill, through Nicholaston Wood to the road, and back along it through the marsh to the Reserve Centre. The car park is a good vantage point from which to scan the Bay, especially the sheltered area in the lee of the headland. Oxwich Point also gives views of the Bay and can be reached by following the footpath SE from the village past the church and through Oxwich Wood.

Access
(see map)
OS Sheet No. 159

In winter there are sometimes Great Northern Divers or Common Scoters offshore, and on the marsh small numbers of Gadwall and Shoveler. Green Sandpiper may winter, and there are occasionally Bitterns, especially in early spring. Turnstones and Purple Sandpipers frequent the rocks and Sanderlings the beach. Mediterranean, Glaucous, and Iceland Gulls are occasionally found in the gull roost. Kingfishers and Grey Wagtails are regular. The woodland and carr usually have Siskin and Redpoll, and often Woodcock, Blackcap, Chiffchaff, and Firecrest too.

Birds

Marsh Harriers and Purple Herons are nearly annual spring visitors, and more regular migrants include Common and Sandwich Terns. Offshore, Fulmar, Manx Shearwater, Gannet, Shag, and Common Scoter may appear in spring and summer. Ospreys have been recorded in autumn, and Hobbies may appear in late summer evenings, hunting the hirundine roost.

Breeding birds on the marsh include Teal, Pochard, and Water Rail. Several hundred pairs of Reed Warblers are joined by Sedge and Grasshopper Warblers and, since 1972, a small number of Bearded Tits; the best chance of seeing one is from the marsh road in late summer and autumn. Cetti's Warblers are the most recent colonists, though more difficult to see. The woods have Buzzard, Sparrowhawk, all three woodpeckers, Nuthatch, Treecreeper, and Marsh and Willow Tits.

Between Worms Head and Port-Eynon Point c 7 miles of coast are managed by the NCC, Glamorgan Trust for Nature Conservation, and National Trust. 109 acres of cliffland around the Worm form the NNR proper. The whole area provides fine cliff-top walking, but the real attractions are the Worm from late April to July for breeding seabirds, and Port-Eynon Point for summer and autumn seawatching.

Gower Coast
National Nature
Reserve

Habitat

Worms Head is a mile-long grass-topped promontory at the SW tip of Gower, and is cut off from the mainland at high tide. The adjacent coast has areas of scrub along the cliff-tops, terminating at Port-Eynon Point, Gower's most southerly point.

Access
OS Sheet No. 159

1. Worms Head (see map). Park in the large car park in Rhossili and walk c 1 mile along the cliff-top path to the disued coastguard's lookout overlooking the Head. The rocky causeway is only passable for 2½ hrs each side of low water. Check the times of the tides before you cross or risk being stranded for 7 hrs. Tide tables are posted at the coastguard houses in Rhossili, and there is usually an NCC warden at the lookout in summer who can advise. The best route across the causeway is on the N side. The seabirds are on the N of the Head, visible from certain points on Middle Head, and there is no access to Outer Head from mid-March to the end of July. Visitors must keep to the footpath.
2. A footpath runs E along the coast from the Worm to Port-Eynon Point, and is accessible in several places from the B4247.
3. Port-Eynon is at the terminus of the A4118. Park just S of the village and follow the footpath S for ½ mile past the Youth Hostel to the Point.

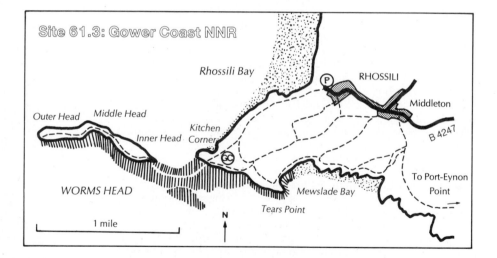

Site 61.3: Gower Coast NNR

Rhossili Bay

RHOSSILI

Middleton

Outer Head   Middle Head

Kitchen

Inner Head   Corner

B 4247

WORMS HEAD

Mewslade Bay

To Port-Eynon Point

Tears Point

1 mile

N

Birds

At the Worm there are breeding Fulmars, Shags, Razorbills, Guillemots, and Kittiwakes, and small numbers of Puffins may be present in summer. Non-breeding Cormorants, Gannets, and Manx Shearwaters can often be seen offshore in spring and summer, shearwaters most commonly in early morning. Erratically, at any time except mid-summer, large flocks of Common Scoter, sometimes with a few Velvets, are off the Worm. With luck, a Peregrine may be seen, and other breeding birds include Rock Pipit, Stonechat, Wheatear, and Raven on the cliff tops.

A few Arctic and sometimes Great Skuas, as well as Gannets, shearwaters, auks, and terns occur on passage. At Port-Eynon particularly, SW gales may bring one or two Storm Petrels (June–August), Sooty Shearwaters (late July to early August), and

Pomarine Skuas (most likely in September). Passerine migrants such as Wheatears, warblers, and sometimes (in late autumn and winter) Black Redstarts occur along the cliff tops.

In winter there are Red-throated Divers offshore, and occasionally Great Northerns, as well as Eider and Red-breasted Mergansers. The rocks at the Worm usually attract a flock of Purple Sandpipers and Turnstones.

Information

NCC Oxwich, Whiteford, and S Gower coast, wardens: Oxwich Reserve Centre, Oxwich, Swansea SA3 1LS. Tel. 0792–390320 or –390626.
References:
The Natural History of Gower by M. E. Gillham (1977).
A Guide to Gower Birds by H. E. Grenfell and D. K. Thomas (1982). Published by Gower Ornithological Society and Glamorgan Naturalists' Trust.
Recorder: West Glamorgan.

Site No. 62 West Pembrokeshire (Dyfed)

62.1 Skomer Island

One mile offshore, Skomer has a large and easily accessible seabird colony. It is best late April to mid-July, though migrants may be seen in autumn. The island is a National Nature Reserve, managed by the West Wales Trust for Nature Conservation (WWTNC).

Habitat

Skomer covers 720 acres. The central plateau of grassland, bracken, and heath has masses of bluebells and red campions in spring, when the cliffs are a blaze of thrift and sea campion. This sward is dissected by a maze of rabbit, Puffin, and shearwater burrows.

Access (see map) OS Sheet No. 157

Skomer is open daily (except Mondays, but including bank holidays) from April to late September, 10.00 – 18.00. The *Dale Princess*, operated by the Dale Sailing Co., sails from Martin's Haven where there is a car park (fee). The boat leaves several times a day from 10.00 onwards depending on demand, allowing c 5 hrs on the island. Access is restricted to the 4-mile nature trail and there is a limit of 100 visitors per day until the end of July. The boat fare is £3, and a landing fee of £2 is payable to the island warden. There are no facilities (toilets, etc.) on the island. During rough weather, especially likely in April, May, and September, the boat may be delayed or even cancelled. Check on sailing times. The Lockley Lodge Information Centre at Martin's Haven can advise on sailings and is open from Easter to late September or October. Basic chalet accommodation is available on Skomer for WWTNC members. It is also possible to stay on the island on a weekly basis as a voluntary assistant warden — in return for help in the running of the reserve, volunteers get free accommodation and boat crossings. Contact the Trust for details.

Birds

Breeding seabirds include Fulmar, over 100,000 pairs of Manx Shearwaters, Shag, Puffin, Guillemot, Razorbill, Kittiwake, and Herring, Lesser, and Great Black-backed Gulls. Other breeders are Oystercatcher, Buzzard, Little and Short-eared Owls,

Wheatear, Raven, and Chough. The shearwaters are largely nocturnal, only returning to land after dark. Though they may come inshore in rough weather and can sometimes be seen from the boat, an overnight stay is essential to experience them *en masse.*

Skomer attracts numbers of passerine migrants but its size and extensive cover make them harder to find than on Skokholm.

62.2 Skokholm Island

In 1933 Ronald Lockley established Britain's first bird observatory on Skokholm, building the country's first Heligoland traps. Ringing ceased in 1976, and the island is now managed as a reserve by the WWTNC. The best time to visit is May – June, and late August or September.

Habitat

One mile long, the island covers 262 acres, with cliffs rising to 160 feet. The exposed W and SW sides have a short sward, extensively excavated by rabbits, Puffins, and Manx Shearwaters. The more sheltered E side is dominated by bracken, with some rocky outcrops. The island's summit has a network of dry stone walls and dykes which, together with the rocky scree and cliffs, shelter nesting Storm Petrels. There are two ponds, the more southerly of which is surrounded by a marsh. The only buildings are the lighthouse and the old farm buildings.

**Access
(see map)**
OS Sheet No. 157

Accommodation is available on a weekly basis, Saturday to Saturday, April–September (and sometimes for weekends in June–July). Up to 15 people can be accommodated observatory-style (full-board) at £100 per week each in May–July; £80 in April and August–September. Contact the WWTNC Islands Booking Officer. The *Dale Princess* leaves Martin's Haven at 13.00 each Saturday. The trip costs £10. Check with the Dale Sailing Co. in rough weather as the boat may be delayed or depart from Dale. Cars can be left at Martin's Haven car park (fee).

Birds

Breeding birds include over 35,000 pairs of Manx Shearwaters, and c 6,000 pairs of Storm Petrels. Other seabirds include Razorbill, Guillemot, Puffin, and Herring and Lesser Black-backed Gulls, as well as Oystercatcher and Wheatear.

Manx Shearwaters

Passage periods bring the usual thrushes, chats, warblers, and flycatchers. Spice is added by the regular autumn occurrence of Wryneck, Black Redstart, Bluethroat, Icterine, Melodious, and Barred Warblers, Red-breasted Flycatcher, and Lapland Bunting, and there have been numerous other rarities.

Lying 10 miles offshore, Grassholm covers 22 acres. As of 1984, its 28,500 pairs of Gannets formed the third largest colony in the world. Other seabirds include Shag, Razorbill, Guillemot, Kittiwake, and Herring and Great Black-backed Gulls. The island is (frustratingly) very good for small birds on passage. An RSPB reserve, landing is permitted from mid-June onwards. Visits are

62.3 Grassholm Island
OS Sheet No. 157

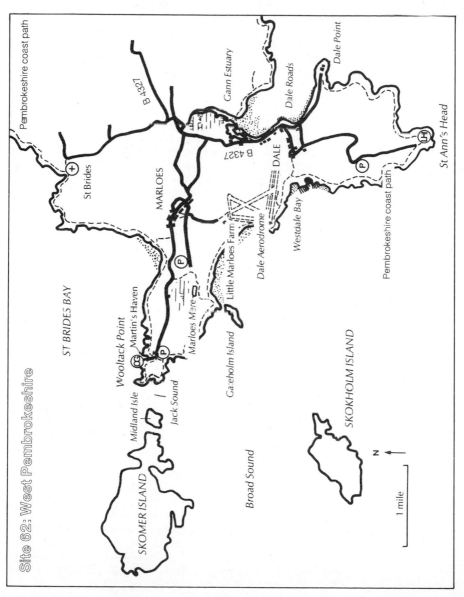

Site 62: West Pembrokeshire

possible only in very calm weather and are consequently infrequent. The authorised boatman is Campbell Reynolds of the Dale Sailing Co.

62.4 Marloes Peninsula (see map)
OS Sheet No. 157

1. It is possible to see some seabirds without getting into a boat. Large numbers of Manx Shearwater assemble offshore each evening in the breeding season, and depending on the weather may be seen from the mainland. Seabirds are best seen around high tide from Wooltack Point (follow the footpath a few hundred yards NW from Martin's Haven); at other times they tend to congregate in Broad Sound and St Brides Bay and views are more distant.
2. From the coastal footpath, on either the N or S sides of the peninsula E of Marloes, Peregrine, Buzzard, Raven, and Chough may be seen and Stonechat and Grasshopper Warbler breed in the rough ground. Passerine migrants occur, and have included rarities. The S path turns N opposite Gateholm and continues past Marloes Mere (a WWTNC reserve) to the road.
3. Dale Aerodrome is worth checking in autumn. Buff-breasted Sandpipers have been seen several times in September. From Marloes a narrow track runs S to Little Marloes, and then a footpath follows the runways S and E to Dale.
4. Westdale Bay and St Ann's Head are spots for Chough. Westdale Bay is accessible from Dale by following the track W from Dale Castle for ½ mile. For St Ann's Head take the minor road S to the lighthouse.

62.5 Gann Estuary (see map)
OS Sheet No. 157

This small estuary is heavily disturbed in summer, but can be interesting in winter and passage periods. The lower reaches can be seen from the B4327 N of Dale and a track leads down to a ford across the river. Winter brings a few Red-throated Divers and the occasional Slavonian Grebe to Dale Roads, especially in rough weather. Duck include Goldeneye and Red-breasted Merganser and there are regularly wintering Greenshank in the upper part of the estuary.

Other Sites in the Area
62.6 Strumble Head

Rising to a maximum of c 100 feet, the main attraction of the Head is seawatching. From the A40 at Fishguard Harbour minor roads lead W to Goodwick and on to Pen Caer, from where a track leads to the lighthouse on the Head. There is a small car park directly opposite the lighthouse rock. The best place to seawatch from is the disused bunker reached by taking a path on the right just before the car park.

Manx Shearwaters can often be seen offshore in the evening March – September. In autumn the best conditions are a SW gale veering W or NW. Shearwaters, including Sooty and occasionally Great, may occur, together with Leach's Petrel, and Cory's and Little Shearwaters have been recorded. Red-throated Diver, Gannet, Common Scoter, Kittiwake, Great and Arctic Skuas, auks, and terns are other possibilities, and there are often Peregrines around. Passerine migrants should not be ignored. Breeding birds include Chough and Raven, with Fulmar on the Head, and Stonechat on the cliff tops.

Site No. 63 Dinas and Gwenffrwd (Dyfed)

The RSPB reserves of Dinas and Gwenffrwd, c 10 miles N of
Llandovery, total 6,828 acres. Their range of habitats and birds is
typical of this part of the principality. May–June is the best time to
visit; the summer visitors will have arrived and be singing and
there is a chance of Red Kite if the weather is good.

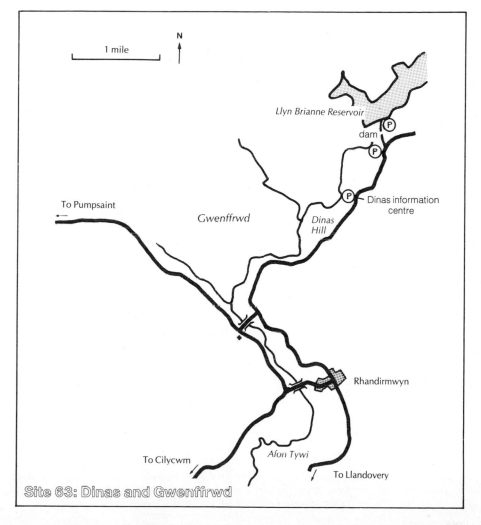

Site 63: Dinas and Gwenffrwd

Habitat

Dinas reserve covers 129 acres and rises to over 1,000 feet, with hanging oakwoods and small areas of alder carr and marshland. Gwenffrwd, far larger, reaches higher elevations — 1,343 feet at Cefn Gwenffrwd — and has areas of moorland, hanging oakwoods, and farmland, as well as woodland in the valleys.

**Access
(see map)**
OS Sheet Nos.
146 or 147

Leave Llandovery N on unclassified roads to Rhandirmwyn and continue towards the Llyn Brianne dam. The Dinas Information Centre is at Nant-y-ffin, a further 4 miles, and is open 10.00 – 17.00 from Easter to the end of August. The nature trail and the reserve itself are open at all times. For access to Gwenffrwd (Easter – August, daily except Friday) report to the Dinas Information Centre. The number of visitors to Gwenffrwd is restricted by limited parking.

Birds

A speciality of mid-Wales is the Red Kite, which can sometimes be seen in this area. The best chance is in the first half of the year and good weather is essential; even so there are few birds and a good deal of luck is needed. The resident Buzzard and Sparrow-hawk are much commoner, and Merlin and Peregrine can sometimes be seen, as can Raven. A few Red Grouse are resident on the moors, and in summer are joined by Wheatear and Whinchat. Along the streams and rivers Goosander, Common Sandpiper, Grey Wagtail, and Dipper breed, and Kingfisher may also visit. Summer visitors to the woodland include Redstart, Wood Warbler, and Pied Flycatcher, with Tree Pipit in the areas of scattered trees. These join the resident Woodcock, Green and Great Spotted Woodpeckers, Marsh and Willow Tits, Nuthatch, and Treecreeper.

Dippers

Information

Warden: Troedrhiwgelynen, Rhandirmwyn, Llandovery SA20 OPN. Recorder: Carmarthenshire.

Site No. 64 Tregaron (Dyfed)

Tregaron, c 15 miles SE of Aberystwyth, is a good area for Red Kites, especially in winter. Ccrs Caron National Nature Reserve N of the village covers 1,957 acres of Tregaron Bog.

Cors Caron contains areas of raised bog covered with heather, grass, moss, and patches of birch and willow carr. Peat cutting has created some small flashes, and a scrape has been built in front of the observation tower. The surrounding area is a mixture of deciduous woodland and pasture rising up to more rugged hills.

Habitat

1. Owned by the NCC, access to the NNR is restricted, but the nature trail along the disused railway line leading to an observation tower is open at all times. In winter wildfowl and raptors, notably kites, can be seen from here. The trail starts from the B4343 c 2½ miles N of Tregaron, just past Maes-llyn

Access (see map) OS Sheet No. 146

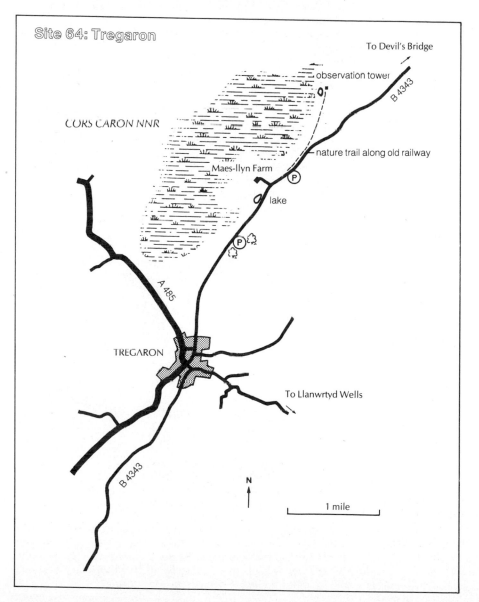

Site 64: Tregaron

To Devil's Bridge

observation tower

B 4343

CORS CARON NNR

nature trail along old railway

Maes-llyn Farm

P

lake

P

A 485

TREGARON

To Llanwrtyd Wells

B 4343

N

1 mile

Farm; there is limited roadside parking. A permit is required to enter the rest of the reserve, but the interesting species can be seen from the road or nature trail.

2. There is a private rubbish dump, adjacent to the B4343 c 1 mile S of the village which attracts kites, especially in winter. They can be seen from the B4343 and A485.

3. The minor road E from Tregaron to Llanwrtyd Wells crosses hill country, with oak woods and plantations. Red Kite is possible as well as the usual woodland species in summer.

Birds

Red Kite, Sparrowhawk, Buzzard, Peregrine, and Raven are resident in the area. A few Red Grouse breed on the bog and Barn Owls, Water Rails, and Dippers can be seen all year. A good spot for Dipper is Tregaron Bridge.

Winter brings wildfowl: up to 50 Whooper Swans occur November–March, and irregularly there are small numbers of Bewick's. Wigeon, Teal, and Mallard form the bulk of the wintering duck. The resident raptors are joined by Hen Harrier, Short-eared Owl, and sometimes Merlin. Other visitors include Stonechat and Redpoll.

Summer visitors to the bog include Sedge Warbler, with Grasshopper Warbler and Redpoll in the scrubbier areas. Teal breed and there is a Black-headed Gull colony. Small numbers of Tree Pipit, Redstart, Whinchat, Wood Warbler, and Pied Fly-catcher breed in the remnant oakwoods and scrubby hillsides, especially on the E side of the B4343, joining the resident Nuthatch, Treecreeper, and Willow Tit. On passage small numbers of waders may be seen on the scrape.

Red Kites with Sparrowhawk

Other Sites in the Area
64.1 Tregaron to Devil's Bridge
OS Sheet Nos. 135 or 147

Continuing N from Tregaron to Devil's Bridge, the triangle formed by the B4343 between Pont-rhyd-y-groes and Devil's Bridge and the minor road that leaves the B4343 at Pont-rhyd-y-groes to the NW and bends back after 2 miles NE to Devil's Bridge, is a good area to look for kites, especially in early spring.

This attractive valley has a good variety of woodland and riverside birds. About 5 miles E of Aberystwyth on the A44 take the minor road S at Capel Bangor to Dolypandy. Continue, paralleling the Afon Rheidol, for 3½ miles to the CEGB Reception Centre at the dam, from where a nature trail runs around the reservoir. Common Sandpiper, Dipper, and Grey Wagtail frequent the river, and Redstart, Wood Warbler, and Pied Flycatcher the woods.

Devil's Bridge can be reached by narrow-gauge steam train from Aberystwyth as well as on the A4120. At the bridge there is a 400 foot cascade. From the car park (fee) above the falls a path descends through mixed woodland, and in summer the usual species occur and there are Sparrowhawks, Buzzards, Ravens, and occasionally kites overhead.

64.2 The Vale of Rheidol and Devil's Bridge
OS Sheet No. 135

NCC Tregaron, warden: Minawel, Ffair Rhos, Pontrhydfendigaid, Ystrad Meurig, Dyfed SY25 6BN.
Recorder: Cardinganshire.

Information

Site No. 65 Dyfi Estuary (Dyfed, Gwynedd)

The Dyfi is the largest estuary opening into Cardigan Bay. The small flock of wintering Greenland White-fronted Geese is of special interest, and at all times of year the range of habitats in the area guarantees an interesting day. The estuary, Ynyslas Dunes, and Cors Fochno (Borth Bog) are a National Nature Reserve covering 5,000 acres. Ynys-hir, an RSPB reserve covering 770 acres, lies on the S shore of the estuary with an additional 309 acres in the adjacent Llyfnant Valley.

About 4½ miles long by 1½ miles at the widest, three-quarters of the estuary are sandflats and the remainder saltmarsh, concentrated on the S shore and near the mouth. This is guarded on the S side by the dune system of Ynyslas. The N shore of the estuary is bordered by oak woods, while the S has estensive water meadows. South of the A487 are open hillsides and conifer plantations, as well as deciduous woodland. Cors Fochno covers 1,360 acres and has one of the largest areas of raised bog in Britain.

Habitat

1. Managed by the NCC, access to the NNR is on the roads and public footpaths. A permit is needed to enter Cors Fochno. The car park, information centre (open daily 09.30–17.00, April–September), and nature trail at Ynyslas are on the minor road N off the B4353. From here you can view the river mouth and look out to sea. Several shingle ridges attract concentrations of gulls and waders at high tide, especially during passage periods. Gulls also roost on the sea anywhere between Ynyslas and the start of the cliffs at Borth.
2. The sand flats behind the dunes attract waders and a good place to watch from is the mouth of the Afon Leri. A short track N off the B4353 follows the W bank of the river and a footpath the E, both giving views of the flats.

Access (see map)
OS Sheet No. 135

3. Ynys-hir is off the A487 7 miles W of Machynlleth; the entrance is signed in Furnace village opposite the mill. Report to reception on arrival. The reserve is open daily 09.00–21.00 (£2 for non-members). There are nature trails and four hides

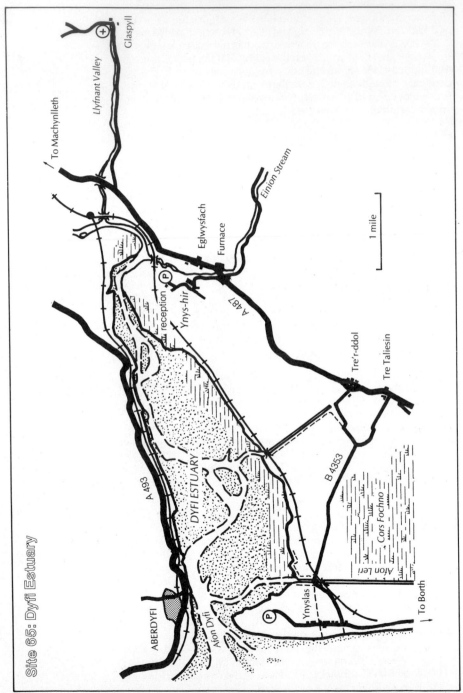

Site 65: Dyfi Estuary

Glaspyll

Llyfnant Valley

To Machynlleth

Einion Stream

Eglwysfach

Furnace

reception

Ynys-hir

A 487

1 mile

Tre'r-ddol

Tre Taliesin

B 4353

DYFI ESTUARY

A 493

Cors Fochno

Afon Leri

ABERDYFI

Afon Dyfi

Ynyslas

To Borth

giving views of the estuary and wader scrape — the best place on the Dyfi to watch waders is the Saltings Hide on a rising tide.

4. The minor road off the A487 up the Llyfnant Valley to Glaspwll is an excellent walk for woodland species with Dippers on the small river.
5. The Einion stream also has Dippers and Grey Wagtails, with Red-breasted Merganser and Common Sandpiper on the higher reaches. A minor road from Furnace follows the stream (well above it in places) and there is a good tea shop at the end.

Birds

Winter brings a small flock of Greenland White-fronted Geese (106 in 1986). These feed on the saltmarsh and adjoining arable and roost on the estuary sands. Present early October to early April, they can be seen best from the RSPB reserve on a good rising tide. Bewick's Swans sometimes appear in February–March and there are small numbers of Pintail and Goldeneye, and Red-breasted Mergansers are always to be seen in the channel. There are often Red-throated Divers off the estuary mouth, occasionally with a few Scaup and Common Scoter. The odd Merlin, Peregrine, and Hen Harrier are present in winter, and waders include small numbers of Sanderling.

Spring passage brings a slightly wider variety of waders, and up to seven Mediterranean Gulls have been seen in early spring in the Borth gull roost, where there have also been records of Ring-billed Gull.

Shelduck, Red-breasted Merganser, Buzzard, Sparrowhawk, Barn Owl, Woodcock, the three woodpeckers, Tree Pipit, Stonechat, Whinchat, Redstart, Grasshopper, Sedge, and Wood Warblers, many Pied Flycatchers, and Raven all breed on the RSPB reserve at Ynys-hir. Red Kites are only seen irregularly in the area, mostly in spring and summer, and do not breed.

Mid-summer is rather quiet, but autumn brings passage waders, including Black-tailed Godwit and Spotted Redshank. Terns, which can include Little, favour the river mouth, while in late summer huge numbers of Manx Shearwaters can be seen in the bay from Ynyslas, particularly in early morning and late evening.

Other Sites in the Area
65.1 Dyfi Forest
OS Sheet Nos. 124 and 135

The area bounded by the Afon Dyfi to the S and E and the A470 and A487 to the N and W is worth exploring. Hills rise to 2,213 feet, with areas of moorland fragmented by conifer plantations. Access is from the roads and footpaths, especially from the A487 and a minor road which parallel the River Dulas on the W and E sides respectively of its well wooded valley. Red Grouse, Wheatear, and the occasional Golden Plover and Ring Ouzel breed on the moors, while the plantations have Redpoll, Siskin, and sometimes Crossbill. Black Grouse can, with a lot of luck, be found around the young plantations; early morning is best. Try the area W of the A487, especially N of Pantperthog; this is also good for Crossbills. The deciduous woods hold the usual Redstart, Wood Warbler, and Pied Flycatcher, with Common Sandpiper and Dipper on the river and streams. Buzzard may be seen anywhere.

65.2 Aberystwyth – Borth

Chough occur on the cliffs between Aberystwyth and Borth, usually nearer to Borth, while the small outflow at Clarach Bay attracts gulls, occasionally including Mediterranean. Take the minor road to the sea off the B4572 at Clarach, 4 miles S of Borth.

65.3 Aberystwyth Harbour

Ring-billed Gull has been recorded several times here, usually January to early April. The best time to check the harbour is on a falling tide when the gulls congregate on the newly exposed mud. Glaucous and Iceland Gulls are also sometimes seen in winter, and there are often Purple Sandpipers by the promenade. Wintering Black Redstarts are almost annual.

65.4 Broad Water
OS Sheet Nos. 124
and 135

1. The estuary of the Afon Dysynni, N of Tywyn, has small numbers of wintering wildfowl and can be good for waders at low tide. At the river mouth there is a small Little Tern colony, wardened during the breeding season, and this area is generally good for other gulls and terns plus seaduck. Take the minor road N from Tywyn, paralleling the railway, to reach the estuary near its mouth. A public footpath follows the S shore of the Dysynni (in places) E from the mouth to Bryncrug.
2. Inland along the Dysynni Valley a precipitous crag, Bird Rock (Craig-yr-Aderyn), has breeding Cormorant and Chough. Leave the A493 at Bryncrug (2½ miles NE of Tywyn) on a minor road along the valley. The rock is on the right after 3 miles and is a reserve of the North Wales Naturalists' Trust.

65.5 Llangranog
OS Sheet No. 145

On the coast SW of New Quay, this is a good spot for Chough. Walk N out of Llangranog on the coastal path to the small peninsula of Ynys-Lochtyn.

Information

RSPB Ynys-hir, warden: Cae'r Berllan, Eglwysfach, Machynlleth SY20 8TA.
NCC warden: Llwyn Awel, Tal-y-Bont, Dyfed SY24 5EQ.
NCC Information Centre, Ynyslas: Tel. 097081-640.
Recorder: Cardiganshire (S of the Dyfi), Merioneth (N of the Dyfi).

Site No. 66 Lake Vyrnwy (Powys)

The largest remaining area of heather moorland in Wales is in the Berwyn Mountains, and the RSPB has a reserve at Lake Vyrnwy, c 15 miles E of Dolgellau. Most is managed by agreement with the Severn-Trent Water Authority, and the total area is c 17,320 acres. The best time to visit is May–June.

Habitat

Lake Vyrnwy covers 1,100 acres and was formed when the Afon Vyrnwy was dammed. Fringed by scrub woodland and meadows, heather and grass moorland then rise to nearly 2,000 feet, with a network of streams and large areas of conifer plantations and deciduous woodland.

**Access
(see map)**
OS Sheet No. 125

Take the B4393 from Llanfyllin (NW of Welshpool) to Llanwddyn, from where the road continues on to circumnavigate the lake. The RSPB information centre is on the minor road 100 yards S of the W end of the dam. It is open at weekends from 11.00–18.00 Easter to Spring Bank Holiday, and from then until the end of

September also on weekdays 12.00–18.00. There is a public hide on the NE side of the lake, and there are nature trails and a woodland hide. The reserve is open at all times, with access along the public roads and footpaths.

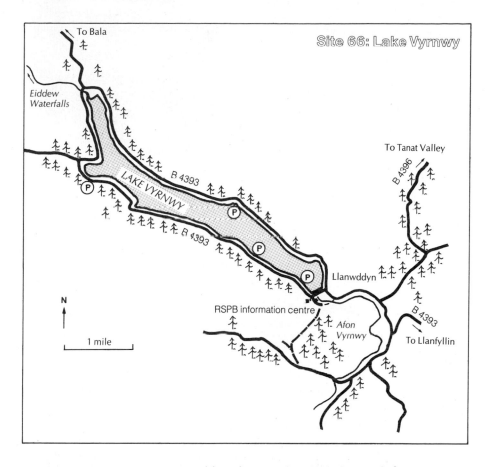

Birds The moorland has a fine range of breeding species, including Buzzard, Hen Harrier, Merlin, Red Grouse, Golden Plover, Short-eared Owl, Wheatear, Whinchat, Stonechat, and Raven. Ring Ouzel is scarce but can often be found near the Eiddew Waterfalls. The areas of deciduous woodland hold Green and Great Spotted Woodpeckers, Willow Tit, Nuthatch, and Tree-creeper and these are joined in the summer by Redstart, Wood Warbler, and Pied Flycatcher. In the conifers there are Sparrow-hawk, Long-eared Owl, Crossbill, Redpoll, and Siskin, and Firecrest has bred. The woodland fringes attract Tree Pipit — sometimes also Black Grouse, though these can be devilishly hard to find. Along the streams and around the reservoir Great Crested Grebe, Goosander, Teal, Common Sandpiper, Grey Wagtail, and Dipper occur.

Waders occasionally appear on passage, especially at the N end of the reservoir, and an oddity like Great Northern Diver may turn up in winter.

Ring Ouzel

Information

RSPB warden: Bryn Awel, Llanwddyn, Oswestry, Salop SY10 OND.
Recorder: Montgomeryshire.

Site No. 67 Bardsey Island (Gwynedd)

Bardsey lies 2 miles off the Lleyn Peninsula and the bird observatory was established in 1953. Some of the scarcer migrants are nearly annual, and Bardsey has a very long list of rarities to its credit. The best times to visit are late April to early June, and August to early November, and ideally a visit should be timed to coincide with the first ten days after a new moon to have the best chance of witnessing a lighthouse 'attraction'.

Habitat

Bardsey covers 444 acres, and is dominated by the 548-foot-high Mynydd Enlli (the 'Mountain'), the upper areas of which are covered by bracken with rocky outcrops. The steep E slopes are riddled with Manx Shearwater and rabbit burrows. The observatory garden, the four withy beds, and a small pine plantation provide cover for migrants. The S section of the island has a lighthouse, which in certain weather conditions following a new moon can attract hundreds or even thousands of night-migrants. Nights with thick cloud cover or a 'smoke-haze' obscuring the horizon are best, but used to result in many fatalities. A false light has now been built nearby and has greatly reduced the death-toll. Large numbers of birds are trapped and ringed and an 'attraction' is certainly a unique experience.

Access
OS Sheet No. 123

The island boat, *Mary K*, leaves Pwllheli harbour at 08.30 on Saturday or the first suitable day thereafter; delays are possible both going to and coming from the island during bad weather. The crossing takes c 2 hrs and costs £11 return. Parking is available at Pwllheli harbour. The observatory is open late March to early November and bookings are taken on a weekly basis, Saturday to Saturday. Up to twelve people can be accommodated in the large stone-built farmhouse in single, double, or triple rooms on a self-catering basis at £27 per week. Two mid-summer courses are run on a full-board basis at £80 per week. There are two seawatching hides.

Birds

Spring migration begins in late March with the usual assortment of chats, warblers, and flycatchers as well as diurnal migrants, but late spring is best for rarities.

Ten species of seabird breed, notably over 2,500 pairs of Manx Shearwaters, as well as small numbers of Fulmar, Shag, Razorbill, Guillemot, and Kittiwake. Oystercatcher, Little Owl, Raven, and about seven pairs of Chough also add interest.

The return passage begins in late July with a trickle of warblers, and these are joined by chats, Goldcrests, and flycatchers as the autumn progresses — light E or SE winds are best. October is the best month for migration, with the possibility of large falls of night-migrants, such as Redwings and Blackbirds, and movements of Skylarks, Starlings, and finches — and Yellow-browed Warbler, Firecrest, and Red-breasted Flycatcher are all nearly annual. Bardsey also has potential for seawatching. Sooty Shearwater, Leach's Petrel, Little Auk, Great Skua, and Sabine's Gull are all scarce but regular; the largest and most varied movements occur in September and early October after strong W or NW winds.

Other Sites in the Area
67.1 Lleyn Peninsula

This can be as good as Bardsey for migrants, and rarities have also been recorded. The best spots are:
1. The sheltered track to the cove at Porth Meudwy. Leave Aberdaron W on the minor road to Uwchmynydd and turn left after ½ mile; the track is on the left after a further ½ mile.
2. The headland opposite Bardsey, reached along a maze of footpaths and tracks from Uwchmynydd.

Information

Bookings secretary (s.a.e. please): Mrs. H. Bond, 21a Gestridge Road, Kingsteignton, Newton Abbot, Devon.
Reference: *Birds of Bardsey* by Peter Roberts (1985).
Recorder: Caernarvonshire.

Site No. 68 Anglesey (Gwynedd)

Five areas have been selected from the many interesting localities on Anglesey. They provide year-round interest with a range of seabirds, wildfowl, raptors, and waders. The three specialities are Roseate Tern, Black Guillemot, and Chough. All sites are to be found on OS Sheet No. 114.

68.1 Rhosneigr

The offshore islets at Rhosneigr have one of Britain's largest colonies of Roseate Terns, which can be seen from the end of April to July.

Access

Rhosneigr is on the A4080 and access to the seafront is straightforward. The terns breed on the offshore islands and sitting birds are visible and just identifiable with a telescope from the beach. Fortunately they often fly much closer, giving good views.

Birds This is the largest colony of Roseate Terns in Britain, currently *c* 100 pairs. Common and sometimes Sandwich Terns also breed, and there are often Arctic Terns around in summer. During passage periods, the beach here is quite good for waders, including Sanderling and Whimbrel.

68. 2 Holyhead Harbour The harbour is worth visiting in winter. Divers are usually present, especially Black-throated, and less often Great Northern. Red-necked Grebes are also sometimes seen, late winter being the favoured period. One or two Black Guillemots are regular. Access is straightforward along the breakwater.

68.3 South Stack Cliffs Three miles W of Holyhead, South Stack Cliffs are an RSPB reserve of 780 acres. The best time to see the seabirds is May–June.

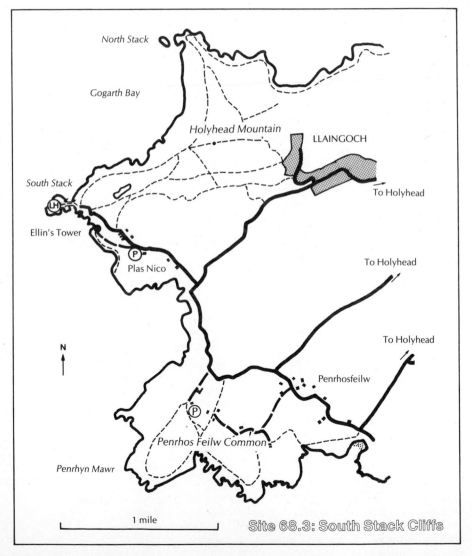

Site 68.3: South Stack Cliffs

The reserve includes both North and South Stacks, and these rise to nearly 400 feet. South Stack is connected to the mainland by a footbridge and the flight of steps that gives access to its lighthouse. Landward of the cliffs, areas of heather and gorse heath rise to 853 feet at Holyhead Mountain and there is a separate area of heath to the S, at Penrhos Feilw Common.

Habitat

From the A5 in Holyhead follow the signs to South Stack. There is a car park and access is possible at all times along the public paths. The information centre at Ellin's Tower has windows overlooking the main auk colony and there are also good views from the steps to the lighthouse. The Tower is open daily April–September; during this period a warden is present. There is open access to Penrhos Feilw Common along tracks from the road S of South Stack. Penrhyn Mawr is a good spot to seawatch from; boulders and shattered rocks provide some cover.

Access (see map)

Nine species of seabird breed, including Fulmar, Kittiwake, a few pairs of Shags, large numbers of Razorbills and Guillemots, and rather fewer Puffins. Other breeding species include Peregrine, Raven, and four or five pairs of Chough, which can be seen around the cliffs and RSPB car park, and in winter in the fields along the approach road. The heathland has breeding Stonechats.

Birds

Choughs

Gannet and Manx Shearwater can sometimes be seen at sea during summer and autumn, shearwaters being commonest July–August when up to 1,000 a day occur; they are especially numerous in early morning and evening. In spring, Great Northern and Red-throated Divers, Common Scoter, and Arctic Skua are regular, and Pomarine Skua probably annual. No special winds are required for seawatching at this season, and interesting birds may be seen at any time of day. In autumn, by contrast, an early morning watch in strong NW winds is recommended: Sooty Shearwater, Storm and Leach's Petrels, and Pomarine Skua are possibilities, while Great and Arctic Skuas and large numbers of

Kittiwakes and auks are regular. On passage the heaths attract harriers, Short-eared Owl, Whimbrel and other waders, and warblers, and there can be big movements of diurnal migrants in late autumn.

**68.4
Newborough
Warren
(see map)**

The Warren and adjacent coast harbour a good variety of wildfowl, waders, and raptors. The treeless SE section of the Warren and much of its coastal perimeter is a National Nature Reserve of 1,565 acres, managed by the NCC. The best time to visit is during winter and passage periods.

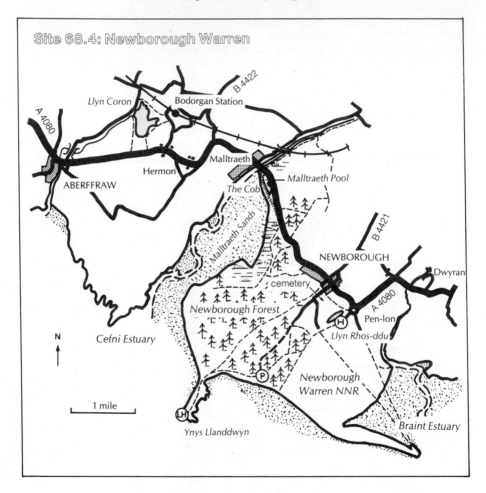

Habitat

The Warren covers over 3,000 acres, two-thirds of which have been planted with Corsican pine. To the SW of the dunes is Ynys Llanddwyn, an island connected to the mainland by a narrow strip of sand which is covered on the highest tides. N is the Cefni estuary with the extensive Malltraeth Sands and some saltmarsh along its S shore. At the head of the estuary, and separated from it by an embankment known as the Cob, is Malltraeth Pool. This is an excellent spot for passage waders, as are the adjacent fields when flooded (though recently the water levels have varied erratically, and when high there are few waders). In the dunes to the S is Llyn Rhos-ddu, while S of the Warren is the Braint estuary. Llyn Coron, another larger lake, lies N of the Warren.

In the NNR, permits are required for areas away from the **Access** designated routes and public rights of way.
1. Malltraeth Pool can be viewed from the A4080 and the Cob.
2. Walk S from the Cob along the seaward side of the forest for views of the saltmarsh. In winter a few Hen Harriers roost in this area, as well as Ravens; other raptors are also frequent.
3. Ynys Llanddwyn is an excellent spot in winter. Divers are often present offshore, together with Slavonian and Black-necked Grebes and Common Scoter. Purple Sandpipers and Turnstones occur on the rocky shore. Drive SW from Newborough on a minor road past the cemetery and then follow the track through the forest to the Forestry Commission car park (fee). Walking W along the shore, the island is reached after 1 mile. Alternatively, walk for 2½ miles from Newborough directly to the island through the forest.
4. A public hide overlooks Llyn Rhos-ddu. In winter Ruddy Duck, Gadwall, and Water Rail can all be seen, and raptors hunt the surrounding dunes. Access is along the short track to the small car park from the A4080 at Pen-lon.
5. Llyn Coron. Leave Aberffraw E on the A4080 and turn left onto a minor road just after crossing the River Ffraw. Follow this for 1½ miles for views from the road. Footpaths run along the N, SE, and W shores of the lake. Llyn Coron supports wintering duck, as well as breeding Great Crested Grebes and summering Ruddy Ducks.

In winter, Cormorant, Shag, all three divers (particularly Great **Birds** Northern and Red-throated), and Slavonian and Black-necked Grebes are joined offshore by numbers of Common Scoter and occasionally other seaduck. There are up to 250 Pintail and lots of Wigeon, plus Goldeneye and a few Shoveler, Gadwall, and Ruddy Duck. Flocks of Canada and feral Greylag Geese roam the area, and odd Pink-footed and White-fronted Geese often join them. Peregrine, Merlin, Hen Harrier, and Barn and Short-eared Owls may be seen, and waders can include wintering Spotted Redshank and Greenshank.
Passage can be good, with a wide variety of waders. Little Stint, Sanderling, Curlew Sandpiper, Black-tailed Godwit, and Spotted Redshank may all occur.
Breeding birds include Great Crested Grebe, Shelduck, Oystercatcher, and Ringed Plover, while Herring, Lesser Black-backed, and Black-headed Gulls nest in the dunes, together with Whinchat and Stonechat. At Ynys Llanddwyn there are breeding Cormorants and a few Shags, Rock Pipits, and Stonechats. Often there are terns offshore, mostly Common, Arctic, and Sandwich, but occasionally also Little or Roseate.

A handful of pairs here at Anglesey's E tip are the only breeding **68.5 Fedw Fawr** Black Guillemots S of St Bees Head. Leave Beaumaris N on the B5109 to Llangoed and then follow a minor road N for 1 mile to Mariandyrys. Fork right at the end of the houses and take the minor road immediately on the left to Fedw Fawr. There is a very small car park at the end of the road. Black Guillemots are usually in the boulder scree under the cliffs below the car park. There are also a few Razorbills and Guillemots.

Information

RSPB South Stack, summer warden: Plas Nico, South Stack, Holyhead, Anglesey, Gwynedd.
NCC Newborough Warren, warden: 'Serai', Malltraeth, Bodorgan, Anglesey, Gwynedd LL62 5AS.
Recorder: Anglesey.

Site No. 69 Aber (Gwynedd)

The Lavan Sands, NE of Bangor, hold internationally important numbers of Oystercatcher and Redshank, and specialities are the wintering Black-necked and Slavonian Grebes. Traeth Lafan Local Nature Reserve covers 6,000 acres of the sands.

Habitat

The mouth of the Afon Ogwen, together with Bangor Flats, forms the muddy W extremity of the Lavan Sands, which can be up to 3 miles wide at low water and extend to Llanfairfechan.

Access
(see map)
OS Sheet No. 115

A footpath follows the shore from Aber Ogwen to Llanfairfechan, with access at the following points.
1. Aber Ogwen. Leave the A55 N on the A5122, turning right after 1 mile to Tal-y-bont, and then taking a minor road left after a further mile to the coast beyond Aber Ogwen Farm. At the bottom of this lane is a car park and just before this a track leads through the gate to a hide overlooking the estuary and a small pool. This is a good spot for wintering Water Rail, Black-tailed Godwit, Spotted Redshank, Greenshank, and Kingfisher, and is generally good for ducks and waders.
2. North off the A55 at Aber a minor road passes under the railway to the shore. Walk NE to the mouth of the Afon Aber, another good area for waders and duck. From 1979 to 1984 a drake American Black Duck was resident and left a number of hybrids with Mallard as a legacy.
3. Leave Llanfairfechan W on the A55. After ¾ mile there is a farm shop on the left and directly opposite a lane leads down to the railway. Follow this and on the right is a sewage farm. The filter beds can be seen from the lane and regularly attract wintering Chiffchaff and Firecrest. Continue on foot over the railway to the small promontory where there is a wader roost, and often Twite on the saltmarsh.
4. Offshore from Llanfairfechan promenade there are regularly small numbers of divers, Black-necked and Slavonian Grebes, and seaduck.

Birds

In winter there are numbers of Great Crested Grebe and Red-throated Diver offshore, as well as a few Great Northerns. Black-throated Diver is uncommon, tending to occur only on passage. Small numbers of Slavonian and Black-necked Grebes are regular, together with Red-breasted Merganser, Goldeneye, and Common Scoter, and a few Long-tailed Duck. Other

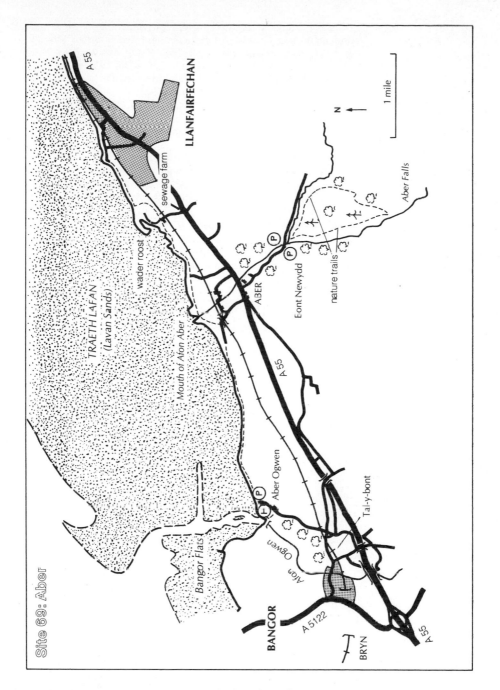

Site 69: Aber

A 55

LLANFAIRFECHAN

sewage farm

1 mile

N

Aber Falls

TRAETH LAFAN
(Lavan Sands)

wader roost

Mouth of Afon Aber

Pont Newydd

ABER

nature trails

A 55

Aber Ogwen

Tal-y-bont

Bangor Flats

Afon Ogwen

BANGOR

A 5122

BRYN

A 55

wildfowl include a few Pintail and Shoveler. The commoner waders are joined by Greenshanks and the odd Spotted Redshank and Black-tailed Godwit. Water Rail, Kingfisher, Chiffchaff, and Firecrest may be found in small numbers around the marshy areas and pools and there are occasionally Water Pipits at the sewage farm. A flock of up to 30 Twite often winters on the shore.

Passage brings a greater variety of waders and there is a concentration of Great Crested Grebe and Red-breasted Merganser on the sea in autumn; over 500 of the former have been recorded. Common and Sandwich Terns are also present on passage. Breeding birds include Shelduck, while Peregrines are resident in the area and seen all year.

Other Sites in the Area
69.1 Coedydd Aber
(see map)

From Aber, the river valley climbs to Aber Falls and the Carneddau uplands, passing through extensive areas of deciduous and coniferous woodland, 420 acres of which are a National Nature Reserve. Park at Bont Newydd and proceed from here on the nature trail or road; a permit is necessary away from these. On the rivers and streams there are Dipper and Grey Wagtail, while the woods have resident Green and Great Spotted Woodpeckers, Nuthatch, and Treecreeper, with Siskin in the conifers. Summer visitors include Redstart, Wood Warbler, and Pied Flycatcher, with Ring Ouzel, Whinchat, and Wheatear on the moors; the scree slopes around Aber Falls are a particularly good spot for Ring Ouzels. Look out for Buzzard, Sparrowhawk, Peregrine, and Raven overhead.

Information

Recorder: Caernarvonshire.

NORTHERN ENGLAND

Site No. 70 Dee Estuary (Clwyd, Cheshire, Merseyside)

The Dee estuary supports internationally important populations of ten species of wader and three of wildfowl. Around its perimeter are several excellent places to see these in winter. In autumn, NW gales push large numbers of seabirds onshore, notably Leach's Petrels, and the Wirral is one of the best sites in the country for these.

Habitat

The W shore has small areas of saltmarsh, reclaimed in places, but E of the canalised Dee are the large Burton and Parkgate Marshes. At Hoylake there is a small group of rocks, Red Rocks, and c 1½ miles offshore are the three islands of Hilbre.

Access
70.1 Point of Ayr (Clwyd)
OS Sheet No. 116

Extensive sandy flats and a small area of dunes guard the NW mouth of the estuary at the Point of Ayr. An RSPB reserve with open access, the Point is not wardened. Take the minor road (Station Road) to Talacre off the A548, 3 miles E of Prestatyn, and proceed to the shore and park. Walk out over the sands, but do not disturb the high-tide roosts. Seawatching from the lighthouse just W of the Point can be interesting, but the Wirral shore is much better in gale conditions. The area is badly disturbed in summer.

Small numbers of wildfowl winter, and up to 20,000 waders roost on the shingle spit and adjoining saltmarsh. A few Twite and Snow Buntings may occur, together with Water Pipits and occasionally Shorelarks. In late summer and autumn there are large gatherings of terns which attract Arctic Skuas.

Up to 50 pairs of Little Terns breed at Gronant, W of the Point. Take the road to the caravan site N of the A548 1½ miles W of the Talacre turning. There is an RSPB summer warden.

70.2 Connah's Quay (Clwyd)
OS Sheet No. 117

90 acres of saltmarsh, mudflat, and grassland scrub around Connah's Quay Power Station are a reserve, owned by the CEGB and managed by the Deeside Naturalists' Society (DNS). A scrape and raised bank (for roosting waders) have been constructed, and large numbers can be seen in the 2 hrs before high water, when the tide is 29½ feet and above. There is a field-studies centre, three hides overlooking the estuary, and nature trail. An advance permit is necessary and will be checked on the gate. Apply to the DNS or the Power Station manager. Casual visitors may visit on a Public Open Day; these are held once a month on Saturday or Sunday, generally when tides are suitable. Take the A548 NW from Connah's Quay towards Flint; the Power Station entrance is on the right.

In winter, wildfowl, raptors, and waders may be seen, including up to 1,000 Black-tailed Godwits and a few Spotted Redshanks. Twite are irregular visitors to the saltmarsh. On passage there is a greater selection of waders, including up to 100 Spotted Redshanks in autumn.

70.3 Shotton Pools (Clwyd)
OS Sheet No. 117

BSC Shotton Steelworks is built on reclaimed marshland at the head of the estuary. Freshwater and brackish lagoons remain in the immediate vicinity of the works and there are several large, open, water-cooling tanks. 55 acres of the most interesting area is managed as a reserve by the Merseyside Ringing Group. Access is via the steelworks' main entrance, signed on the A550 at Garden City. A permit must be obtained in advance from BSC. Permit holders receive a map showing the areas to which they have access. The nearby rifle-range pools are also attractive to passage waders. These are reached by walking S along the bank from Burton Point (leave the A540 SW into Burton and take the minor road W over the railway to the shore, walking S to the Point), with no access when the red flag is flying.

Up to 250 pairs of Common Terns nest on specially built platforms in the pools, and other breeders include Oystercatcher, Little Ringed Plover, Stonechat, Whinchat, and Reed and Sedge Warblers, with a high density of Yellow Wagtails and Corn Buntings in the adjacent farmland. On passage the area attracts an excellent variety of 'fresh' waders.

70.4 Gayton Sands/Parkgate (Cheshire)
OS Sheet No. 117

Gayton Sands is an RSPB reserve covering 5,040 acres of mudflat and saltmarsh on the NE shore of the estuary. Take the B5135 to Parkgate and turn right at the Bistrot Restaurant to the Old Baths car park. There are good views from here, and a footpath runs NW along the shore.

Winter brings wildfowl, especially Pintail, and the occasional small flock of Pink-footed Geese or Bewick's Swans. On high spring tides, roosting waders include up to 200–300 Black-tailed Godwits. Water Rails and Jack Snipe are forced to leave the marshes on the highest tides, and Grey Herons then prey extensively on the Water Rails. Raptors regularly patrol the area, and there is a harrier roost at Parkgate. Twite and Brambling can be found feeding in mixed finch flocks on the saltmarsh, together with up to 20 Water Pipits. A small reedbed has Grasshopper, Reed, and Sedge Warblers in summer.

70.5 Hilbre (Merseyside)
OS Sheet No. 108

There are three rocky islands, the ½-acre Little Eye, Little Hilbre, and Hilbre, the largest at 11 acres. About 1½ miles offshore, they are cut off from the mainland for 3 hrs each side of high water. Hilbre is reached on foot from West Kirby. Start from the slipway on the promenade opposite Dee Lane (just N of the Marine Lake), walk NW to Little Eye, and then, keeping Little Eye on your right, continue over the top of Little Hilbre and on to the gate at the S end of Hilbre. This takes about 1 hr and you should start, at the latest, 3 hrs before high tide. The islands are a reserve of the Wirral Borough Council, and a permit is required. The paddocks and bungalows are private. The wader roost, publicised by legions of bird photographers, remains one of the attractions of Hilbre, though it has declined in recent years. Others are the small falls of migrants and, particularly, the seawatching. Hilbre

Bird Observatory operates a ringing station and seawatching hide. No accommodation is available.

Winter brings divers, seaduck, and Purple Sandpipers and other waders. In spring and autumn there are small falls of migrants. The best conditions are light to moderate SE – SW winds, coupled with poor visibility and perhaps rain or drizzle. However, by 2 hrs after dawn, most birds will have left, though some falls occur later in the day. The visible migration of passerines can also be interesting and usually takes place in the first 4 hrs after dawn. Autumn is the best time for seawatching. The hide is available by arrangement, otherwise the N end of Hilbre, above the Lifeboat House, is a good spot to watch from, providing conditions are not too bad. After two or three days of NW gales Leach's Petrels are virtually guaranteed, as well as other seabirds. The period around high tide is most productive.

70.6 The Wirral Coast (Merseyside)
OS Sheet No. 108

This coast has occasional patches of cover suitable for migrants, but numbers are small. The main interest centres on autumn seawatching and winter gulls.

1. West Kirby Marine Lake may hold one or two seaduck, especially in the early morning. Access is straightforward from the promenade. Up to 350 Scaup can be seen off Caldy beach road, to the S.
2. Bird Rock, off Red Rocks Point at the mouth of the Dee, becomes an island at high tide, and when not disturbed holds roosting waders. To the S a line of dunes extends to West Kirby; they provide a home for the Royal Liverpool Golf Course. Between the dunes and the shore is a small reedbed, managed as a reserve by the Cheshire Conservation Trust. This attracts migrant passerines, as do the areas of buckthorn and trees and the gardens along Stanley Road. Access is as follows: from West Kirby, walk N along the foreshore, past the reedbed to the Point; from the A540, turn NW towards the coast at the roundabout by Hoylake Station and after 200 yards turn left into Stanley Road and park. Stay on the foreshore or board-walk on the inland side of the reedbed, which is strictly out of bounds.
3. Leasowe Promenade is a good place to seawatch from, but Leasowe lighthouse is better. This is W of Wallasey on the A551. At the sharp left-hand bend a few hundred yards past the hospital, take the rough track along the seawall; the lighthouse is clearly visible ½ mile ahead. It is possible to drive onto the seawall and use the car as a shelter. Meols promenade, to the SW, also offers this facility.
4. New Brighton is also good for seawatching in the right weather. The A554 runs along the coast for 1 mile to the marine lake and lighthouse – the best place to seawatch from. Leach's Petrels regularly occur, sometimes in large numbers, and often there are more prolonged views than at Leasowe. Gulls should be carefully checked. Mediterraneans are frequent, with small numbers of Glaucous, and an Iceland Gull appeared in mid-winter every year from 1957 to 1985.

Birds

In winter there are small numbers of divers off the estuary mouth, mostly Red-throated; Great Northerns are scarce and Black-throated only occasional. Wildfowl on the estuary sometimes include small flocks of Brent and Pink-footed Geese, or a party of Bewick's Swans. Pintail are often the commonest duck, and the river channel is frequented by Scaup, Red-breasted Merganser, and Goldeneye, and these also occur off the mouth, together with a few Common Scoter — also Guillemots and Razorbills. Hen Harrier, Sparrowhawk, Peregrine, Merlin, and Short-eared Owl are all regularly seen hunting over the marshes. Winter waders include up to 30,000 Dunlin and Knot, large numbers of Black-tailed Godwit, smaller numbers of Purple Sandpiper and Sanderling, and a few Spotted Redshank. Gulls regularly include the odd Mediterranean, Little, or Glaucous, but Icelands are quite rare. On the saltmarshes there are often Water Pipits and finch flocks, which should be checked for Bramblings and Twite, and a few Snow Buntings; the latter also favour the areas of dunes at the mouth of the Dee.

From September to early November strong NW gales may bring good numbers of Leach's Petrels onshore, as well as Manx Shearwaters and occasionally Sooty Shearwaters and Sabine's Gulls. A deep low centred around the Faeroe Islands and moving slowly E will produce the necessary gales. Gannets, Kittiwakes, and Arctic Skuas are regular offshore in autumn, but Great and Pomarine Skuas are scarce and Long-tailed rare. There is the odd shearwater or skua in early spring, and Little Gulls may be seen from June onwards. There are late-summer congregations of terns off the mouth, occasionally including Roseate, and up to 1,000 Little occur in mid-August off Red Rocks and Hilbre. Black Terns are frequent, especially in the upper estuary. Passage periods also bring large numbers of waders, with a greater variety than the winter. Whimbrel are more frequent in spring, but autumn is generally better; Curlew Sandpiper, Little Stint, Spotted Redshank, and Wood Sandpiper may all occur. Numbers of migrant passerines are seen around the estuary especially at Red Rocks and Hilbre, but scarce migrants are rare.

Other Sites in the Area

70.7 Frodsham Lagoons and the Weaver Bend (see map).
OS Sheet No. 117

Dredgings from the River Mersey are pumped into embanked lagoons at Frodsham. These and the surrounding pasture form a complex of freshwater and brackish habitats and on big tides waders roost on the lagoons. When wet they can also attract feeding waders, but as they dry out they become less interesting, though No. 5 Sludge Bed and the ICI Tank are usually good in late summer and autumn. Backing onto the lagoons at the Weaver Bend are areas of mud attractive to waders; the patch around the small island by the ICI Tank is favoured. Access to the area is from the A56 in Frodsham, crossing the M56 via Ship Street or Marsh Lane. In winter there are numbers of duck as well as occasionally Common Sandpiper and Short-eared Owl. On passage an exceptional variety of waders occurs and the area is especially good for Curlew Sandpiper and Little Stint in autumn; American waders are annual. Other regular migrants include Black Tern.

70.8 Halkyn Churchyard
OS Sheet No. 117

Halkyn is just off the A55 SW of Flint. The churchyard, on a slight hill, is a regular spot for Lady Amherst's Pheasant and Hawfinch. These can be seen at any time of day, but early morning when there is least disturbance is best, and January–March is the optimum period. Do *not* wander into nearby back gardens.

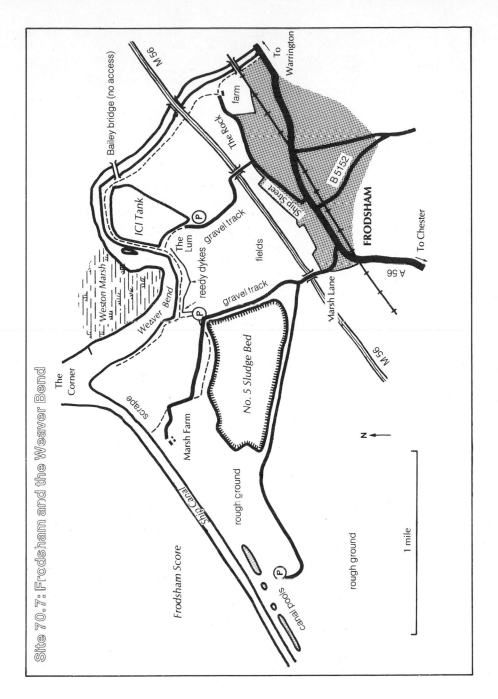

Site 70.7: Frodsham and the Weaver Bend

Connah's Quay, warden: R. A. Roberts, 38 Kelsterton Rd, Connah's **Information**
Quay, Deeside, Clwyd CH5 4BJ.
RSPB, Gayton Sands: Marsh Cottage, Denhall Lane, Burton, Wirral,
Merseyside L64 0TG
Shotton Pool, permits: Personal Relations Manager, BSC, Shotton
Steelworks, Deeside, Clwyd.

Hilbre: Visits to the Observatory by arrangement with J. C. Gittins, 17 Deva Rd, West Kirby, Wirral, Merseyside L48 4DB (s.a.e. please). Yearly permits for the island are available free from the Wirral Country Park Centre, Station Rd, Thurstaston, Wirral L61 0HN.
Cheshire Conservation Trust, c/o Marbury Country Park, Northwich, Cheshire CW9 6AT.
Reference: *Hilbre, the Cheshire Island. Its History and Natural History* edited by J. D. Craggs (1982).
Recorder: Clwyd (Point of Ayr, Connah's Quay, Shotton, Halkyn), Cheshire (all other sites).

Site No. 71 Martin Mere (Lancashire)

Martin Mere is a Wildfowl Trust Refuge covering 363 acres. Intensive management has produced an excellent wetland area that attracts large numbers of ducks, Pink-footed Geese, and swans. The best time to visit is winter.

Habitat

Formerly a large lake, the Mere was drained to leave an area of winter flooding. Purchased by the Wildfowl Trust in 1969, the area of flooding was increased and permanent pools established.

Access
OS Sheet No. 108

The refuge is on a minor between the B5246 at Holmeswood (S of Mere Brow on the A565) and the A59 at Burscough Bridge, and is signposted from Burscough Bridge and Mere Brow. Open daily 09.30 – 17.30 (or dusk if earlier) and by prior arrangement on Tuesday and Wednesday evenings in June–July, entrance is £2 for non-members. There is an education centre, exhibition hall, and a collection of captive wildfowl and flamingos, as well as nine hides overlooking the area of the Mere.

Birds

In early winter the Lancashire Pink-feet converge on Martin Mere, and can peak at 34,000 before dispersal. Many leave Lancashire, but some feed on Altcar Moss and some move to Marshside (see p. 211), but large numbers still spend the day at Martin Mere, and these are augmented by others coming to roost. A flock of c 200 Whooper Swans has built up, together with around 300 Bewick's, some of which fly in from the Ribble in the evening. Ducks are numerous – Teal and Pintail can both peak at 10,000; Pintail are especially common in early winter. There may be small numbers of Gadwall, Shoveler, and Goosander. Short-eared Owl, Hen Harrier, and Merlin are all regular and the area is especially good for Peregrine. A flock of Ruff winter, and can number 250.

Waders are not numerous on passage, and mainly comprise the longer-legged species. Breeding birds have included Little Ringed Plover, Black-tailed Godwit, and Ruff, and up to 150 godwits and a few Ruff usually summer, together with one or two Marsh Harriers.

Information

The Wildfowl Trust, Martin Mere, Burscough, Ormskirk, Lancs L40 OTA. Tel. 0704–895181.
Recorder: Lancashire.

Site No. 72 Ribble Estuary (Lancashire)

Between Southport and Blackpool, this is one of the most important estuaries in Britain and supports internationally important populations of Pintail and nine species of wader, particularly Knot, Sanderling, and Bar-tailed Godwit. This provides excellent birdwatching, especially in autumn and winter. 5,688 acres of the S shore are a National Nature Reserve.

Habitat

The outer estuary is sandy, attracting tourists to Southport, Lytham St Anne's, and Blackpool. The inner estuary is also mostly sandy, but fortunately attracts fewer people. The Ribble has one of the largest areas of tidal flats and saltmarsh in the country, the latter mainly on the S shore.

Access
(see map)
OS Sheet Nos.
102 and 108
The South Shore

1. Southport marine lake at the base of the pier is rather disturbed and only Goldeneye are regular. In autumn NW gales can push seabirds onshore, and at high tide a few Leach's Petrels and Manx Shearwaters may be seen from the pier, but it is not as good as Squires Gate on the N shore.
2. Marine Drive follows the coast NE from Southport. The golf course at Marshside attracts small numbers of migrants during passage periods, such as Garganey, White Wagtail, and Ring Ouzel. ½ mile N of the sand depot, the fields inland of the road are excellent. From Christmas onwards large flocks of Pink-feet spend the day feeding here, usually roosting on Southport Sands. Bewick's Swans, as well as the occasional Whooper, also frequent the fields, but roost at Martin Mere. The area attracts raptors, including a roost of c 5 Hen Harriers. When the fields are wet they may hold Golden Plover and Black-tailed Godwit, and sometimes Little Stint. Crossens Marsh is not attractive to feeding waders, but has a huge roost on the highest tides of the year in spring and autumn (30 feet or more). Twite are occasionally present on the saltings, and sometimes also Lapland Buntings. Parking is limited on Marine Drive, but possible near the sand depot.
3. In the NNR, Crossens, Banks, and Hesketh Out Marshes are visible from a public footpath along the seawall. Access is from Crossens Pumping Station, just off the A565, and also at Hundred End (on a minor road N from the A565). There are no restrictions on access to Crossens and Banks Marshes, except for the study–sanctuary zone. Access to this and Hesketh Out Marsh is by permit only. While a nice walk, you are unlikely to see more than at the more convenient Marine Drive.

The North Shore

1. At Squires Gate on the S outskirts of Blackpool, the beach is only ½ mile wide, and in autumn and winter divers, grebes, and seaduck can all be seen at high tide. Autumn also brings terns to the area, and NW gales push numbers of seabirds onshore. Seawatch from the beach shelter on the front opposite Pontin's Holiday Camp.
2. The 2-mile section of shore from Squires Gate to St Anne's is sandy and holds thousands of waders, notably Sanderling. On a reasonably high tide waders roost along the foreshore in this

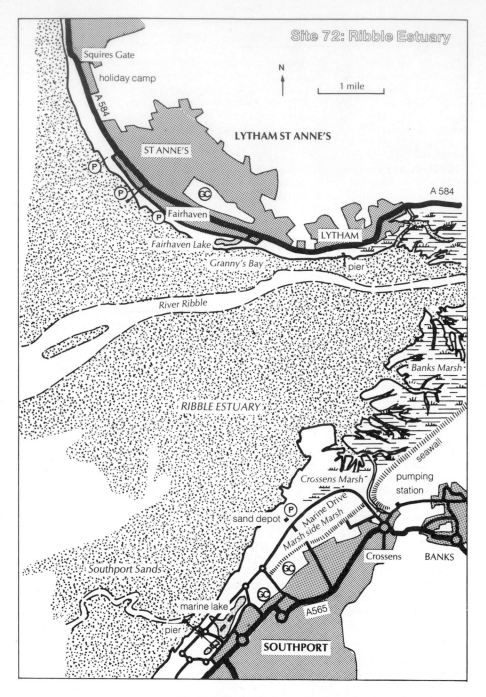

area. The A584 runs S along the shore from Blackpool, and a
minor road parallel to it on the seafront between St Anne's and
Fairhaven Lake gives views of the shore.
3. The foreshore from Fairhaven to Lytham is muddier and on the
'lower' high tides waders roost at Granny's Bay. This section is

especially good for Black-tailed Godwits (as is the area E of Lytham pier), and Turnstones are regular on the mussel beds. Access is from the promenade.

Birds

In winter there are small numbers of Red-throated Divers on the sea, and seaduck include several hundred Common and a few Velvet Scoters, as well as Goldeneye and Red-breasted Merganser. By late December numbers of Pink-footed Geese appear at Marshside, where they are joined by up to 200 Bewick's and a few Whooper Swans. Other wildfowl include large numbers of Pintail, as well as a few Gadwall and Shoveler. Waders are dominated by Knot, up to 70,000 of them, as well as hordes of the other common species. There are usually 2,000 – 3,000 Sanderling and up to 1,000 Black-tailed Godwit — both species predominantly on the N shore. Hen Harrier, Merlin, and Short-eared Owl can all be seen, but Peregrines are quite scarce. There are sometimes Twite or even Lapland Buntings on the saltmarshes, while the rather erratic Snow Bunting prefers the sandier areas.

Spring movements of waders are rapid, but autumn passage is more leisurely, with big influxes from late July onwards, and huge flocks of moulting waders on the estuary. The wintering species are joined by Curlew Sandpiper, Little Stint, and up to 4,000 Black-tailed Godwits. In September – October a NW gale can result in excellent seawatching. Leach's Petrels and Manx Shearwaters are regular, as are Arctic and small numbers of Great Skuas, but Pomarines are uncommon (the chance of seeing one increases later in the autumn). Kittiwakes are the commonest seabird after gales, and there are often Little Gulls with them. The latter occur right though the winter until April, and up to 100 a day have been seen.

Breeding birds include several thousand pairs of Black-headed Gull and a few hundred pairs of Common Tern on the marshes, as well as large numbers of waders, particularly Redshank.

Other Sites in the Area
72.1 Marton Mere
OS Sheet No. 102

On the outskirts of Blackpool, Marton Mere is an area of open water, marsh, and reedbeds. It holds breeding Great Crested Grebe and Sedge and Reed Warblers, but the main attraction is passage waders, which include species like Green Sandpiper that are difficult to find on the estuary. There is also a variety of passerines on spring migration. Winter wildfowl include Shoveler, and Short-eared Owls are also sometimes seen. There is public access to the Mere which is a Local Nature Reserve. Leave the A583 N at Great Marton towards Stanley Park, and after ½ mile take Lawson Road on the right. Park two-thirds of the way down the road and walk across the football pitch to the Mere.

Information

NCC warden: Nature Reserve Office, Old Hollow Farm, Banks, Southport, Merseyside PR9 8DU.
Recorder: Lancashire.

Site No. 73 Leighton Moss (Lancashire)

Leighton Moss holds the largest population of Bitterns in Britain, as well as Bearded Tits, and in winter a wide variety of wildfowl is present. A visit is worthwhile at any time, other than when the moss is completely frozen in hard weather, but to see Bitterns May – June is probably best. Leighton Moss is an RSPB reserve, covering 321 acres.

Habitat

Once an arm of the sea, it was embanked, drained, and ploughed, but allowed to re-flood in 1917. It is now a freshwater marsh, extensively overgrown with reeds, willow, and alder carr, with areas of open water.

**Access
(see map)**
OS Sheet No. 97

Off the minor road between Silverdale and Yealand Redmayne, the car park and visitor centre are at Myers Farm, near Silverdale Station. A public causeway runs across the reserve, with a public hide that is always open. Access to the rest of the reserve is by permit only, available from Reception (£2 for non-members). The reserve is open daily (except Tuesdays), 09.00 – 21.00 (or dusk if earlier).

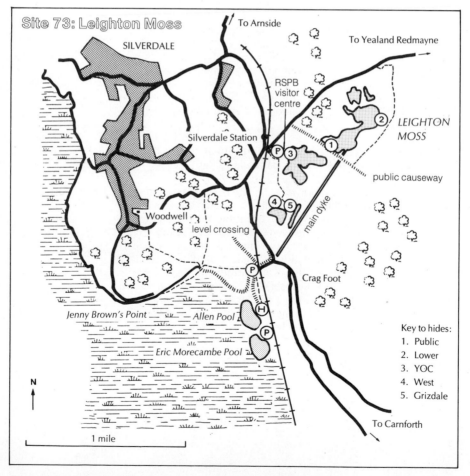

Site 73: Leighton Moss

To Arnside
SILVERDALE
To Yealand Redmayne
RSPB visitor centre
LEIGHTON MOSS
Silverdale Station
public causeway
Woodwell
level crossing
main dyke
Crag Foot
Jenny Brown's Point — Allen Pool
Eric Morecambe Pool
To Carnforth

N

1 mile

Key to hides:
1. Public
2. Lower
3. YOC
4. West
5. Grizdale

Birds

Winter brings large numbers of duck, including Wigeon, Pintail, Shoveler, and a few Gadwall, Goldeneye, and Goosander. Feral Greylag Geese are resident, and other (probably wild) birds fly in to roost. Bitterns are present, even if difficult to see, as are Water Rails, and there are occasionally Water Pipits, with Siskins and Redpolls in the carr. Hawfinches are resident in Silverdale, and can often be seen in the vicinity of Woodwell.

Breeding species include Buzzard and Sparrowhawk, and c 10 pairs of Bittern. Teal, Shoveler, Pochard, and occasionally Gadwall or Garganey also breed, and Spotted Crakes have done so twice. The reedbeds hold Bearded Tit and Reed Warbler, with Sedge and Grasshopper Warblers in the scrubbier areas.

Bittern

A lucky visitor may see a Jack Snipe in early spring or late autumn, feeding quietly along the edge of the reeds, or perhaps a Garganey. Ospreys are also reasonably regular on passage, as are Marsh Harriers. Little Gulls favour the spring, but Black and Common Terns are equally likely in autumn, which is best for waders — these can include Green Sandpiper and Spotted Redshank. The autumn roost of Swallows, martins, and Starlings attracts hunting Sparrowhawks, and sometimes a Merlin, Peregrine, or even a Hobby.

Other Sites in the Area

The N end of the RSPB's Morecambe Bay reserve is adjacent to Leighton Moss; the Eric Morecambe and Allen Pools are especially convenient (see map opposite).

Information

RSPB warden: Myers Farm, Silverdale, Carnforth, Lancashire LA5 0SW. Tel. 0524–701601
Recorder: Lancashire.

Site No. 74 Morecambe Bay (Lancashire, Cumbria)

Morecambe Bay is the largest and, for birds, the most important intertidal area in Britain, attracting up to 200,000 waders in winter. It is of international importance for Shelduck, Wigeon, Pintail, and nine species of wader, particularly Knot. In addition,

Heysham harbour is probably the only mainland site in Britain guaranteed to produce Leach's Petrels after SW to W gales (W to NW elsewhere). The best time to visit the bay is in the winter and passage periods. The RSPB has a 6,141-acre reserve between Silverdale and Hest Bank.

Habitat

Morecambe Bay covers c 120 square miles of tidal mud and sand, and is a complex of five estuaries – Wyre, Lune, Keer, Kent, and Leven. There are large mussel beds, and the flats are fringed by heavily grazed saltmarsh, especially in the upper reaches of the rivers.

Access
(see map)
OS Sheet Nos. 96
(access points
9, 10, 16-19),
97 (9–18), and
102 (1–8)

It is important to note the state of the tide, as the sea can be up to 7 miles away at low water. The fortnightly spring tides are generally best and predictions for Liverpool more or less correct. Access is at the following points.

1. Fleetwood. Rossall Point, at the W end of the promenade near the Coastguard Station, attracts a few Purple Sandpipers as well as Turnstones – which number up to 1,000 by the spring. There are often Red-throated Divers offshore, usually a flock of Twite, and sometimes Snow Buntings. The regular wintering Glaucous Gull usually appears on the mussel beds near the Marine Hall 2 – 3 hrs after high tide. In September – October NW gales push seabirds onshore, notably Leach's Petrels.
2. Leave the A588 onto the B5377/B5270 to Knott End-on-Sea, from where you can walk E along the shore for 2½ miles to Fluke Hall.
3. The Pilling wader roost is best seen from the Lane Ends car park, on the seawall just N of the village. It is is also worth going to Fluke Hall. Turn off to Pilling from the A588 and follow signs in the village.
4. The low fields in the Cockerham–Pilling–Eagland Hill area are good for Pink-feet, especially mid-February to mid-March. Numbers vary between 500 and 3,000, and it is necessary to drive round the maze of lanes to find the geese.
5. ½ mile N of Cockerham on the A588, a lane leads W to Bank End Farm, from where a path follows the coast NW for c 2 miles to Cockersand Point. There is a wader roost on lower tides, seaduck offshore, and late-summer congregations of terns.
6. Cockersand Point may also be reached off the A588 at Thurnham, taking the signposted road W to the Point.
7. Take the B5290 off the A588 at Conder Green to Glasson dock. Waders are visible from the road over the disused railway embankment and the area is good during passage periods.
8. Middleton Salt Marsh. Follow signs from Heysham S to Middleton, turning right at the first junction in the village, signed Middleton Sands. Park at Potts Corner from where a footpath runs SE through the marsh. There is a large wader roost and late-summer concentrations of terns. Sunderland Point is worth checking for migrant passerines in the correct conditions (see p. 220).
9. Heysham harbour. Straightforward access off the A589. A good area for Purple Sandpiper, it is most notable as a

seawatching station. In September – October SW–WNW gales (especially after strong W winds) should produce Leach's Petrels, as well as Arctic and some Great Skuas. Shearwaters are rare, as are Gannets — Leach's Petrels are commoner. Winter gales are good for Little Gulls, and April – August gales produce Fulmars and terns, while skuas are seen in variable numbers mid-April to mid-May. The N harbour wall is the best place to watch from.

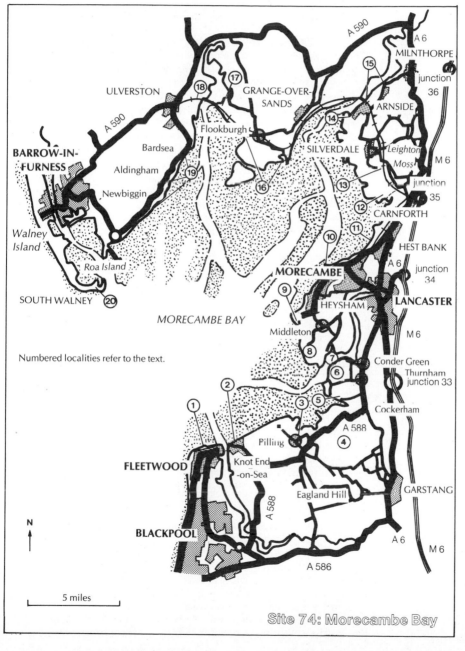

Site 74: Morecambe Bay

10. Morecambe promenade is good for waders at low water. Watch from the stone jetty (just behind the Midland Hotel) especially for seaduck. Red-breasted Merganser, Goldeneye, and a few Scaup are regular and Long-tailed Duck and Common Scoter also occur, along with Great Crested Grebes and Red-throated Divers. A similar range of seabirds as at Heysham harbour may be seen after gales. On the lowest tides numbers of waders roost around the jetty, while on slightly higher tides they roost towards the Teal Bay Restaurant (no Teal here) and on the highest tides at Hest Bank.

11. Hest Bank is the S tip of Carnforth RSPB reserve, and probably the best place to see large numbers of waders, with up to 15,000 roosting on spring tides. Other attractions are wildfowl and raptors. Cross the railway at the level crossing at Hest Bank signal box on the A5105 (plenty of parking space) and walk N for good views of the waders at high tide.

12. Carnforth saltmarsh can be reached by taking the footpath along the N bank of the River Keer near Cote Stones Farm. Leave the A6 into Carnforth and take the minor road past the station towards Silverdale. After c 1 mile turn left at the junction and at a sharp right hand bend take the road straight ahead to Cote Stones, forking left after 100 yards to the riverbank. The old slag heaps provide good vantage points. The pools are good for Jack Snipe, and there is a wader roost.

13. RSPB Allen Pools (see map, p. 214). Two lagoons have been constructed on the saltings of the RSPB reserve, overlooked by hides on the seawall. This is a prime spot to watch waders and a good area for Greylags. Leave the Carnforth – Silverdale road at Crag Foot (near Leighton Moss), passing under the railway bridge to the car park.

14. The lower Kent estuary can be viewed from the footpath to New Barns and Blackstone Point from the W end of Arnside promenade. There is a wader roost, except on higher tides.

15. The S side of the upper Kent estuary can be seen either from the E end of Arnside promenade, looking over the railway wall, or from Sandside promenade, 1½ miles N of Arnside. Waders roost, but not on the highest tides. This area is good on passage and there is a large gull roost.

16. At Flookburgh, off the B5277, either: (a) go W along the main street of the village to a vantage point on the shore past Sandgate Farm to view Sandgate Marsh (the area is a wader roost on the higher tides and is good for wildfowl, especially on a rising tide); or (b) follow signs from the village square to Humphrey Head, then walk along the shore to a point overlooking Out Marsh (there is a wader roost here).

17. The E side of the Leven can be reached from the B5278 1½ miles N of Flookburgh, down the minor road to Old Park and on to Park Head on the shore.

18. The Leven estuary is best seen from the W shore. A minor road leads from the A590 at Newland (just N of Ulverston) to Plumpton Hall. Walk N along the shore from here, under the railway and on towards Ashes Point. There is a wader roost, and it is a good area on passage.

19. The A5087 parallels the coast from near Roa Island to Bardsea. Waders roost at Newbiggin (visible from the main

road), Aldingham (take the minor road into the village to view the shore), and Bardsea (a track runs NE off the main road to Wadhead Scar, just N of the turn off to the village). Seaduck occur off Bardsea, especially Scaup and Common Scoter, as well as Red-throated Divers.

20. Walney Island. See p. 220.

Birds

In winter small numbers of Red-throated Divers appear offshore. Raptors include Peregrine, Merlin, Short-eared Owl, and occasionally Hen Harrier. Pink-footed Geese are regular, feeding inland and roosting in the Bay. 1,000 – 4,000 use the sandbanks in the Lune, and are joined by a handful of White-fronted Geese. The Pilling/Cockerham area is also favoured. Greylag Geese concentrate on the RSPB reserve at Carnforth, roosting on the Keer estuary or at Leighton Moss in the early part of the winter, and the Lune estuary in the latter part. Other wildfowl include Pintail and a few Shoveler. Seaduck occur in small numbers: Scaup, Goldeneye, and Red-breasted Merganser are sometimes joined by Common Scoter, Eider, or Long-tailed Duck. The commonest wader is Knot, which can total 80,000. Oyster-catcher, Curlew, Bar-tailed Godwit, Redshank, and Dunlin are also numerous, with small numbers of Turnstone and a few Ringed Plover and Sanderling. Purple Sandpipers are regularly found at Heysham and Fleetwood. The saltmarshes attract Rock Pipits, but Snow Bunting and Twite are quite uncommon.

Knot

Passage periods produce more waders but fewer wildfowl. Most waders are commoner in autumn, from July onwards, than in spring. Exceptions are Knot (up to 100,000), Ringed Plover, and Sanderling. Autumn passage also produces a greater variety which may include Little Ringed Plover, Curlew Sandpiper, Little Stint, Spotted Redshank, or Black-tailed Godwit. Other passage visitors include terns, and in the autumn the right conditions can produce seabirds at Heysham harbour or Fleetwood.

Small numbers of waders remain in summer. Breeding birds include Shelduck, Red-breasted Merganser, and Shoveler. Common and a few Arctic Terns breed on the saltmarshes, together with Oystercatcher, Redshank, and some Dunlin and Wheatear, but the commonest birds are Meadow Pipit and Skylark.

Other Sites in the Area
74.1 Heysham Power Station
OS Sheet Nos. 96 (or 97) and 102

The power station light acts like a huge lighthouse. Sizeable falls of passerines occur in spring and autumn and have included the odd scarce migrant. The best conditions are either SE winds around the W flank of an anticyclone, or SE winds ahead of a warm front with the edge of the cloud cover coinciding with dawn. Any bushes around the power station can hold birds, especially those by the Observation Tower, along Moneyclose Lane, and bordering the caravan site and golf course. In Heysham, follow the main road to the harbour and turn left at the lights by the Moneyclose pub to the power station's Observation Tower car park.

Information

RSPB Carnforth: Information, including tide details, are available at the Leighton Moss visitor centre or by writing to the warden c/o Leighton Moss reserve (see p. 215).
Reference: *The Birds of Morecambe Bay* by John Wilson (1976).
Recorder: Lancashire (access points 1–13), Cumbria (14–19)

Site No. 75 South Walney (Cumbria)

South Walney, part of Walney Island, projects into Morecambe Bay and shares its huge population of waders. This position also concentrates migrants and has led to the establishment of a Bird Observatory. A few semi-rarities and rarities are recorded annually. The best time for migrants is April to early June and August to early November, but for wildfowl and waders winter is better. South Walney is a 230-acre reserve of the Cumbria Trust for Nature Conservation.

Habitat

There is a variety of habitats. Dunes and sandy beaches are interspersed with areas of gravel, bracken, marsh, and brackish and fresh water. The limited amount of cover is concentrated around the five Heligoland traps and the coastguard cottages. The island is fringed by saltmarsh and mudflats, and the Spit protects the sheltered tidal basin of Lighthouse Bay and is used by large numbers of roosting waders.

Access
(see map)
OS Sheet No. 96

Cross the road bridge from Barrow-in-Furness to Walney Island, turn left at the traffic lights, and fork right into Ocean Road. Turn at Carr Lane (fifth – unsigned – on the left) and continue on through Biggar village and past the rubbish tip. At the caravan site an unmade road cuts across the island to the reserve (stopping not allowed). The reserve is signposted at Walney Bridge and the caravan site, and there is a car park. South Walney Nature Reserve is open all year (except Mondays, but including bank holidays), 10.00 – 17.00 (or 16.00 September – April). There is a permanent warden. Entrance is by permit, available on site at 50p per day, and restricted to the two nature trails. A hide overlooks the gull colony and three others face the Irish Sea and Morecambe Bay, excellent for seawatching in wet and windy weather. A cottage accommodating up to eight people is available all year on a self-catering basis (£57.50 per week from Easter to the end of September, £43.70 the rest of the year). It can sometimes be rented on a daily basis for £6.30 in the latter period, and it may be possible to accept individual bookings at a reduced rate. There is also a six-berth caravan (£63.25 per week in the high season, £43.70 in the low).

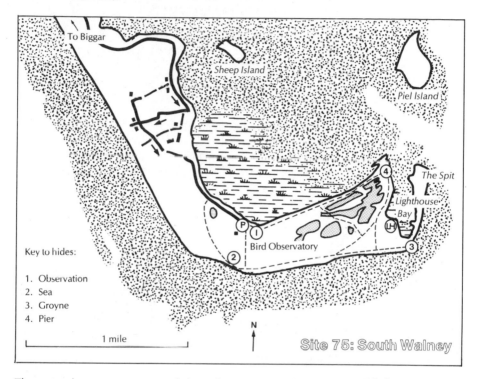

To Biggar

Sheep Island

Piel Island

The Spit

Lighthouse
Bay

Bird Observatory

Key to hides:

1. Observation
2. Sea
3. Groyne
4. Pier

1 mile

N

Site 75: South Walney

Birds

There are large movements of diurnal migrants in the passage periods, and in spring one or two Marsh Harriers are usually recorded. Calm, overcast or hazy weather is most likely to produce a fall of night migrants. As well as the commoner species, Black Redstart, Red-breasted Flycatcher, Yellow-browed and Melodious Warblers, and Firecrest are annual. Seawatching during or after strong W winds August – September can produce Gannets, Manx and sometimes Sooty Shearwaters, and Leach's Petrels, while Great and Cory's Shearwaters are nearly annual. Another possibility is Pomarine Skua, though you are more likely to see Great and Arctic Skuas and large numbers of Common, Arctic, and Sandwich Terns, Guillemots, and Razorbills. Migrant waders may include some of the scarcer species such as Curlew Sandpiper or Little Stint, especially in autumn.

Winter birds include Red-throated Divers on the sea, with large numbers of Eider and sometimes Common Scoter as well as Red-breasted Mergansers and Goldeneye. Merlins and Peregrines are daily visitors, and there are sometimes Short-eared Owls or

Hen Harriers too. The whole of Walney Island attracts raptors, so keep a sharp look-out from the car. Little Auks are almost annual after NW gales, and there have been spectacular hard-weather movements of wildfowl and passerines. Waders include up to 10,000 Oystercatchers and large numbers of the other common species.

Breeding birds include 650 pairs of Eider, 9,000 pairs each of Herring and Lesser Black-backed Gulls, and a few Great Black-backs. There are small numbers of Shelduck, Oystercatcher, Ringed Plover, and Little and Common Terns. Peregrines breed in the area and are often seen.

Information

Warden: Coastguard Cottages, South Walney Nature Reserve, Barrow-in-Furness LA14 3YQ.
Recorder: Observatory recorder.

Site No. 76 St Bees Head (Cumbria)

St Bees Head, W of the lakeland fells, holds a colony of seabirds, including England's only Black Guillemots. The Head is an RSPB reserve covering 55 acres.

Habitat

Red sandstone cliffs rise to 300 feet and are topped with areas of gorse and grassland.

Access
(see map)
OS Sheet No. 89

Leave Whitehaven S on the B5345. At the staggered crossroads in St Bees take the road straight ahead and turn right after 400 yards at the T junction. The car park is a further ½ mile. From there take the cliff path N for c 2½ miles to the lighthouse at North Head. There are safe observation points overlooking the seabird colonies on the way. The reserve is open at all times, and a warden is present April – August.

Birds

Breeding birds include large numbers of Guillemots, but many fewer Razorbills and only a few Black Guillemots and Puffins. There are also Fulmars, Shags, and Kittiwakes, as well as Ravens, Peregrines, Rock Pipits, and Stonechats.

Black Guillemot

The Head can be good for seawatching, especially in strong SW winds. Red-throated Diver and Manx and Sooty Shearwaters are possible, especially in late summer and autumn, together with

Gannet, Great and Arctic Skuas, and Sandwich, Common, and Arctic Terns. Small numbers of passerine migrants may occur along the cliff tops.

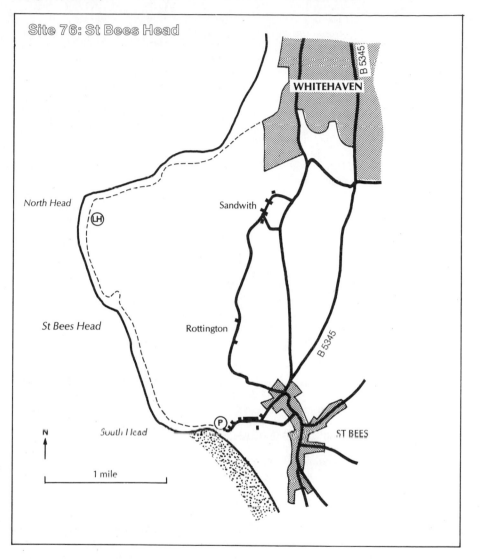

Site 76: St Bees Head

RSPB summer warden: c/o St Bees Head Lighthouse, Sandwith, **Information** Whitehaven, Cumbria.
Recorder: South Cumbria.

Site No. 77 Fairburn Ings (North Yorkshire)

These shallow lakes were formed by mining subsidence and are now an RSPB reserve of 680 acres. The variety of habitats created has proved very attractive to birds in an otherwise industrial area. Fairburn lies alongside the A1, 4 miles N of the A1–M62 interchange. It is best during the migration seasons or in winter.

Habitat

Over a third of the reserve is open water. There is little fringe vegetation at the E end of the reserve and continuing subsidence is causing some loss of reedbeds. Floating islands have been introduced to help compensate for this loss. Unsightly disused spoil heaps are being colonised by a variety of plants and a programme of tree planting is being carried out which helps stabilise the heaps as well as providing a useful habitat. At the W end, low-lying farmland is subject to occasional flooding and subsidence and the resulting shallow flashes are attractive to wildfowl and waders.

Access
(see map)
OS Sheet No. 105

Turn W off the A1 at Fairburn. A footpath from Cut Lane in the centre of the village leads S across the E end of the reserve. Three public hides are situated along this and the riverbank footpath. The reserve can also be viewed from the Fairburn–Allerton Bywater road on the N boundary. The information centre at Newton, c 1½ miles W of Fairburn, is open on Saturdays and Sundays, 10.00 – 17.00.

Birds

Many wildfowl winter including a regular herd of Whooper Swans. These tend to feed in fields during the day, coming in to roost in the evening. Small numbers of Goldeneye and Goosander are usually present but Scaup and Smew are only occasional. A large gull roost frequently attracts the odd Glaucous Gull. Redpolls feed on the alders and birches and are sometimes joined by a few Siskins.

Small numbers of waders occur on passage, sometimes including Spotted Redshank, and Green and Wood Sandpipers. Tern passage is sometimes notable, particularly in spring after E winds. The main species are Common, Arctic, and Black Terns. A few Little Gulls are regular at these times. In the autumn large numbers of hirundines can be seen, many of them roosting on the reserve.

Summer is comparatively quiet. Several species of wildfowl breed including the occasional Garganey. Lapwing, Snipe, and Redshank favour the shallow flashes at the W end of the reserve, and Little Ringed Plover and Reed Warbler are here almost at the N limit of their breeding range. A colony of Black-headed Gulls nests on Priest-holme and in 1978 a pair of Little Gulls attempted to breed amongst them. The scrub and deciduous woodland attracts a variety of the commoner warblers.

Information

Warden: 2 Springholme, Caudle Hill, Fairburn, Knottingley, Yorkshire WF11 9JQ.
Recorder: Yorkshire.

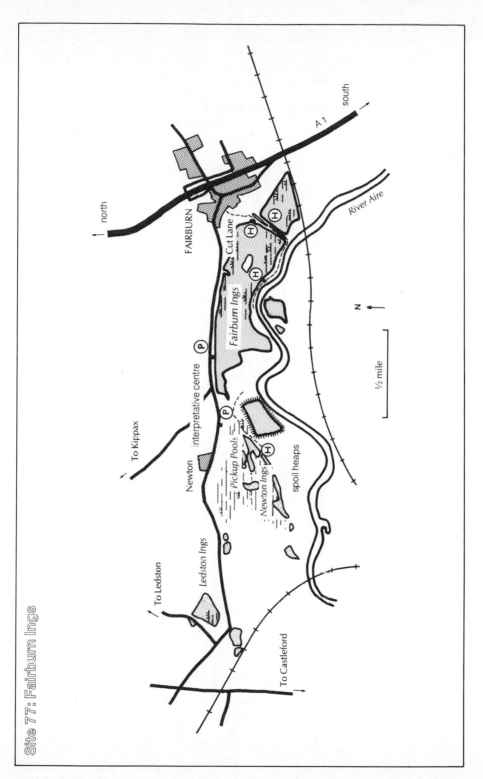

Site 77: Fairburn Ings

Site No. 78 Blacktoft Sands (Humberside)

Blacktoft Sands is an RSPB reserve of 460 acres lying at the confluence of the Rivers Ouse and Trent on the S side of the Humber estuary. Several uncommon species breed and the recently dug lagoons have attracted a wide variety of waders.

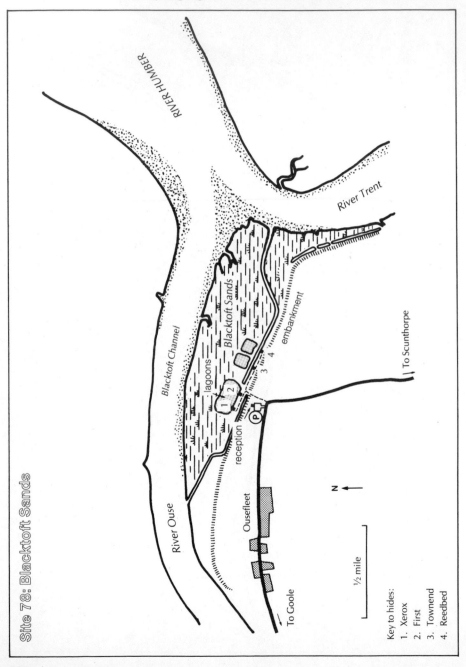

Site 78: Blacktoft Sands

Key to hides:
1. Xerox
2. First
3. Townend
4. Reedbed

The majority of the reserve is tidal reedbed, and an area of mudflats lies at the confluence of the two rivers. In order to create further habitats, parts of the drier W end have been excavated to create a series of brackish lagoons with islands and carefully controlled water levels.

Habitats

Leave Goole on the A161 to Swinefleet and Crowle. Fork left in Swinefleet onto a minor road signed Reedness. Continue on this for c 5 miles, through Reedness, Whitgift, and Ousefleet. About ½ mile E of Ousefleet, turn left into the signed reserve car park, immediately before the road bends sharply right. A reception hut is situated in the car park. The reserve is open daily (except Tuesdays), 09.00 – 21.00 (or sunset when earlier). Non-members are charged £2. Four hides are sited beyond the embankment overlooking the lagoons and reedbed. Access is restricted to the hides and embankment, and visitors are asked to walk along the bottom of the bank to avoid disturbance.

Access
(see map)
OS Sheet No. 112

Large numbers of the commoner duck winter on the Humber estuary and are occasionally seen on the reserve, and flocks of Pink-footed Geese and wild swans sometimes fly over. A few waders winter, and Merlin, Short-eared Owl, and Hen Harrier are regularly seen. In the reedbeds, Bearded Tit and Reed Bunting are resident.

Birds

During the migration seasons, a wide variety of waders stops over and these are best viewed from the hides. Many are often only visible at high tides when their feeding areas on the Humber estuary are covered. Characteristic species include Little Stint, Curlew Sandpiper, Ruff, Black-tailed Godwit, Greenshank, and Spotted Redshank, and a number of rare waders have been found at Blacktoft in recent years. The best time for waders is May and July – August with greater numbers during the latter period. In spring, Marsh Harrier, Temminck's Stint, Black Tern, and Little Gull are seen occasionally.

In summer, Redshank, Lapwing, and Snipe nest on the lagoons alongside Teal, Shoveler, and Gadwall. A few pairs of Little Ringed Plovers have recently colonised the lagoons. One or two pairs of Short-eared Owl and Grasshopper Warbler nest in the grassy areas. Large numbers of Reed Warblers breed in the reedbeds together with Sedge Warbler and a few pairs of Water Rail. Blacktoft's reedbeds are an important breeding site for Bearded Tits with up to 100 pairs in some years. They are most active September to early November. Marsh Harriers have bred in the past and are still occasional in summer.

Warden: Hillcrest, High St, Whitgift, Goole, Humberside DN14 8HL. Recorder: Lincolnshire.

Information

Site No. 79 Spurn Head (Humberside)

The first bird observatory to be established on mainland Britain, in 1946, Spurn is an excellent place to see migrants and probably the premier site on the mainland for rarities. Spurn Nature Reserve is owned by the Yorkshire Wildlife Trust.

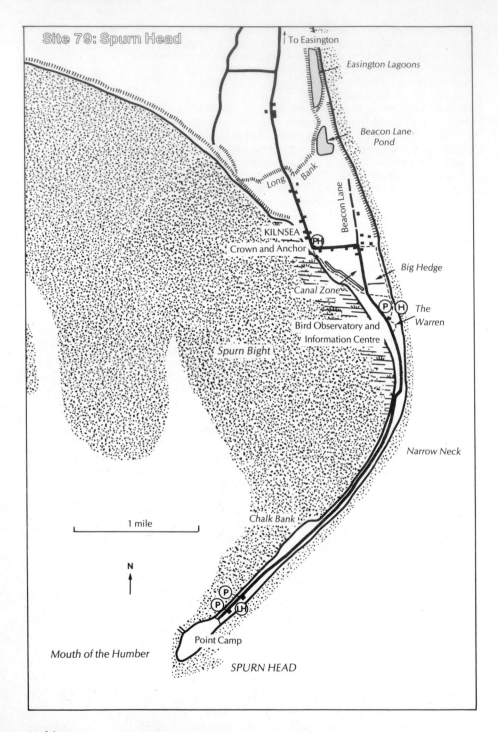

Site 79: Spurn Head

To Easington

Easington Lagoons

Beacon Lane Pond

Long Bank

Beacon Lane

KILNSEA

Crown and Anchor

PH

Big Hedge

Canal Zone

P H

The Warren

Bird Observatory and Information Centre

Spurn Bight

Narrow Neck

1 mile

Chalk Bank

N

P

P LH

Mouth of the Humber

Point Camp

SPURN HEAD

Habitat

Spurn is a narrow sand and shingle spit, c 3½ miles long, extending into the mouth of the Humber. The base of the peninsula is farmed, and includes Beacon Lane Pond and

Easington Lagoons, but the spit really begins at the Observatory, and is less than 40 yards wide at the Narrow Neck. Sea buckthorn forms extensive and largely impenetrable thickets, with occasional elder bushes and areas of marram grass. To seaward there is a narrow beach, whilst on the Humber shore are the extensive mudflats of Spurn Bight.

Leave Hull on the A1033 to Patrington and then take the B1445 to Easington, continuing on a minor road to Kilnsea and Spurn. Access to the peninsula is unrestricted, apart from the Observatory garden, the various RNLI, pilot's, and coastguard's buildings, and the Point Camp area. There is a charge (£1.30) for cars using the road along the peninsula. An Information Centre is situated outside the Observatory; there is a car park here and at the tip of the peninsula. Basic self-catering accommodation is available for up to 17 people at £1.50 per night. There is a seawatching hide for the use of Observatory residents, and a resident warden.

Access (see map)
OS Map No. 113

Visible migration is best watched from the Narrow Neck. Movements usually peak in the first few hours of the morning and W winds are the most productive. Otherwise migrants can occur anywhere but the buckthorn is difficult to work. It is better to concentrate on:

1. The hedges around Kilnsea.
2. The Big Hedge and the Canal Zone.
3. Beacon Lane Pond and the Lagoons, accessible along Beacon Lane. These are good for waders if the water levels are low, especially at high tide. In winter they attract the odd duck or grebe and there are often lots of Snow Buntings, and sometimes Lapland Buntings and raptors, in the area.
4. The area around the Observatory and Warren.
5. Chalk Bank, especially good for larks, pipits, and Snow Buntings.

Birds

Visible migration begins in March with Lapwings, Starlings, Rooks, and Jackdaws on the move. A peculiarity of Spurn is that birds appear to be going the 'wrong' way in spring — S or SSE. In March and April Rock Pipits of the Scandinavian race may occur on the saltmarsh and Lagoons. E winds in late March and April will bring Black Redstarts, and later on flycatchers, chats, and warblers; Wryneck and Bluethroat are seen most years. Easterlies also bring movements of Black, Common, and Arctic Terns in the first few hours of daylight.

Late summer sees passages of waders and terns offshore, especially with strong W or SW winds, as well as large movements of Swifts. From late August to early November, NW–NE winds may prompt a passage of seabirds. There are regularly Sooty Shearwaters, skuas (sometimes including Pomarine and occasionally Long-tailed), and (from October onwards) Little Auks, while Little Gulls can peak at 100 on a very good day. Large numbers of waders frequent the estuary, with a good variety on Beacon Lane Pond and the Lagoons. Spotted Redshank are regular, with Little Stints and Curlew Sandpipers in some years. Autumn passerine migration starts in late July with movements of Sand Martins, Swallows, and Pied and Yellow Wagtails. August produces a trickle of warblers, mainly Willow, but towards the end of the month and into September the pace increases with

Redstart, Whinchat, Wheatear, and Pied Flycatcher joining a wide variety of warblers. E winds are most likely to produce good birds and there is a chance of Wryneck, Red-backed Shrike, Bluethroat, Icterine, or perhaps even an Aquatic Warbler. Spurn is *the* locality on the British mainland for Barred Warbler. Into October, diurnal migrants (pipits, Linnets, Greenfinches, and sometimes Twite) increasingly dominate the scene, but there can still be large falls of Robins, thrushes, or Goldcrests. Meadow Pipits may occasionally be joined by a Richard's, and in late October Spurn has consistently produced records of Pallas's Warbler, as well as Yellow-browed Warbler and Red-breasted Flycatcher. Long-eared Owls are regular, and may be flushed from the buckthorn; Short-eared Owls tend to go straight through. There can be large arrivals of thrushes in bad weather, especially Blackbirds, and Spurn is one of the best places in Britain to see Great Grey Shrikes; up to 5 birds have been present at once.

Great Grey Shrike

The winter months are comparatively quiet. Large numbers of Red-throated Divers can occur offshore, and wildfowl on the Humber include Brent Geese, often around the Narrow Neck. At Chalk Bank, as at the Narrow Neck, there is a roost of the common estuarine waders. Hen Harrier, Merlin, and Short-eared Owl may, with luck, be seen and in early winter there are often large numbers of thrushes feeding on the buckthorn berries. Snow Buntings are regular, numbers varying from a few dozen to a few hundred. Hard-weather movements can occur: fleeing birds can be seen moving S in early morning, especially if it is clear, and some may stop to feed.

Other Sites in the Area
79.1 Stone Creek/ Cherry Cobb Sands
OS Sheet No. 107

On the Humber NW of Spurn, Cherry Cobb Sands are signposted off the A1033 at Thorngumbald. Carry on down this minor road for 2½ miles, passing the hamlet of Thorney Crofts and follow the road left, parallel to the Humber Bank. Continue for c 3 miles until you reach Stone Creek. Park and walk N along the Humber Bank. The lagoons in the saltmarsh attract waders such as Black-tailed Godwit, and in winter small numbers of Pintail are regular, together with a few Bewick's Swans.

Warden (bookings): Spurn Nature Reserve, Kilnsea, Patrington, Hull, **Information**
Humberside HU12 0UG (s.a.e. please).
Recorder: Yorkshire.

Site No. 80 Hornsea Mere (Humberside)

Hornsea Mere is an RSPB reserve of 580 acres. Very attractive to wildfowl and migrants, it is worth a visit at any time.

A natural lake lying ⅔ mile from the sea, there are 300 acres of **Habitat** open water, and the surrounding vegetation includes large reedbeds, especially at the W end, and areas of carr. The fringe of the Mere is wooded on the N and W sides. The open water is used for sailing and fishing.

1. From the B1242 in Hornsea follow signs to 'The Mere' out to **Access** Kirkholme Point. An information centre is situated in The **(see map)** Bungalow and is open at weekends, May – August. Parking is OS Sheet No. 107 available during business hours. The Point is a good spot to look for gulls and terns over the Mere.

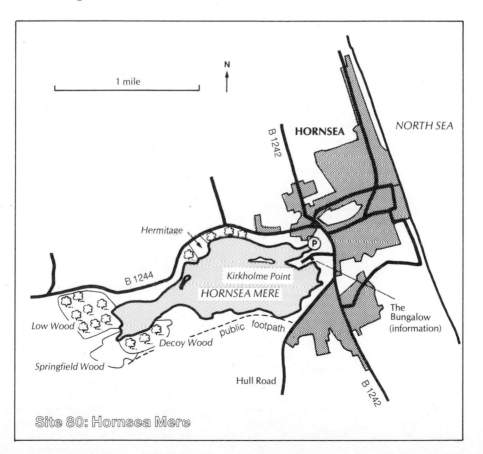

Site 80: Hornsea Mere

2. A public footpath runs along the S shore of the Mere from Hull Road in Hornsea. The first ½ mile gives the best views, after this the water is obscured by reeds and trees. There is no other access to the reserve.

Birds

In winter there are large numbers of Wigeon and notable concentrations of 100 – 200 Goldeneye, Gadwall, and Shoveler. A few Goosander are also regular. The resident feral Greylag Geese and Mute Swans are sometimes joined by small numbers of Bewick's or Whooper's Swans. Around the Mere's fringe a few Jack Snipe find cover, and occasionally a Hen Harrier may be seen. Bitterns and Bearded Tits are recorded rather irregularly.

In early spring a few Rock Pipits of the Scandinavian race occur. Later, passage brings Garganey and possibly Marsh Harrier and terns, including Black.

Breeding birds include Great Crested Grebe, Pochard, Shoveler, and Gadwall. In the waterside vegetation are Reed and Sedge Warblers and there are Corn Buntings in the fields. Sparrowhawk, Great Spotted Woodpecker, and Treecreeper nest in the areas of trees. There are late-summer concentrations of Cormorants, gulls, and terns, most notably Little Gulls, which are generally present early May to October and can peak at over 100. In mid-summer quite good numbers of Manx Shearwaters may be seen off the coast at Hornsea.

Red-necked, Black-necked, and Slavonian Grebes may occur in ones and twos in autumn and winter, but are irregular, as is Red-throated Diver. In autumn both Ferruginous Duck and Red-crested Pochard have turned up several times and a careful check through the ducks is worthwhile. Little Gulls continue to occur, often with migrant terns and, as in spring, Black Terns are regular. If water levels fall exposing some mud a variety of waders may be seen. There is a large roost of hirundines in the reedbeds, and these are hunted by Sparrowhawks and occasionally Hobby. There may be migrants in the surrounding woods, fields, and hedges, and sometimes these include scarcer species such as Wryneck or Red-backed Shrike.

Information

RSPB warden: 15 Burton Lane, Hornsea, Humberside HU18 1TN.
Recorder: Yorkshire.

Site No. 81 Flamborough Head and Bempton Cliffs (Humberside)

Flamborough Head provides the best seawatching on the east coast, and is rivalled in Britain only by St Ives. As a bonus, landbird migrants also occur in good numbers, and have included many rare and exciting species. The adjacent Bempton Cliffs support one of the largest seabird colonies in Britain; to see them visit May to mid-July. The cliffs are an RSPB reserve.

Habitat

Bempton Cliffs rise to 400 feet and extend for 4 miles to Flamborough Head. This is 250 feet high and projects over 6 miles into the North Sea. Along the top of the cliffs the network of hedges provides cover for migrants. Danes' Dyke, an ancient fortification, runs N – S at the base of the headland and at its S end, as at South Landing, there are more extensive areas of cover.

Leave Bridlington N on a minor road to Buckton and then turn E on the B1229 to Bempton, from where you take Cliff Lane to the reserve car park. Access to the cliffs is unrestricted, but they can be very dangerous, especially when wet. A footpath runs along the cliff top for the length of the reserve with several safe observation points. Bempton is wardened April – August.

**Access
(see map)**
OS Sheet No. 101
Bempton Cliffs

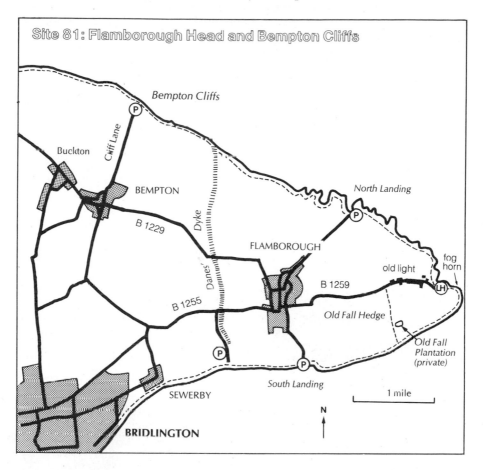

Site 81: Flamborough Head and Bempton Cliffs

Leave Bridlington on the B1255, past the S end of Danes' Dyke and on to the village; the Head can be reached from here along the B1259. There are car parks at the S end of Danes' Dyke, South Landing (reached on a minor road from Flamborough village), North Landing, and the lighthouse near the Head. A track leads from the lighthouse down to the foghorn; the best spots to seawatch from are the grassy ledges just below this. Seabirds can be seen at all times, but the best numbers and variety are likely when there is a strong NW to E wind coupled with poor visibility.

The hedges and fields at the Head should be checked for migrants. The large areas of cover at South Landing and the S end

**Flamborough
Head**

of Danes' Dyke are probably the best, but the southern cliff path and the public footpath running S from the road near the old light to the cliffs, passing Old Fall Hedge, are also interesting. Old Fall Plantation is private and any temptation to enter must be resisted. The areas of low scrub along the N cliff path from the lighthouse to North Landing may also be worth a look. Flamborough Head is private farmland, with access along the roads and public footpaths only.

Birds

In summer there are as many as 80,000 pairs of Kittiwakes between Bempton and Flamborough, as well as Guillemot, Razorbill, Puffin, Herring Gull, Fulmar, and a few Shags. 650 pairs of Gannets at Bempton form the only mainland gannetry in Britain. Rock Doves also breed on the cliffs, and Peregrines are sometimes seen around the colonies. Corn Buntings nest in the cliff-top fields.

There are always Gannets offshore at Flamborough, and Fulmars are common all year, with larger numbers in spring and early autumn. Occasionally 'Blue' Fulmars, dark birds from the northerly populations, are seen. Manx Shearwaters are also quite common March – November, and sometimes birds of the Mediterranean race (Balearic Shearwaters) occur. Of the less common shearwaters, Sooty are regular July – October, and can total several hundred on good days. Great (August – October) and Cory's (scattered records, April – October) are both much rarer. Little Shearwater, the rarest of all, has been seen June – October. Arctic is the commonest skua; peak passage is in the last 10 days of August and the first half of September. Great Skuas too can appear in large numbers, up to 100 in a good day, especially in September and sometimes October. Though Pomarine Skuas occur in spring, autumn is better for them. They usually occur in small numbers, only a handful even on a good day. Odd ones are present at the end of August, and are increasingly frequent in September. Occasionally, they can appear in large numbers, and in these 'invasions' most are seen October to early November. Long-tailed Skuas are very uncommon (perhaps 25 a year) and tend to be associated with the main Arctic Skua passage. Sabine's Gulls are also uncommon, about 15 a year, but sometimes as many as 100 Little Gulls can be seen in a day, especially in late autumn. Other species that appear on spring and autumn seawatches are divers (mainly Red-throated), ducks, waders, gulls, and terns, especially Common, Arctic, and Sandwich, but including Black.

During passage periods there are occasionally large falls of migrants on the Head. These follow the same pattern as at other east-coast sites. Wryneck, Redstart, Ring Ouzel, Whinchat, Wheatear, and Pied Flycatcher occur regularly, together with a variety of warblers. Icterine and Yellow-browed Warblers, Red-breasted Flycatcher, and Ortolan Bunting are annual in very small numbers, and in fact Flamborough is *the* locality on the east coast for Yellow-browed Warbler. Late spring and late autumn are generally best for good birds.

In winter, fishing boats going to and from Bridlington pass close to the Head and their attendant gulls should be checked for Glaucous and Iceland. All three divers are regular in winter, though Great Northern is scarce. A regular group of Black-throated Divers winter in Bridlington Bay and can sometimes be seen from the Head. Scaup and scoters are frequent offshore in small numbers. The odd Arctic or Great Skua may appear, and much less often a Pomarine Skua or even Sabine's Gull. There may be big movements of seabirds in severe weather. Peregrine can appear anywhere in the area.

Yellow-browed Warblers

N of Scarborough on the A165, Scalby Mills is interesting in winter and early spring. A good walk is S along the sea front; if you have left your car at Scalby Mills, there are regular buses back from Scarborough. There are Purple Sandpipers on the rocks in North Bay, which is good for divers (usually Red-throated but sometimes Great Northern, especially in early spring). Often one or two wintering Little, Mediterranean, Iceland, or Glaucous Gulls may be seen. The beach and sewage outfall are always worth a careful look, not only for gulls, but also for auks, including Little Auk. In March and April Rock Pipits of the Scandinavian race are regularly seen along the stream on the beach. The concentrations of wintering gulls in Scarborough harbour are worth a careful check and during passage periods Scarborough Castle should be investigated for passerines. Situated on a tiny peninsula, the slopes have areas of bushes. At the crossroads of Westborough and Northway outside the railway station, go straight across on to Northway and take Victoria Road, the first on the right. This eventually runs into Castle Road which takes you to a small car park. Walk through into the grounds of the castle; there are footpaths which explore most of the interesting areas.

Other Sites in the Area

81.1 Scarborough and Scalby Mills

This lies between Filey and Scarborough and is a good place to look for Common Scoter, Eider, and sometimes Velvet Scoter or Long-tailed Duck in winter. A footpath runs the length of the Bay, and access to the coast is along footpaths off the A165 at three points: Cayton Cliff, High Killerby, and Redcliffe Farm, respectively 2½, 3½, and 4½ miles S of Scarborough station.

81.2 Cayton Bay

81.3 Filey Brigg

This is a good seawatching point, though it cannot compare with Flamborough. Together with Filey Bay it is worth a look in winter for the scarcer gulls, Little Auk, and regular Purple Sandpipers. At the roundabout on the A1039 in Filey follow the sign to the Church Cliff Country Park and park (fee). From the car park a footpath leads to the sailing club, from where you can check the gulls resting on the beach and in the N part of Filey Bay. For access to the Brigg, walk N from the car park along the top of the cliff and follow the path around until it leads down to the base of the Brigg. There is a seawatching hide here and this is the best place to seawatch from.

Seabird passage involves essentially the same species as at Flamborough. Red-throated Divers are regular in winter, and there are sometimes Great Northerns in early spring, as well as small numbers of Eider, Common Scoter, and maybe Long-tailed Duck. In late autumn and winter Grey Phalaropes and Little Auks may be seen sitting on the sea close inshore or flying low over the water. Both occur irregularly and in small numbers. Glaucous, Iceland, and Little Gulls are regular, and can be seen from the Brigg or sitting on the beach and around fishing boats in the harbour. There are sometimes wintering Snow Buntings around the car park. In autumn up to 30 Lapland Buntings occur in the cliff-top fields NW of the Brigg (which are used by other migrants); occasionally small numbers winter. The fields are viewable by following the Cleveland Way coastal footpath.

81.4 Bridlington

Bridlington harbour and beach are worth a look in winter. There are sometimes Glaucous and Iceland Gulls and there is a semi-resident Mediterranean Gull. Small numbers of Purple Sandpipers are usually present around the harbour, which can also be good for seaduck and Little Gulls in rough weather. Both North and South Bays also have good numbers of seaduck and grebes, especially Great Crested.

81.5 Fraisthorpe Sands
OS Sheet Nos. 101 and 107

To the S of Bridlington and N of Hornsea Mere, this section of coast with low cliffs is a good site for wintering Lapland Buntings. The best access is from Barmston, off the A165. Walk N from the car park at the cliffs and you will see some lagoons just behind the beach ½ mile in front of you. The first ploughed field on the left sometimes has Shore Larks, but even if present they can be difficult to find. The marshy areas around the lagoons themselves may hold Jack Snipe and, in irruption years, Bearded Tits. The sand and shingle area between the sea and pools is a good spot for Lapland and Snow Buntings, as are the fields around the pools; Laplands also use the fields further N. Check the bay for divers (there are often a few Black-throated along with the commoner Red-throats) and Common and sometimes Velvet Scoters. On passage the lagoons attract a variety of waders.

Alternative access to the N end of the Sands is from the A165 2 miles S of Bridlington. Opposite the turning to Carnaby there is public access to Wilsthorpe. Park near the cliff top and scan the bay. It is possible to walk S along the coastal footpath all the way to Barmston.

Information

RSPB Bempton, summer warden: c/o Bempton Post Office, Bempton, Bridlington, Humberside.
Recorder: Yorkshire.

Site No. 82 Teesside (Cleveland)

Although no one site is of outstanding interest, the complex of habitats on Teesside attracts a variety of ducks, gulls, and terns, and an astonishing number of rare waders have been found. On the coast any area of cover can attract migrants. Hartlepool Head is especially favoured, and it also provides a fine seawatching point. Winter, spring, and autumn are the best times to visit, and you should cover as much ground as possible rather than concentrate on one area that may be unproductive on that particular day. Cowpen (160 acres) and Coatham Marshes (134 acres) are both reserves of the Cleveland Nature Conservation Trust (CNCT).

Habitat

The mouth of the Tees is protected by two breakwaters, North and South Gares, as well as areas of dunes. Within these the estuary has been extensively reclaimed for industry. Despite this the remaining areas of Seal Sands have retained their attraction for wildfowl and waders, with internationally important populations of Shelduck, Knot, and Sanderling. Separated from the mudflats by slag reclamation banks are a number of areas of marsh and rough grazing and several small pools. Hartlepool's geographical position makes it first landfall for many migrants, and these frequent any cover that is available.

Access
OS Sheet No. 93 and 94

North of the River Tees (see map)

1. Hartlepool. The harbour is attractive to grebes, divers, seaduck, auks, and gulls, the last favouring the Fish Quay. North View Cemetery is good for passerine migrants, but the headland is better. The Teesmouth Bird Club runs a small observatory, based near the lighthouse. The tennis courts, bowling green, allotments, and back gardens should all be checked; many have public access or can be viewed from the outside, but if in doubt, ask before entering. Seawatching can also be good from the Head, especially in NW – E winds; NE is most productive but in spring SE may also be good. Turnstones and Purple Sandpipers winter on the rocks around the headland.
2. Seaton Carew. The sewage outfall attracts ducks, and the rubbish tip is also worth a look in winter. Sometimes there are Glaucous or Iceland Gulls, and occasionally Shore Larks. The churchyard holds passerine migrants, including annual Yellow-browed Warblers.
3. The most convenient route to North Gare is along the minor road which leaves the A178 1 mile S of Seaton Carew. Follow the road round to the base of the Gare; from here you can either walk onto the breakwater or along the seawall past the power station for 1 mile for views of Greatham Creek. North Gare is good for seaduck, Purple Sandpipers, and Snow Buntings in winter and for seabirds in autumn. A large tern roost on Seaton Snook attracts numbers of skuas.
4. Cowpen Marsh has areas of fresh and saltmarsh, and is a reserve of the CNCT. There is no access September – January, but for the rest of the year members of the CNCT, Teesmouth Bird Club, and RSPB may walk along Greatham Creek wall as far as the rubbish tip fence, preferably below the level of the

seawall. Access is from the car park on the A178, where a warden's hut is manned Monday – Friday, 09.00 – 17.00. From there you can also walk directly to the Gatenby hide overlooking the Creek. On the opposite side of the main road there is public access to the Tidal Pool and Seal Sands hides.

5. The three Saltholme Pools are visible from the road.

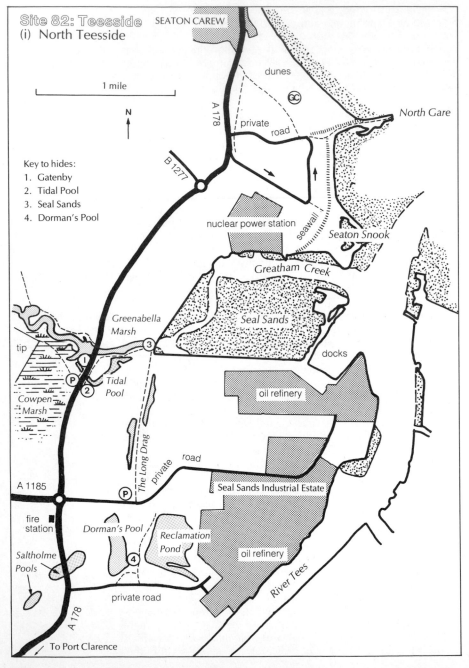

Site 82: Teesside
(i) North Teesside

SEATON CAREW

1 mile

N

Key to hides:
1. Gatenby
2. Tidal Pool
3. Seal Sands
4. Dorman's Pool

A 178

B 1277

dunes

private   road

North Gare

nuclear power station

Seaton Snook

seawall

Greatham Creek

Greenabella Marsh

Seal Sands

docks

tip

Tidal Pool

Cowpen Marsh

The Long Drag

private   road

oil refinery

A 1185

Seal Sands Industrial Estate

fire station

Dorman's Pool

Reclamation Pond

Saltholme Pools

oil refinery

private road

River Tees

A 178

To Port Clarence

6. The Long Drag is the W perimeter of the reclaimed area of Seal Sands, and the Long Drag Pools are accessible by walking N from the road to Seal Sands Industrial Estate off the A178. Park at the private sign c ½ mile from the main road and proceed on foot; access is by permit from Philips Petroleum. It is possible to continue along the Long Drag to Greatham Creek for views of Seal Sands.

7. Dorman's Pool is a shallow flash, probably the best wader pool on North Teesside. The Reclamation Pond is an embanked lagoon which also sometimes attracts interesting waders. Both pools are accessible along a private road E off the A178 near Saltholme Pools. Access is by permit, issued on behalf of ICI by the Teesmouth Bird Club (s.a.e. please); the Club also supplies a key for the Dorman's Pool hide.

In winter there are sometimes Ruff as well as Golden Plover and raptors on and around these pools. Seal Sands has waders and duck, including hundreds of Goldeneye and often Scaup and Long-tailed Duck on the creeks. During passage periods migrant waders frequent the pools.

1. At South Gare a few bushes provide cover for migrants and there is a marshy area, the Lagoon. To the SW, Bran Sands and its system of creeks hold waders. In winter divers, seaduck, waders, raptors, and Snow Buntings can be seen on and around the breakwater, while on passage there are sometimes shearwaters and almost always skuas offshore, waders on the beach and pools, and passerine migrants. Access to South Gare is from Redcar: along Coatham Sands, or via a private road, a NW continuation of Tod Point Road. **South of the River Tees (see map)**

2. Coatham Marsh, off the A1085 immediately W of Redcar, has several pools and c 50 acres of fresh marsh. In winter it attracts wildfowl, raptors, Jack Snipe, and Ruff. On passage, Garganey, waders, terns, and passerine migrants may be found. A reserve of the CNCT, access is by permit only, available to non-members at £1 per year. There are two hides. The marsh can be seen from the outside at the reserve car park on Tod Point Road, from the A1085 near the fire station, and from the footpath along the E boundary.

3. Locke Park lies just E of Coatham Marsh. Its many mature trees and bushes attract passerine migrants. Yellow-browed Warbler is annual. Access is off Locke Road and Corporation Road (A1085).

4. There are several spots where it is possible to park on the seafront between Redcar and Marske. From N to S (with specialities indicated) they are: Majuba Road car park (divers); opposite the Coatham Hotel; town-centre beach, especially if fishing boats are gutting (rarer gulls); opposite the Zetland Hotel (waders, especially on a middle tide; Goldeneye at the sewage outfall; seawatching); the large car park on the Stray, just S of Redcar (divers, seawatching); the pull-off half way to Marske; the 'Fox Coverts' car park (divers); the Marske sewer, S of Cliff House.

5. The large coastal field between Redcar and Marske has flocks of wintering Lapwing and Golden Plover and small numbers of Ruff. It is the best site in NE England for wintering Lapland Bunting, up to 100 having been recorded. There are also often

a few Snow Buntings here or on the beach, sometimes with a handful of Shore Larks (which may also frequent the short turf on the Stray).

Birds

In winter Red-throated is the common diver offshore; Black-throated and Great Northern are both quite scarce, as is Red-necked Grebe. On the estuary and marshes small numbers of Bewick's and Whooper Swans are quite often seen, and wildfowl include Pintail and Shoveler. Diving duck congregate off the mouth of Greatham Creek, while on the sea Common Scoter, Eider, and Red-breasted Merganser are regular, the first two in good numbers. Scaup, Velvet Scoter, and Long-tailed Duck are less numerous and more erratic and there is a scattering of Cormorants, Guillemots, and Razorbills. Raptors include Merlin and Short-eared Owl, and often Peregrine as well. The estuary holds the commoner waders, with Sanderling on the beaches and Purple Sandpipers along all the rockier coasts. Around the marshy pools there may be Water Rails and Jack Snipe, as well as Ruff. Gulls are abundant and often include Kittiwake, sometimes Glaucous and more rarely Iceland and Mediterranean. South Gare has recently had a regular wintering Mediterranean Gull. Hooded Crows are frequent, as are quite large numbers of Snow Buntings on the beaches and dunes, and there are sometimes Lapland Buntings and Shore Larks.

Passage periods are the most exciting. Manx and Sooty Shearwaters are regular offshore in late summer and autumn (especially if the wind has a N component), together with Gannets, Fulmars, and Kittiwakes. There are gatherings of up to 2,000 terns off the estuary mouth, mostly Sandwich and Common but sometimes also Black or even Roseate, and these attract skuas — Arctic and Great are both quite frequent, but Pomarine are uncommon and Long-tailed rare. Little Auks are occasionally seen in late autumn, sometimes in good numbers. Black Terns and Little Gulls are regular, both on the sea and marshland pools, where Garganey are also regular. The real specialities are waders: all the commoner species are seen, and Temminck's Stint, White-rumped and Pectoral Sandpipers, and Wilson's Phalarope are nearly annual. Among landbird migrants, the usual chats, warblers, and flycatchers are sometimes joined in autumn by Wryneck, Black Redstart, Barred Warbler, or Red-backed Shrike, and a handful of Icterine and Yellow-browed Warblers are seen each year.

Breeding species include numbers of duck in the marshes, and some of Britain's most northerly Little Ringed Plovers.

Other Sites in the Area
82.1 Scaling Dam Reservoir
OS Sheet No. 94

This is on the A171 W of Whitby, and views are possible from the road as well as the public hide. There is a car park at the E end of the reservoir. Red Grouse are resident on the adjacent moors, and the area is good for raptors, especially in winter. Hen Harrier, Peregrine, and Short-eared Owl are regular. Wintering wildfowl include Goldeneye and Goosander, and the gull roost may have Glaucous. In spring and summer, Tree Pipit, Whinchat, Wheatear, and Redpoll occur, and the water attracts migrant waders and duck.

Information

Cleveland Nature Conservation Trust: Old Town Hall, Mandale Rd, Thornaby, Stockton on Tees TS17 6AW.

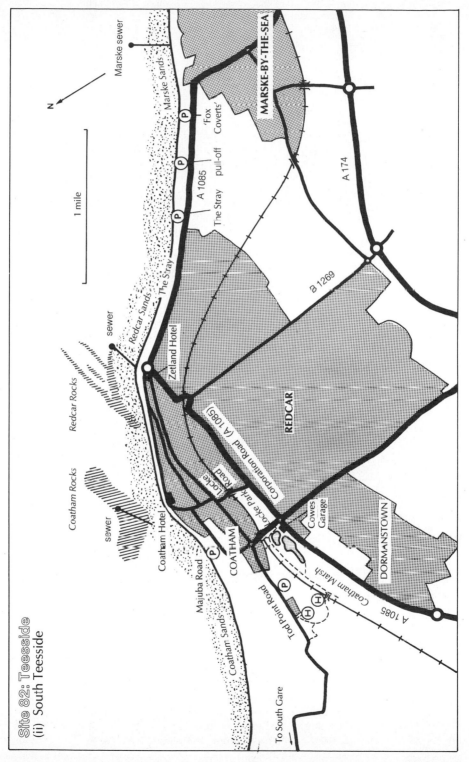

Site 82: Teesside
(ii) South Teesside

Marske sewer

N

1 mile

MARSKE-BY-THE-SEA

Marske Sands

'Fox Coverts'

A 1085   pull-off

The Stray

A 174

The Stray

Redcar Sands

B 1269

Sewer

Zetland Hotel

REDCAR

Redcar Rocks

Corporation Road (A 1085)

Coatham Rocks

Locke Road

Locke Park

sewer

Coatham Hotel

Cowes Garage

DORMANSTOWN

Majuba Road

COATHAM

Coatham Marsh

A 1085

Coatham Sands

Tod Point Road

To South Gare

Teesmouth Bird Club: Mrs Rita Dunnett, 43 Hemlington Rd, Stainton, Middlesborough, Cleveland TS8 9AG.
Recorder: Cleveland.

Site No. 83 The Farne Islands (Northumberland)

Off the coast at Bamburgh the Farnes have excellent seabird colonies, and the short boat trip is guaranteed to add to the excitement. The best time to visit is May – June. The islands belong to the National Trust.

Habitat

These small rocky islands, 28 in all, lie 1½ miles or more offshore. Most are rocky stacks, but Inner Farne and Staple Island are flatter, providing habitat for nesting terns.

Access
OS Sheet No. 75

Weather permitting, boats run daily from Seahouses harbour, tickets available from the boatmen. It is best to book seats in advance, especially during holiday periods. The National Trust's information centre in Seahouses can advise. Seahouses is reached from the A1 via the B1341/B1342 to Bamburgh, turning S on the B1340 to the harbour. From 15 May to 15 July Staple Island is open 10.30 – 13.30, and Inner Farne (probably the best island) 13.30 – 17.00. Outside this period, from Good Friday to the end of September, both islands are open 10.00 – 18.00. An entrance fee of £2.40 in the breeding season and £1.50 during the rest of the year is payable on landing.

Birds

14 species of seabirds breed. Puffins are the most numerous, with about 15,000 pairs, and Kittiwakes, Lesser Black-backed and Herring Gulls, and Sandwich and Arctic Terns also number thousands. There are several hundred pairs of Cormorants, Shags, Fulmars, and Common Terns, but just a handful of Roseate Terns. The terns breed on Inner Farne and Brownsman. Other breeding birds include 1,000 – 1,500 Eider, Ringed Plover, Oystercatcher, and Rock Pipit. Passage brings divers, shearwaters, waders, and skuas to this coast, as detailed under Lindisfarne – Seahouses.

Information

NT warden: 8 St Aidan's, Seahouses, Northumberland NE68 7SR.
National Trust information centre: 16 Main St, Seahouses. Tel. 0665–720424.
Recorder: Northumberland.

Site No. 84 Lindisfarne – Seahouses (Northumberland)

Lindisfarne, on the Northumberland coast, is an excellent area for birdwatching during winter and the passage periods, especially for divers, grebes, wildfowl, and waders. The area supports internationally important populations of Knot, Dunlin, and

Bar-tailed Godwit. On passage a wide variety of passerines has been recorded. Lindisfarne National Nature Reserve covers 8,101 acres, and includes Budle Bay. The adjacent coast from Bamburgh to Seahouses has essentially the same population of divers, grebes, and seaduck as Lindisfarne, and also attracts passage migrants.

Habitat

The intertidal flats are sheltered from the sea by the dune systems of Goswick Sands, Holy Island, and Ross Links. Budle Bay is another sheltered tidal basin, while the 4-mile stretch of coast from Bamburgh to Seahouses has several rocky sections.

Access (see map)
OS Sheet No. 75

In the NNR, permits are not required for access to the shore or causeway, but remember that farmland is private. The tidal flats (the area for swans, Brent Geese, and waders) can be seen from the following points:
1. From the A1 at West Mains, take the minor road to Beal. Continue to the shore and causeway, from the base of which a public footpath runs along the shore.
2. The causeway to Holy Island.
3. The Snook on Holy Island.
4. Turn off the A1 on a minor road to Fenham and the shore, opposite the B6353 turning to Fenwick.
5. A minor road off the A1 S of Buckton leads to Fenham-le-Moor and on to Lowmoor Point.
6. From the minor road to Ross a footpath runs N to Heather Law, giving views of the shore, and a track runs N from Elwick to the shore.

Ross Links

A footpath runs E from Ross, over Ross Links to Ross Back Sands, with access N and S along the shore to view Skate Road for divers, grebes, seaduck, Sanderling, Snow Bunting, and occasionally Shore Lark.

Budle Bay

From Budle a footpath runs to Heather Cottages and on to the golf course, past Budle Point, a good spot to view the bay and look out to sea. The path then continues to meet a minor road to Bamburgh. The bay is very good for waders and ducks, especially if the flats are disturbed by shooting.

Bamburgh – Seahouses

The B1340 parallels the coast from Bamburgh to Seahouses, with open access to the foreshore. At Bamburgh you can drive up the minor road to the lighthouse, using the wall as shelter to view the sea. This is an excellent area for divers, grebes, and seaduck. Seahouses harbour attracts small numbers of gulls, including Glaucous and occasionally Iceland. The public park/bowling green opposite the N pier should be checked for passerine migrants in season. The Farne Islands are reached by boat from Seahouses.

Holy Island

It is impossible to cross to Holy Island between 2 hrs before and 3½ hrs after high water. Tide tables are displayed on the causeway. The following areas are worthwhile.
1. At the Snook there is a scattering of bushes and clumps of willows which attract migrants.
2. Off Sandon Bay and North Shore look for Red-breasted

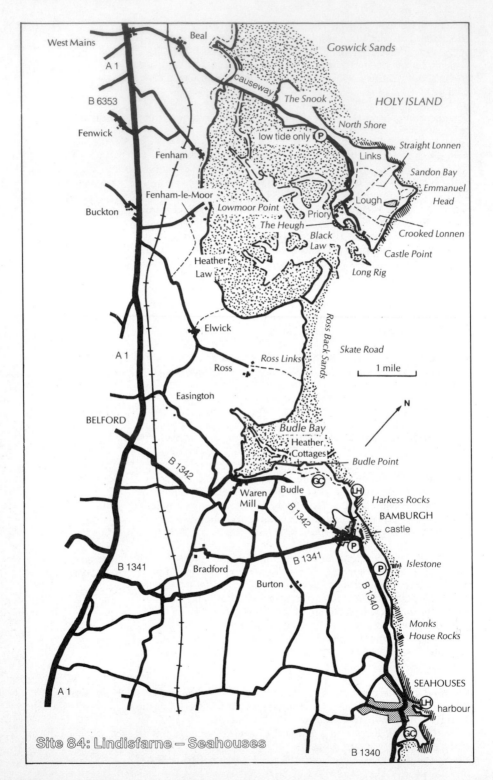

West Mains

A 1

B 6353

Fenwick

Fenham

Fenham-le-Moor

Buckton

Beal

causeway

Goswick Sands

The Snook

HOLY ISLAND

North Shore

low tide only

P

Links

Straight Lonnen

Sandon Bay

Emmanuel Head

Lowmoor Point

Priory

The Heugh

Lough

Black Law

Heather Law

Crooked Lonnen

Castle Point

Long Rig

Elwick

Ross Links

Ross Back Sands

Skate Road

1 mile

N

Ross

Easington

BELFORD

B 1342

Budle Bay

Heather Cottages

Budle Point

Waren Mill

Budle

B 1342

Harkess Rocks

BAMBURGH

castle

B 1341

Bradford

Burton

B 1341

P

P

Islestone

B 1340

Monks House Rocks

A 1

SEAHOUSES

harbour

B 1340

Site 84: Lindisfarne – Seahouses

244

Merganser and Shag, and Sanderling on the beach.
3. The Links and dunes area attract migrants.
4. The Lough attracts 'fresh' waders and duck.
5. You can seawatch from Castle Point or Emmanuel Head, but they are probably no better than Bamburgh or Seahouses.
6. The harbour and the Heugh are worth checking for divers and grebes, especially on a rising tide. From here you can also view Long Rig and Black Law for roosting waders and gulls. The harbour also attracts gulls and the freshwater pools in the nearby fields attract passage waders.
7. The cover on the farms and gardens around the Priory and village, as well as along the Straight and Crooked Lonnens, attracts migrants. These tend to drift off the island during the day, so that in suitable weather an early morning visit is best.

Birds

In winter Red-throated Diver and Slavonian Grebe are quite common offshore; Black-throated is the second commonest diver but distinctly scarce. Red-necked Grebes are regular, but uncommon, and on the sea there are also Cormorant, Shag, and many Eider and Common Scoter, with smaller numbers of Long-tailed Duck and Red-breasted Merganser and a few Goldeneye, Velvet Scoter, and Scaup. Up to 4,000 Greylag Geese occur, mainly in the fields between Budle Bay and Ross, and are sometimes joined by a few Pink-footed or Bean Geese. The flats hold the largest flock of wintering pale-bellied Brent Geese in Britain. They belong to the declining Svalbard and Franz Josef Land populations, which number only 2,500 – 3,000. These mainly winter in Denmark but, depending on weather, the numbers at Lindisfarne range from a few hundred to 1,800. Up to 440 Whooper Swans use the fields and flats and are sometimes joined by a few Bewick's. Wigeon have recently peaked at 40,000, and Shelduck and Teal are also common, with a few Pintail and Pochard. Peregrine, Merlin, and Short-eared Owl are regular, and there are sometimes Hen Harriers. Of the waders, Dunlin are by far the commonest, and Knot are also abundant together with the usual estuarine species, but Sanderling and Purple Sandpiper occur in relatively small numbers. There are occasionally wintering Spotted Redshanks or Greenshanks. The odd Glaucous Gull puts in an appearance, and sometimes Iceland is seen. Snow Buntings can be quite common, especially on Ross Links. Shore Larks, Twite, and Lapland Bunting are only occasional.

Purple Sandpipers

Seawatching can be good during passage periods. Gannet and Manx and sometimes Sooty Shearwaters are noted offshore in autumn, together with six species of tern, though Roseate and Little are quite rare. Arctic Skuas are almost constantly present in the autumn, and there are sometimes Great too, but Pomarine are unusual. There are waders on the flats, but it is worth checking any area of freshwater as well. Black-tailed Godwit, Spotted Redshank, and Wood Sandpiper occur at both seasons, but Little Stint and Curlew Sandpiper almost exclusively in autumn. There are occasionally large falls of migrants in autumn, including arrivals of large numbers of thrushes, and sometimes Woodcock, Jack Snipe, and Long-eared Owl in late autumn. Wryneck, Shore Lark, Black Redstart, Bluethroat, Red-backed Shrike, and Ortolan and Lapland Buntings may occur in both spring and autumn, but all are scarce and a visitor would be lucky to see any of these. The equally elusive Barred and Yellow-browed Warblers, Red-breasted Flycatcher, and Great Grey Shrike are almost entirely confined to the autumn period, as are the sporadic appearances of Waxwings.

Breeding birds include small numbers of Fulmar, Eider, Shelduck, Ringed Plover, and Oystercatcher, as well as Common, Arctic, and Little Terns. Seabirds from the Farnes can be seen moving up and down the coast, as well as Gannets and Manx Shearwaters from further afield.

Information

NCC Reserve Office: Tel. 06683–386.
Reference: *Lindisfarne's Birds* by Ian Kerr (1984). Tyneside Bird Club.
Recorder: Northumberland.

SCOTLAND

Site No. 85 St Abb's Head (Borders)

12 miles north of Berwick-upon-Tweed, St Abb's has breeding seabirds, is a good seawatching station, and, during passage periods, numbers of migrants are recorded. The best time for breeding seabirds is May to mid-July, and for migrants April to early June and mid-August to October. The coast from St Abbs village to Pettico Wick is a National Nature Reserve, covering 192 acres, owned by the National Trust for Scotland and managed in co-operation with the Scottish Wildlife Trust.

Habitat

The cliffs rise to 300 feet, and immediately behind the Head is a man-made pool, Mire Loch, surrounded by bushes and trees that are attractive to migrants.

Access
(see map)
OS Sheet No. 67

From Coldingham take the B6438 to St Abb's Head Nature Reserve and park on the right at Northfield Farm. From here take the footpath E for 300 yards to the track to the lighthouse and Head. This skirts the cliff and has seabirds en route. There is a very small car park (fee) at the Head itself. Seawatch from the lighthouse, and during passage periods explore the cover around the loch.

Birds

50,000 breeding seabirds include Fulmars, Shags, Kittiwakes, Herring Gulls, Guillemots, Razorbills, and a few Puffins. Other breeders are Rock Pipit and Wheatear, while Turnstone and Purple Sandpiper haunt the rocks for much of the year. Offshore there are always Gannets, but seawatching is most productive in autumn, when Manx and sometimes Sooty Shearwaters, Arctic, a few Great, and occasionally Pomarine Skuas, and terns can be seen. In late autumn and winter Little Auks occasionally occur, but Red-throated Divers are regular, with the odd Great Northern and Black-throated and small numbers of Common Scoter and Eider, the last especially in Starney Bay and Pettico Wick.

As well as the commoner chats, flycatchers, and warblers, scarce migrants are recorded each year on passage. Any wind from the E quarter is good, but SE is best, especially if coupled with rain or drizzle. Wryneck and Red-backed Shrike are annual in spring, and Barred and Yellow-browed Warblers and Red-breasted Flycatcher in autumn.

Information

Warden: Ranger's Cottage, Northfield, St Abbs, Berwickshire TD14 5QF. Tel. 08907–71443.
Recorder: Borders.

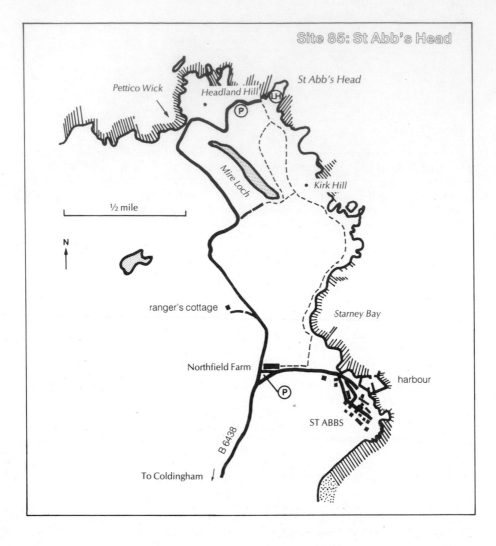

Site 85: St Abb's Head

Pettico Wick

Headland Hill

St Abb's Head

LH

P

Mire Loch

Kirk Hill

½ mile

N

ranger's cottage

Starney Bay

Northfield Farm

harbour

P

B 6438

ST ABBS

To Coldingham

Site No. 86 Gosford, Aberlady, and Gullane Bays (East Lothian)

This section of the Firth of Forth attracts a wide variety of species and is worth a visit the whole year round. In winter seaduck, divers, and grebes are prominent, and a speciality is Red-necked Grebe, which may appear as early as July. Aberlady Bay is a reserve of the East Lothian District Council, covering 1,439 acres.

Habitat   Aberlady and Gosford Bays have an extensive foreshore, with rocky areas at Port Seton and Gullane Point, but Gullane Bay itself has a relatively narrow foreshore. The beach is backed by areas of dunes and patches of sea buckthorn, most extensive in Gullane Bay.

1. Gosford Bay can be viewed from the road. The B1348 runs E from Port Seton, joining the A198 just before Ferny Ness, and this continues along the shore of the bay. The best spot is Ferny Ness, where you can park.
2. A footpath accessible from the A198 follows the shoreline from Gosford Bay to Aberlady along the SW shore of Aberlady Bay. At low tide it is best to watch Aberlady Bay from the road or this footpath. The key for the hide can be obtained from the warden by prior arrangement.
3. On a rising tide the E shore of Aberlady Bay is best. Leave Aberlady on the A198 and after ½ mile there is a small car park (free permits to park from the Department of Leisure). A footbridge over the stream leads to a signposted footpath to Gullane Point, and there is no general access away from this.
4. Gullane Point itself is an excellent seawatching spot. Continue from there along the shore of Gullane Bay to the car park, which is also accessible N off the A198 through Gullane. The bay often has an evening roost of up to 50 Red-throated Divers.

Access
(see map)
OS Sheet No. 66

Birds

Red-necked and Slavonian Grebe, as well as Red-throated Diver occur offshore and there can be as many as 65 Slavonians along this stretch of coast. Great Northern and Black-throated Divers are however infrequent. A small flock of Whooper Swans winters, and up to 12,500 Pink-footed Geese, especially in early winter. The swans and geese feed inland, usually on the fields around Fenton Barns and Drem, and roost in Aberlady Bay. Seaduck occur mainly in Gullane and Gosford Bays, with smaller numbers in Aberlady Bay. Eider and Common Scoter are both present in large numbers, with up to 250 Velvet Scoter, 200 Long-tailed Duck, and a few Goldeneye and Red-breasted Merganser. Waders include Grey Plover and Purple Sandpiper, and sometimes Ruff in the Port Seton and Aberlady areas. There is often a Glaucous Gull around Port Seton – Ferny Ness, and Redwings, Fieldfares, and Blackcaps in the sea buckthorn.

There is a good variety of waders on passage. Little Stint, Curlew Sandpiper, Sanderling, Black-tailed Godwit, and Green Sandpiper occur annually, with the best variety in autumn.

Red-necked Grebes

249

Breeding birds include 200 pairs of Eider, and numbers of non-breeding Eider and Common and Velvet Scoter are also present. Late summer and autumn is the peak period for Red-necked Grebe, with up to 40 birds present. The best spot is Ferny Ness. Arctic Skuas regularly occur offshore in late summer, and irregularly, Great and Pomarine.

Other Sites in the Area
86.1 Leith – Musselburgh

The sea between Musselburgh and Leith on the outskirts of Edinburgh formerly attracted vast numbers of seaduck. Though these no longer occur, there are still divers, grebes, and a variety of duck. The ash lagoons E of the mouth of the River Esk at Musselburgh are being infilled and landscaped, and a wader scrape is to be built. The sea can be viewed from their embankments, or from the coast road between here and Leith, with roadside parking at Musselburgh on the W side of the

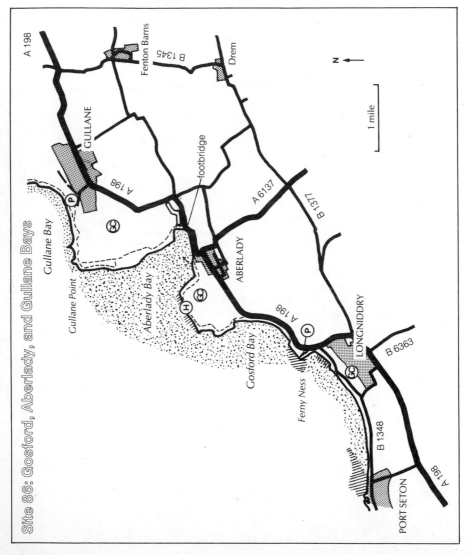

Site 86: Gosford, Aberlady, and Gullane Bays

lagoons (W and N off the A1 past the W perimeter of the racecourse).

In winter there are small numbers of Red-throated Divers and Slavonian Grebes, as well as several hundred Great Crested Grebes. Scaup peaked at 30,000 – 40,000 in 1968–69, but now rarely reach 100. Other seaduck include Red-breasted Merganser, Long-tailed Duck (100–200), Eider, Common Scoter, Goldeneye, and usually a few Velvet Scoter. Waders occur along the shore, and sometimes Snow Buntings; much less frequently, Lapland Buntings are also present. Throughout the year, waders, gulls, and terns roost on the lagoons at high tide.

86.2 The Bass Rock
OS Sheet No. 67

Probably the most accessible large gannetry in Britain, the Bass Rock is only 3 miles off North Berwick. During the breeding season there are regular boat trips around the island from North Berwick — contact the boatman for details. Over 21,000 pairs of Gannet are joined by Shag, Guillemot, Razorbill, a few Puffins, and Kittiwakes.

Information

Aberlady, warden: 1–3 Craigielaw Cottages, Longniddry, East Lothian EH32 0PY. Tel. 08757–588.
Car park permits: Dept of Leisure, Recreation and Tourism, Brunton Hall, Musselburgh EH21 6AF.
Bass Rock boatman: Mr Fred Marr. Tel. 0620–2838.
Recorder: East Lothian.

Site No. 87 Loch Leven (Tayside)

E of Kinross, Loch Leven attracts large numbers of wintering wildfowl, especially Pink-footed Geese. The loch is a National Nature Reserve covering 3,946 acres and the RSPB have a reserve at Vane Farm covering 458 acres. The best time for geese is October–March.

Habitat

The loch covers c 3,900 acres and has seven islands, which hold large numbers of breeding duck. Surrounded by farmland, the fields provide feeding areas for the thousands of geese which roost on the loch. At Vane Farm there are areas of marsh and a scrape on the shore, while farmland, birch woods, and heather moor cloak the slopes of the Vane, a 824-foot high hill.

Access (see map)
OS Sheet No. 58

1. Access to the shore is permitted at three places: Kirkgate Park, Burleigh Sands, and Findatie. All are well signposted. Wildfowl however are best seen at Vane Farm.
2. Vane Farm. Leave the M90 at junction 5 and take the B9097 Glenrothes road for 2 miles to the RSPB car park and nature centre. The reserve is open all year, and access is restricted to the car park, hide, and nature trail, which stretches from the loch to the top of the Vane. There is a charge of 60p for non-members. The nature centre is open daily 10.00–17.00, except January – March, when opening is limited to Saturday and Sunday, 10.00–16.00.

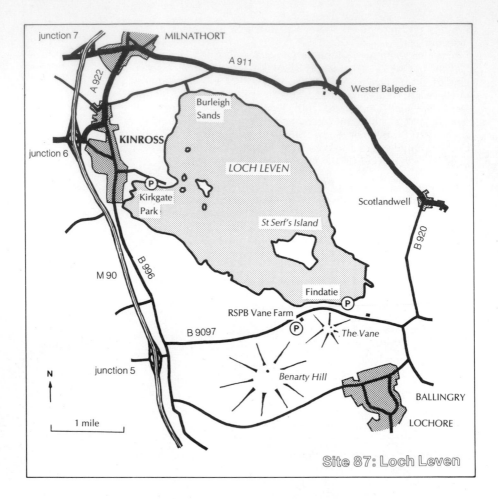

junction 7   MILNATHORT

A 911

Wester Balgedie

A 922

Burleigh
Sands

KINROSS

junction 6

LOCH LEVEN

Scotlandwell

P

Kirkgate
Park

St Serf's Island

B 920

M 90

B 996

Findatie

P

RSPB Vane Farm

P   The Vane

B 9097

N

junction 5

Benarty Hill

BALLINGRY

1 mile

LOCHORE

Site 87: Loch Leven

Birds

The numbers of Pink-footed Geese peak in late autumn and March, when up to 14,000 have been counted. Lower numbers winter. They are joined by hundreds, sometimes thousands, of Greylag Geese and several hundred Whooper Swans, but the latter are erratic in their appearances. There are often ten species of duck wintering on the loch, including Goosander, Goldeneye, Wigeon, Shoveler, Gadwall, and occasionally Pintail. Raptors may include Sparrowhawk and Peregrine, and there are often Siskins and Redpolls in the areas of birch.

On passage the loch shore at Vane Farm attracts small numbers of waders, sometimes including Black-tailed Godwit and Green and Wood Sandpipers.

1,000 pairs of duck nest on St Serf's Island. Mostly Mallard and Tufted Duck, they include Shelduck, Gadwall, Wigeon, and Shoveler. There are a few pairs of Common Tern as well as the usual breeding waders. The surrounding moorland has Curlew and Red Grouse, with Redpoll and Tree Pipit in the woods. An unusual sight is the handful of Fulmars that breed on nearby crags — 8 miles from the sea.

Well W of Loch Leven, Braco lies on the A822 NE of Dunblane. The area is excellent for Black Grouse, and large numbers are sometimes seen from the road, especially in hard weather. Leave Braco SW towards Dunblane on the B8033. The best area is after c 2 miles, and the roadside moorland and fields should be checked, preferably in early morning.

NCC warden: 'Benarty', Vane, Kinross, Tayside.
RSPB warden: Vane Farm Nature Centre, Kinross KY13 7LX. Tel. 0577–62355.
Recorder: Fife.

Other Sites in the Area
87.1 Braco
OS Sheet No. 57

Information

Site No. 88 Largo Bay and Kilconquhar Loch (Fife)

Largo Bay attracts large numbers of wintering seaduck, and other interesting species include a variety of divers and grebes. The nearby Kilconquhar Loch is famous for concentrations of Little Gulls in July – August, as well as holding good numbers of wintering and breeding wildfowl.

The only notable habitat of Largo Bay is the sea. Kilconquhar Loch covers c 135 acres. Shallow and fertile, it is largely surrounded by trees and, to the N, back gardens.

Habitat

1. Leven. Seaduck are usually best seen from here. Park in the car park on the NE side of the River Leven, just over the river from Methil Power Station, and look out over the seawall. Seaduck may also be seen at Lower Largo.
2. Ruddons Point and Shell Bay. Leave the A917 near Kilconquhar Loch and drive through Earlsferry caravan site to the point, from where you can view more seaduck. From here walk along the E shore of Shell Bay for waders.
3. Kilconquhar Loch. Leave the A917 N of Elie on the B941 to Kilconquhar. Park in the village and go to the churchyard, from where the loch can be seen.
4. Elie. In winter there are occasionally Glaucous Gulls in Elie harbour. Elie Ness, a small promontory, is the best place for seawatching around the bay. Little Gulls sometimes occur on passage, as well as divers, Shags, auks, and terns. There is direct access from the E side of Elie to the coastguard's lookout and lighthouse.

Access (see map)
OS Sheet No. 59

On the sea, wintering Red-throated Divers are often joined by small numbers of Black-throated, and there are usually also Great Crested and Slavonian Grebes, though Red-necked are only occasional. There are lots of Common Scoter, Scaup, Eider, and Goldeneye, together with several hundred Long-tailed Duck and some Velvet Scoter. On the beaches and rocks there are usually Grey Plover and Purple Sandpiper, and Glaucous Gull can occasionally be seen. January – March often produces records of Little Gull. Kilconquhar Loch holds wintering duck, though being shallow, it freezes quite quickly in hard weather. Notable are

Birds

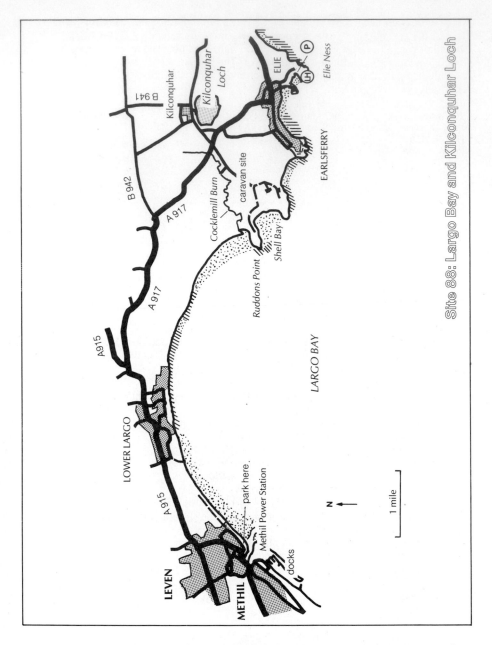

Site 88: Largo Bay and Kilconquhar Loch

large numbers of Goldeneye, immatures often staying into late spring and summer. Other species include small numbers of Gadwall and Shoveler. Greylag Geese roost on the loch, and there are occasionally also parties of Barnacle Geese.

On passage at sea there are numbers of Common, Arctic, and Sandwich Terns, and often a few Roseates, which can be seen on the beach just about anywhere in the bay. Small numbers of Eider and scoter remain all summer. The numbers of Little Gulls that visit Kilconquhar Loch on passage vary greatly. Only a few occur in some years, and over 500 at once in others. The biggest numbers generally turn up when evening coincides with a high tide. Passage Little Gulls are also sometimes seen in the bay.

Breeding birds on the loch include Great Crested and Little Grebes and numbers of duck, including Gadwall and Shoveler.

Recorder: Fife.

Information

Site No. 89 Isle of May (Fife)

The Isle of May lies at the entrance to the Firth of Forth. It has colonies of seabirds, but the main attraction lies with migrants. The May rose to fame through the work of Evelyn Baxter and Leonora Rintoul from 1907 to 1933, and the Bird Observatory was established in 1934. It is now a National Nature Reserve, and the best time to visit is in late spring and autumn.

The island covers just 141 acres and there is little vegetation; most of the cover is concentrated in the observatory garden. The coastline varies from low on the E shore to cliffs topping 180 feet on the W.

Habitat

During April – October basic self-catering accommodation is available for up to six people at the observatory at £2 per night. The usual period for a visit is a week. The crossing from Anstruther on the Fife coast takes c 1 hr, and can be organised when booking. The return fare is £8, and delays are possible in bad weather. Day trips can also be arranged from Anstruther.

Access
OS Sheet No. 59

Small movements of diurnal migrants are seen in both spring and autumn, but potentially more interesting are the falls of night migrants in E or SE winds during poor weather (see p. 14). These often include some of the scarcer species: Wryneck, Bluethroat, Icterine, Barred and Yellow-browed Warblers, Red-breasted Flycatcher, Great Grey and Red-backed Shrikes, Scarlet Rosefinch, and Lapland and Ortolan Buntings are all almost annual, mainly in autumn, and Yellow-breasted Bunting is also reasonably regular. There are also large falls of birds destined to winter in Britain and Ireland, especially thrushes. These can be spectacular, for example 15,000 Goldcrests at once in October 1982. The May has an excellent list of rarities.

Birds

Seawatching can be interesting. Gannets are almost always present offshore, and divers, Manx and Sooty Shearwaters, ducks, Arctic and Great Skuas, and Common, Arctic, and Sandwich Terns are all regular. Few birds use the island in winter; most notable is a flock of several hundred Purple Sandpipers and Turnstones, and there are sometimes Black Guillemots or Little Auks offshore.

Breeding seabirds include Fulmar, Shag, Guillemot, Razorbill, Kittiwake, Herring and Lesser Black-backed Gulls, a few Common and Arctic Terns, and large numbers of Puffins, as well as Eider, Oystercatcher, Swallow, and Rock Pipit.

Information

Bookings Secretary: Mrs Rosemary Cowper, 9 Oxgangs Rd, Edinburgh EH10 7BG. Tel. 031–445 2489.
Day trips: Ian Gatherum, 27 Glenogil Gardens, Anstruther. Tel. 0333–310860.
References:
One Man's Island by Keith Brockie (1984).
The Isle of May: a Scottish Nature Reserve by W. J. Eggeling (1960, reprinted 1985).
Recorder: Observatory recorder.

Site No. 90 Fife Ness (Fife)

Fife Ness is the E tip of the Fife peninsula, which explains its attractiveness to migrants. Both on land and sea, interesting birds can be seen. The Ness is worth visiting during spring and autumn, but only in a NE, E, SE, or SW wind, being otherwise usually very quiet. 20 acres of the Kilminning coast and Fife Ness Muir are a reserve of the Scottish Wildlife Trust.

Habitat

As at any migration watch-point, anywhere that could shelter a bird is worth checking. Particularly good areas are Denburn Wood, the walled garden and large trees at Balcomie Castle, the small walled garden at Craighead Farm, the quarry below the golf club, and Fife Ness Muir, the last-mentioned being the best. Also below the golf club there is a small beach and pool, both of which attract waders. Inland of the Ness, Crail Airfield is worth a look for pipits, larks, thrushes, buntings etc.

**Access
(see map)**
OS Sheet No. 59

Please behave with the greatest consideration; in the past relations between locals and birders have been strained. Park *only* at Kilminning or the car park near the golf club. Around the golf course, keep to the road or coastal footpath. Always ask permission before entering private property, notably at Balcomie and Criaghead Farms. When inspecting areas of cover around habitations, respect peoples' privacy, especially in the early morning.

1. Leave Crail NE on the minor road to Balcomie Golf Course. Park at Kilminning (turn into the road for the go-karts, and follow the signs). From here you can walk the ½ mile to the coastguards (the best seawatching point), check-out the airfield, and walk back up the road and on to Balcomie Castle.
2. Alternatively, continue on to the golf club. Just before the entrance there is a car park (fee) on the left. Park and walk through the gate to the right of the road and then left down towards the sea. The quarry lies on the left below the club house; Fife Ness Muir is the gorse-patch on the hill to the right. Approach the latter along the edge of the golf course, not the fields.
3. Denburn Wood lies on the outskirts of Crail. There are a number of paths in the wood with free access from the road.

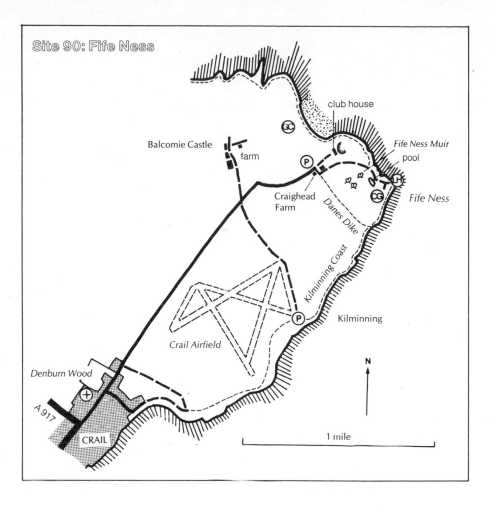

Site 90: Fife Ness

club house

Balcomie Castle

farm

Fife Ness Muir

pool

Craighead Farm

Fife Ness

Danes Dike

Kilminning Coast

Kilminning

Crail Airfield

N

Denburn Wood

A 917

CRAIL

1 mile

On passage, the usual chats, thrushes, warblers, and flycatchers **Birds**
are sometimes joined by scarce migrants. In spring, Wryneck and
Bluethroat have been recorded, and Black Redstart and Red-
backed Shrike are regular. Additional possibilities in autumn are
Icterine, Barred and Yellow-browed Warblers, Red-breasted
Flycatcher, and Great Grey Shrike. Occasionally Snow or even
Lapland Bunting join the regular Golden Plover and Lapwing on
the airfield in late autumn and winter.

Seawatching can be productive. Gannet and Shag are almost
always present offshore, but in spring and autumn E–NE winds are
best, though too strong a NE wind in spring may delay the passage
of terns — Common, Arctic, Sandwich, and sometimes Little.
Autumn brings Manx and (regularly) Sooty Shearwaters, Little
Gull, terns, and skuas — mostly Arctic, with some Great and a
small number of Pomarine. The small beach and pool attract
passage waders.

Red-breasted Flycatcher

In winter seawatching can produce all three divers, auks, and seaduck. There are Purple Sandpipers and Turnstones on the rocks and large numbers of Golden Plover on the airfield.

Summer is quieter, but large numbers of Eiders can still be seen, as well as some of the seabirds that breed locally — Gannets, auks, Kittiwakes, and terns. Corn Buntings are fairly common breeders but Stonechats are only sporadic.

Information   Recorder: Fife.

Site No. 91 Eden Estuary (Fife)

Good numbers of seaduck occur offshore at St Andrews, whilst the adjacent Eden estuary is easy to work and holds, for Scotland, an excellent selection of waders, with internationally important numbers of Shelduck, Bar-tailed Godwit, and Redshank. The whole area is good in winter and passage periods. 2,200 acres of the estuary are a reserve of the North East Fife District Council.

Habitat   The Eden estuary is relatively small and flanked at the mouth by areas of dunes. By contrast, the shore at St Andrews is very rocky.

Access
(see map)
OS Sheet No. 59

1. In St Andrews there is straightforward access to the seafront. A good place to watch from is the Castle.
2. Follow signs in St Andrews to West Sands. Continue to the road's end near Out Head and park. From here view the sea and lower reaches of the estuary.
3. The main concentration of birds in the estuary can be seen from Guardbridge, where the A91 crosses the River Eden. Park in the large lay-by and view from there.
4. For further views, take the track to the stables off the main road slightly nearer to St Andrews. This leads to a footpath

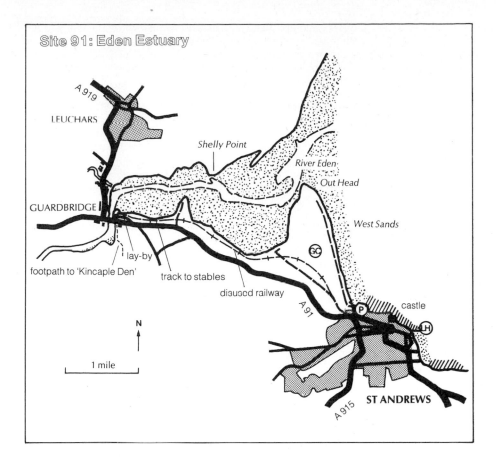

overlooking the estuary. Waders roost on the saltmarshes in this area. A rising or high tide is best here.

5. Wintering Greenshank, Black-tailed Godwit, and Goosander are sometimes seen up-river from Guardbridge. Take the footpath signposted 'Kincaple Den' to the river S off the A91.

In winter Red-throated, Black-throated, and sometimes Great **Birds** Northern Divers can be seen on the sea, together with Slavonian, Great Crested, and occasionally Red-necked Grebes. There are large numbers of Eider and Common Scoter, and several hundred Velvet Scoter, whilst Surf Scoter have been recorded several times. Other seaduck include Goldeneye, Long-tailed Duck, and Scaup. The estuary shelters a few Pintail, with Goosander on the river. Waders are abundant, and include Grey Plover (a scarce bird in Scotland), Sanderling around the estuary mouth, up to 100 Black-tailed Godwits, and a few Ruff and Greenshank. The rocky coast at St Andrews is frequented by Purple Sandpipers and Turnstones. There are generally few raptors in the area, but you may see a Merlin or perhaps Peregrine.

On passage, Grey Plover, Black-tailed Godwit and Greenshank occur in larger numbers, and Little Stint, Curlew Sandpiper, Ruff, and Spotted Redshank are usually seen a few times each autumn. The concentrations of terns off the river mouth in early autumn attract skuas, mostly Arctic.

In summer, numbers of Eider and scoter remain offshore, as well as a few waders.

Other Sites in the Area
91.1 Cameron Reservoir

3 miles SW of St Andrews this water covers c 100 acres, and in winter attracts wildfowl, including Gadwall and Goldeneye. Notably, up to 10,000 Pink-feet and 1,000 Greylags fly in or over to roost. Other possibilities in winter are Sparrowhawk and Short-eared Owl. Access is W off the A915 along a minor road to Cameron, turning S after ½ mile for views of the reservoir. Contact the Scottish Wildlife Trust for a permit and key for the hide (SWT and SOC members only).

Information

LNR Countryside Ranger: Crigtown Country Park, St Andrews, Fife. Tel. 0334–73666 (office).
Scottish Wildlife Trust: 25 Johnston Terrace, Edinburgh EH1 2NH.
Recorder: Fife.

Site No. 92 Loch of Lowes (Tayside)

Loch of Lowes was the first Scottish Osprey's eyrie to be widely publicised away from Loch Garten, and they can be seen between early April and August. The loch is a Scottish Wildlife Trust reserve covering 242 acres.

Habitat

The loch is shallow and very fertile, and the margins have areas of reed-grass, sedge, and waterlily. It is surrounded by mixed woodland.

Access
OS Sheet No. 53

Leave the A9 at Dunkeld onto the A923 to Blairgowrie, and after 1½ miles take the minor road on the right. The loch is immediately to the N of this road, and access is restricted to the S shore adjacent to the road, where there are a number of lay-bys, and to the hide, visitor centre, and car park at the W end. The visitor centre is open 10.00–17.00 April – September (10.00–19.00 June to mid-August). The hide is always open.

Birds

Apart from the Ospreys, raptors in the area include Sparrowhawk and Buzzard. Great Crested Grebe, Teal, Common Sandpiper, and Sedge and Grasshopper Warblers breed around the loch, and Slavonian Grebe has bred once. The surrounding woodland has Capercaillie and Black Grouse, though due to the restricted access these are unlikely to be seen. The resident Woodcock, Green and Great Spotted Woodpeckers, Treecreeper, Redpoll, Siskin, and Common Crossbill are joined in summer by Tree Pipit, Redstart, Wood Warbler, and Spotted Flycatcher. In autumn over 1,000 Greylag Geese roost on the loch.

Information

Ranger: Loch of Lowes Centre, Dunkeld, Tayside. Tel 03502–337.
Recorder: Perthshire.

Site No. 93 Cairngorms and Speyside (Highland)

The range of habitats and birds in this area is reminiscent of the high arctic and boreal forests of northern Eurasia, and supports all the Scottish specialities. The best time to visit is April – July, though some of the more interesting species (e.g. Dotterel) do not arrive until May. There are three National Nature Reserves: Cairngorms (64,000 acres), Abernethy Forest, and Craigellachie (642 acres). The RSPB has three reserves: Loch Garten (2,216 acres), Insh Marshes (1,258 acres), and Upper Glen Avon on the Cairngorm massif, covering 5,300 acres of Cairn Gorm and Ben Macdui.

Habitat

The highest of the Cairngorms top 4,000 feet, and form a plateau of arctic-alpine heath, with a characteristic flora and fauna. This expanse of mountain and moorland is difficult to penetrate, except around the heavily disturbed Cairngorm ski-lift. In the valleys the pinewoods are remnants of the primeval Forest of Caledon that once covered much of Scotland. The pines shade a mixture of juniper, bilberry, and heather, and support Britain's only endemic bird, the Scottish Crossbill. Apart from these natural forests, there are plantations of both native and introduced species of conifer. Not as unique as the pinewoods, the birchwoods are equally attractive. Around the forests and on the lower slopes of the massif there is moorland, peatland, and bog.

Access
OS Sheet Nos. 35 and 36
Outdoor Leisure Map 1:25,000
OLM3

Access to the Cairngorm NNR is unrestricted, except in some areas in the deer-stalking season, August – October. The weather on the high tops is very changeable, and walkers should be properly equipped and leave notice of their intended route (even a note on the car windscreen) if they stray far from the populous areas.

1. Findhorn Valley is good for Golden Eagle. From the A9 12 miles N of Aviemore, take the minor road signposted Raigbeg and Alralad (and check the river at Findhorn Bridge for Dipper). Drive as far as the 'No Entry' sign. Golden Eagles are usually further up the valley, and there are often Peregrines in the area as well.
2. Grantown-on-Spey is excellent for Capercaillie. The area immediately SE of the golf club and village is best, and there are Crested Tits and Scottish Crossbills too.
3. Loch Garten. The RSPB's Osprey Observation Post is signposted off the B970 and open mid-April to August, 10.00 – 20.00 (as long as the Ospreys nest). There is no other access to the statutory bird sanctuary. The area around the entrance to the sanctuary is good for Crested Tit and, sometimes, Scottish Crossbill. Away from the loch, access to the reserve is unrestricted, and the track W of Loch Garten to Loch Mallachie is a fine walk. In winter up to 1,000 Greylags and small numbers of Goldeneye and Goosander roost on Loch Garten.
4. At Forest Lodge, in Abernethy Forest NNR SE of Loch Garten, Capercaillies are often seen around the track N to the river,

and this is often good for Scottish Crossbill too. Visitors should stay on the tracks.

5. Tulloch Moor (Mhor Cottage on recent OS maps). This lies SW of Loch Mallachie, on the minor road to Tulloch from the B970 just N of Auchgourish. This is a well-known Black Grouse lek, though numbers have declined in recent years. If you see them, keep a good distance to avoid disturbance.

6. At Aviemore, Peregrines can often be seen on the high cliffs of Craigellachie Rock. Craigellachie NNR covers the birchwood on its lower slopes and entrance is from the Youth Hostel or the Aviemore Centre. There is a signposted nature trail.

7. Loch an Eilein, off the B970 S of Inverdruie, occasionally holds Black-throated Diver and there is often Peregrine in the area, as well as Crested Tit and Scottish Crossbill.

8. Glenmore Forest Park includes Loch Morlich, which is often visited by Ospreys, and there are Dippers on the loch and tributary streams. Scottish Crossbill can sometimes be seen in the area of the loch, and with perseverance, Crested Tit and Capercaillie too. A map-guide and booklet for the park is available from the Aviemore Tourist Office or the Glenmore Forest Office.

9. The easiest access to the high plateau is the Cairngorm ski-lift. Take a minor road off the B970 at Coylumbridge and follow it for c 8 miles, past Loch Morlich, to a car park at the foot of the ski-lift. In winter there are often Snow Buntings around this, and Ptarmigan as well as Red Grouse may be in the area. A good place to look is the valley S of the ski-lifts. In summer take the ski-lift to near the top of Cairn Gorm. Ptarmigan and Dotterel both occur, but because of the disturbance may be difficult to find. Try walking S along the ridge towards Ben Macdui; the further you get from the most accessible areas, the better the birds.

10. Carn Ban Mor is more difficult to get to and consequently excellent, with most of the upland specialities. Access is from Achlean, down tracks from Feshiebridge on the B970.

11. The RSPB's Insh Marshes reserve stretches along 5 miles of the Spey's floodplain between Kingussie and Loch Insh. There is fen, rough pasture, willow carr, and pools, with stands of birch and juniper on the higher ground. Stopping places on the B970 and B9152 give views over the marshes, and this should be adequate in the winter. The reception centre and car park are on the B970 1½ miles SE of Kingussie; there are two hides and a network of tracks through the marshes. The reserve is open daily (except Tuesday), 09.00 – 21.00 (or dusk if earlier). The whole area regularly floods in winter and attracts Greylag Geese, up to 200 Whooper Swans, and a variety of duck. There is a small Hen Harrier roost, usually three or four (sometimes 15), and Peregrines are often seen. Occasionally Marsh Harriers appear in spring, but Ospreys are regular visitors. Spotted Crakes are sometimes heard in summer, but rarely seen. Wood Sandpipers also breed nearby and sometimes feed on the reserve. In 1968 a female Bluethroat with a nest and eggs was found, the only British breeding record. The wooded areas may have a few Pied Flycatchers and 16 pairs of Goldeneye bred in nest-boxes in 1985.

12. Glen Tromie, running S from Drumguish on the B970, has Black Grouse and sometimes Golden Eagle as well.

Residents include Goshawk, Sparrowhawk, Hen Harrier, Buzzard, a few Golden Eagles, and Peregrine. The Ptarmigan are on the tops in summer and move down in winter, often to below the snow-line, to the same altitude as Red Grouse. Black Grouse favour the forest edge and areas of scattered trees, as well as birch woods. Capercaillies also prefer more open, heathery woodland. Long-eared Owls are resident, but hard to find. No so Woodcock, which can be very conspicuous in early spring when roding. Crested Tits are quite common and often located by call; they tend to move into the more open, heathery areas in winter. Other small woodland passerines are Siskin, Redpoll, and Scottish Crossbill; the last can be scarce one year and abundant the next, but tend to be most obvious April — July. Snow Buntings occur all year, though they are much commoner in winter. A few pairs breed on the tops, favouring corries, boulder fields, and scree slopes.

Birds

Crested Tit

Summer visitors include Slavonian Grebe in small numbers to some of the lochs. They are present early April to August. Red and Black-throated Divers have also bred, but are usually only irregular visitors. Breeding duck include Wigeon, Shoveler, Red-breasted Merganser, and Goosander. Goldeneye is a recent colonist, and has dramatically increased in the last ten years. Ospreys are present early April to August, and Honey Buzzard and Merlin are both summer visitors to the area in very small numbers. A few Water Rails breed, for example at Loch Garten and Insh Marshes. Waders include Golden Plover and Dunlin on the moors and tops, and Dotterel, which favour short grass, moss, and lichen heath, on the flat summits of the hills. Common Sandpipers and Dippers haunt the streams, and Greenshank and Wood Sandpiper inhabit the forest bogs in very small numbers. Temminck's Stint, Green Sandpiper, and Red-necked Phalarope have all bred in the past, and should be watched for. Green and

Great Spotted Woodpeckers are joined by a handful of Wrynecks in open pine and birch woodland, though these are very difficult to find — the best chance is early spring, when newly arrived birds are calling. Tree Pipits favour woodland clearings and areas of scattered trees, and Redstart and Wood Warbler are reasonably common, with Whinchat and Wheatear on the open ground and Ring Ouzels around rocky valleys and scree slopes high on the hills.

Dotterel

In the last 20 years several species, presumably of Scandinavian origin, have colonised Scotland, and there is potential for others to do so. On the tops Snowy Owl, Purple Sandpiper, Sanderling, and Shore Lark are all possibilities, with Red-backed Shrike, Scarlet Rosefinch, and Brambling in the valleys, though the attempts by Shore Lark, Red-backed Shrike, and Lapland Bunting to colonise may well have failed.

Large numbers of Pink-footed and Greylag Geese pass through on passage, and there are sometimes Waxwings in autumn. In winter smaller numbers of Greylags occur, as well as Whooper Swan, and if you are very lucky, you may see a Great Grey Shrike, though you are more likely to see the much commoner Brambling.

Osprey

Information   RSPB Loch Garten, warden: Grianan, Nethybridge, Inverness-shire PH25 3EF.
RSPB Insh Marshes, warden: Ivy Cottage, Insh, Kingussie, Highland PH21 1NT.

NCC Head Warden: NCC Sub-regional Office, Achantoul, Aviemore
PH22 1QD. Tel. 0479–810477.
Reference: *The Birds of Badenoch and Strathspey* by Roy Dennis (1984).
Recorder: Inverness-shire.

Site No. 94 Fowlsheugh (Grampian)

Fowlsheugh holds one of the largest seabird colonies in the
country and is readily accessible. The best time to visit is April to
mid-July. 1½ miles of cliff are an RSPB reserve.

The grass-topped cliffs are over 200 feet high in places. **Habitat**

Fowlsheugh is signposted E off the A92 4 miles S of Stonehaven. **Access**
Park at Crawton at the end of the road and walk N along the OS Sheet No. 45
footpath to the cliffs, with good views of the colonies at several
points. There is no warden.

Fulmar, Shag, and Eider are joined by nearly 30,000 pairs of **Birds**
Guillemots, 5,000 pairs of Razorbills, and small numbers of
Puffins. The 30,000 pairs of Kittiwakes vastly outnumber the few
Herring Gulls. Outside the breeding season there is little of
special interest.

Recorder: Aberdeenshire. **Information**

Kittiwakes and Guillemots

Site No. 95 Deeside (Grampian)

The River Dee drains the S flank of the Cairgorm massif, and the forests and mountains of upper Deeside have a similar range of birds to Speyside with the notable exception of Crested Tit. They are, however, less disturbed and more convenient for the traveller to E Grampian. The best time to visit is March–April for residents, and May–June for summer visitors.

Habitat

The Dee's wooded valley has areas of relict Scots pine and birchwood. The surrounding slopes are bog and moorland, and as the river winds westwards the hills rise higher and eventually reach 3,924 feet at Beinn A Bhuird. In the valley bottom are Lochs Davan and Kinord.

Access

W from Braemar parts of the area are in the Cairngorm National Nature Reserve, and in it, as on the other estates, there are restrictions on access in the deer-stalking season, July–February.

Glen Tanar
OS Sheet No. 44

Leave the B976 at Bridge o'Ess (just SW of Aboyne) and follow the road for 1½ miles to Braeloine. Park here and continuing on foot to Glen Tanar House follow any of the tracks into the forest. There are often Scottish Crossbills in the woods immediately beyond Glen Tanar House and Capercaillies are common, with Black Grouse in the more open woodland and scattered pines. Golden Eagle may be seen over the surrounding ridges, as well as Goshawk, Sparrowhawk, Hen Harrier, and Merlin, the latter two species in the open areas above the forest. Mount Keen lies at the head of Glen Tanar, and holds Ptarmigan. Follow the old Mounth drove-road to the summit or, perhaps better, the Firmounth Road along the valley of the Water of Allachy towards the high ground around Hill of Cat or Cock Cairn. Glen Tanar NNR covers 10,330 acres of the glen and adjacent hills. Glen Tanar Charitable Trust runs a visitor centre across the Water of Tanar from Braeloine. They can give information on access, particularly relevant in the grouse shooting/deer stalking seasons. Otherwise, visitors are asked to keep to the tracks, especially May–June.

Muir of Dinnet National Nature Reserve
OS Sheet Nos. 37 and 44

This covers 3,479 acres of woodland, bog, and moorland surrounding Lochs Kinord and Davan, which hold Goosander and sometimes summering Goldeneye. In late autumn and winter up to 2,000 Pink-footed and 8,000 Greylag Geese use the lochs. Access is from the A93, B9119, and A97 at Dinnet, and visitors should keep to the marked footpaths.

Glen Muick and Lochnagar
OS Sheet No. 44

Leave the B976 just S of Ballater at Bridge of Muick and follow the road to the car park at Spittal of Glenmuick, 8 miles from the junction. From here you can walk to Lochnagar, where there are Ptarmigan, Dotterel, Peregrine, Merlin, Hen Harrier, and Golden Eagle. Glen Muick itself is an excellent area. Black Grouse are relatively numerous, and if you are very lucky, you may see Honey Buzzard or Wryneck in late spring. A good walk is to cross the River Muick NW of Spittal to Allt-na-giubhsaich and follow tracks through the wood on the W bank of the river, this being a good area for Black Grouse. 6,355 acres of the area is a reserve of the Scottish Wildlife Trust by agreement with the Royal Estate. Visitors should keep to the paths.

Mar Lodge
OS Sheet No. 43

Leave Braemar W on the minor road paralleling the River Dee on the S shore. Park along the road, or after 3½ miles cross the river at Victoria Bridge and park at Mar Lodge. Recrossing the river on foot, Linn of Corriemulzie to the E is good for Capercaillie, and Craig an Fhithich to the W for Peregrine. Scottish Crossbills can be found anywhere from Victoria Bridge W to the Linn of Dee in areas of Scots pine, and are often quite easy to find.

Beinn A Bhuird
OS Sheet No. 43

From Mar Lodge drive E to the Linn of Quoich and park at the Punch Bowl. There is usually a barrier across the road here, but you can walk W and N along this track to the foot of the mountain. Black Grouse occur on both sides (especially the NE) of Glen Quoich, and there are also Capercaillies. Continue to the tops for Golden Eagle, Ptarmigan, and Dotterel.

Birds

The high tops support Ptarmigan, which are often found around corries, and move lower down in winter. They are joined in summer by Dotterel, which may be relatively numerous, and other breeding waders here and on the surrounding moorland include Golden Plover and a few Dunlin. Wheatears are widespread and Ring Ouzels are quite common, but Snow Buntings are very rare — Beinn A Bhuird is probably the likeliest peak to support them. Raptors in the area include Golden Eagles, which prefer the more rugged and remote areas. Buzzard, Goshawk, Sparrowhawk, Hen Harrier, and Peregrine are resident, and in summer there may be one or two Honey Buzzards and more regularly Merlins. The forest areas support Capercaillies and Black Grouse, and Woodcock are quite common. Among the smaller birds Siskin and Scottish Crossbill are resident, and Common Crossbill may breed in the conifer plantations. In summer there are also Tree Pipit, Redstart, Wood Warbler, Spotted Flycatcher, and perhaps Wryneck, or even a migrant

Capercaillie

267

Red-backed Shrike. In the forest meadows there are a few pairs of Greenshanks, and along the river and its tributaries Goosander, Common Sandpiper, Grey Wagtail, and Dipper, and these may also be seen on the lochs.

Scottish Crossbills

Information

NCC NE Scotland Region: Wynne Edwards House, 17 Rubislow Terrace, Aberdeen AB1 1XE.
NCC Muir of Dinnet: New Kinord House, Dinnet. Tel. 033985–369.
Recorder: Aberdeenshire.

Site No. 96 Ythan Estuary and the Sands of Forvie (Grampian)

The Ythan lies 12 miles N of Aberdeen, and together with the sea and the adjacent Sands of Forvie is an excellent area for large numbers of wildfowl, waders, and terns, with the largest colony of breeding Eiders in Britain. It is worth a visit at any time of year. The area is a National Nature Reserve covering 2,516 acres.

Habitat

The estuary is c 5 miles long but only a few hundred yards wide. Flanked for half its length by the A975, it is surprisingly undisturbed, and very good views are possible. The extensive mussel beds at the mouth provide food for the hordes of Eiders, whilst there are small areas of saltmarsh in the middle reaches. The Sands of Forvie, an area of dunes and moorland, lies between the river and the sea. N of Rockend the coast is flanked by cliffs, rising to 130 feet at Collieston. Three small Lochs, Meikle, Cotehill, and Sand, lie in the N of the area.

**Access
(see map)**
OS Sheet Nos. 30
and 38

There is open access to the NNR, though you should keep to the paths.
1. There are good views of the estuary from the A975. Heading N from Newburgh, park at the near end of Waterside Bridge to view the Sleek of Tarty and Inch Geck, which is used by

roosting waders. A track follows the shore of the Sleek W from the bridge, giving the best chance of interesting waders. Continuing N there are more parking places giving views of the upper estuary. Accessible on minor roads off the A975, Logie Buchan Bridge is a good spot for wintering Water Rail.

2. For access to the N section of the Sands of Forvie turn off the A975 onto the B9003 to Collieston. Cotehill Loch is adjacent to the road soon after you turn and is good for duck and, if the water level is low, passage waders. Nearer Collieston, Forvie Centre, the NNR HQ, has a car park. A path leads from here past Sand Loch to the coast and Rockend Track. Sand Loch often has breeding Great Crested Grebe, but is otherwise uninteresting.

3. Continuing, you come to Collieston. The village gardens can attract migrants, and the height of the cliffs make this a good spot to seawatch from.

4. Meikle Loch is the main goose roost, and also good for duck. Continue on the A975 for 1 mile past the B9003 turning and take a track on the left just before the crossroads. To avoid disturbing the geese, stay on this track. Small numbers of

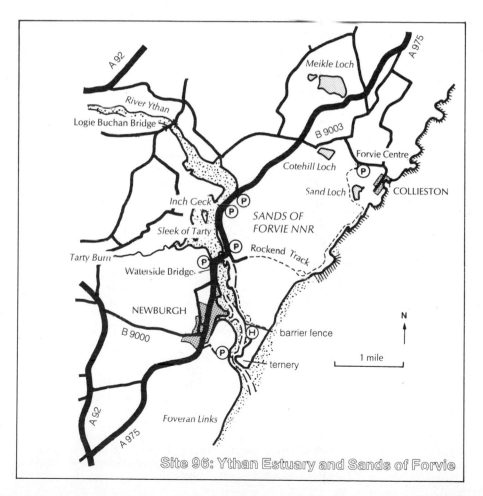

Site 96: Ythan Estuary and Sands of Forvie

269

passage waders regularly include Ruff and Green Sandpiper, and there is further access on the track along the E shore.

5. From April to August the S end of the NNR is fenced off to protect breeding terns. These can be watched from a hide, reached by walking S from Waterside Bridge.

6. Access to the S side of the estuary is from Newburgh. Turn off the A975 just S of the village to the car park and follow the shore round to the mouth of the river. From here you can see the terneries in summer and in winter it is an excellent spot to view divers and seaduck out to sea. Areas of bushes which attract passage migrants lie around the car park and golf course, in the dunes at the estuary mouth, and further S on Foveran Links.

Birds

Wintering wildfowl include up to 250 Whooper Swans, which feed on the estuary and surrounding fields. Up to 10,000 Pink-footed and Greylag Geese occur in autumn, though far fewer winter, and there are sometimes Shoveler. Offshore, there are small numbers of Long-tailed Duck, Common and Velvet Scoters, Goldeneye, and Red-breasted Merganser, and the 1,000 Eider in early winter build up to the full summer strength of over 6,000 by February. There are also Red-throated Divers. Waders sometimes include small numbers of wintering Ruff. On the beach and dunes there are often Snow Buntings.

In summer there may still be several hundred Common Scoter offshore, often joined by Velvets, and occasionally a King Eider is found (usually in spring or early summer). Eider concentrate on the mussel beds in the lower estuary. Common, Arctic, Little, and large numbers of Sandwich Terns breed, together with Black-headed Gulls. The terns attract skuas, and both Great and Arctic are frequently present in small numbers. On the cliffs to the N there are small numbers of Fulmar, Kittiwake, and a few Razorbills, with Shelduck, Oystercatcher, Ringed Plover, and Curlew on the dunes and moorland.

A variety of waders are recorded in spring and autumn, and can include Greenshank and Ruff, and occasionally Little Stint, Curlew Sandpiper, Black-tailed Godwit, Spotted Redshank, and Green Sandpiper, but by southern standards the variety is usually quite poor. Little Gulls, which favour Meikle Loch, are another possibility. In late spring and autumn, SE winds, especially combined with rain or poor visibility, may bring falls of migrants which regularly include some of the scarcer species such as Wryneck, Bluethroat, Black Redstart, and Red-backed Shrike.

Other Sites in the Area
96.1 Blackdog
OS Sheet No. 38

Blackdog lies E of the A92 5 miles N of Aberdeen, and a track runs from the main road down to the shore. There are always large numbers of Eider and Common and Velvet Scoter in July–August, and these are joined in winter by Red-throated Diver, Red-breasted Merganser, and Long-tailed Duck. This area is much better for seaduck than the Ythan, and regularly attracts King Eider, especially in late summer.

96.2 Mains of Murcar
OS Sheet No. 38

Mains of Murcar has a similar range of species offshore as Blackdog. Leave the A92 directly opposite its junction with the B997 in Bridge of Don, fork left to the golf course, and follow the track for 1 mile to its end, proceeding to the shore. To the S, the mouth of the Don is a likely spot for Glaucous Gull, and sometimes also Iceland in late winter. It can be good for passage waders. A minor road runs alongside the river from the A92 immediately S of the bridge, and from it you can walk out to the mouth.

On the E outskirts of Aberdeen, access is from the A956. Take the second left after crossing the bridge over the Dee from the N. Follow the road past the docks and along the edge of the golf course to the lighthouse. Seawatching in autumn can be good. Manx and Sooty Shearwaters and skuas occur in E winds, and Little Auks are possible in late autumn and winter, when there are also divers offshore, regularly Glaucous Gull and Purple Sandpiper, and sometimes Iceland Gull too. Small falls of migrants occur on passage, but there is little cover and they usually disperse quickly.

96.3 Girdleness
OS Sheet No. 38

N of the Ythan, there are several thousand breeding seabirds here, including Fulmar, Shag, Kittiwake, Guillemot, Razorbill, and Puffin. Take a short track E off the main road to the cliffs at Robie's Haven, just N of Cruden Bay on the A975. Cruden Bay itself is better for passerine migrants than the Ythan. The small wood along the stream to Port Errol attracts birds, as do the gardens in the village. Access to the wood is from the village, or on a track S off the A975 just N of Cruden Bay, immediately after a sharp right-hand bend.

96.4 Bullers of Buchan
OS Sheet No. 30

NCC warden: Little Collieston Croft, Collieston, Ellon, Aberdeenshire. Recorder: Aberdeenshire.

Information

Site No. 97 Loch of Strathbeg (Grampian)

Midway between Fraserburgh and Peterhead, the Loch of Strathbeg is Britain's largest dune-slack lake and forms part of a 2,327-acre RSPB reserve. Only ½ mile from the sea, it is used by a large variety of wintering wildfowl. The adjacent Rattray Head is a good spot in winter for all three divers, and in spring and autumn the area attracts small numbers of migrants.

The loch covers c 550 acres and is very shallow; a small rise in the water level can flood the surrounding marshes and farmland. Around it are areas of freshwater marsh, large stands of reed-grass, some reeds, and scattered patches of willow carr and fen woodland. To seaward, the dunes of Back Bar lead to the low-lying Rattray Head.

Habitat

The loch lies NE of the A952, and access to the reserve is across MOD land by advance permit only, available on written application to the warden. Non-members pay £1. There are two hides and a reception centre overlooking the loch. Casual visitors can view the S of the loch from the unclassified road that leaves the A952 NE between Blackhill and Crimond; a short track leads towards the S corner. Continue on to the coastguard's cottages

Access (see map)
OS Sheet No. 30

where there are small areas of cover which should be checked for migrants after SE winds in spring and autumn, preferably in early morning. Except during foggy weather, migrants tend to disperse quickly. Continue on to the lighthouse and Rattray Head and walk either N or S along the shore, looking out to sea for divers.

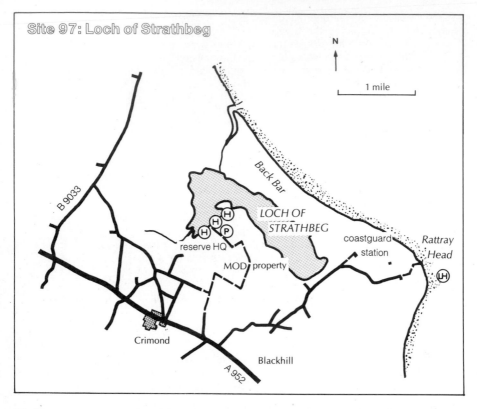

Birds

Several hundred Whooper Swans use the loch in winter, peak numbers occurring in November; sometimes there are also a few Bewick's in early winter. Large numbers of grey geese roost at Strathbeg and, again, numbers peak during passage: up to 10,000 Greylags and 28,000 Pink-feet may be present, and small numbers of Barnacle Geese also pass through. Eider are resident and up to 500 Goldeneye winter, together with large numbers of Wigeon. Goosander occur for much of the year, with Red-breasted Mergansers on passage, and there are occasionally Smew in late winter. Hen Harrier and Short-eared Owl are sometimes seen, and, rather less often, Merlin. All three divers winter off Rattray Head, as well as Eider and Long-tailed Duck, and there are frequently Snow Buntings on the shore and dunes.

Breeding birds include Fulmar in the dunes, Eider, Shelduck, and, in 1984, Ruddy Duck. Others are Water Rail at the reserve, Common Tern, and (irregularly) large numbers of Sandwich. Sedge and Willow Warblers frequent the surrounding marsh and carr.

On passage, Ospreys are annual visitors, as are Marsh Harriers, especially in spring. A few waders occur if the water level drops, and other migrants can include Little Gull and Black Tern, the latter a scarce bird in NE Scotland. At Rattray Head a NW–SE wind may produce Sooty Shearwater and skuas in August – September.

Fraserburgh attracts wintering Glaucous and Iceland Gulls, sometimes in good numbers. There are usually Black Guillemots on the sea and lots of Purple Sandpipers. Explore the coast from the harbour W to Broadsea, where the two fish factories and sewage outfall are especially attractive to gulls. Access is along a maze of roads N off the A98 in the town. Kinnaird Head, the N tip of Fraserburgh, is a good spot to seawatch from in NW–SE winds. In winter there are divers, often including Great Northern and Black-throated, and Black Guillemots amongst the masses of Guillemots and Razorbills. In autumn Sooty Shearwaters are seen regularly.

Information

RSPB warden: The Lythe, Crimonmogate, Lonmay, Fraserburgh AB4 4UB.
Recorder: Aberdeenshire.

Site No. 98 Spey Bay and Lossiemouth (Grampian)

This area holds large numbers of seaduck, and up to eight Surf Scoter have been recorded. Winter and spring are the best times to visit, though seaduck are present all year.

Habitat

The Rivers Lossie and Spey discharge into a long shallow bay. There are no large tidal flats, rather a sand and shingle beach between Lossiemouth and Portgordon, and a rocky foreshore from Portgordon E to Portknockie.

**Access
(see map)**
OS Sheet No. 28

1. Speymouth. Take the B9104 off the A96 at Fochabers, and drive to the coast at Spey Bay. Scan the bay to see where the duck are, and make a move if necessary.
2. Take the B9015 off the A96 N to Kingston. View the sea from here, or take the track W along the beach. Seaduck are usually numerous here.
3. Take the A941 to Lossiemouth and follow the road until it ends at Branderburgh pier and harbour. This is a good place to look for seaduck in the bay. Surf Scoter has been seen quite frequently.
4. The best access to the middle of the bay is to take the track to Speyslaw. Park there and walk N to Boar's Head Rock. Seaduck and, in autumn, divers are often numerous offshore.
5. The A990 follows the coast from Portgordon to Portknockie, and at Buckie the harbour attracts gulls in winter.
6. Lossie Forest is owned by the Forestry Commission, and access is from the beach W of Kingston or along several tracks N off the A96. Cars are not allowed into the forest, and entry may be restricted because of activity on the firing range. The forest may be closed at times of severe fire-risk.

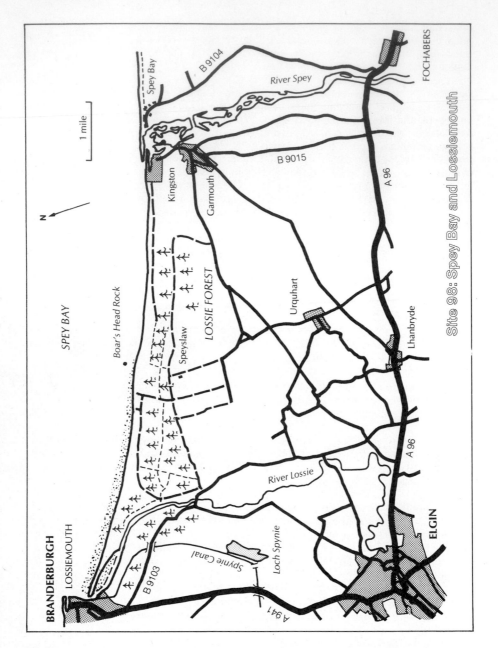

Site 98: Spey Bay and Lossiemouth

Birds   Red-throated Diver can be abundant offshore, especially in autumn, but wintering Black-throats and Great Northerns are only present in small numbers, though with persistence both may be seen. Common Scoter may peak at 5,000, and Velvet Scoter and Long-tailed Duck can both manage 1,000 – 3,000 each, though in some years there are many fewer. A few hundred Eider are joined by small numbers of Scaup and Red-breasted Merganser, and quite often Surf Scoter. As always, the duck can be well offshore at times. Waders include large numbers of Purple

Sandpipers and Turnstones E of Portgordon and at Branderburgh. Otherwise the mouth of the Lossie holds numbers of the commoner species. There are sometimes Glaucous and occasionally Iceland Gulls along the beach, especially at Lossiemouth, and in Buckie harbour. In Lossie Forest, Crested Tit and Scottish Crossbill are resident, though neither are numerous.

Common, Velvet and Surf Scoters

Numbers of Common and Velvet Scoter remain in summer, together with Goosander and sometimes also Surf Scoter. A few Common and Arctic Terns breed, usually on islands in the lower reaches of the Spey. In autumn there are small numbers of passage waders and Sandwich Terns may be abundant. Especially in a strong NE wind, Manx and Sooty Shearwaters, Gannet, and Great, Arctic, and (occasionally) Pomarine Skuas may also be seen offshore.

Recorder: Morayshire.

Information

Site No. 99 Findhorn Bay and Culbin Bar (Grampian, Highland)

This area is excellent in winter. Within a short distance there are concentrations of seaduck and waders and all three Scottish specialities. During the summer there is less to see on the coast, but from April to June the forest is at its best. The E end of Culbin Sands is an RSPB reserve of 2,130 acres.

Culbin Sands is the largest dune system in Britain and has been extensively planted with Corsican and Scots pines, resulting in a large area of monotonous woodland. Sand-bars totalling nearly 5 miles border the coast, with some areas of saltmarsh. Findhorn Bay is an almost completely enclosed tidal basin, attractive to wildfowl and waders.

Habitat

1. RSPB Culbin Sands. Leave Nairn on the A96 and turn E just before the railway bridge to Kingsteps. Take the unsignposted track from here to the shore, park, and walk E along the coast. There is no warden, and access is possible at all times.
2. Loch Loy and Cran Loch are accessible on tracks N off the minor road past Kingsteps. They attract wildfowl, including wintering Whooper Swan.

Access (see map)
OS Sheet No. 27

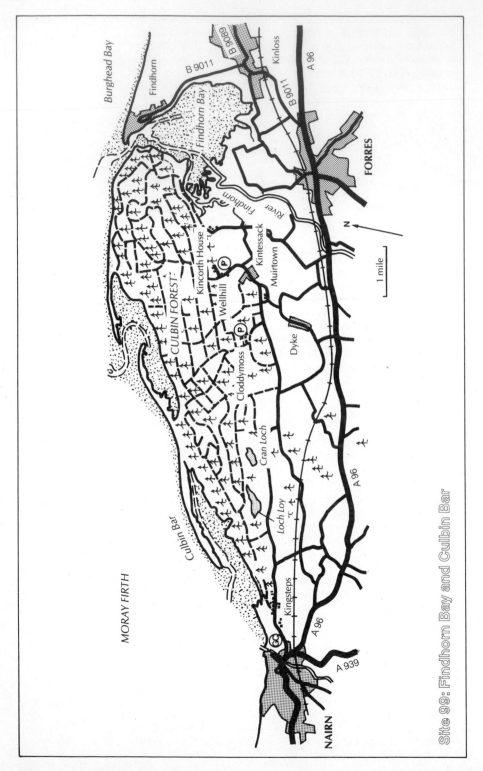

Site 99: Findhorn Bay and Culbin Bar

3. Culbin Forest is owned by the Forestry Commission and can only be entered on foot, from either Wellhill or Cloddymoss. These are accessible along a maze of lanes N off the A96. Tracks lead from the car parks through the forest to the shore and bar.
4. Findhorn Bay. View the E shore from the B9011 Findhorn – Kinloss road. The W side can be seen by following tracks through the forest from Kincorth House. Access to the S side is more complicated, with several minor roads leaving Forres N to the shore.
5. From Findhorn village itself you can view seaduck in Burghead Bay.
6. Burghead harbour, on the B9089 NE of Kinloss, occasionally holds wintering Black Guillemot.

Birds

On the sea, all three divers are regular in winter, though Red-throated far outnumber Black-throated and Great Northern. Large numbers of Common and Velvet Scoter and Long-tailed Duck join the local Red-breasted Mergansers, and Black Guillemot are reasonably frequent. Greylag Geese and Whooper Swans frequent the fields. Waders involve the usual species.

Breeding birds include small numbers of Eider, Oystercatcher, and Ringed Plovers, as well as a few Common and Arctic Terns at Culbin and in Findhorn Bay. Ospreys quite often fish in Findhorn Bay in summer. In the plantations Buzzard, Sparrowhawk, falling numbers of Capercaillie, Long-eared Owl, Crested Tit, Scottish Crossbill, and Siskin are resident. Common Crossbills may appear in late summer, especially in invasion years.

Passage brings some waders, and these can include Whimbrel, Spotted Redshank, and Greenshank, and less frequently Curlew Sandpiper or maybe Black-tailed Godwit. Findhorn Bay is the best place for these. Offshore there are often Gannets and Common, Arctic, and Sandwich Terns. Skuas may appear, especially in NE winds.

Information

Recorder: Morayshire.

Site No. 100 Golspie, Loch Fleet, and Embo (Highland)

N of the Dornoch Firth, this area holds large numbers of seaduck, often including one or two King Eider and Surf Scoter. The best time to visit is probably early spring when numbers are at their peak. The loch and its N shore are a Scottish Wildlife Trust reserve covering 1,750 acres.

Habitat

The coast is sandy towards Golspie, with dunes along the shore. About 3 miles long, the shallow salt-water basin of Loch Fleet is almost completely enclosed. An attempt to drain it resulted in the development of an extensive alder carr at the head of the loch beyond the Mound (the embanked A9), and there are areas of both semi-natural and planted pines adjacent to the coast.

Access
(see map)
OS Sheet No. 21

1. The sea and beach at Golspie are of straightforward access from the A9.
2. The upper part of Loch Fleet, together with the freshwater pools and carr beyond the Mound are also visible from the A9.
3. Most seaduck congregate N of the loch's mouth. Access is along the beach, either walking S from Golspie or, better, taking the minor road off the A9 signed 'Ferry Road' S to Littleferry and walking around the loch's mouth. A permit is necessary away from the footpaths.
4. Loch Fleet can also be viewed from the minor road to Skelbo off the A9. This skirts the S shore.
5. Continue past Skelbo to the shore at Embo, a collection of caravans and chalets. The seaduck are usually off the makeshift pier; if not, walk N along the beach to the mouth of Loch Fleet.

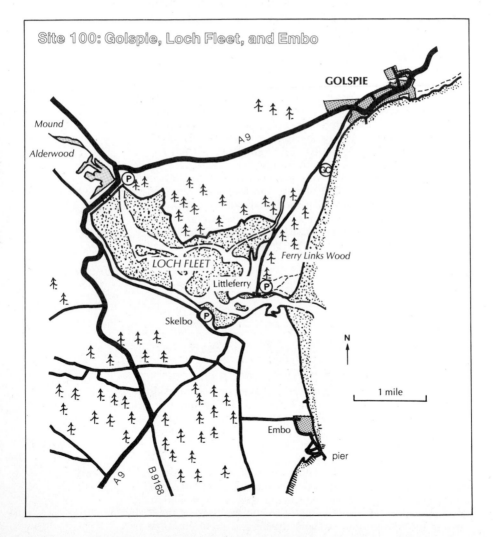

Site 100: Golspie, Loch Fleet, and Embo

Birds

In winter all three divers occur in small numbers, though Red-throated is commonest. There are also Slavonian and sometimes Red-necked Grebes. Variable numbers of Eider winter, sometimes as many as 2,000, together with several hundred Long-tailed Duck, Common Scoter, and Red-breasted Merganser. Lots of Eider spend time loafing around the loch. Velvet Scoter and Goldeneye both occur in smaller numbers.

Seaduck peak in spring and autumn, with up to 2,000 Long-tailed Duck in April – May, but only Eider are numerous in summer. A drake King Eider is present all year, usually at Littleferry or Loch Fleet in summer, and off Embo October – April. Surf Scoter are less regular in their appearance, but one or two seem to be resident. There are numbers of Greylag Geese in the area, and a flock of up to 60 Whooper Swans use the surrounding fields. Sparrowhawk, Buzzard, and Short-eared Owl are seen quite frequently, Hen Harrier and Peregrine less often. The usual waders are present in winter, with small numbers of Purple Sandpipers, especially at Embo. One or two Glaucous Gulls are regular, and there are sometimes Icelands as well. Small numbers of Snow Bunting and, irregularly, Twite may be found in the dunes and along the shore.

Eider and King Eider

On passage a few interesting waders occur, but are generally few and far between. In autumn, NW or N winds, especially if it is misty or hazy, can push seabirds onto the coast, and Sooty Shearwater and skuas may occur.

Breeding birds include Fulmar, Shelduck, Eider, and Arctic Tern. The surrounding woodland has resident Siskin and Scottish Crossbill, and they are joined in summer by Redstarts. Ospreys can quite often be seen fishing in Loch Fleet or the Dornoch Firth in summer.

Other Sites in the Area

100.1 Dornoch

The Dornoch Firth holds large numbers of seaduck. The populations of Embo/Loch Fleet and the firth are closely linked and both King Eider and Surf Scoter can find their way here. To reach Dornoch either continue on minor roads S from Embo or take the B9168/A949 off the A9 S of Loch Fleet. At Dornoch, several tracks lead to the shore, and Dornoch Point can be reached on foot along a track S past the small airstrip. Ard na Cailc, in the inner Firth, is accessible along minor roads WSW from Dornoch to Meikle Ferry (from where you can also view the firth), turning S on foot down a track to the shore 1½ miles before the Ferry.

100.2 Tarbat Ness   This promontory is quite good for seawatching. Take the B9165 to Portmahomack from the A9 3 miles S of Tain, and continue on a minor road to the lighthouse. In autumn, quite large numbers of Sooty Shearwater, as well as skuas, auks, and terns, are seen.

Information   Scottish Wildlife Trust, permits: 25 Johnston Terrace, Edinburgh EH1 2NH.
Recorder: Inverness-shire (Tarbat Ness), Sutherland (all other sites).

Site No. 101 Shetland

Shetland has two major attractions for the birdwatcher: breeding seabirds and waders, and migrants, particularly rarities. There is immense potential for those who wish to find their own birds. The best times to visit are late May to mid-July for breeding birds, and mid-May to early June and mid-August to the end of October for migrants.

Habitat   The Shetland archipelago has 117 islands, of which 13 are inhabited. Six degrees S of the arctic circle, the islands have a landscape of interlocking peninsulas and voes (inlets). The rolling, dark, peat-covered hills are bordered by a rocky coast and with over 2,500 freshwater lochs as well as the labyrinthine coast, water forms a very important part of the Shetland environment. The sheltered voes often have sandy beaches, but the outer coastline consists of cliffs, occasionally rising to over 1,000 feet. The sun is above the horizon for nearly 19 hrs a day in summer, and it is easy to read a book in the twilight at midnight, but its rays are not strong at these latitudes. In winter there are barely 5½ hrs of daylight, and Shetland can be very bleak indeed. There have been no indigenous trees for 2,000 – 3,000 years, apart from relic patches protected from sheep, in steep valleys or on small islets. There are, however, small areas of planted woodland, the largest stand being at Kergord. The lack of cover means that migrants have to go for what they can find, and any crops, trees, or bushes are worth investigating. In particular, any and all gardens and areas of cover on the E coast of Shetland will hold migrants; which you choose to work is a question of accessibility and convenience.

Access   A P&O car ferry sails overnight to Shetland three times a week: the *St Clair* leaves Aberdeen at 18.00 on Monday, Wednesday, and Friday, arriving at Lerwick at 08.00 next morning; it departs from Lerwick at 18.00 on Tuesday, Thursday, and Saturday (but Sunday April – June and September). From the end of May to mid-September a weekly ferry connects Orkney to Shetland and can carry a number of cars: the *Orcadia* leaves Kirkwall at 09.00 on Saturday and arrives at Scalloway at 17.00; on the return journey the departure from Scalloway is 09.00 on Sunday.

Advance booking may be necessary. A round-trip ticket is available (in advance only), Aberdeen – Lerwick, Scalloway – Kirkwall, Stromness – Scrabster (or vice versa). British Airways fly Aberdeen – Sumburgh daily, with a connecting bus service to Lerwick. Loganair fly Edinburgh – Lerwick (Tingwall) daily; on Saturdays from mid-May to October the flight goes via Kirkwall and Fair Isle.

Public transport is very limited, but it is possible to hire cars or bring your own. Accommodation is available on all the islands detailed below (except Mousa), but away from Lerwick and Scalloway is limited. There is a youth hostel in Lerwick and cheap hostels at Uyeasound (Unst) and on Foula. Camping wild is not discouraged, but ask permission before setting up. There are official camp sites on Fetlar, at Graven (North Mainland), and Levenwick (South Mainland). Full details of all transport and accommodation from the Shetland Tourist Organisation.

Many of the areas described below are private. Especially when searching for migrants, the nature of the habitat — gardens and crofts — calls for discretion. Do not enter these without permission, and even when looking in from the outside remember that not everyone may appreciate you peeping over their garden wall. In general, you will get a friendly reception if you ask first.

The Lerwick Area
OS Sheet No. 4

1. Lerwick is the point of arrival for most visitors coming by sea. The harbour is well worth a look, with resident Black Guillemots and gulls, including wintering Glaucous and Iceland. The gulls sit around on warehouse roofs, and a good spot is the sewage outfall directly S of Loch of Clickimin. The short grass on the E shore of the loch is also used by loafing gulls. W of the loch, at Helendale, there are several large wooded gardens which attract migrants. In Lerwick itself there are also good gardens, but they are scattered. At Gremista, just N of the town, the few gardens and thick sycamore copse W of the road along the North Burn of Gremista (just N of the A970) also hold migrants.
2. Scalloway has similar attractions to Lerwick. The best area for gulls is the fish dock pier on the E side of the harbour near the castle, and the adjacent fish factories. Long-tailed Duck are present in winter, together with small numbers of auks, Tufted Duck, and occasionally Scaup. The gardens in the town hold migrants, and formerly Long-eared Owls in winter.
3. Veensgarth, Gott, and Strand plantations, N of Lerwick on the A970, are excellent areas for migrants and sometimes hold wintering Long-eared Owls. Strand is owned by the Shetland Bird Club, with open access. Other good areas in the Tingwall Valley include the Lochs of Tingwall and Asta, adjacent to the B9074, and the crofts on the W side of that road, for migrants, breeding Red-throated Diver (sometimes), and small numbers of wildfowl (including Whooper Swan on passage).

South Mainland (see map)
OS Sheet No. 4

1. Sumburgh Head has good colonies of seabirds that are readily accessible, and is also a good seawatching station. Sooty Shearwaters are regular in late summer and autumn, and Pomarine or even Long-tailed Skua could also occur. Watch from the shelter of the lighthouse. Nearby stone dykes and quarries often hold migrant passerines.

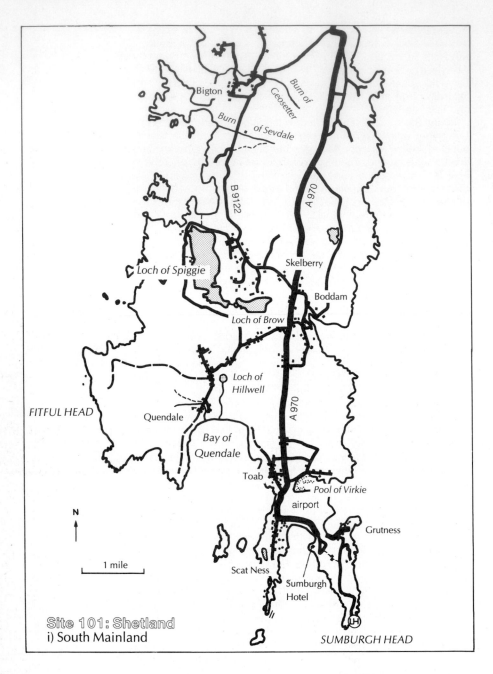

Site 101: Shetland
i) South Mainland

2. Sumburgh Hotel gardens used to be attractive to migrants, but have declined as the habitat was destroyed. The tiny marsh at the back is still worth checking.
3. Grutness, from where the *Good Shepherd* leaves for Fair Isle, has attractive areas of cover around the gardens.
4. Pool of Virkie also has good gardens on its N shore. The pool is one of Shetland's few tidal basins, and usually has a wider

variety of waders than anywhere else. It is the best site for Shelduck in the islands.

5. Scatness Loch also has waders and ducks, and the adjacent gardens attract migrants. Other good areas for migrants include the gardens at Toab (Tolob) and the streams that run from Quendale and the Loch of Hillwell to the sea. These last are favoured by Bluethroat and Marsh Warbler in spring, or maybe even Aquatic Warbler in August.

6. The Bay of Quendale is good for Long-tailed Duck and Great Northern Diver in spring. View from the road on the W side.

7. Loch of Hillwell is very good, with marshy edges, and holds numbers of wildfowl. Corncrakes sometimes sing in the area.

8. Fitful Head has spectacular cliffs with associated seabird colonies, and Great Skuas breed on the moors. It is rather more difficult to reach than Sumburgh Head, involving a hard cross-country climb.

9. Loch of Spiggie, a fertile loch surrounded by areas of marshland, is an RSPB reserve covering 284 acres. It holds wintering wildfowl, up to 300 Whooper Swans on passage, and small spring gatherings of Long-tailed Duck. Breeding birds include several species of duck, and the loch is used by bathing seabirds. There are good views from the road on the N and W sides. The summer warden can be contacted at the boat shed at the N end of the loch.

10. Boddam's slaughterhouse attracts lots of Great Skuas and Ravens, and its gardens shelter migrants.

11. Two particularly good areas for migrants away from the coast are the Burn of Geosetter and the Burn of Sevdale, E of the B9122. Patches of willow follow the course of the streams and are easy to work.

North Mainland
OS Sheet No. 3

1. A good area for migrants is Tresta, on the A971 just W of its junction with the B9075. It has gardens and sycamore trees by the chapel. Tresta Voe is good for divers, Slavonian Grebe, and ducks, and Weisdale Voe has a similar range of birds.

2. Kergord on the B9075 in the Weisdale Valley has plantations of sycamore, larch, and spruce. These support breeding Woodpigeon, Rook and sometimes Jackdaw, Tree Sparrow, Goldcrest, or even Fieldfare. They also attract migrants, but due to the extent of the cover they are difficult to work. The plantations are private; ask permission at Kergord House before entering.

3. The gardens at Voe on the B9071 are very good. It is a large area with lots of houses.

4. The peninsula of Lunna Ness in the NE is an excellent area for migrants, especially Lunna itself with its line of sycamores (on the left of the road 300 yards before Lunna House). The gardens and stream at the head of Swining Voe, W of Lunna Ness, are also good.

5. Sullom Voe has wintering Great Northern Diver, Slavonian Grebe, and Velvet Scoter. The sewage outfall just before the main gate of the oil terminal is good for gulls, and the Houb of Scatsta, N of the B9076 just past the airfield, attracts waders.

6. Ronas Hill in the far N is the largest wilderness area in Shetland. The W flank has spectacular cliffs, and at 1,475 feet it is the archipelago's highest point, with areas of arctic-alpine

habitats. The going is very rough, and it is possible to get lost quite easily, especially in the very changeable weather. Snowy Owls are regularly seen, the best area being around Mid Field and Roga Field. Dotterel are occasionally recorded in spring, and Snow Buntings have been seen in summer and may be numerous in autumn. Access is from the A970. The track W off the road just N of North Collafirth goes to Collafirth Hill, giving access W to Mid Field and Roga Field. The scenic Ronas Voe has the usual species. A minor road runs along the shore from the A970.

7. Sandness is Mainland's westernmost village, and the surrounding lochs have potential for vagrant American waders and ducks, and have a 'resident' Ring-necked Duck. It is also a good seawatching point, with the possibility of Pomarine or Long-tailed Skua.

Bressay
OS Sheet No. 4

The island of Bressay is immediately E of Lerwick and accessible by frequent car ferry. There is a colony of Arctic Skuas on the SE side of the island, but the main attraction is migrants. The best areas are the crofts on the W side. However, a lot of walking is required to cover them without a car.

Noss
OS Sheet No. 4

A few hundred yards E of Bressay, Noss is a National Nature Reserve covering nearly 1,000 acres. This green and fertile island rises to 594 feet at the Noup. There are spectacular seabird colonies. Over 100,000 birds of twelve species breed, including 6,900 pairs of Gannet, 65,000 Guillemots, and both Great and Arctic Skuas. Noss is open to visitors mid-May to the end of August, 10.00 – 17.00 daily except Monday and Thursday. The resident wardens provide a ferry service from Bressay, 75p return, but check with the Tourist Office whether or not it is operating.

Mousa
OS Sheet No. 4

This 450-acre island is just over ½ mile off the E coast of Mainland, opposite Sandwick. It has the best Pictish broch in Britain, and this archeological attraction is not without its birds — Storm Petrels nest in the walls. The island has several small pools which are good for migrant waders. It is necessary to stay overnight to see and hear the petrels — contact the Tourist Office.

Whalsay
OS Sheet No. 2

Whalsay has breeding Red-throated Divers, Whimbrels, and Arctic Skuas, but its main attraction is passage migrants. A large island, over 5 miles long, a certain amount of leg-work is necessary to cover all the better areas. Skaw in the NE is where most of the goodies have been found, and all the crofts here should be checked. Those on the seaward side of Isbister and around Brough are also worth a look. Symbister bay is good for gulls in winter, attracted by the fish factory. Loganair operate daily flights (except Sunday) from Lerwick (Tingwall). The Whalsay car ferry leaves Mainland from Laxo, just S of Lunna Ness, and regularly passes small groups of Little Auks in winter. It has also been the best bet recently for White-billed Diver.

Out Skerries
OS Sheet No. 2

Skerries is a group of small, rocky islands. Their position at the easternmost point in Shetland and the ease of coverage has resulted in a list of rare birds unequalled in Shetland away from Fair Isle. A passenger ferry runs between Lerwick and Skerries on

Tuesday and Friday (and from Whalsay on Sunday if booked), and there are weekly flights in summer from Lerwick (Tingwall).

Papa Stour
OS Sheet No. 3

This small island off W Mainland has the largest Arctic Tern colony in Shetland, as well as Arctic Skuas, seabird cliffs, spectacular coastal scenery, and massive sea caves. Several small lochs are good for wildfowl and waders, and though under-watched it has great potential for interesting migrants. A passenger ferry runs from West Burrafirth, weather permitting, on Monday, Wednesday, Friday, and Sunday.

Foula
OS Sheet No. 4

Foula is one of the most isolated inhabited islands in Britain. 14 miles W of Mainland, it has a spectacular, precipitous coastline. At 1,220 feet the Kame is the second highest sea cliff in Britain. Its main attraction, apart from its splendid isolation and superb atmosphere, is the large number of breeding seabirds, including Manx Shearwater, Storm and Leach's Petrels, c 200 pairs of Gannets, and Britain's largest colony of Great Skuas. Despite limited coverage it has turned up many interesting migrants. A passenger ferry sails on Tuesday and Friday, weather permitting (and it often doesn't) from Walls in W Mainland, and there are weekly flights in summer from Lerwick (Tingwall).

Yell
OS Sheet Nos. 1 and 2 (or 3)

Yell is the second largest island in Shetland and has a covering of blanket-bog over its low, rounded hills. The RSPB have a 4,000-acre reserve at Lumbister, W of the A968 and NE of Whale Firth. Moorland, several lochs, and sea cliffs support breeding Red-throated Diver and both species of skua as well as Merlin, seabirds, and occasionally Whimbrel. There are good views from the A968, but otherwise access is from the lay-by 4 miles N of Mid Yell. The reserve is always open and there is a summer warden. There are good areas for migrants on Yell, including the gardens in Burravoe and Otterswick in the SE. Other attractions are the peninsula of Horse of Burravoe, which has breeding Manx Shearwater, and Copister Broch in the S, which has a large colony of Storm Petrels. Access from Mainland is by car ferry across Yell Sound, where several islands are owned by the RSPB and have breeding Storm and Leach's Petrels. However, visiting is not permitted. In winter Great Northern Diver, Long-tailed Duck, and sometimes Little Auk may be seen from the ferry, but it is poor when compared to the Unst or Whalsay crossings.

Fetlar
OS Sheet Nos. 1 or 2

The W of Fetlar, especially Lamb Hoga, is heather moorland and peat bog, while the E has grassy moorland and dry heath, all interspersed with lochs, pools, marshes, and patches of cultivated land. There is a fine coastline of cliffs and beaches. The RSPB reserve, originally established to protect Snowy Owls, covers 1,727 acres of Vord Hill, Stackaberg, and the surrounding slopes, and the coastline from East Neap to Urie Ness. Entrance is only by arrangement with the warden, whose house is signposted 2½ miles along the road from the pier. If there are owls on the reserve in summer, the warden will escort visitors to see them.
   Snowy Owls no longer breed, but females may be present in the area N of Crossbister or, probably better, between Skutes Water and Waters of Cruss. Red-necked Phalarope and Whimbrel are Fetlar's other specialities. There are less than 20 pairs of

phalarope, which can often be seen feeding on roadside lochs, especially Loch of Funzie. Whimbrels are quite widespread, good areas being the roadside moorland W of Loch of Funzie and moorland W of the airstrip and E of the school. With such rare birds, you should take special pains to avoid disturbance. Do not linger in the Whimbrels' territories and do not try to find the phalaropes' breeding areas. Red-throated Divers breed on many lochs, and can often be seen on Loch of Funzie (watch from the road) and Papil Water. Merlins also sometimes breed.

There are large colonies of Arctic Terns, as well as Great and Arctic Skuas. Seabirds breed in small numbers around the coast, the S tip of Lamb Hoga having a good selection. Fetlar is *the* place to see Manx Shearwater and Storm Petrel. Shearwaters breed on Lamb Hoga and a good place to watch the evening gatherings in the Wick of Tresta is the beach adjacent to Papil Water, especially the Tresta end. Storm Petrels cannot be seen in daylight, but the colonies along the W slopes of Lamb Hoga are accessible with care, especially at Stack of Grunnigeo. From Velzie walk past the N shore of Papil Water, directly over the saddle of the hills to Grunnigeo. Descend on the N side of Grunnigeo to the grassy ridge that connects the stack to the main slope. This ridge is a good vantage point, and petrels can be seen and heard around midnight. They favour overcast nights, and in clear, bright conditions none may come ashore. A torch is essential.

Fetlar attracts its fair share of migrants, and there are good crofts around the E of the island, especially at Funzie.

Access is by frequent ferry from Yell to Unst and thence to Fetlar (Oddsta). Loganair operate daily flights (except Sunday) from Lerwick (Tingwall).

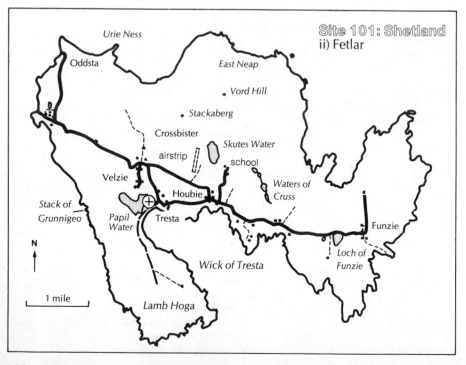

Site 101: Shetland
ii) Fetlar

Unst is the third largest and northernmost main island in Shetland. The main attraction is Hermaness, whose cliffs rise to 400 feet, overlooking Muckle Flugga and Out Stack, Britain's most northerly point. Seabirds include over 10,000 pairs of Gannets, huge numbers of Puffins, and both species of skua. A solitary Black-browed Albatross has returned each year since 1972 to build its nest among the Gannets. It can be seen well from the cliff top immediately over Saito, as well as from slightly to the N, but great care must be taken on the steep and slippery grass slopes, which are especially treacherous when wet. There is a hut c 1½ miles NE of Saito, on the S slopes of Hermaness Hill, which can provide shelter in wet weather (and overnight). The cliffs are accessible along a track across the moorland from the road at Burrafirth. It is difficult to avoid dive-bombing skuas, but a hat or stick (a telescope will do) to hold above your head helps. Hermaness is a National Nature Reserve covering 2,382 acres, with no restrictions on access.

Unst
OS Sheet No. 1

S of Burrafirth, the Loch of Cliff attracts bathing seabirds, and in winter may hold a few roosting Glaucous or Iceland Gulls. Between Norwick and Haroldswick, in NE Unst, there are marshy areas and several shallow pools by the roadside which sometimes attract migrant waders. Baltasound has some of the best areas of cover for passerine migrants.

Snowy Owls are frequently seen on Unst, usually in the S around Uyeasound, in the Breck of Mainland area, especially near Dam Loch, or on Gallow Hill. Uyea Sound often has late Great Northern Diver.

Loganair operate daily flights (except Sunday) to Unst from Lerwick (Tingwall). Access from Yell is by car ferry across Bluemull Sound. Large numbers of seabirds pass through the sound on their way to and from the colonies. In the winter there are large numbers of Eider and Long-tailed Duck, as well as divers, Black Guillemot, and sometimes Little Auk.

Fulmars first bred on Foula in 1878 and now number over 150,000 pairs in Shetland; they include occasional 'blue' Fulmars. There are three known colonies of Manx Shearwater. Storm Petrels are widespread, and Leach's Petrels breed on Foula and on Gruney in Yell Sound. The gannetries at both Noss and Hermaness are increasing, and Shags outnumber Cormorants by 20 to 1. Guillemot, Razorbill, and Puffin are all common, with smaller numbers of Black Guillemot. Common and Arctic Terns, six species of gull, and Arctic and Great Skuas complete the complement of breeding seabirds.

Birds

Great Skua chasing Kittiwake

Several hundred pairs of Red-throated Diver nest on the lochs and pools, and marshes and wetlands also support Teal, Tufted Duck, and Red-breasted Merganser, with Eider on heather moorland. There are odd pairs of Wigeon and Common Scoter. Twelve species of wader breed, notably Red-necked Phalarope, c 400 pairs of Whimbrel, and often one or two pairs of Black-tailed Godwit. The phalaropes usually arrive in late May and leave by early August. Corncrakes have just about disappeared; few, if any, now breed on Shetland. Red Grouse have been introduced, and there are small numbers of Merlin and Peregrine. Skylark and Rock and Meadow Pipits are common, but Swallow and House Martin breed only irregularly, and White Wagtails occasionally. Blackbird, Wheatear, Wren (the endemic Shetland subspecies), Starling (a subspecies shared with the Outer Hebrides), Raven, and Hooded Crow are common, and Rooks breed at Kergord. Twite and House Sparrow are both common around crofts, and sometimes a few pairs of Reed and Corn Buntings nest.

Red-necked Phalarope

Occasionally individuals of species which breed in Iceland or Scandinavia summer and may even nest. These include Great Northern Diver, Whooper Swan, Long-tailed Duck (which bred several times last century), Velvet Scoter, Purple Sandpiper, Turnstone, Glaucous Gull (has hybridised with Herring Gull), Snowy Owl (bred 1967–75), Redwing (bred five times 1953–83), Fieldfare (bred most years 1968–73 and a few times since), and Snow Bunting.

Sooty Shearwaters are regularly seen on passage in late summer and autumn, especially from Sumburgh Head. Other seabirds to look for include Pomarine and Long-tailed Skuas, in both spring and autumn, and there is a notable late-autumn passage of 'blue' Fulmars. Flocks of Pink-footed and Greylag Geese, and small numbers of Barnacles, occur in both spring and autumn, as well as Gadwall, Pintail, and Shoveler. Migrant raptors include Long- and Short-eared Owls; less often, Honey Buzzard, Hen Harrier, Sparrowhawk, Buzzard, Rough-legged Buzzard, and Osprey. Grey Plover, Sanderling, Bar-tailed Godwit, and Knot occur almost exclusively on passage, joining the usual array of migrant waders. Woodcock, thrushes, chats, Blackcap, Willow Warbler, Goldcrest, Pied Flycatcher, etc., all occur in quite large numbers given suitable weather. The best conditions are SE winds. Among

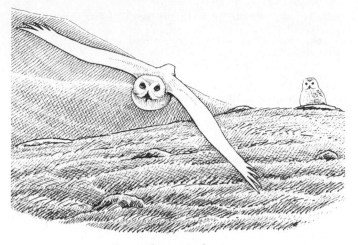

Snowy Owls

the scarcer migrants, those usually more frequent in spring than autumn are Bluethroat, Marsh Warbler, Golden Oriole, Red-backed Shrike, and Ortolan Bunting. Icterine Warbler, Lapland Bunting, and Scarlet Rosefinch are much more frequent in autumn, though they can occur in spring, but Barred and Yellow-browed Warblers, Red-breasted Flycatcher, and Yellow-breasted Bunting are nearly unknown in spring. Wrynecks are recorded equally at both seasons, and Waxwing can put in one of its erratic appearances at either season too. Some species common on the mainland, but rare or absent as breeding birds on Shetland, occur on migration. These include Dunnock, Robin, and finches (apart from Twite), while Great Spotted Woodpecker, tits, and northern Bullfinches are rare and erratic visitors. South Mainland and Out Skerries are probably the most productive areas for migrants, but birds can, and are, found almost anywhere.

500–600 Great Northern Divers winter around the islands, with many fewer Red-throated. Slavonian Grebes occur in small numbers, especially in Tresta Voe. Up to 400 Whooper Swans pass through on migration, but in general there are few in winter unless it is very mild. They, like most of the duck (with the exception of Eider and Long-tailed Duck) move S early in the season. King Eider are seen most winters, with records widely scattered around the islands. Large numbers of Turnstone and Purple Sandpiper winter along the shore, and away from the coast there may be Golden Plover, Curlew, Snipe, Jack Snipe, and sometimes numbers of Woodcock in late autumn. Small flocks of Little Auk can occur October–February, and both Glaucous and Iceland Gull are regular visitors, especially to the fishing harbours. A few Long-eared Owls winter, mainly in the Tingwall Valley, and small numbers of Snow Buntings sometimes stay on and may be found almost anywhere.

RSPB Shetland Officer: Peter Ellis, 'Seaview', Sandwick, Shetland ZE2 9HP. Tel. 09505–506. **Information**
Fetlar, summer warden: Bealance, Fetlar, Shetland ZE2 9DJ. Tel. 095783–246.

NCC Shetland: 1 Albert Buildings, Alexandra Wharf, Lerwick. Tel. 0595–3345.
Shetland Tourist Organisation: Market Cross, Lerwick ZE1 0LU. Tel. 0595–3434.
P&O Ferries: PO Box 5, Jamiesons Quay, Aberdeen AB9 8DL. Tel. 0224–572 615.
Loganair, Tingwall: Tel. 059584–246/7
Loganair, Unst: Tel. 095781–620.
British Airways, Sumburgh: 0950–60345.
British Airways, Lerwick agent: J. Leask & Sons. Tel. 0595–3162.
References:
The Natural History of Shetland by R.J. Berry and J.L. Johnston (1980).
A Guide to Shetland Birds by Bobby Tulloch and Fred Hunter (1970).
The Birds and Mammals of Shetland by L.S.V. and U.M. Venables (1955).
Recorder: Shetland.

Site No. 102 Fair Isle (Shetland)

Fair Isle is justly famous for the numbers of rare and unusual birds that turn up year after year, and further attractions in spring and summer are the excellent seabird colonies. After the pioneering studies of Eagle Clark in the early years of the century, George Waterston bought the island and established a Bird Observatory in 1948; the island now belongs to the National Trust for Scotland.

Habitat

The island is c 3 miles long and covers 1,890 acres. The cliffs of the magnificent coastline reach c 500 feet. The S of the island is crofted, while the N is mostly heather moor rising to 712 feet at Ward Hill, with nesting skuas. Migrants can occur anywhere, but generally favour the crops, ditches, and a tiny area of trees, as well as the geos (inlets) on the coast (which can be very good, especially in spring).

Access
OS Sheet No. 4

Loganair fly Shetland (Tingwall) to Fair Isle on Monday, Friday, and Saturday May–October, and Monday and Friday only for the rest of the year. These flights connect with Shetland–Edinburgh services. In summer Loganair operate an Edinburgh–Kirkwall–Fair Isle–Tingwall service on Saturdays. The *Good Shepherd* mail boat runs between Fair Isle and Shetland (Grutness) on Tuesday and Saturday, May–September, Tuesday only during the rest of the year. The boat leaves Fair Isle at 07.00 and returns from Grutness at 11.30 at the latest. The voyage takes c 2½ hrs and costs 40p return. Bookings are essential, and sailings are affected by bad weather — this trip is to be avoided if you are a bad sailor. For details of transport to Shetland, see pp. 280–1. Accommodation is available at Fair Isle Lodge and Bird Observatory from mid-March to the end of October, prices starting at £74 a week full board. By observatory standards, Fair Isle Lodge is luxurious.

Birds

Spring migration begins in March, but despite the occurrence of several outstanding rarities in early spring, it is in late May and early June that the most exciting range of species has been recorded. Golden Oriole, Bluethroat, Icterine and Marsh Warblers, Red-backed Shrike, Scarlet Rosefinch, and Ortolan and Lapland Buntings are annual, and sometimes occur in comparatively large numbers. Thrush Nightingale is something of a speciality in the last week of May, and Red-throated Pipit, Short-toed Lark, Subalpine Warbler, and Rustic Bunting are regularly recorded, though perhaps not every year.

Breeding seabirds include a few pairs of Storm Petrel, and many more non-breeding petrels come ashore at night. There are vast numbers of Fulmar and c 260 pairs of Gannet. Shag, Kittiwake, four other species of gull, a few pairs of Common and Arctic Terns, and all four auks also breed. There are several dozen pairs of Great and Arctic Skuas, and in mid-summer single Long-tailed Skuas are occasionally seen in the colonies. The commonest breeding landbirds are Skylark, Meadow and Rock Pipits, and Wheatear, while the Fair Isle subspecies of Wren is ubiquitous.

Yellow-browed Bunting

Corncrake, Wryneck, Richard's Pipit, Bluethroat, Icterine, Barred, and Yellow-browed Warblers, Red-breasted Flycatcher, Red-backed and Great Grey Shrikes, Scarlet Rosefinch, and Lapland Bunting are all annual during the autumn, and several rarities are nearly annual. In August and early September, Aquatic Warbler and Black-headed Bunting have appeared a number of times, and there have also been several Booted Warblers. Arctic and Greenish Warblers and Red-throated Pipit may be seen from now onwards, but it is in the latter half of September that things usually start to warm up. However, the quality of birds is very weather-dependent. Just a hint of a SE wind can, and does, produce rarities, and Yellow-breasted Buntings are almost guaranteed. W or SW winds may spell disaster, with very few birds at all. It is a risk you have to take. With the right winds regulars include Short-toed Lark, Olive-backed Pipit, Citrine Wagtail, 'Siberian' Stonechat, and Little and (more erratically) Rustic Buntings. The rarest specialities also favour this period. Pechora Pipits have been seen in late September and early October, and Lanceolated Warblers occur in the same period, mostly in late September. If these are not enough, the most sought-after species, for example Siberian Rubythroat, Red-flanked Bluetail, and Pallas's Grasshopper Warbler, have occurred. There are common migrants too, and sometimes large numbers of Woodcock, Redwing, and Fieldfare. Others include Pink-footed and Greylag Geese, Whooper Swan, a trickle of

Merlins, and some interesting subspecies — Greenland Redpoll and northern Bullfinch.

Seawatching is best from the *Good Shepherd* and South Light. Storm Petrels are regular from the boat in summer, and Manx Shearwaters are joined in autumn by Sooty Shearwater and occasionally, Leach's Petrel. Seaduck may also be interesting.

Lanceolated Warbler

Information

Bookings: Bookings Dept, Fair Isle Lodge and Bird Observatory, Fair Isle, Shetland ZE2 9JU. Tel. 03512–258.
Loganair, Tingwall: Tel. 059584–246.
Loganair, Edinburgh: Tel. 031–344 3341.
Good Shepherd: Mr J. W. Stout, Fair Isle, Shetland. Tel. 03512–222.
References:
The Birds of Fair Isle by John F. Holloway and Roderick H. F. Thorne (1981).
Fair Isle and its Birds by Kenneth Williamson (1965).
The *Fair Isle Bird Observatory Report* is produced annually, and is recommended.
Recorder: Observatory recorder.

Site No. 103 Orkney

Orkney comprises 67 islands and at the nearest is only 6 miles from mainland Scotland. Its attractions for the visiting birdwatcher are vast numbers of breeding seabirds, the moorland specialities, and passage migrants. The best time to visit to see breeding birds is May to early July, and for migrants May and early June and late August to October.

Habitat

The islands, with the exception of Hoy, are rather low and fertile. In places the coast has cliffs, sometimes spectacular, as at St John's Head on Hoy. Other parts have beaches and sheltered bays, while Deer Sound and Scapa Flow provide a haven for large numbers of divers and seaduck. The original vegetation of Orkney was scrubby woodland, but this was cleared by neolithic and Viking settlers and replaced by moorland and bog. These form an invaluable habitat, but it would be a mistake to think that Orkney is cloaked in moorland. Since the early 18th century the moors have been reclaimed for farming, and the major land-use is now cattle pasture. However, large areas remain on Mainland and

Hoy, often with scattered lochs, streams, and marshes. Some of the smaller islands are still crofted, and there are tracts of maritime heath, a habitat unique to Orkney and parts of Caithness. Exposure to the wind has dwarfed shrubs such as heather and crowberry, and these mix with sedges and small herbs.

Access

A P&O roll-on/roll-off ferry runs from Scrabster to Stromness (Mainland). The *St Ola* sails every day except Sunday, usually leaving Scrabster at 12.00 and Stromness at 08.45. The voyage takes 2 hrs. There are extra sailings 9 June–25 September, including Sundays July–August. From 5 May to 25 September there is a passenger-only service from John o'Groats to Burwick (South Ronaldsay) operated by Thomas & Bews. There are two sailings daily, with extra services July–August. The voyage lasts 40 min. Check sailing times in advance. Daily flights (except Sunday) to Kirkwall are operated by Loganair from Edinburgh, Glasgow, Inverness, and Wick. British Airways operates daily services (except Sunday) to Kirkwall from Glasgow, Inverness, and Aberdeen. Inter-island flights are operated by Loganair serving the northern isles, and ferries to the northern islands are run by the Orkney Island Shipping Co. (OISCo.) and Wide Firth Ferries.

Care should be taken not to disturb breeding birds, especially divers, raptors, and terns. Many of the sites described below are on private land, and if in doubt ask permission before entering. In general you will get a very friendly reception. In addition, when searching for migrants, the nature of some of the habitat — crops and gardens — means that extra caution is called for.

Mainland
OS Sheet No. 6

In winter there is an abundance of birds, with large numbers of waders, especially Curlew, throughout the whole island. Otherwise, Mainland can be conveniently divided into E and W along a line through Kirkwall.
1. Both Stromness and Kirkwall harbours are worth a look in winter for Glaucous and Iceland Gulls, and at Kirkwall the abbatoir on Hatston Industrial Estate also attracts gulls.
2. Binscarth wood near Finstown has a rookery as well as a variety of small passerines and wintering Long-eared Owls, but there is so much cover that it is difficult to work for migrants.
3. E Mainland is mainly farmland. Though there is some moorland remaining, with the typical species, the main attraction is passage migrants. Any areas of bushes, crops, or other vegetation should be checked.
4. The outstanding areas for divers, grebes, and seaduck are Scapa Flow and Deer Sound. In winter these may hold over 200 Great Northern Divers and 2,500 Long-tailed Ducks. Waders are also numerous. The causeways that connect Mainland to Burray and South Ronaldsay are good vantage points for Scapa Flow.
5. Though much of W Mainland has been reclaimed for beef cattle, some large areas of moorland remain, especially around Orphir in the S, between Finstown and Kirkwall, and the area from Finstown N to the Loch of Swannay. A large part of the last is now the RSPB reserve of Birsay Moors and

Cottascarth which covers 4,719 acres astride the B9057. Breeding species include Short-eared Owl, Hen Harrier, a few Merlins, and Great and Arctic Skuas — in 1985, also Greylag Goose and Whimbrel. There is a winter harrier roost at Durkadale on Birsay Moors. Access is at two points. (i) A hide on Burgar Hill overlooks Lowrie's Water, which has breeding Red-throated Diver and other waterbirds. The entrance is signposted from the A966 at Evie, ½ mile NW of the B9057 turnoff, and the hide is near the wind generators. (ii) Lower Cottascarth. Turn W off the A966 on a minor road 3 miles N of Finstown, and then right along the track to the hide at Lower Cottascarth. There is a summer warden.

6. The RSPB reserve at Hobbister, SW of Kirkwall, covers 1,875 acres and includes areas of moorland as well as low cliffs and the large, sandy Waulkmill Bay. It lies between the coast, the A964, and the Loch of Kirbister. Breeding birds include Red Grouse, Hen Harrier, Merlin, Black Guillemot, Short-eared Owl, and Raven. Waulkmill Bay, which can be watched from the car, attracts passage waders, and in winter Great Northern and Black-throated Divers and Slavonian Grebe are regular, as well as seaduck. The reserve lies 4 miles from Kirkwall on the A964. Access is only permitted to the area between the road and sea, and visitors should keep to the paths. Enter via a track at HY396070 or the minor road to Waulkmill Bay. There is a summer warden.

7. Of the marshes and lochans, one of the best is also an RSPB reserve, the Loons in Birsay, covering 164 acres in NW Mainland. It is a waterlogged basin with reed and sedge beds adjacent to the Loch of Isbister. Breeding birds include Pintail, Wigeon, seven species of wader, Arctic Tern, Sedge Warbler, and perhaps still Corncrake. In winter up to 50 Greenland White-fronts use the area, as well as waders and other wildfowl. The only access is to the hide at HY246242: leave the A986, turning W 3 miles N of Dounby; the hide is off this minor road c 400 yards before the junction with the B9056, and the reserve can also be viewed from this road.

8. The large Loch of Harray holds up to 7,000 wintering duck, mostly Pochard, while the adjacent tidal Loch of Stenness has Long-tailed Duck and Goldeneye. Between these two lochs and around the Loch of Skaill there are often several hundred Greylags in winter, together with Whooper Swans.

9. Marwick Head on the NW coast is an RSPB reserve, with a mile of cliffs rising to 280 feet. Breeding birds include over 35,000 Guillemots and 10,000 pairs of Kittiwakes, while Peregrine is occasionally seen. Access is on foot from two points: either the end of the minor road off the B9056 to Mar Wick bay, or the car park at Cumlaquoy (similarly off the B9056 to the N of the Mar Wick turning) from where it is a short walk to the cliffs.

Copinsay
OS Sheet No. 6

This 375-acre island lies 1¾ miles off E Mainland. It was bought in memory of the late James Fisher and is an RSPB reserve. The grassy interior is bounded by cliffs that rise to 250 feet, and the whole of the SE side is one big seabird colony. As well as the main island, Corn Holm, Black Holm, and Ward Holm are accessible at low tide. Seabirds include 30,000 Guillemots and these are joined by Razorbill, Black Guillemot, and a few pairs of Puffin, as well as Kittiwake and other gulls, Shag, Fulmar, and Arctic Tern. There are more Puffins on Corn Holm and Black Holm. Other species of note are Raven and Corncrake, and Copinsay also attracts passage migrants.

From Skaill in Deerness, at the terminus of the B9050, a small boat makes day trips to the island by arrangement. A converted farmhouse makes an information and display centre, and provides very basic self-catering accommodation for an overnight stay. Contact the RSPB Orkney Office for details.

Hoy
OS Sheet No. 7

This island is rather different in character to the rest of Orkney. Mainly rugged, bleak moorland, the Cuilags and Ward Hill, rising to 1,577 feet, are the highest points in Orkney. There are few people. The scenery is spectacular, and includes the sheer 1,100-foot cliffs of St John's Head and the Old Man of Hoy, which, at 450 feet, is the highest sea stack in Britain. The RSPB has a 9,700-acre reserve at North Hoy; moorland is bounded by superb cliffs which are home to large numbers of seabirds. There is a small colony of Manx Shearwaters on Hoy, and Storm Petrel may also breed. Evening gatherings of shearwaters can be seen from Rackwick, on the W coast, accessible by road. There are c 1,500 pairs of Great Skua and 400 pairs of Arctic Skua. Many are on North Hoy, but the valleys on the W side of the island are also good, especially those around Heldale Water. The continual bombardment by skuas is something to consider in advance — wear a hat. There are 1,500 pairs of Arctic Terns near Tor Ness. Red-throated Diver, Buzzard, Hen Harrier, Peregrine, Merlin, and Short-eared Owl all breed, though there are few harriers and owls because of the lack of Orkney voles. Golden Eagle is occasionally present and a good place to look is the footpath between Ward Hill and the Cuilags. Winter birds include up to 500 Barnacle Geese on South Walls.

There is a daily boat service to Moness Pier on Hoy from Stromness, and a roll-on/roll-off ferry to Lyness from Houton, operated by the OISCo.

South Ronaldsay
OS Sheet No. 7

South Ronaldsay and Burray are connected by road to Mainland by the Churchill Barriers. The E and W coasts have colonies of seabirds, including small numbers of Puffin, and there are also Ravens. Otherwise the island is mainly farmed, with small areas of heath that support nesting gulls and a few skuas, and some lochans and marshes with breeding duck and waders. Lying on the E side of the archipelago, the major attraction is passage migrants.

Rousay
OS Sheet No. 6

In contrast to South Ronaldsay, Rousay is predominantly moorland, and has a fine range of breeding birds, including Red-throated Diver, Hen Harrier, Merlin, Short-eared Owl, and Raven. The RSPB has a reserve of c 1,000 acres at Trumland in the S with most of the moorland specialities. There is open access, but visitors should contact the summer warden at Trumland Mill Cottage. There are areas of maritime heath at Quandale and Brings in the NW, and they support 4,000 pairs of Arctic Tern and 100 pairs of their attendant Arctic Skuas, as well as a few Great Skuas. The cliffs have Guillemot, Razorbill, Kittiwake, and

Fulmar; the last also nests inland on scattered rocks in the moorland. Around Westness and Trumland House there are areas of trees with the common woodland species. Offshore, the sounds between Rousay, Egilsay, and Wyre support numbers of wintering Great Northern Diver and Long-tailed Duck. The island is served by Flaws Ferries.

Shapinsay
OS Sheet No. 6

This island is almost all agricultural land, though in the SE there is a small area of moorland with a few pairs of Arctic Skuas. In winter up to 100 Whooper Swans may be seen around Mill Loch, and the woodland in the grounds of Balfour Castle supports a variety of small passerines.

Stronsay
OS Sheet No. 5

Mainly farmland, the area of moorland on the SW peninsula of Rothiesholm supports Red-throated Diver, large numbers of breeding gulls (especially Great Black-backed), Arctic Tern, and small numbers of both Great and Arctic Skuas. There is a small colony of seabirds on this coast. The E cliffs are also good for seabirds, and the small lochs have breeding wildfowl, including Pintail. There are still a few Corncrakes and Corn Buntings. Well placed to receive migrants, though underwatched, Stronsay has produced some good birds.

Eday
OS Sheet No. 5

There is a large amount of moorland on Eday which supports a good number of Arctic Skuas, as well as Greats, and six to eight pairs of Whimbrel breed. Seabird colonies around the coast include the Calf (with large numbers of Great Black-backed Gull, Grey Head for auks, and the S cliffs with a large colony of Cormorants). Near Carrick in the N are two small woods which attract migrants.

Sanday
OS Sheet No. 5

There is almost no moorland on Sanday and a low-lying coast means that there are few cliff-nesting seabirds. There are however, large colonies of terns, mainly Arctic, at Westayre Loch, Start Point, and Els Ness, as well as breeding Arctic Skuas. Ravens breed regularly and Short-eared Owls occasionally, while the island, with Stronsay, forms the last Orkney home for Corn Bunting. It is ideally placed to receive migrants, especially Lady Parish in the NE.

Westray
OS Sheet No. 5

There are spectacular numbers of seabirds breeding along 5 miles of the W coast between Noup Head and Inga Ness, including over 60,000 pairs of Kittiwake and 60,000 Guillemots. The N end of the colony is the RSPB reserve of Noup Head, which forms the NW extremity of the island. Here, Peregrine and Raven haunt the cliffs and there are 2,000 pairs of Arctic Tern on the adjacent maritime heath, together with 50 pairs of Arctic Skua. Follow a minor road W from Pierowall to Noup Farm, and then the track NW for 1½ miles to the lighthouse on Noup Head. There is no warden. Puffins may be difficult to see at Noup Head, and if so try Stanger Head in the SE of the island. There are several lochs with breeding waterbirds, the best probably being the Loch of Burness, which has Britain's most northerly Little Grebes, and the rough ground harbours a few Corncrakes. The island attracts migrants during passage periods, though being on the W side of the archipelago, it is not ideally placed.

Known in Orkney as 'Papay', Papa Westray is still largely crofted and Corncrake has consequently maintained a small population here. The RSPB has a 510-acre reserve covering the N unculti-vated quarter of the island at North Hill. This includes an area of maritime heath, with one of the three largest colonies of Arctic Tern in Britain (often over 6,500 pairs) together with about 100 pairs of Arctic Skua. Visitors must not walk through the tern colonies. The coast has low cliffs with Kittiwake, Guillemot, Razorbill, and Black Guillemot. The best area is in the SE of the reserve at Fowl Craig. There is a summer warden at North Hill, based at Gowrie, 100 yards SE of the reserve entrance (which is at the N end of the island's main road). If contacted in advance he will escort visitors around the colonies. There are other large tern colonies in the S of the island at Sheepheight and Backaskaill, and there is a large colony of Black Guillemots on the Holm, off the E coast; this island also has a small colony of Storm Petrels.

Papay attracts migrants, and any area of cover could produce birds. There is also excellent seawatching, especially from Mull Head on North Hill. Sooty Shearwaters are regular in late summer, up to 1,300 having been seen in a day. Other species include skuas and the remarkable day-total of 40 Long-tailed Skuas was once logged.

Papa Westray
OS Sheet No. 5

This small island is mostly crofted and very flat, with several small lochs and areas of marshland. The coastline is bounded by a dry stone wall, the 'Sheep Dyke', which keeps the kelp-eating North Ronaldsay sheep on the foreshore. This is mostly rocky, with some sandy beaches on the E and S coasts. There are no big seabird colonies, but there are small numbers of Black Guillemot, Arctic, and, erratically, Sandwich and Common Terns. Other breeding birds include waders and ducks, notably Gadwall and Pintail, and a few Corncrakes.

The area between Orkney and Fair Isle is probably the main route for seabirds moving between the North Sea and Atlantic. North Ronaldsay, the northernmost of the Orkney archipelago, is well placed to witness these movements. Fulmars pass in vast numbers — up to 20,000 per hr. Sooty Shearwaters regularly peak at over 100 per hr, and Leach's Petrels also occur. The best seawatching point is the old beacon in the NE corner of the island, and the best conditions are following a NW gale when the wind returns to SE at first light.

Despite the lack of intensive coverage, many rarities have been found. The walled garden at Holland House with fuchsias and sycamores is attractive, but most migrants frequent the crops. There are large falls of the commoner species, and several scarce migrants are annual. A good variety of passage waders and ducks includes large numbers of Whooper Swans and geese in late September and October. North Ronaldsay Bird Observatory has been established, with some limited accommodation, and pro-spective visitors should contact Kevin Woodbridge.

North Ronaldsay
OS Sheet No. 5

Four other islands are worth mentioning. Sule Skerry has 44,000 pairs of Puffin, as well as breeding Storm Petrel, but is very difficult to get to. Sule Stack is even more difficult to reach, and has 4,000 pairs of Gannet. The Pentland Skerries, accessible from South Ronaldsay, have a huge colony of Arctic Terns. Auskerry,

Other Islands

off Stronsay, was the site of some of Eagle Clark's pioneering studies of migration.

Birds

Fulmar, Cormorant, Shag, Kittiwake, Guillemot, Razorbill, Black Guillemot, and Puffin are widespread on cliffs and small islands, which they share with Rock Dove and Raven. On the moorland and heaths there are Arctic and Great Skuas, five species of gull, and Sandwich, Common, and Arctic Terns, these last also favouring beaches. Gannets breed on Sule Stack and are widespread offshore, but Manx Shearwater and Storm Petrel are rather elusive, though petrels are in fact common.

Breeding duck include Wigeon, Gadwall, Shoveler, Eider, and Red-breasted Merganser, and a large proportion of Britain's Pintail. Scaup, Long-tailed Duck, and Common Scoter have bred in the past. Wildfowl share the marshes and lochs with Red-throated Diver, of which there are c 95 pairs on the islands, half on Hoy. Waders include Golden Plover, Dunlin, and a few Whimbrel on Eday, but Curlew are the most conspicuous species, being abundant on the moors. Black-tailed Godwit and Red-necked Phalarope have bred. Small birds in the marshy areas include Sedge Warbler and Reed Bunting.

The moorland supports Red Grouse and ground-nesting Kestrel, Woodpigeon, Starling, and Hooded Crow. Orkney was the last refuge for the Hen Harrier when persecution had all but eliminated it from the rest of the country. Now, in a good year, 100 females of this polygamous species may lay, though it has to be a very good year for more than one female in each harem to raise young. Sparrowhawk, Buzzard, Peregrine, and Short-eared Owl also breed, but there are only a handful of Merlins remaining. Other birds on the moors, apart from the abundant Meadow Pipits and Skylarks, are Stonechat, Wheatear, and a few Ring Ouzels. Twite are widespread, often being found along roadside verges. A speciality of the areas of crofted land as well as of rush and iris beds is the Corncrake, which retains a foothold on the N islands of the archipelago. There has been a recent average of 25 pairs. The areas of trees and plantations support Rook, Willow Warbler, and occasionally other woodland passerines such as Spotted Flycatcher or Garden Warbler, and Fieldfare first nested in Britain in 1967 on Orkney. Redwing has also bred.

Hen Harrier

Offshore, wintering Great Northern Divers are common, and there are much smaller numbers of Black-throated Diver, which probably occur most frequently in late winter and spring. There is a good winter population of Slavonian Grebe, and small numbers of Little Auk around the islands. Wildfowl include Whooper Swan, though many or most of these go S after early winter unless the weather is very mild. About 125 Greenland White-fronted Geese are joined by much larger numbers of Greylags and Barnacles. These geese and swans occur more abundantly on passage, when they are joined by Pink-feet. The breeding ducks are joined by several thousand Long-tailed and a few hundred Scaup, Velvet Scoter, and Goldeneye, but Common Scoter only occur on passage. As in summer, Curlew are abundant, and Orkney supports a quarter of the British wintering population; although ubiquitous, they favour the pasture fields. Also notable are large numbers of Turnstone and Purple Sandpiper, as well as Knot, Sanderling, and Grey Plover. The gulls in the harbours and along the coast should be carefully checked for Glaucous and Iceland. Miscellaneous wintering species are Long-eared Owl and Snow Bunting, and the latter may be abundant.

In spring and autumn many of the breeding and wintering birds may be seen but there are several species which are more or less confined to these periods. A variety of waders occurs, Green-shank and Whimbrel being the most frequent, and these are joined by small numbers of Curlew Sandpiper, Black-tailed Godwit, Spotted Redshank, and Green Sandpiper. Offshore there is a large, sometimes very large, autumn passage of Sooty Shearwaters, especially off the N isles. Pomarine and Long-tailed Skuas and Little Gull are also possible, though they are distinctly uncommon. Other scarce migrants include Honey Buzzard and Rough-legged Buzzard. A wide variety of passerines occurs; among the commonest are Robin, Blackbird, Fieldfare, Redwing, Blackcap, Willow Warbler, Chiffchaff, Goldcrest, Brambling, Chaffinch, and Siskin, and with these there are small numbers of scarcer species — the more regular include Wryneck, Black Redstart, Bluethroat, Icterine, Barred, and Yellow-browed Warblers, Red-breasted Flycatcher, Great Grey and Red-backed Shrikes, Scarlet Rosefinch, and Ortolan and Lapland Buntings. The best conditions, in both spring and autumn, as on Fair Isle and Shetland, are SE winds. As the cream on the cake, a wide variety of rarities has been recorded, and, like Shetland, Orkney has immense potential for those who wish to find their own.

Information

RSPB Orkney Officer. Eric Meek, Smyril, Stenness, Stromness, Orkney KW16 3JX. Tel: 0856–850176.
RSPB North Hoy, warden: K. Fairclough, Ley House, Hoy, Orkney.
RSPB North Hill, summer warden: c/o Gowrie, Papa Westray KW17 2BU.
North Ronaldsay Bird Observatory: Dr. Kevin Woodbridge, NRBO, Twingness, North Ronaldsay, Orkney KW17 2BE.
P&O, Stromness: Tel. 0856–850 665.
Thomas and Bews, John O'Groats: Tel. 095581–353.
British Airways, Kirkwall: Tel. 0856–2420.
Loganair, Kirkwall: Tel. 0856–3457.
Copinsay Ferry: contact S. Foubister, tel. 085674–252.
Orkney Islands Shipping Co: 4 Ayre Rd, Kirkwall. Tel. 0856–2044; The Ferry Office, Houton, Orphir. Tel. 0856–81397.
Flaws Ferries, Rousay: Tel. 985682–203.

Wide Firth Ferries, Deerness: Tel. 085674–351.
Orkney Tourist Organisation: Broad St, Kirkwall, Orkney KW15 1NX. Tel.
0856–2856.
For accommodation on Papa Westray, contact Papa Community Co-op,
Beltane House, Papa Westray, Orkney KW17 2BU. Tel. 08574–267.
References:
Birds of Orkney by Booth, Cuthbert, and Reynolds (1984).
Island of Birds. A guide to Orkney Birds by Eric Meek. RSPB pamphlet.
Recorder: Orkney.

Site No. 104 Dunnet Head and Thurso (Highland)

Dunnet Head is the most northerly part of the Scottish mainland
and has good seabird colonies, best visited May to mid-July.
Nearby Thurso harbour regularly attracts white-winged gulls in
winter and early spring, and also, together with Dunnet Bay, a
variety of divers and seaduck.

Habitat

The head is topped by moorland with a few small lochs, and there
are good cliffs, especially on the N and E flanks. St John's Loch
and Loch of Mey at the base of the head attract waterfowl, and, to
the W, Dunnet Bay is sandy, with a rocky stretch of coast between
it and Thurso harbour.

**Access
(see map)**
OS Sheet No. 12

1. Leave Dunnet N on the B855, which ends after 4½ miles at
   the car park at Easter Head.
2. St John's Loch lies NE of Dunnet and can be seen from the
   A836.
3. Loch of Mey is 3 miles E of Dunnet. Access is either from
   Scarfskerry (permission must be sought to cross the intervening
   crofts) or N from the roadside pull-off on the A836 along an
   old peat track. The water level on the loch may be high and
   uninteresting, or low, attracting passage waders.
4. Castletown pier at the SW corner of Dunnet Bay gives views of
   the bay, and the A836 parallels the shore from here to Dunnet,
   with a car park at the E end of the bay.
5. In Thurso a track runs N from the A836 along the E bank of the
   River Thurso towards the ruined castle, and a footpath
   continues along the shore.
6. The breakwater in Thurso harbour itself is of straightforward
   access from the town, and the A836 also gives views of the sea
   and shore. Scrabster Harbour to the W is the departure point
   for the Orkney ferry, and sometimes holds a few divers,
   seaduck, and gulls.

Birds

Breeding seabirds on Dunnet Head include Fulmar, Guillemot,
Razorbill, Black Guillemot, Puffin, and Kittiwake. Great Skuas
summer and often attempt to breed on the moorland, especially
on the W flank, but they are usually thwarted by peat cutting and
muir-burn. Rock Dove and Raven haunt the cliffs, and Twite can
be found around the crofts. Small numbers of Arctic Terns breed

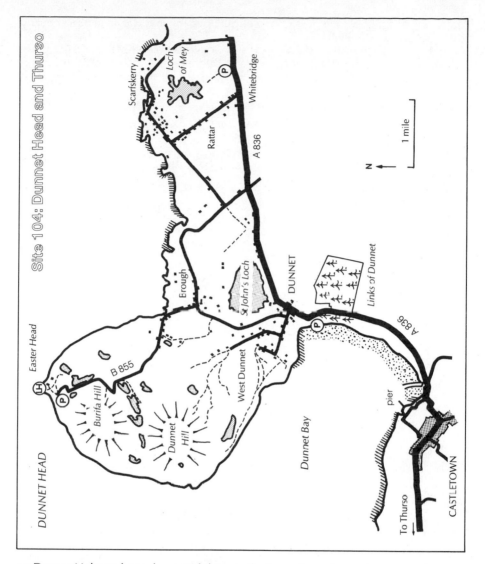

Site 104: Dunnet Head and Thurso

on Dunnet Links and may be seen fishing in the bay, where there are often summering Great Northern Divers.

In winter there are numbers of Red-throated Divers offshore at Thurso and Dunnet Bay, together with a few Black-throats and Great Northerns. Shag, Common Scoter, Long-tailed Duck, Goldeneye, Eider, and Red-breasted Merganser are also frequent, and are joined by Black Guillemot, Razorbill, and Guillemot. In the area there are small numbers of Whooper Swans, which, together with a variety of wildfowl, can be seen on St John's Loch. A flock of up to 100 Greenland White-fronted Geese regularly winter in the area of the Loch of Mey and Loch Heilen (to the S of our area). Greylag Geese are also regular, and there are occasionally Brent Geese in Dunnet Bay. There are few waders, but they include Turnstone and Purple Sandpiper. Glaucous and Iceland Gulls are usually present, sometimes several of each. A

Peregrine is often seen and, occasionally, large numbers of Snow Buntings.

The Loch of Mey is attractive during passage periods and has held several rarities, and Dunnet Bay is also worth checking for migrant waders, but St John's Loch is disturbed by fishermen in summer.

Iceland, Herring and Glaucous Gulls

Information   Recorder: Caithness.

Site No. 105 Clo Mor (Highland)

Mainland Britain's highest sea cliffs, Clo Mor rises to 921 feet and lies *c* 3 miles SE of Cape Wrath. It is truly spectacular and has huge seabird colonies. A visit from May to mid-July is recommended.

Habitat   The cliffs are backed by a typical Sutherland landscape of moors and hills.

Access   Leave the A838 at the Kyle of Durness to Keoldale. From here a
(see map)   passenger ferry crosses the Kyle, connecting with the road to Cape
OS Sheet No. 9   Wrath lighthouse. A minibus service runs to Cape Wrath several times a day in summer. Ask to be dropped off at the Kearvaig track and walk to Kearvaig, approaching Clo Mor from the W. Follow the cliffs E for *c* 3 miles and meet the minibus, by arrangement, at Inshore. This is a rough cross-country walk. Access is sometimes restricted because of the activity on the firing range.

Ptarmigan

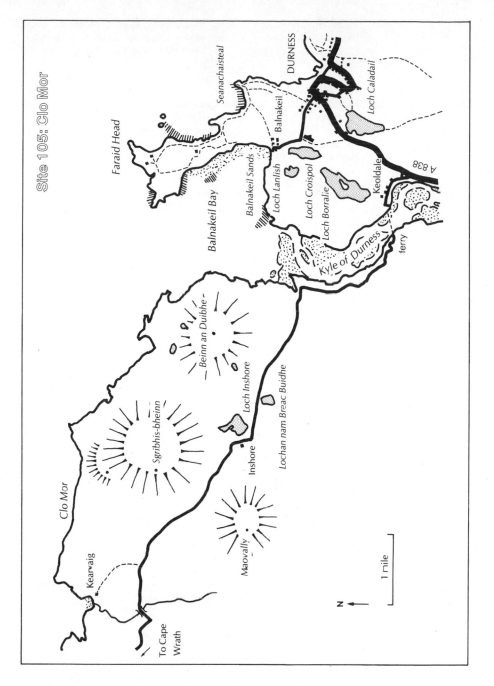

Site 105: Clo Mor

Breeding seabirds include Fulmar, Guillemot, Razorbill, Black **Birds** Guillemot, and one of the largest British colonies of Puffin. There are also large numbers of Gannet offshore. Golden Eagle, Peregrine, and Rock Dove also nest on the sea cliffs, and there are Ptarmigans on the rocky areas on the adjacent hills, sometimes as low as 600 feet, together with Red Grouse. Greenshanks occur along the river valleys, and there may be summering or even breeding Great Skuas. The Kyle of Durness holds Red-throated Diver, and wintering Great Northerns sometimes stay until late spring.

Other sites in the area
105.1 Faraid Head
(see map)

This has smaller and less spectacular seabird colonies than Clo Mor, but is easier to get to. Continue on the A838 to Durness and turn NW to Balnakeil. Park and walk along Balnakeil Sands to the head. On the grassy E slopes there are Puffins, and other seabirds include Fulmar, Kittiwake, Black Guillemot, Guillemot, and Razorbill. During late summer and autumn Sooty Shearwater may be seen offshore.

Information

Kyle of Durness ferry: Tel. 097181–377.
Minibus service to Cape Wrath: Tel. 097181–287.
Recorder: Sutherland.

Site No. 106 Sutherland (Highland)

An area of sombre hills, vast expanses of moorland, and flow country, this bleak but grand area is difficult to work. Distances are large and the going is rough, but the place has its own special attractions. The best time to visit is between the last week of May and early July; during the rest of the year there are few birds on the hills.

Habitat

The flow country of E Sutherland and Caithness is a mosaic of small lochans, peaty burns, and blanket bogs. The stronghold of breeding Greenshanks in Britain, it is threatened by afforestation. One third is owned by forestry interests, and large areas have been planted with exotic species of conifer. There are small areas of native birchwood, mainly along water courses, and other habitats include lochs and sea lochs, and the high tops, with several 'arctic' species breeding and the potential for others to do so.

Access

In this vast area it is impossible to single out any one place, because the birds are scattered over the available habitat. It is more a question of the convenience of access. The following areas are suggested as a beginning:
1. Loch Eriboll (OS sheet no. 9). The A838 parallels most of the loch's shore, approaching closest on the E side.
2. Loch Hope (OS sheet no. 9). A minor road runs along the E shore from Hope, on the A838.
3. Ben Hope (3,040 feet, OS sheet no. 9). A minor road runs S along the W flank of the mountain from the A838 at Hope.
4. The Kyle of Tongue (OS sheet no. 10) is a tidal inlet with extensive mudflats which attract passage waders. Tongue Pier is a good place to look from, and the A838 bisects the Kyle before paralleling the E shore for a short distance and connecting with an unclassified road.
5. Loch Loyal (OS sheet no. 10). This lies E of the A836.
6. Ben Loyal (2,509 feet, OS sheet no. 10). Access W from the A836.

7. Loch Naver (OS sheet no. 16). The B873 runs along the N shore.
8. Ben Klibreck (3,157 feet, OS sheet no. 16) lies E of the A836.
9. Loch Shin (OS sheet no. 16). The A838 runs along the E shore, and Lairg, on the A836, is at the S end.

Exploration away from the road is necessary to see at least some of the birds, and you should be properly equipped to deal with the sometimes harsh conditions. Although access is generally not a problem, grouse shooting and deer stalking take place in late summer and autumn; notices are often posted at access points giving details of stalking. You will not be welcome if you disturb either the hunters or the hunted, and as a general rule you should keep off the moors from the beginning of July.

Birds

The larger lochs have nesting Black-throated Diver and sometimes Red-throated as well, though these tend to favour the smaller, isolated pools and lochans, flying to the bigger lochs and sea to feed. The sea lochs have Eider and Arctic Tern.

Especially in the E, Hen Harrier and sometimes Short-eared Owl breed, favouring young conifer plantations, usually abandoning them once the trees are more than 6–8 feet high. These plantations also attract Black Grouse when they are young, again mainly in the E, though it is a difficult bird to find. Siskins frequent the older conifer woods. Buzzards are uncommon, but Golden Eagle, if not common, is widespread. The way to see one is to find a mountain and climb it, though they can be seen from the roads. Peregrine is also widespread, favouring the vicinity of cliffs and crags, especially near woodland. Merlins are scattered over the moorland areas in small numbers. Ptarmigan breed on every hill over 2,500 feet, and may sometimes be seen at lower elevations. They like areas with rocks, scree, or boulder piles, and overlap altitudinally with Red Grouse. Rocky screes and corries also attract the rare Snow Bunting, and you may even find Dotterel on the tops, though there have been very few recent records of either.

Golden Eagles

Greenshanks breed in broad marshy valleys in the moors, and often frequent the edges of freshwater lochs after they have brought off young; Dunlin are also scattered in marshy areas. Oystercatcher, Golden Plover, Curlew, and Snipe are widespread, but Whimbrel, Wood Sandpiper, and Red-necked Phalarope are rare and erratic breeding birds. Other species that may have nested, and are worth keeping an eye out for are Temminck's Stint, Sanderling, Green Sandpiper, and Turnstone. Common Gull, Teal, Wigeon, and sometimes Greylag Goose breed on scattered lochs on the moors and flows. Red-breasted Merganser is commonest near the coast, but may breed right up at the head of the glens, while Goosander favour the larger rivers and lochs. Common Scoter have bred on isolated small lochs on the moors, but there are few recent records. Common Sandpiper and Dipper occur on most streams and rivers. W Sutherland is the only area of mainland Britain to support more than a handful of Corncrakes; areas with a mosaic of habitats, including hay meadows, marshy ground, and other tall cover are favoured.

The commonest small birds are Meadow Pipit and Skylark. Wheatear is widespread, but Whinchat more scattered. Ring Ouzels are found around crags and rocky gullies on the hills. In birchwoods look for Woodcock, Tree Pipit, Wood and Willow Warblers, Redstart, Spotted Flycatcher, and Redpoll. These, and areas of rhododendron (usually found around houses), also attract Redwing — Britain's first breeding record was in Sutherland in 1925. Brambling bred in 1920, and may do so again. Twite favour the vicinity of old buildings, rough pasture, and moorland edge, especially on the coast. They particularly like to feed on short grazed turf around crofts, cliffs, and roadsides.

Information

Reference: *Sutherland Birds* edited by S. Angus (1983).
Recorder: Sutherland.

Site No. 107 Handa (Highland)

This superb island off NW Sutherland holds over 100,000 breeding seabirds and is easily accessible. It is an RSPB reserve, and the best time to visit is May to early July.

Habitat

The island covers 766 acres and is only a few hundred yards offshore. On the N coast, cliffs rise to over 400 feet, but the other shores have sandy beaches and dunes. Inland is rough sheep pasture and heather moor, with six small lochans. There is a small plantation by the bothy.

Access
OS Sheet No. 9

Handa is open 1 April–10 September, except Sunday. Boats leave from Tarbet, which is reached from the A894 by taking a minor road NW c 3 miles NE of Scourie. The first boat is usually at 10.00. There is a shelter and display on the quay, and a warden is present in summer. Members of the RSPB may stay overnight in the bothy by arrangement with the Society's Scottish Office. Keep to the marked paths.

Black-throated Diver is usually present offshore in summer, and wintering Great Northerns sometimes stay until mid-May. Red-throated Diver, Eider, and Shelduck breed on the island. The 25,000–30,000 Guillemots vastly outnumber the Fulmars, Shags, Black Guillemots, and several hundred pairs of Puffin, but Razorbill and Kittiwake are both very common. Both Great and Arctic Skuas breed and are increasing, together with Great Black-backed and Herring Gulls. Peregrine and Buzzard visit, and Stonechat and Wheatear nest on the grassland and moor.

Birds

Passage periods see small numbers of waders on the shore, and there are occasionally movements of interesting seabirds offshore. Pomarine Skua is possible in early May, and Manx and Sooty Shearwaters in autumn.

The region S of Loch Laxford holds some of the typical Sutherland specialities — Black and Red-throated Divers, raptors, and Greenshank. The A894 and A838 cross the area, as well as the minor roads to Tarbet. Be prepared for heavy going, and have an OS map to hand if you leave the road. Stalkers' paths and tracks are clearly marked, and there are few restrictions on access outside of the deer-stalking season, mid-August onwards.

Other Sites in the Area
107.1 Tarbet

RSPB summer warden: c/o Mrs A. Munro, Tarbet, Foindle, Lairg, Sutherland IV27 4SS.
RSPB Scottish Office, 17 Regent Terrace, Edinburgh EH7 5BN. Tel. 031–556 5624/9042.
Boatman: William MacRae, Scourie. Tel. 0971–2156.
Recorder: Sutherland.

Information

Site No. 108 Inverpolly (Highland)

Inverpolly is magnificently scenic. A National Nature Reserve covers 26,827 acres, and holds the usual range of highland species. It is best April–June.

This remote, almost uninhabited area has a range of habitats. Lochs, including the large Loch Sionascaig, streams, bog, and moorland rise to the hills — Cul Mor reaches 2,787 feet. There are many small areas of remnant birch-hazel woodland, and the high tops form an arctic-alpine habitat. Sandy beaches and small islands flank the coast.

Habitat

The NNR covers a roughly rectangular area of land between Enard Bay in the NW and the A835 between Drumrunie and Elphin in the SE. It is managed by the NCC in co-operation with the estate owners. Access is unrestricted, though permission is required from the Assynt Estate Office to visit Drumrunie (the area adjacent to the A835) from 15 July to 21 October. The NCC's Knockan Information Centre, signposted on the A835 c 2½ miles SW of Elphin, is open Monday–Friday, 10.00–18.00 from May to mid-September, and can provide information and leaflets for the adjacent nature trail. No roads penetrate the reserve, and there are few tracks; access is difficult and walkers should be properly equipped. Try walking the peripheral roads and the nature trail, and from the road on the W side of the reserve, just S of

Access
OS Sheet No. 15

Inverkirkaig, walk up the N bank of the River Kirkaig to the falls. A variety of woodland species may be seen in the glen.

Birds

Breeding birds include Black-throated Diver, which favour the larger lochs, including Sionascaig, and may sometimes be seen on the lochs adjacent to the A835. Red-throated Diver, Red-breasted Merganser, Goosander, and Wigeon, with small numbers of Greylag Goose, also frequent the lochs, especially on the coast, where Fulmar, Shag, Eider, and Black Guillemot breed. The high tops have Ptarmigan, with Red Grouse lower down. Snow Buntings, which are winter visitors to the area, can stay late into spring and may even breed. Golden Eagle, Buzzard, Merlin, and Peregrine occur, together with Raven. Although eagles may be seen from the road, exploration on foot can be more productive. Golden Plover and Greenshank breed on the moors, with Ring Ouzel in the higher, rockier gullies. The birch woodland has Woodcock, Wood Warbler, Spotted Flycatcher, and sometimes Redwing. Twite occur on the moorland edge and around crofts near the coast.

Peregrine chasing Red Grouse

Other Sites in the Area

108.1 Loch Broom
OS Sheet Nos. 19 and 20

This is used by Soviet factory ships in winter, and these attract hordes of Kittiwakes. The number of ships varies, but even with just a handful it is possible to find double figures of both Iceland and Glaucous Gulls in winter and into early spring; after NW gales in mid-winter large numbers of Icelands could well occur. The ships stretch the whole length of the loch and out to sea. The A835 runs along the N shore, to the SW of Ullapool, while the mouth of Loch Broom is visible from a minor road to the Rubha Cadail lighthouse, which leaves the A835 2 miles NW of the town.

Information

Wardens: Knockan Cottage (tel. 085484–234) or Strathpolly (tel. 05714–204).
Assynt Estate Office: Tel. 05714–203
Recorder: Ross-shire.

Site No. 109 Beinn Eighe (Highland)

Beinn Eighe was the first National Nature Reserve to be declared by the NCC, established to protect remnant areas of Caledonian pinewood. The 11,860 acres also incorporates uplands, and is best visited May to early July.

There are c 450 acres of natural pinewoods with an understorey of **Habitat**
heather, as well as about 150 acres of birchwood. A further 1,200
acres has been re-planted with native tree species. Woodland is
concentrated along the SW shore of Loch Maree. The hills rise to
over 3,000 feet; the highest is Ruadh-stac Mor, which peaks at
3,313 feet just outside the reserve. The unwooded areas are
mostly heather and grass moorland and bog, but on the high tops
this gives way to dwarf shrubs, which mix with mosses and
liverworts to form an arctic-alpine heath.

There is unrestricted access to the hills in a large area S of Loch **Access**
Maree and N of the A896 which incorporates the NNR; this is OS Sheet Nos. 19
except for 1 September – 21 November when deer stalking takes and 25
place and permission must be sought from local estates to enter
certain areas. Birdwatchers however are unlikely to visit during
this period. The A832 runs along the SW flank of Loch Maree, and
there are several car parks along the shore. The reserve is
bordered to the SE by the A896, but within this area there are no
roads, and walkers should be properly equipped. The NCC's
Aultroy Visitor Centre is at Kinlochewe, on the A832 1 mile N of
the junction with the A896. Information and advice are available,
as well as leaflets for two nature trails which start at the car park
1¾ miles further NW. These are I and 4 miles long and run
through some typical woodland, moorland, and mountain
habitats. The pony trail which runs W from the Visitor Centre
gives the best access to the highest ground. The Centre is open
June–September.

Black-throated Diver

The areas of relic woodland have resident Sparrowhawk, Wood- **Birds**
cock, and Great Spotted Woodpecker, while Tree Pipit, Redstart,
and Wood and Willow Warblers are summer visitors, and these
join Siskin and Redpoll. Both Common and Scottish Crossbills
can sometimes be seen, and a really lucky observer may find
singing (and breeding) Redwings in the birchwoods. On the

lochs, streams, and rivers there are Red- and Black-throated Divers, Goosander, Red-breasted Merganser, Greylag Goose, Common Sandpiper, and Dipper. Golden Eagle, Buzzard, Merlin, Peregrine, and Short-eared Owl occur, as well as Raven. Probably the best chance to see an eagle is to regularly scan the mountainsides. The common birds on the moorland are Skylark and Meadow Pipit, and these are joined by smaller numbers of Golden Plover, Ring Ouzel, Wheatear, Whinchat, and a few Twite. In the wetter, boggier valley bottoms you may find Greenshank. Higher on the hills, Red Grouse are joined by Ptarmigan, and a thorough search of the tops may reveal summering Snow Bunting.

Information

Warden: Anancaun Field Centre, Kinlochewe, Ross-shire IV22 2PD. Tel. 044584–244/254.
Aultroy Visitor Centre: Tel. 044584–258.
Recorder: Ross-shire.

Site No. 110 North and South Uists (Western Isles)

These islands are undoubtedly one of the most attractive parts of Britain. Supporting a range of raptors, wildfowl, and large numbers of breeding waders, the star bird is perhaps Corncrake, which maintains its British stronghold here. The best time to visit is May–July for breeding birds, but autumn could be productive for migrants. Loch Druidibeg National Nature Reserve covers 4,145 acres, and the RSPB's Balranald reserve is 1,625 acres.

Habitat

The long sandy beaches of the Atlantic seaboard back onto the fertile machair, level grassland formed by a mixture of wind-blown shell-sand and peat, which supports the highest density of breeding waders in Britain. Often cultivated, the crops may still provide cover for nesting birds. In the machair and extending towards the E flank of the islands is a mosaic of lochs, marshes, and wet grazing. The land gets more acidic and peaty as it rises to the E hills, which peak at 2,033 feet on South Uist, but at only 1,139 feet on low-lying, watery North Uist. The islands are almost treeless, with only small, isolated stands.

Access

Caledonian MacBrayne operate car ferries to the islands. From Skye (Uig) to North Uist (Lochmaddy) the voyage normally takes 2 hrs, with sailings once or twice daily (except Sunday) from mid-May to mid-September, but not Tuesday and Thursday (or Saturday and Thursday) Uig to Lochmaddy during the rest of the year. From Oban to South Uist (Loch Boisdale) the journey takes 5½ – 9 hrs, with daily sailings (except Sunday) in summer, but only on Monday, Wednesday, and Friday in winter. Cars are advised to book well in advance in summer. Both crossings are good for seabirds, with a good chance of Storm Petrel and shearwaters. There are flights from Glasgow: Loganair operates a weekday service to Barra, and an inter-island service from Barra to Benbecula. British Airways fly daily (except Sunday) to Benbecula. For details of accommodation, contact the tourist board. Crofting land in the Hebrides, as elsewhere in N and W Scotland, is often unfenced. Due care should be taken, and if in doubt about access to any particular area please ask first.

North Uist, Benbecula, and South Uist are all connected by two causeways, and there are large areas of essentially similar habitat bisected by the main N–S road. The following areas deserve special mention, but are ony representative of the whole area.

South Uist
OS Sheet Nos.
22 and 31

1. Lochboisdale harbour attracts Glaucous and Iceland Gulls in winter, as well as divers and seabirds.
2. Loch Hallan at Daliburgh, at the junction of the A865 and the B888, often has summering Whooper Swan. Take the road W at the crossroads in the village and after 1 mile follow a track N to view from the cemetery (which avoids disturbance). Do not approach the loch over agricultural land.
3. Rubha Ardvule peninsula is a good spot for seawatching. Access is down a road and track from the main road. Visitors must keep clear of the point when in use by the military, but this is infrequently the case.
4. The Howmore area. Formerly much visited because of the drake Steller's Eider that was resident 1972–84. It has a typical range of coast/machair/marshland species, with cheap accommodation at Howmore Hostel.
5. Loch Druidibeg NNR. View the loch from the main road and B890. Access away from these requires a permit during the breeding season. Birds include divers, breeding Greylag Geese, waders, and sometimes summering Whooper Swan. The trees around Grogarry Lodge provide some cover for migrants.
6. On the B890 to Loch Skipport is a grove of rhododendrons and deciduous and coniferous trees which attract migrants and have breeding Long-eared Owl, Goldcrest, and Greenfinch. It is a good spot to scan for eagles over the slopes of Hecla.
7. Hecla and Beinn Mhor support Golden Eagle, Red Grouse, etc. Look for eagles from the main road or the road to Loch Skipport.
8. Loch Bee is excellent for wildfowl, with up to 500 Mute Swans. View from the main road crossing the loch.
9. Ardivachar is a good seawatching spot. Take the road W from the A865 in the N of the island to the peninsula. The best birdwatching is in North Bay.

Benbecula
OS Sheet No. 22

1. The sewage outfall at Balivanich on the B892 attracts gulls, and is good for Glaucous and Iceland, even in mid-summer. Waders frequent the adjacent foreshore and aerodrome (check with Air Traffic Control before entering the latter).
2. The causeway from Benbecula to North Uist gives views of the intertidal flats for waders.

North Uist
OS Sheet Nos. 18 and 22

1. Balranald RSPB reserve has areas of beach, dunes, machair, pools, and marshland, and is largely crofted. All three divers are often present in summer, and several species of raptor regularly visit. There is a dense population of breeding ducks and waders (and sometimes non-breeding Red-necked Phalarope) as well as 10–15 pairs of Corncrake. Arctic Terns breed, and an excellent seawatching spot is the headland of Aird an

Runair, the most westerly spot in the Outer Hebrides. Turn W off the A865 2 miles NW of Bayhead, signed Hougharry, and fork left to the reception cottage at Goular. The reserve is open at all times, but visitors should contact the summer warden and keep to the paths marked on the map at the cottage.

2. Loch Scadavay, N of the A867, is good for divers, and Arctic Skua breeds in the vicinity.

3. Loch Skealtar, N of the A867 just W of Lochmaddy, is another good spot for divers; up to 21 Black-throated have been counted in August.

4. Lochmaddy harbour is worth checking for gulls, Black Guillemots, and other seabirds, and eagles may be seen to the S over the Lees.

5. The trees around Newton House and at Clachan attract migrants. Both are on the B893 in the NE of the island. Permission to enter should be sought from Newton House and Clachan Farm respectively, but both can be seen well from the road. Other areas that have proved useful in recent years are the conifer plantation on Ben Langass, S of the A867, and that on Ben Aulasary, just E of the minor road between Bayhead and Sollas.

6. The extensive foreshore at Valley Strand and Vallaquie Strand on the N coast (off the A865) are good for waders.

Birds

Red-throated is the commonest diver and can often be seen flying between its tiny nesting pools and fishing grounds on the sea. There are about five pairs of Black-throated Divers, almost all on North Uist. They breed and fish on the larger lochs and are less often seen in the air. Great Northern are present until June, almost always on the sea. Fulmar, Cormorant, and Shag can be seen around the coast at any time, but most other seabirds are summer visitors. Arctic Skua breeds mainly in the centre of North Uist, with a few on Benbecula and South Uist. Five species of gull are joined by non-breeding Kittiwakes offshore, as well as the odd summering Glaucous or even Iceland Gull. Arctic, Common, and Little Terns are widespread in that order of abundance, as are Black Guillemots. There are small numbers of Razorbills and Guillemots and these share the cliffs with Rock Doves.

A speciality is several hundred pairs of Greylag Geese, deemed 'wild', rather than 'feral'. Their stronghold is Loch Druidibeg, which has 60–70 pairs. Outside the breeding season the flock grazes around Grogarry. Though several Whooper Swans may summer, they have not been proved to nest since 1947. Shelduck, Teal, Shoveler, Eider, and Red-breasted Merganser, and small numbers of Wigeon and Gadwall, are regular breeders. Raptors include Hen Harrier, with about a dozen nesting females, Buzzard, Golden Eagle, Kestrel, Merlin, Peregrine, and Short-eared Owl. These may be seen hunting anywhere, though eagles favour the mountains and harriers are best seen around Loch Hallan on South Uist and Loch Mor on Benbecula. Wandering White-tailed Eagles from Rhum are now a possibility on the E coast. Red Grouse occur thinly on the moorland, together with small numbers of Golden Plover and Greenshank. Commoner breeding waders are Oystercatcher, Ringed Plover, Lapwing, Dunlin, Snipe, Redshank, and Common Sandpiper, and a few Red-necked Phalaropes still hang on. Corncrakes arrive in mid-April and can best be seen early in the season before the vegetation has grown up. Rush, sedge, and iris beds are favoured on arrival, and later on hay meadows. They call most frequently 00.00–04.00, and only irregularly during the day. The common passerines are Skylark, Meadow and Rock Pipits, Pied Wagtail, Wren (the Hebrides subspecies), Stonechat, Wheatear, Sedge Warbler, Hooded Crow, Raven, Starling (the Shetland subspecies), Twite, House Sparrow, and Reed and Corn Buntings. The Hebridean race of Song Thrush can be quite elusive, favouring heathery hill country as well as areas of shrubs, and Blackbirds are also confined to gardens and pockets of woodland on the W coast, together with Long-eared Owls in the latter.

Corncrake

In spring, N–NW winds can prompt movements of skuas. Up to 271 Long-tailed and 436 Pomarine Skuas have been seen at Balranald in a day, as well as the more regular Great and Arctic. Every year since this skua passage was discovered (in 1971) and that observers have been present, Long-tailed and Pomarine have been seen, usually in the third week of May, though numbers are obviously weather-dependent. Manx Shearwaters can be seen, sometimes in large numbers, April–August, as well as Sooty from June onwards. Storm and sometimes Leach's Petrels occur off the W coast in strong onshore winds, but, as for the shearwaters, the boat crossings are a better bet, especially for Storm Petrels. Gannets are common offshore March–November. Pink-footed, Brent, and Barnacle Geese pass through on passage, but usually do not stop. Migrant waders may include Little Stint, Curlew Sandpiper, Black-tailed Godwit, and Whimbrel, while Ruff favour the machair and crofts. Only small numbers of migrant passerines occur, notably the Greenland race of Redpoll, and Snow Bunting, which may be abundant.

In winter, Great Northern Diver and Slavonian Grebe are widespread offshore, with just a few Red-throated Divers. Several hundred Whooper Swans winter, and Greenland White-fronted Geese are erratic visitors in small numbers; Nunton on Benbecula, Loch Hallan, and Loch Bee are the most regular areas. Other wildfowl include Scaup, Long-tailed Duck (especially between Rubha Ardvule and Grogarry on South Uist), and Goldeneye. There are internationally important populations of Ringed Plover, Sanderling, and Turnstone, and smaller numbers of Knot and Purple Sandpiper are joined by a few Greenshanks and the odd Grey Plover. Glaucous and Iceland Gulls are both regular, and after persistent NW gales Iceland Gulls may be relatively common. Small flocks of Rooks and Jackdaws winter.

Other Sites in the Area
110.1 Skye
OS Sheet Nos. 23, 32, and 33

Skye is the northernmost of the Inner Hebrides and is huge, nearly 50 miles long, with dramatic scenery. Mostly sheep-walk with some areas of forestry, no one site is outstanding. Divers, Peregrine, Golden Eagle, Ptarmigan, Black Grouse, Black Guillemot, Greenshank, and Dipper all breed, and exploration on foot can be worthwhile in many places, though the Cuillin Hills in the S have Ptarmigan and eagles.

Information

RSPB Balranald, summer warden: c/o Visitor's Cottage, Goular, near Hougharry, Lochmaddy, North Uist, Outer Hebrides.
NCC Loch Druidibeg, warden: Stilligarry, South Uist, Outer Hebrides.
Caledonian MacBrayne: Ferry Terminal, Gourock PA19 1QP, tel. 0475–33755; Lochboisdale, tel. 08784–288; Lochmaddy, tel. 08763–337.
Loganair Ltd: Glasgow Airport, Abbotsinch, Renfrewshire, tel. 041–889 3181; Stornoway, tel. 0851–3067.
British Airways: 134 Renfrew St, Glasgow. Tel. 041–332 9666.
Outer Hebrides Tourist Board: 4 South Beach St, Stornoway, Isle of Lewis. Tel. 0851–3088.
Reference: *The Birds of the Outer Hebrides* by Peter Cunningham (1983).
Recorder: Inverness-shire (Skye), Outer Hebrides (all other sites).

Site No. 111 Rhum (Highland)

Rhum was the centre for the successful re-introduction of White-tailed Eagles into Britain. It has many other attractions, however, including numbers of breeding seabirds. The best time to visit is April–June. The island is a National Nature Reserve covering 26,400 acres, managed by the NCC.

Habitat

The basic habitats are the coast (with rugged cliffs, sandy bays, and maritime grassland), moorland, the higher more exposed hilltops, relic woodland, and, importantly, reafforestation. The NCC is trying to re-establish woodland and has planted extensive areas with native trees, notably in the E.

Access
OS Sheet No. 39

A passenger ferry from Mallaig run by Caledonian MacBrayne serves Rhum. The boat sails on Monday, Wednesday, Thursday, and Saturday, and the journey takes 3–4 hrs. The boat returns the same day, and landing on a day-trip is only possible on summer Saturdays. Occasionally, between June and September, day-trips may be organised from Mallaig or Arisaig. Day visitors land at Loch Scresort and may explore the area around Kinloch, including the nature trails, with no formalities. However, a day-trip allows too little time on Rhum to be worthwhile (though the crossing has many birds — all three divers, Manx and sometimes Sooty Shearwaters, and Storm Petrel are possibilities). Prior permission is needed to stay overnight, and all intended visitors are asked to contact the warden. Full-board accommodation is available in Kinloch Castle, and there are bothies and a camp site (but camping is uncomfortable July–October because of midges). Apply well in advance to the chief warden.

Breeding species include Red-throated Diver, Fulmar, Shag, **Birds** Common, Lesser and Great Black-backed, and Herring Gulls, Kittiwake, Guillemot, Razorbill, Black Guillemot, and Puffin, and occasionally Common or Arctic Tern. However, the Kittiwake and auk ledges are fairly inaccessible, hidden at the base of the cliffs. There are c 100,000 pairs of Manx Shearwaters, which breed on mountain tops in the centre of the island. Storm Petrels occur offshore, but there is no evidence of breeding. Small numbers of Greylag Geese nest, and are also regular on passage. Other wildfowl include Shelduck, Teal, Eider, and Red-breasted Merganser. There are two to five pairs of Golden Eagles, as well as Peregrine, Merlin, and Sparrowhawk. 82 White-tailed Eagles were released on Rhum between 1975 and 1985, but most have now dispersed and can occur anywhere in the Inner Hebrides, or indeed, as far away as Shetland, the Outer Hebrides, and Northern Ireland. They may still be seen on Rhum, but are not guaranteed, and indeed the chances are better on some of the other Inner Hebrides. Red Grouse and Raven breed on the hills, and waders include Oystercatcher and Ringed and Golden Plovers, with Woodcock in the wooded areas, occasionally together with Long- or Short-eared Owl. Common Sandpiper and Dipper nest along the streams. On the open ground the common birds are Meadow Pipit and Skylark, together with Stonechat, Whinchat, and Wheatear, and Ring Ouzel in the hills. Whitethroat, Willow Warbler, Chiffchaff, a few pairs of Wood Warbler, and Siskin nest, and the number and variety of woodland birds is likely to increase as the forest develops.

White-tailed Eagle

Offshore, especially in late summer, you could see Sooty Shearwater, Gannet, and Great and Arctic Skuas. On passage Rhum records a variety of waders and wildfowl, including Whooper Swan, Pink-footed, White-fronted, and Barnacle Geese, Sanderling, Whimbrel, Greenshank, and Turnstone, and numbers of the common passerines. In winter there are Great Northern Divers and small numbers of seaduck offshore.

Information

NCC warden: The White House, Kinloch, Isle of Rhum, Scotland.
Day-trips from Arisaig, MV *Shearwater*: Tel. 06875–224.
Day-trips from Mallaig: Mr Bruce Watt, tel. 0687–2233.
Recorder: Records should be sent or handed to the island's warden.

Site No. 112 Islay (Strathclyde)

Islay's major draw is its geese. Up to 70% of Greenland's breeding Barnacles and 25% of its White-fronts winter here. A visitor to Islay is guaranteed not only a wide diversity of species, but also a superb spectacle. The RSPB's Loch Gruinart reserve covers over 4,050 acres.

Habitat

The southernmost of the Inner Hebrides, Islay is a large island. The varied habitats include deciduous plantations around houses and farms, conifer plantations, extensive areas of scrub, moorland, cliff (including the spectacular Mull of Oa), dunes, machair, freshwater and sealochs, rivers, streams, marshes, and arable land. The extensive areas of peat bog are important to the Greenland White-fronts. The island lacks high hills, but the Paps on neighbouring Jura dominate the N horizon.

Access
OS Sheet No. 60

Caledonian Macbrayne operates car and passenger ferries from Kennacraig, Kintyre, to Port Ellen and Port Askaig, and the 2-hr voyage is good for divers and other seabirds. There are daily services, with two sailings Monday–Saturday. Loganair operates two flights each weekday from Glasgow, with one on Saturday. The Islay Field Centre (funded by the Islay Natural History Trust) offers self-catering accommodation for up to 15, with specialist facilities for birdwatchers. For full details of accommodation, contact the tourist board. The geese and raptors are widespread, and exploration with the OS map is strongly recommended, but the following spots are worth mentioning:
1. Loch Gruinart. Gruinart Flats, at the S end of the loch is an important area for geese, especially Barnacles, and forms a part of the RSPB reserve. The B8017 crosses the flats and gives good views of the S of the reserve, while the minor road N along the Ardnave peninsula gives views of the W. Park at Aoradh or Gruinart Farms. Numbers of Barnacles roost on the loch's saltings, and the tidal flats are used by a variety of waders. The whole area attracts raptors.
2. The hummocky moorland and areas of birch along the stream that flows into the E side of Loch Gruinart are good for Black Grouse. Take the minor road N off the B8017 that follows the E shore of Loch Gruinart to Bun-an-uillt and follow the stream E from there.

3. Loch Gorm has breeding terns on its islands, and the area supports Greenland White-fronts. The loch is circumnavigated at a distance by minor roads. Breeding seabirds can be seen at Sanaigmore: drive to the end of the B8018 and walk W.
4. The Rinns. The dunes at Machir Bay on the NW coast often have feeding Chough, and the W cliffs attract Peregrine and Chough, especially the area N of Lossit Point around Cnoc Breac. Seawatching from Rubha na Faing can be interesting. Take the track W off the minor road which runs N out of Portnahaven.
5. Port Charlotte often has Black Guillemot in winter.
6. Bruichladdich, on the W shore of Loch Indaal, is a spot for Greenland White-front, and the mudflats adjacent to the A847 at Traigh an Luig to the N are good for waders.
7. There are waders on the flats at Bridgend, on the shore of Loch Indaal; view from the A847 and A846 to the N and S of Bridgend. Barnacle Geese roost in Bridgend Bay. The bridge over the River Sorn is a good spot to look for Dipper.
8. Bowmore harbour in Loch Indaal attracts waders and seaduck, with divers and grebes offshore, the effluent from the distillery being a particular attraction. The coast to the SW from Ralneach Mhor to Gartbreck is good for waders.
9. The B8016 crosses an extensive area of mosses, and there is a Hen Harrier roost in the Loch Tallant area, just N of the Laggan Bridge; up to ten birds may be seen, as well as other raptors. This road is good for Greenland White-fronts, especially the N end. At Avenvogie the road runs alongside extensive plantations, and a minor road heads NE through the trees. These plantations hold Black Grouse, which should be looked for along the edges.
10. Port Ellen has divers and grebes in the mouth of the harbour as well as seaduck.
11. The S cliffs of The Oa are good for Golden Eagle, Peregrine, and Chough, and can be reached along a minor road SW from Port Ellen.
12. Port Askaig has Black Guillemot, often the whole year round, and there are often Arctic Skuas in the Sound.

Birds

In winter, Great Northern Divers are quite common offshore, and there are a few Red-throated and good numbers of Slavonian Grebe. Wildfowl include Whooper Swan and up to 20,000 Barnacle Geese. Barnacles usually peak October–November, immediately after their arrival in Britain; numbers then fall slightly as they disperse. They favour the pasture around the head of the two sealochs, and are joined by up to 5,000 Greenland White-fronts. These tend to be more scattered, occurring in small, secretive flocks on the rougher grassland. A small flock of Greylags frequents the Bridgend area. There may be one or two 'wild' Snow Geese, as well as vagrant Canada Geese of one of the small subspecies. Up to 1,200 Scaup frequent the harbour at Bowmore, and sometimes move to Bruichladdich or Port Charlotte. They are joined by Goldeneye, Eider, Red-breasted Merganser, and a few Common Scoter. Dabbling duck concentrate on the shores of inner Loch Indaal, and this area also attracts small numbers of waders. The odd Glaucous and Iceland Gulls appear in winter and, like Black Guillemots, they can be found in the harbours.

Black-throated Divers are scarce summer visitors, seen mainly around the coast. Red-throated Divers are resident, and frequent small lochs as well as the sea and sealochs. Breeding seabirds include Fulmar, Cormorant, Shag, Kittiwake, Common, Arctic, and Little Terns, Razorbill, Guillemot, and Black Guillemot. These are joined on the cliffs by Rock Dove, and non-breeding Arctic Skuas may be present offshore. Shelduck, Teal, Eider, and Red-breasted Merganser are widespread, but Common Scoter is distinctly uncommon, with only a handful of pairs, and there are occasionally summering Whooper Swans. Breeding waders include Oystercatcher, Ringed and Golden Plovers, Common Sandpiper, and a few Dunlin. A few pairs of Golden Eagle are resident, as well as Buzzard, Hen Harrier, Peregrine, Merlin, and Barn and Short-eared Owls, and these may be joined in winter by wandering White-tailed Eagles from the re-introduction programme on Rhum. Red Grouse breed on the moors, while Black Grouse favour birch scrub and the tussocky grass on the edges of conifer plantations, which hold Siskin and Redpoll. In summer, Tree Pipit, Whinchat, and Wood Warbler are present. Rock Pipit, Twite, and Stonechat are all widespread residents. There are up to 100 pairs of Chough, and Ravens are widespread.

Black Grouse lekking

Other Sites in the Area
112.1 West Loch Tarbert
OS Sheet No. 62

West Loch Tarbert has all three divers in winter, as well as Slavonian Grebe, Glaucous, and sometimes Iceland Gull. These can be seen around the harbour and from the ferry as you leave for Islay.

Information

RSPB warden: Bushmill, Gruinart, Isle of Islay, Argyllshire PA44 7PW.
Islay Field Centre: Port Charlotte, Isle of Islay, Argyllshire PA48 7TX. Tel. 049685–288.
Mid-Argyll, Kintyre and Islay Tourist Board: The Pier, Campbeltown, Argyll PA28 6EF. Tel. 0586–52056.
Caledonian MacBrayne Ltd: The Ferry Terminal, Gourock PA19 1QP. Tel. 0475–33755.
Loganair, Glasgow Airport: Tel. 041–889 3181.
Reference: *Birds in Islay* by Gordon Booth (1981).
Recorder: Argyllshire.

Site No. 113 Loch Ryan (Dumfries and Galloway)

This large, sheltered sealoch holds small numbers of divers, grebes, and seaduck. The best time for a visit is winter.

The loch has a rather narrow shoreline, with only two significant areas of mud, around the Wig and on the S shore.

Habitat

The A77 follows the E and S shores as far as Stranraer, while the A718 hugs the W shore N to the Wig. Most of the diving duck and Wigeon occur on the S shore, but Eider are scattered in several areas, which can make location of any King Eider present time-consuming. Cairnryan has been favoured by the species. Most birds can be seen by stopping at regular intervals and scanning the shore and loch.

Access
OS Sheet Nos. 76 and 82

Winter brings small numbers of both Slavonian and Black-necked Grebes and all three divers, though Red-throated are dominant. Seaduck include several hundred Eider, with smaller numbers of Common Scoter, Scaup, Goldeneye, and Red-breasted Merganser, and sometimes Long-tailed Ducks. There have been several King Eiders over the years. Wigeon can peak at around 2,000. A handful of Black Guillemots winter, together with small numbers of waders. Glaucous Gulls are occasional visitors, and parties of Twite may be found, especially on the Wig.

Birds

Portpatrick, SW of Stranraer on the A77, is a good spot for Black Guillemot. The area around the harbour is best — they nest in the harbour walls. Check the gulls here at the same time.

Other Sites in the Area
113.1 Portpatrick
OS Sheet No. 82

Up to 30 Hen Harriers roost here in late October, numbers falling to about twelve in winter. Sparrowhawk, Peregrine, Merlin, and Short-eared Owl can also be seen. Leave Stranraer S on the A77 and turn SE on to the A716 and then take the A757 towards Glenluce. Finally, after 4 miles, turn SW onto the A715. The harriers can be seen on the N side of this road, 1 mile S of the junction with the A757. You should not attempt photography in this sensitive MOD area. About 500 Greenland White-fronts occur around West Freugh, but are difficult to pinpoint. Try the fields N of the A757, E of Lochans. There are also up to 3,000 Greylags, as well as several feral Snow Geese, based on Lochinch, Castle Kennedy.

113.2 West Freugh Airfield
OS Sheet No. 82

To the N of Stranraer, this is a good seawatching point with a constant stream of Gannets passing in summer and autumn, as well as Cormorants and Shags. From mid-August to October, Manx Shearwater, Storm Petrel, and skuas may also be seen, especially in strong W winds. Leave Stranraer N on the A718 and then follow an unclassified road NW to the lighthouse.

113.3 Corsewall Point
OS Sheet No. 76

Recorder: Kirkcudbrightshire.

Information

Site No. 114 Loch Ken (Dumfries and Galloway)

To the NW of Castle Douglas, Loch Ken attracts Greenland White-fronted and Greylag Geese. To the W, the National Trust for Scotland has a wildfowl refuge near Threave Castle, covering 1,300 acres. The RSPB has two reserves totalling 390 acres, adjacent to the loch. For wintering wildfowl, October–March is the peak period, and for breeding birds May–June.

Habitat

The River Dee has been dammed in a hydro-electric scheme to form Loch Ken, with areas of freshwater marsh, especially at the head of the loch. The surrounding area has farmland, open hillsides, and woodland.

Access (see maps)

OS Sheet Nos. 77, 83, and 84

1. Carlingwark Loch, a 105-acre pool visible from the A75 immediately S of Castle Douglas, holds duck, including Goldeneye and Goosander.
2. Castle Douglas to Bridge of Dee. Greylags and a few Pink-feet are regular, but although Bean Geese may be seen around Threave and S of Castle Douglas (anywhere between Gelston and Netherhall), they are erratic and unpredictable. Pink-feet can usually be seen in the pastures W of the B736, 1–2 miles S of Castle Douglas. The geese move around and you have to be prepared to search the area.
3. Threave Wildfowl Refuge is open November–March. Enter at Kelton Mains Farm or Lodge of Kelton Farm, off the A75 1 and 1¾ miles W of Castle Douglas. There are footpaths to four observation points overlooking the marshes and river, and maps showing their location are posted at the access points. Entrance is free. Ducks, including Goosander, Red-breasted Merganser, and Shoveler, use the river, and Hen Harrier and Kingfisher are occasionally seen.
4. W side of Loch Ken. The S section is visible by leaving the A713 W at Townhead of Greenlaw. Cross the river on the B795 and turn right immediately. This unclassified road gives good views of the loch as far as Mains of Duchrae, and this is the best area for geese and swans. Greenland White-fronts favour the rough grazing immediately S of Mains of Duchrae. Be careful not to block the road with your car here.
5. The A713 between New Galloway and Crossmichael gives views of the entire E shore of the loch. Greenland White-fronts favour the permanent pasture on the drum SW of Cogarth Farm.
6. The RSPB's two Ken–Dee Marshes reserves comprise water meadows and freshwater marshes at Kenmure Holms and adjacent to the loch SE of Black Water of Dee. Visitors are escorted round the reserve by arrangement with the warden; there is a £2 charge.
7. The conifer woods W of the loch are worth exploring. Following the disused railway line that runs W from Mossdale, there is a roost of up to ten Hen Harriers in the area of Stroan Loch (best in early winter, with few after January), and it is also good for Crossbill, Siskin, and Redpoll. Continuing along the railway, you come to Loch Skerrow. Black Grouse may be seen around this but there is little else *en route* to compensate

for the 4-mile walk from the main road. The Raiders Road forest drive also passes Stroan Loch. This leaves the A762 at Bennan, 1 mile N of Mossdale, and passes through Cairn Edward Forest to emerge on the A712 at Clatteringshaws Loch. There are three forest walks. The road is open from late May to October (£1 toll). A thorough tramp around Clatteringshaws Loch itself may also turn up Black Grouse.

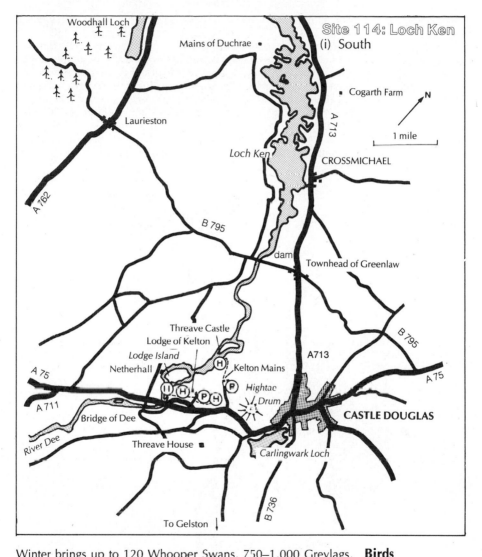

Birds Winter brings up to 120 Whooper Swans, 750–1,000 Greylags, and 300 Greenland White-fronts to the area. Bean Geese now occur only irregularly in the New Year, with a recent maximum of 60 birds. Ducks include Goldeneye, Goosander, Pintail, and Shoveler. Buzzard, Sparrowhawk, and Barn Owl are regularly seen, while Peregrine, Merlin, and Hen Harrier are occasional, as is Great Grey Shrike. Black Grouse, Siskin, and Common Crossbill occur in and around the conifer plantations.

In summer the marshy areas, loch, and river hold breeding Great Crested Grebe, Oystercatcher, Curlew, Goosander, Teal, Shoveler, and Sedge and a few Grasshopper Warblers, with Willow Tits in the areas of damp scrub. Summer also brings migrant Tree Pipits, Redstarts, Wood Warblers, and a few Pied Flycatchers. On passage, almost any species of wader can occur, and Osprey is reasonably regular, as are terns.

Other Sites in the Area
114.1 Murray's Monument
OS Sheet No. 77

This landmark on the A712 c 12 miles W of New Galloway is a good spot to look for Golden Eagle, especially in the late afternoon. The monument stands on a small hill in the bottom of a scenic valley, and behind it are conifer plantations. Eagles can be seen anywhere, though it is usual to stand at the monument and scan the valley sides. Goshawks are sometimes seen from here or the road to the W, and Peregrines are regular, especially around the cliffs N of the road just before the monument. Golden Pheasants occur in the conifers, though most, if not all, have some Lady Amherst's Pheasant blood. Black Grouse can also sometimes be seen in these woods, and Dippers are regular on the river.

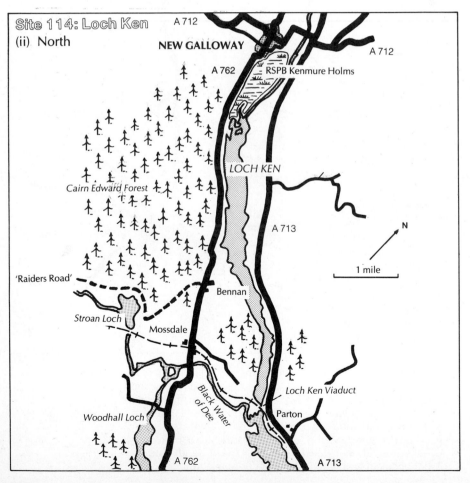

Site 114: Loch Ken
(ii) North

A 712

NEW GALLOWAY

A 712

A 762

RSPB Kenmure Holms

LOCH KEN

Cairn Edward Forest

A 713

N

1 mile

'Raiders Road'

Bennan

Stroan Loch

Mossdale

Woodhall Loch

Black Water of Dee

Loch Ken Viaduct

Parton

A 762

A 713

Part of Galloway Forest Park, this attractive valley is worth exploration. Hen Harrier, Peregrine, and occasionally Golden Eagle and Black Grouse can be seen in winter from the road, and in summer the woods around Loch Trool hold Redstart, Wood Warbler, and Pied Flycatcher, with Common Crossbills and Siskins in the conifers. Leave Newton Stewart on the A714 Girvan road and turn E after c 9 miles onto a minor road at Bargrennan, bearing right at Glentrool village to the glen. There are three way-marked trails.

114.2 Glen Trool
OS Sheet No. 77

This large oakwood on the slopes of the Cree valley is an RSPB reserve covering 524 acres. It lies 4 miles NW of Newton Stewart, via a minor road through Minnigaff on the N side of the town, running parallel to, and E of, the A714. About halfway through the reserve is an open grassy parking area, with paths leading into the woods. In May–June, Buzzard, Sparrowhawk, Woodcock, Barn Owl, Tree Pipit, Redstart, Wood Warbler, and Pied Flycatcher can all be seen, with Goosander, Dipper, and Grey Wagtail on the streams and river and Grasshopper Warbler and Willow Tit in the riverside scrub.

114.3 The Wood of Cree
OS Sheet Nos. 77 and 83

RSPB Ken–Dee Marshes, warden: Ray Hawley, Midtown, Laurieston, Castle Douglas, Dumfries & Galloway DG7 2PP.
RSPB Wood of Cree, warden: Gairland, Old Edinburgh Rd, Minnigaff, Newton Stewart, Wigtownshire DG8 6PL.
NTS Threave, warden: Threave Wildfowl Refuge, Kelton Mill, Castle Douglas.
Recorder: Kirkcudbrightshire.

Information

Site No. 115 Southerness Point – Caerlaverock (Dumfries and Galloway)

On the N shore of the Solway Firth, this area holds thousands of wintering Barnacle and Pink-footed Geese. Caerlaverock National Nature Reserve covers 13,593 acres of saltmarsh and mudflats along 6 miles of coast between the mouth of the River Nith and Lochar Water. Eastpark Wildfowl Trust Refuge covers 1,495 acres, with excellent viewing facilities. The whole area provides superb birdwatching in the winter months, especially for those of us who are deprived of the spectacle of large numbers of geese nearer home.

There are five main habitats for birds in the area. The sea, extensive mudflats, saltmarsh or 'merse' (especially at Caerlaverock), rocky coastline (from Carsethorn to Southerness), and finally farmland, both arable and pasture.

Habitat

1. The B725 from Dumfries to Caerlaverock Castle gives views, firstly of Kirkconnell Merse, a good area for Whooper Swan, and secondly of the mudflats and merse in the N of the NNR. Pink-feet are often visible from the road near the Castle.
2. Eastpark. Take the signposted turning from the B725 to the Wildfowl Trust's Refuge. There are 20 hides, an observatory, and two observation towers. The pond in front of the

Access (see map)
OS Sheet Nos. 84 and 85

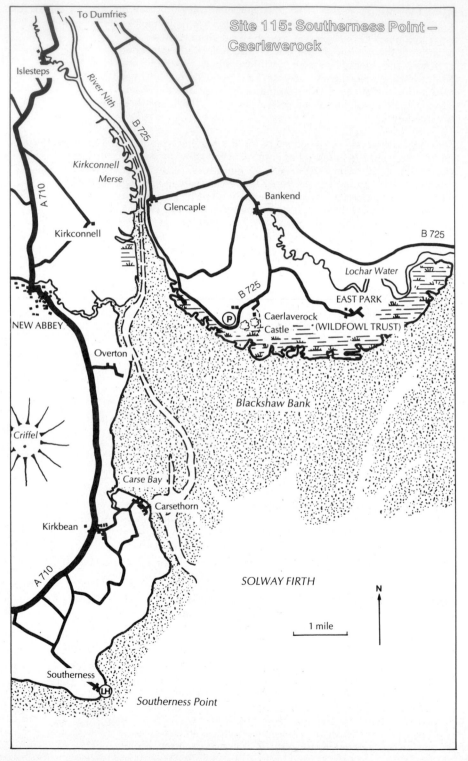

Site 115: Southerness Point – Caerlaverock

To Dumfries

Islesteps

River Nith

B 725

Kirkconnell Merse

A 710

Kirkconnell

Glencaple

Bankend

B 725

Lochar Water

B 725

EAST PARK

Ⓟ

Caerlaverock Castle

(WILDFOWL TRUST)

NEW ABBEY

Overton

Blackshaw Bank

Criffel

Carse Bay

Carsethorn

Kirkbean

A 710

SOLWAY FIRTH

N

1 mile

Southerness

Ⓛ

Southerness Point

observatory holds up to 17 species of wildfowl in winter. Open daily mid-September to late April, visitors are escorted around the refuge at 11.00 and 14.00, at other times they should report to the observatory on arrival. Admission is £1.40.

3. The fields around Islesteps, on the A710 just S of Dumfries, are good for Whooper Swan.

4. On the A710 12 miles S of Dumfries, take the turning at Kirkbean to Carsethorn and drive down to the waterfront. Check the sea and rocky coastline — Scaup sometimes occur in good numbers.

5. Southerness Point. Leave the A710 S on an unclassified road 1 mile SW of Kirkbean and park at the end of the road. Divers (mainly Red-throated), Scaup, scoter, auks, and the occasional skua occur off the point, with Purple Sandpiper and Turnstone on the rocks. There is a wader roost, often holding Grey Plover and Greenshank (both on passage and in winter), and the area is generally very good for waders. It is worth exploring the mudflats and sandbanks both E and W of the point, and the fields in the area sometimes hold Pink-feet and Barnacles, especially in late winter.

Barnacle Geese

Birds Red-throated and sometimes Black-throated Divers winter offshore, together with Cormorant and Shag. Up to 350 Whooper Swans use the area from late September to April, and these are joined by smaller numbers of Bewick's in late October. Both Pink-feet and Barnacle Geese arrive in late September or early October and depart in mid-April. Barnacles can peak at 10,500, this being the whole of the Svalbard population. Pink-feet peak late in the season; the numbers depend on the severity of weather in the rest of Scotland — they reached 35,000 during the severe winter of 1984. Barnacles favour the merse, while the Pink-feet and several hundred Greylags use the surrounding farmland to feed. In many years there are one or more Snow Geese, though these are likely to be feral birds, perhaps the ones that breed near Stranraer. Confusingly, there are also often several albino Barnacle Geese. Other wildfowl include large numbers of Pintail (up to 2,500 in autumn — Carse Bay is especially good), and small numbers of Shoveler. The sea formerly held thousands of Common Scoter at Southerness, but only a handful are now seen, though up to 500 Scaup occur at Carsethorn and at Southerness, together with Red-breasted Merganser. Raptors present in winter include Hen Harrier, Sparrowhawk, Peregrine, and Merlin. Waders are plentiful on the mudflats, especially Oystercatcher, and there are thousands of Golden Plover, Curlew, and Lapwing in the fields. Purple Sandpiper and Turnstone occur on the rocky coasts, especially at Southerness Point.

Passage brings a greater variety of waders. Large numbers of Sanderling pass through in May, and in autumn they may be joined by Little Stint, Curlew Sandpiper, Black-tailed Godwit, Whimbrel, and Spotted Redshank. Breeding species include Shelduck, sometimes Pintail or Wigeon, and Oystercatcher, with Common Terns and gulls on the saltmarsh.

Information

NCC warden: Tadorna, Hollands Farm Rd, Caerlaverock, Dumfries.
The Wildfowl Trust, Eastpark Farm, Caerlaverock, Dumfriesshire DG1 4RS. Tel. 038777–200
Recorder: Dumfriesshrie (Caerlaverock), Kirkcudbrightshire (Southerness and W of the River Nith).

Key to Status Codes:

RB	Resident Breeder	PM	Passage Migrant
MB	Migrant Breeder	IB	Introduced Breeder
WV	Winter Visitor	FB	Former Breeder

An 'S' prefix to the above codes indicates a scarce or sporadic species. Codes are arranged in approximate order of abundance. Where two or more codes are used together (e.g. 'RB, MB' or 'RB, PM'), this indicates that part of the population is migratory.

An approximate indication of abundance is given using the following terms, listed here from least to greatest: rare, scarce, uncommon, fairly common, common, very common, abundant. Population figures and average numbers of the scarcer migrants have been taken from various sources and are included to provide a more precise assessment of a species' status.

For species with local or restricted distributions, a list of numbered sites is given at the end of an account. This is not usually exhaustive, rather a selection of the best areas. Sites are not given for those species which are widespread, even if they are considered difficult to see. We think it more useful to give hints on habitat and how to see the bird close to home. Some subspecies are mentioned where birds are readily identifiable for at least part of the year.

Red-throated Diver
Gavia stellata
WV, PM, MB

Local breeder (c 1,000–1,200 pairs) in N and W Scotland, including Hebrides, Orkney, and Shetland. Prefers small lochs and moorland pools. Vulnerable to disturbance; the appearance of one or two on a loch where there were none before may indicate that they have been put off eggs — withdraw out of sight immediately. Offshore in winter, most frequently off E and S coasts and scarce in SW England and N Scotland. Occasional inland. The commonest and most familiar diver.

Black-throated Diver
Gavia arctica
WV, PM, MB

Very local breeder (c 100 pairs) in N and W Scotland including Hebrides. Favours larger lochs than Red-throated Diver. Very vulnerable to disturbance and great care is needed to avoid putting sitting birds off eggs. Coastal in winter, most frequently off Scotland, and NE and SW England. Always less common than Red-throated except in SW England. Passage birds occur off S coast April–May.
Sites: Winter 6.1, 68.2, 81.5, 84, 88, 91, 97, 98, 99, 100, 104
Summer 107, 108, 109, 110, 112

Great Northern Diver
Gavia immer
WV, SMB

A few summer off Scottish coasts, particularly the NW, Shetland, Orkney, and Hebrides, and bred in 1970 in NW Scotland. Mainly a winter visitor in small numbers around all coasts, the majority off N and W Scotland; also regular SW England.
Sites: Winter 1, 3, 5.1, 6.1, 68.4, 69, 97, 98, 99, 100, 101, 103, 104, 110, 112

Little Grebe
Tachybaptus
ruficollis
RB, WV

Common, widely distributed breeder on fresh water, less frequent in N Scotland, Wales, and SW England. Absent Shetland. In winter also on estuaries.

Great Crested Grebe
Popiceps cristatus
RB, WV

A fairly common breeder on ponds and lakes, most frequent in central and S England. Absent N Scotland and extreme SW England. In winter widely distributed on both fresh and salt water.

Red-necked Grebe
Podiceps
grisegena
WV

Regular in very small numbers, mainly October–March. Most frequent off E coast, especially from Norfolk to Edinburgh, and parts of S coast. Occasional inland. Has summered, but no proven breeding.
Sites: 39, 40, 41, 84, 86

Slavonian Grebe
Podiceps auritus
WV, SRB

Up to 75 pairs breed on large freshwater lochs mainly in the Inverness region. In winter small numbers are widely distributed around coasts and estuaries; occasional inland.

Black-necked Grebe
Podiceps
nigricollis
WV, PM, SMB

Breeds regularly at only a handful of sites (10–25 pairs) but subject to sporadic short-term colonisations. Favours lowland lakes. Regular in small numbers August–May off coasts and estuaries, but rare in N England and Scotland. Generally less marine than Slavonian Grebe, preferring sheltered harbours and sometimes inland waters; usually less common.
Sites: Passage/winter 16, 18, 21, 53, 54, 68.4, 69, 113

Black-browed Albatross
Diomedea
melanophris
SPM

Very rare migrant, less than annual. One summered at the Bass Rock gannetry 1967–9, and one (the same?) has been present at the Hermaness gannetry from 1972 to at least 1986, arriving in late February or March and leaving in September.
Sites: 101

Fulmar
Fulmarus glacialis
RB, MB

A common breeder on almost all suitable cliffs, but less common on E and S coasts and almost absent SE England and East Anglia. Disperses outside the breeding season but may be seen off all coasts throughout the year.
Sites: South-east England/East Anglia 22, 44.1

Cory's Shearwater
Calonectris
diomedea
SPM

Occurs mainly July–September, mostly off coasts of SW England. Usually 15–20 a year, occasionally large influxes (e.g. 2,730 seen off Porthgwarra July–August 1980). A hard bird to see in Britain.
Sites: None regular but try 2, 8, 15

Great Shearwater
Puffinus gravis
PM

Uncommon off British coasts, mainly July–September. Most frequent SW Cornwall. Another difficult species to find in Britain, but sea crossings offer the best chance: try Pembroke–Cork.
Sites: Nowhere guaranteed but try 1, 2, 62.6, 81

Sooty Shearwater
Puffinus griseus
PM

Regular offshore August–September. Most numerous off N Scotland but frequent, usually in small numbers, off North Sea coasts and SW England. They may be seen from any seawatching station in these areas. Rare in SE England.

Common breeder on widely scattered W coast islands and Shetland. Largest colonies on Rhum, Skomer, and Skokholm. Resident February–October, dispersing to sea and rarely seen in other months. Large numbers gather offshore at or near colonies in mornings and evenings. Seen regularly offshore at most seawatching sites April–September, though scarce off SE and NW England. The Balearic race *mauretanicus* is a regular visitor in small numbers, mainly July–October, in particular off SW England.

Manx Shearwater
Puffinus puffinus
MB, PM

Common colonial breeder on islands off W and N coasts. Largest colonies on Shetland, Orkney, Skomer, Skokholm, and Scilly. Resident April–November, rarely seen at other times. This pelagic species is best seen on boat crossings but is also occasionally seen from seawatching stations.
Sites: 1, 3, 62.2, 101, 110, 111

Storm Petrel
Hydrobates pelagicus
MB

Breeds on a handful of remote islands off NW Scotland and Shetland. Offshore movements noted mainly September–November after NW gales. 'Wrecks' are most frequent in NW England and Cornwall and individuals are occasionally driven inland.
Sites: 3, 70, 72, 74, 110

Leach's Petrel
Oceanodroma leucorhoa
MB, PM

British gannetries hold 60% of the world's population and almost half the British Gannets breed on St Kilda. Most colonies are on outlying islands but Bempton Cliffs, Bass Rock, Noss, and Hermaness are reasonably accessible. Can be seen around all coasts for most of the year.

Gannet
Sula bassana
MB, RB, PM

Common gregarious breeder, mainly on cliffs and islets off the W coast and largely absent SE and E England. Disperses around all coasts in winter and small numbers are seen inland.

Cormorant
Phalacrocorax carbo
RB, MB, PM, WV

Common colonial breeder on rocky coasts, most numerous in Scotland, where it easily outnumbers Cormorant. Virtually absent NW, SE, and E England. Generally fairly sedentary and more strictly coastal than Cormorant and irregular away from breeding areas.

Shag
Phalacrocorax aristotelis
RB, WV

Rare and decreasing resident of extensive reedbeds. A difficult species to see; most are located by the booming call of the male or seen flying over reedbeds. There is usually a small winter influx, particularly in severe weather when they may be found in unlikely places.
Sites: 25, 33, 34, 38, 39, 42, 61.2, 73

Bittern
Botaurus stellaris
SRB, SWV

A widely distributed and fairly common resident. Normally breeds in small colonies, usually in trees but a few pairs in reedbeds at Minsmere, and others on cliffs. Feeds in any wetland habitat, occasionally even grassland. Disperses widely in winter when the population is augmented by continental visitors.

Grey Heron
Ardea cinerea
RB, WV

Purple Heron
Ardea purpurea
SPM

15–20 recorded per year, mainly in S England and East Anglia, usually April–October, mostly in spring. Shyer than Grey Heron and favours large reedbeds. Unlikely to be found casually but most individuals stay a few days, if not weeks.
Sites: Likely places include 1, 5, 25, 33, 38, 59, 61.2

White Stork
Ciconia ciconia
SPM

Rare annual visitor, *c* 15 a year, mainly S England and East Anglia. Unpredictable due its catholic choice of habitat. Some are probably escapes and individuals may remain for several months.

Glossy Ibis
Plegadis falcinellus
SPM

Small parties were not uncommon in the past, but it is now rare, averaging just one record a year. However, since 1975 and 1979 two have taken up residence in Kent: at Stodmarsh in winter and Sheppey in summer, with at least one still present in 1986.
Sites: 25, 26

Spoonbill
Platalea leucorodia
SPM, FB

Regular visitor in very small numbers. Most records are from coastal wetlands of East Anglia in late spring but individuals may turn up at any time, occasionally overwintering (particularly in SW England).
Sites: Regular localities include 5, 33, 39, 42

Mute Swan
Cygnus olor
RB

Common and widespread breeder over most of Britain, favouring lowland fresh water. Most numerous in S England, and absent Shetland and upland Scotland. In winter often gathers in flocks on large bodies of fresh water or estuaries.

Bewick's Swan
Cygnus columbianus
WV

Localised winter visitor, mainly to E and S England. Favours wetland and damp, open grasslands. May be seen November to early April but peak numbers occur January–February.
Sites: 19.3, 26, 27, 36, 38.1, 47, 58, 71, 72, 115

Whooper Swan
Cygnus cygnus
WV, SMB

Pairs occasionally summer and breed in Scotland, but essentially a winter visitor, October–April, mainly to Scotland, N England, and Wales; much less frequent on E coast of England and very scarce elsewhere. Frequents both coastal and inland locations, often feeding in fields.
Sites: 47, 64, 71, 84, 86, 96, 97, 114, 115

Bean Goose
Anser fabalis
WV

The only regular flock winters in the Yare valley in Norfolk but a few still occur annually in SW Scotland. Elsewhere largely a straggler with odd birds amongst flocks of White-fronted Geese. Present in Norfolk late November to March.
Sites: 37, 114

Pink-footed Goose
Anser brachyrhynchus
WV

Common in Scotland, N England, and Norfolk (the Wash), occurring in large flocks at traditional sites mid-September to mid-May. Rare in S England. Favours arable land and pasture for feeding, roosting on lakes and estuaries.
Sites: 44, 71, 72, 74. Widespread in S and E Scotland

White-fronted Goose
Anser albifrons
WV

The European race *albifrons* mainly occurs in central and SE England and East Anglia but also in Wales. Present October–March (peak numbers in mid-winter) with the bulk of the population at a small number of regular sites. Flat grazing land and coastal marshes are preferred. The Greenland race *A.a.*

flavirostris is much less common, mainly wintering on bogs in W Scotland and Inner Hebrides (9,500 in 1984, over half of them on Islay), though a few still occur at traditional sites in NW England and Wales.
Sites: European White-front 26, 27, 36, 41, 58
      Greenland White-front 65, 103, 104, 112, 113.2, 114

Rare winter visitor, averaging about three birds a year (but recently fewer), usually with the White-fronted Geese at Slimbridge, but occasionally away from there and with other species of geese. Many records of escapes from captivity.
Sites: 58

Lesser White-fronted Goose
Anser erythropus
SWV

The wild breeding population is restricted to NW Scotland and the Hebrides (c 500–700 pairs), but feral birds breed widely in England and Scotland, particularly SW Scotland, the Lake District, and Norfolk. Absent Wales (except Anglesey) and SW England. Winter visitors from Iceland are present October–April, mainly in Scotland.

Greylag Goose
Anser anser
WV, IB, RB

Rare annual visitor October–April, mainly to Scotland, usually singles or very small groups amongst flocks of other species. Many records refer to escapes.
Sites: Regular localities include 112, 115

Snow Goose
Anser caerulescens
SWV

Introduced c 250 years ago, now common and widespread breeder, though less common in SW England and Wales and scarce in Scotland. Largely sedentary. Smaller individuals, probably wild vagrants, occur irregularly amongst flocks of wintering wild geese.

Canada Goose
Branta canadensis
IB, SWV

Regular visitor to a small number of traditional sites, mainly October–May. Greenland birds winter on Hebrides and W Scotland while the whole Svalbard population winters on the Solway Firth. Very small numbers of Siberian birds irregularly visit S England, particularly Kent and East Anglia, but many records in the south are escapes.
Sites: 112, 115

Barnacle Goose
Branta leucopsis
WV

Visitor to the coast, September–April (mainly November–March). Numbers have increased dramatically in recent years. Three distinct races occur. The dark-bellied Siberian form *bernicla* occurs widely on the E and S coasts of England. Pale-bellied birds, *hrota*, from Svalbard and Franz Josef Land are regular in NE England though stragglers of this race from Greenland winter irregularly on the W coast. The Black Brant *B. b. nigricans*, which breeds in E Siberia, Alaska, and NW Canada, occurs as a vagrant.
Sites: Dark-bellied race 10, 18, 19, 28, 30, 39, 40, 41, 44, 50
      Pale-bellied race 84

Brent Goose
Branta bernicla
WV

An uncommon sedentary introduction, long established in a feral state, mainly in East Anglia.
Sites: N Norfolk, especially 41

Egyptian Goose
Alopochen aegyptiacus
IB

Ruddy Shelduck
Tadorna ferruginea
SPM

Rare visitor to many parts of Britain, formerly subject to periodic influxes. Now few records, presumably linked with the species' decline in Europe. Most recent sightings are probably escapes.

Shelduck
Tadorna tadorna
MB, RB, WV

Common and widespread resident on estuaries and flat coastal areas almost throughout Britain. Much less frequent at inland localities. Subject to local movements in autumn, and there is evidence that continental birds winter in Britain.

Mandarin
Aix galericulata
IB

Small feral populations exist in various parts of S (mainly SE) England, also Tayside (Perth city). The stronghold is Virginia Water and numbers have increased recently with an expansion of range. It is now suspected that the numbers in Britain exceed the wild populations of China and Japan. Mandarins nest in holes in trees and frequent lakes, ponds, and streams surrounded by mature deciduous woodland.
Sites: 21.3

Wigeon
Anas penelope
WV, PM, RB

Uncommon breeder, mainly in central and N Scotland, less frequent in S Scotland and N England. Large numbers winter throughout Britain, September–March, particularly at coastal locations, although c 20% winter on the Ouse Washes. Feeds on mudflats, saltmarshes, grasslands, and arable fields.

Gadwall
Anas strepera
IB, RB, MB, WV

Uncommon and local breeder, mainly in East Anglia. Occurs at widely scattered localities elsewhere, partly as a result of introductions. Small numbers arrive in winter from Iceland and the continent.
Sites: 12, 33, 39, 47, 73, 87, 88, 91.1, etc.

Teal
Anas crecca
WV, PM, RB

Fairly common breeder, mainly in Scotland and N England. Thinly distributed elsewhere and scarce in SW England and NW Scotland. Large numbers winter in most wetlands. The distinct American race *carolinensis* (Green-winged Teal) is a regular vagrant.

Mallard
Anas platyrhynchos
RB, WV

Very common resident, breeding throughout Britain in a wide variety of wetland habitats. In winter the population is augmented by immigrants from Europe.

Pintail
Anas acuta
WV, PM, SRB

Very scarce breeder (10–30 pairs) at various widely scattered sites, particularly the Ouse Washes and Orkney. Fairly common winter visitor mainly to coastal locations, especially the Dee, Mersey, and Ribble estuaries. Exceptional inland concentration of over 3,000 on the Ouse Washes.

Garganey
Anas querquedula
SMB, PM

A summer migrant, the first arrivals in late March may be seen at many localities in the S and E. Scarce breeder in S and E England, sporadic elsewhere. Its favoured habitat of well-vegetated shallow pools makes it difficult to locate when breeding. Somewhat greater numbers on passage.
Regular sites include 25, 26, 39, 42, 47, 53, 59, 73

Uncommon but widely distributed breeder, scarce in central and W Scotland, Wales, and SW England. Common winter visitor, November–April, to most wetlands of England and Wales.

Shoveler
Anas clypeata
WV, PM, MB, RB

Presumed wild migrants recorded annually in very small numbers mainly March–April and late July to September, largely in England. Has bred. True status clouded by the occurrence of escapes.
Sites: 12, 29, 53

Red-crested Pochard
Netta rufina
SPM, SMB

Uncommon local breeder mainly in E Britain in well-vegetated lowland freshwater habitats. Common winter visitor, largely on inland waters but also some estuaries.

Pochard
Aythya ferina
WV, PM, MB, RB

Scarce visitor, mainly September–April but especially October–November, when occasional small influxes. Most records in central and S England. Some may be escapes from captivity.

Ferruginous Duck
Aythya nyroca
SWV

Fairly common breeder, though scarce in NW Scotland, Wales, and SW England. Very common in winter, mainly on inland waters.

Tufted Duck
Aythya fuligula
WV, RB

Primarily a winter visitor (October–March), with the largest numbers at a few coastal sites in Scotland. Only small numbers are recorded off E coast of England and uncommon inland. Has bred Scotland.
Sites: 44, 70, 88, 91, 98, 103, 112, 113, 115

Scaup
Aythya marila
WV, PM, SMB

Common and widespread breeder around Scottish coasts, occasionally inland, also Northumberland and Walney Island. Forms large wintering flocks in Scotland and small numbers also seen off E and S coasts of England.
Regular sites in England and Wales include: 44, 61.1, 75, 83, 84

Eider
Somateria mollissima
RB, WV

Rare visitor, almost exclusively to Scottish coasts. Variable numbers (up to 13) arrive each winter, some taking up residence and staying for several years. All concentrations of Eider are worth checking for this species.
Sites: 96, 100

King Eider
Somateria spectabilis
SWV

Primarily a winter visitor (October–April) to E coast of Scotland, Orkney, and Shetland. Smaller numbers are regular off the Hebrides and E England. Has bred Scotland.
Sites: Regular localities include 44, 69, 82, 84, 86, 88, 91, 97, 98, 99, 100, 101, 103, 104, 110

Long-tailed Duck
Clangula hyemalis
WV, SMB

50–100 pairs breed annually in Scotland. Outside the breeding season, flocks are widespread offshore. Generally most numerous off the E coast, particularly E Scotland, but large numbers in Carmarthen Bay and off N Wales. In April, there is an impressive eastward passage in the English Channel, with some birds inland.
Sites: Spring passage 15, 19.1, 22, 23
        Non-breeding concentrations 44, 84, 86, 88, 91, 98, 99, 100

Common Scoter
Melanitta nigra
WV, PM, SMB

333

Surf Scoter
Melanitta
perspicillata
SWV

Rare winter visitor (averages about ten a year) to all coasts. Usually found in large flocks of Common and Velvet Scoter, and any flock should be checked for a Surf. Also occasionally seen flying past on seawatches. Some individuals may stay for several years.
Sites: 98, 100

Velvet Scoter
Melanitta fusca
WV, PM

Widespread offshore, chiefly October–May. Main concentrations off E Scotland and generally small numbers off E England. Scarce off W coast. Always less common than Common Scoter with which it often associates.
Sites: 44, 84, 86, 88, 91, 98, 99, 100, 103

Goldeneye
Bucephala
clangula
WV, PM, SMB

Recently established as a breeding species in central Scotland (c 50 pairs), with numbers increasing due to provision of nest-boxes. Chiefly a widespread winter visitor (October–April), with many on inland waters; particularly numerous in E Scotland.

Smew
Mergus albellus
WV

Uncommon winter visitor in small numbers (probably not more than 100 birds), mainly on inland waters of S and E England; scarce and irregular elsewhere.
Sites: Some of the more regular localities are 7.3, 12, 21.2, 23, 29, 32, 53, 56

Red-breasted
Merganser
Mergus serrator
WV, RB

Fairly common breeder in Scotland, NW England, and N Wales. Shows a preference for coastal areas in the breeding season although some do breed far inland. Widely scattered in winter around the coast (most common in Scotland) and only rarely seen inland.

Goosander
Mergus merganser
WV, RB

A not uncommon breeder on rivers and lochs in Scotland and N England. Has recently colonised central Wales but the population there is still small. Many winter on the Beauly and Moray Firths while immigrants from Scandinavia and NW Russia occur widely on inland waters of central and SE England, usually in small numbers. Scarce in SW England.
Sites: 7.3, 12, 21, 23, 29, 32, 48, 52, 53, 54, 55, 56, 66, 73, 77, 87, 91, 93, 95, 114

Ruddy Duck
Oxyura
jamaicensis
IB

Introduced from N America as recently as 1960, its breeding strongholds are W Midlands reservoirs and Chew Valley Lake, but individuals and small groups are recorded with increasing regularity at many inland waters in S and E England.
Sites: 12, 52, 53, 54, 55, 56, 68.4

Honey Buzzard
Pernis apivorus
PM, SMB

Rare breeder (10–20 pairs), and very small numbers also occur on passage, mainly in E England. A difficult species to see in Britain, the best chances are at Welbeck Park and the New Forest in May–June.
Sites: 17, 51, 93, 95

Red Kite
Milvus milvus
SRB

Restricted as a breeding species to central Wales (46 pairs in 1983). Mostly sedentary but a few wander outside the breeding season. Occasional records in East Anglia may be of continental origin.
Sites: 63, 64, 64.1

Widespread in Scotland, the Lake District, and the Isle of Man in the 18th century, it was decimated by persecution and became extinct in Britain by c 1916. An attempted re-introduction of four birds to Fair Isle in 1968 failed, but 82 were released on Rhum 1975–85, and the first successful breeding occurred in 1985. Birds are now widely scattered in W Scotland. Apart from these, has become a very rare winter visitor (less than annual) to the SE, especially East Anglia.
Sites: 111

White-tailed Eagle
Haliaeetus albicilla
SRB, SWV

Rare breeder (28 nests in 1983), generally in large reedbeds but also a few in arable crops. Most are in East Anglia but nesting has occurred in a number of counties elsewhere in England. Passage birds occur at many sites, usually coastal, and a few regularly winter, mainly in East Anglia.
Regular sites include: 25, 33, 34, 38, 39, 42, 47, 61.2, 78

Marsh Harrier
Circus aeruginosus
SMB, SPM

About 600 pairs breed on Scottish moorlands (especially Hebrides and Orkney, but absent Shetland) and less commonly in N England and Wales. The breeding population is mainly sedentary. Wintering immigrants occur widely in England, in both coastal and moorland areas, and are best seen at their communal roosts at dusk.
Sites: Winter 7, 17, 26, 27, 28, 33, 34, 35, 39, 42, 46, 47, 49,
50, 59, 64, 68.4, 70, 71, 72, 84, 112, 113.2, 115
Summer 66, 93, 95, 103, 110, 112

Hen Harrier
Circus cyaneus
PM, WV, RB, MB

Up to ten pairs breed annually, all in S England. Very small numbers are recorded on passage, mainly in East Anglia and SE England. It is not possible to give any sites.

Montagu's Harrier
Circus pygargus
SPM, SMB

Population c 50 pairs, but subject to severe persecution. Some are known to be escaped falconers' birds. Scattered widely, the species may occur in any area of extensive woodland. Goshawk is a difficult bird to see and is most likely to be found when displaying, March–April.
Sites: 93, 95, 114.1

Goshawk
Accipiter gentilis
SRB, SPM

Common resident with a population of c 20,000 pairs. They occur in any area of suitable tree cover; not surprisingly absent from Orkney, Shetland, and Outer Hebrides. Some individuals from the continent are recorded on passage, occasionally wintering.

Sparrowhawk
Accipiter nisus
RB, PM, WV

Common resident, mainly in W Britain and most numerous in Scotland, NW England, Wales, and SW England, favouring diverse habitats such as wooded farmland and valleys. Their frequent soaring makes them easy to find. E coast records are largely passage migrants, and there are three records of vagrant Steppe Buzzards *B. b. vulpinus*.

Buzzard
Buteo buteo
RB, PM

Scarce winter visitor subject to periodic influxes (e.g. c 60 in 1966–7). Most records are from Scotland and E England with the majority in East Anglia. Most arrive October–November and wintering birds often wander.
Sites: None guaranteed but fairly regular at 34.

Rough-legged Buzzard
Buteo lagopus
SWV

Golden Eagle
Aquila chrysaetos
RB

Uncommon sedentary resident, mainly in the Scottish Highlands and Western Isles, with small numbers in SW Scotland and, since 1969, the Lake District. Current population 400–500 pairs.
Sites: 93, 95, 105, 106, 108, 109, 110, 111, 112, 114.1

Osprey
Pandion haliaetus
PM, SMB

The return of the Osprey as a breeding species to Scotland in 1954 has been well publicised. The population is now c 30 pairs. Passage birds are recorded regularly in very small numbers at many inland waters, especially S England. Two breeding sites are highly accessible.
Sies: 92, 93, 99, 100

Kestrel
Falco tinnunculus
RB, MB, PM, WV

Britain's commonest raptor with a population of c 70,000 pairs. Breeds throughout Britain but largely absent on the Outer Hebrides and Shetland. A familiar sight nowadays, especially over motorway verges.

Merlin
Falco columbarius
RB, MB, PM, WV

Uncommon breeder on moorland and fells in Scotland, N England, and Wales, with a few in SW England. Current population 550–650 pairs but is declining, especially in Wales and N England. Some disperse in winter in lowland areas, especially coastal marshes, and join continental migrants, notably on the E coast. At all seasons Merlins are elusive and difficult to locate; chance sightings in suitable habitat are the rule.
Sites: Winter 1, 2, 7, 8, 11, 26, 27, 34, 47, 49, 50, 59, 61.1, 65, 68.4, 70, 71, 72, 75, 82, 84, 112, 113.2, 115
Summer 66, 93, 95, 101, 103, 109, 110, 111, 112

Hobby
Falco subbuteo
MB, PM

Uncommon summer visitor, May–September. Probably at least 500 pairs, breeding in most counties of central and S England. Hobbies require open country for feeding and trees for nesting. There are few sites where a sighting can be guaranteed and they are perhaps most likely to be seen on passage, or when hunting Swallows and martins at their autumn roosts in reedbeds in the evening.
Sites: Summer 17, 20

Peregrine
Falco peregrinus
PB, PM, WV

Uncommon resident, mainly in the Scottish Highlands, SW Scotland, NW England, Wales, and SW England. Nests on inland crags and sea-cliffs; many eyries are traditional. Population at least 800 pairs and increasing though subject to persecution from falconers. A few disperse in winter, augmented by immigrants from Scandinavia, particularly to coastal localities with large concentrations of waders and wildfowl.
Sites: Winter 1, 2, 6, 7, 10, 26, 58, 59, 65, 70, 71, 72, 82, 84, 113.2, 115
Resident 60, 61.3, 62, 64, 68, 69, 75, 76, 93, 95, 103, 104, 105, 107, 108, 109, 110, 111, 112, 114.1

Red Grouse
Lagopus lagopus
RB

Common resident of open moorland in Scotland, N England, Wales, and SW England. Populations in Shetland and SW England are the result of introductions and numbers remain small.
Sites: England and Wales 65.1, 66, 82.1

Fairly common resident of the arctic-alpine zone of the Scottish Highlands, but in NW Scotland found at lower altitudes than in the Cairngorms. The ski-lifts in the latter area have made it the easiest place to see them.
Sites: 93, 95, 105, 108, 109, 110.1

Ptarmigan
Lagopus mutus
RB

Fairly common resident in Scotland, though absent from NW Scotland, Outer Hebrides, Orkney, and Shetland. Also breeds in N England and Wales, but these populations have recently declined. Black Grouse require a combination of forest and moorland and are often difficult to find. They are best looked for at dawn, especially at their traditional leks (communal display grounds).
Sites: 65.1, 66, 87.1, 93, 95, 112, 114

Black Grouse
Tetrao tetrix
RB

The indigenous population died out *c* 1785. Reintroduced from Scandinavia in the 19th century and not uncommon now in E central Scotland, especially Speyside and the valleys of the Don, Dee, and Tay. Occasionally they frequent plantations of larch and spruce but Scots pine is their favourite tree. Shy, but may with luck be seen in the early morning on forest tracks, otherwise it usually requires a strenuous bash through the undergrowth to get a fleeting glimpse of a flying bird (though this tactic must not be used mid-April to June as the birds are notoriously prone to desertion when disturbed on the nest).
Sites: 93, 95, 99

Capercaillie
Tetrao urogallus
IB, FB

Common introduced resident, mainly in S and E England and most numerous in East Anglia. Found on agricultural land, sandy heaths, chalk downland, and even coastal dunes — drier habitats with lower rainfall than Grey Partridges. They are perhaps easiest to see in early spring when crops are sprouting.

Red-legged Partridge
Alectoris rufa
IB

Common resident over most of Britain except NW Scotland and parts of Wales, mainly in areas of mixed cultivation. Highest densities occur where there is plenty of cover, and their current decline is attributed to changes in land use and increased use of insecticides.

Grey Partridge
Perdix perdix
RB

Uncommon migrant breeder, notoriously difficult to see even when calling birds have been located. Occurs mainly in cereal crops, favouring chalk downland. Breeds regularly only in a small number of counties in S England but subject to occasional invasions when breeding may take place in many additional areas, even in Scotland. No regular sites.

Quail
Coturnix coturnix
MB

Probably introduced in the 11th century, the Pheasant has flourished and spread through most of Britain, but is less common in the W and largely absent from NW Scotland, the Outer Hebrides, and Shetland. Pheasants are both common and conspicuous, with a preference for wooded agricultural areas.

Pheasant
Phasianus colchicus
IB

First introduced in the late 19th century and two well established populations now exist, in Galloway and Breckland, where they are increasing. Other introductions, including Tresco, have met with only limited success or have to be artificially maintained.

Golden Pheasant
Chrysolophus pictus
IB

Found mainly in coniferous woods and plantations, they can often be seen on woodland edges in early morning but are shy.
Sites: 44.3, 45, 114.1

Lady Amherst's Pheasant
Chrysolophus amherstiae
IB

Various introductions since the turn of the century but the only real success has been in Bedfordshire, spreading to Buckinghamshire and Hertfordshire. Favours half-grown coniferous thickets with no undergrowth; shy and skulking. Best looked for at wooded edges and along tracks and rides in the early morning and evening.
Sites: 70.8. Also in Little Brickhill Woods, E of Milton Keynes.

Water Rail
Rallus aquaticus
PM, WV, RB

Fairly common but local breeder throughout most of Britain except highland regions. Its retiring habits in dense reedbeds and other aquatic vegetation make it easy to miss. Birds are often located by their squealing calls and are best seen at dusk along the water's edge. Passage migrants and winter visitors from the continent augment the population September–May, offering a better chance of finding this elusive bird.
Some reliable sites include: 1, 13, 25, 33, 38, 39, 42, 69, 70.4, 73, 78

Spotted Crake
Porzana porzana
PM, SMB

Rare and sporadic breeder at a few widely scattered sites throughout Britain. This extremely elusive inhabitant of densely vegetated wetland areas is usually only located in the breeding season by its nocturnal calling (twelve singing males reported in 1983). Most likely to be encountered on passage mid-August to October, but numbers always very small; probably most frequent in English coastal counties. The edges of reedbeds are favoured, and a careful scrutiny at dusk, perhaps from a hide, provides the best chance of a sighting.
Sites: Impossible to guarantee but regular sites include 1, 5, 13, 39, 42, 47

Concrake
Crex crex
MB, PM

The catastrophic decline of the Corncrake, attributed to agricultural changes, continues. In 1978–9 the estimated population was 700 pairs and numbers are now considerably lower. The bulk of the population is on the Western Isles and Orkney, with small numbers on the mainland of NW Scotland. It is sporadic elsewhere. Corncrakes favour meadows for breeding though they are also found in iris beds at the start of the season. They are most likely to be located by the call which is given most frequently at night. Very small numbers are recorded on passage in most parts of Britain, usually flushed accidentally or seen flying from field to field.
Sites: 103, 110

Moorhen
Gallinula chloropus
WV, RB

Very common in all well-vegetated freshwater habitats in most of Britain, though scarce in NW Scotland, and the Western Isles. The population is augmented in winter by visitors from the continent.

Coot
Fulica atra
WV, RB

Common resident of freshwater habitats throughout most of Britain, though scarce in NW Scotland and the outlying islands. Large flocks congregate on reservoirs and lakes in winter, including many immigrants from the continent.

Bred in East Anglia until c 1600. Since then a rare passage migrant (c 25 a year) subject to occasional influxes (over 500 in late 1963, 201 in late 1982), mainly to E Britain in spring and autumn. Since 1979 a few have been regularly present in Broadland (Norfolk).

Crane
Grus grus
SPM, SRB

Common breeding resident in Scotland and N England, nesting both inland and on the coast. Elsewhere, breeds widely but less commonly, mainly at coastal sites. Large numbers of immigrants swell the population in winter when they are almost exclusively coastal.

Oystercatcher
Haematopus ostralegus
RB, MB, PM, WV

Re-established as a breeding species in Suffolk in 1947, since when it has steadily increased, and now numbers c 250 pairs at nine sites, mainly in East Anglia but also in SE England. Small numbers winter on the S coast, with the largest concentration, up to 100, on the Tamar estuary in Devon. A few also winter in East Anglia. Breeds on shallow brackish lagoons close to the coast, wintering in similar habitats or on estuaries.
Sites: 10, 16, 19, 33, 34, 39

Avocet
Recurvirostra avosetta
RB, PM, WV

Uncommon summer visitor, March October, restricted to East Anglia and S England. Its favoured habitat is chalk downland and sandy heaths, but many now breed on cultivated land. Largely nocturnal and, though they may be heard calling, difficult to locate. 67 pairs were reported in 1983 (at 36 sites), but the true breeding population is likely to be much higher.
Sites: 45

Stone Curlew
Burhinus oedicnemus
MB

First bred in 1938, since when it has increased to c 500 pairs. Most breed on gravel pits or other man-made sites in E and central England, but some as far N as NE England. Irregular elsewhere. Passage birds occur more widely, including coastal lagoons.

Little Ringed Plover
Charadrius dubius
MB, PM

Fairly common breeder around most of the coast, though only locally in SW England and parts of Wales. Nests on sandy or shingle beaches, with a few inland in Scotland, N England, and Breckland. Common in winter on all coasts when the resident population is increased by immigrants from the continent.

Ringed Plover
Charadrius hiaticula
RB, MB, PM, WV

Lost as a regular breeding species as recently as 1956 but still an annual migrant, especially in spring, in very small numbers to the coasts of E and S England, most frequently in East Anglia.
Sites: Nowhere guaranteed, but likely sites include 24, 33, 39, 40, 42

Kentish Plover
Charadrius alexandrinus
PM, FB

Scarce summer visitor, breeding on desolate mountain-tops, mainly in the central Highlands of Scotland, though a few pairs in NW Scotland and N England and recently also N Wales. Population uncertain but almost certainly under 100 pairs. On passage small flocks are noted regularly at traditional sites, especially on farmland in East Anglia and SW England (April–May and September–October).
Sites: Passage 1, 11, 39
    Breeding 93, 95

Dotterel
Charadrius morinellus
SMB, SPM

Golden Plover
Pluvialis apricaria
RB, MB, WV, PM

Common breeder on moorlands of Scotland and N England with smaller numbers in Wales and a few in SW England (Dartmoor). Numbers in winter are swelled by continental and Icelandic birds. Many winter inland on grassland and ploughed fields, but coastal marshes and estuaries are often used, especially in hard weather.

Grey Plover
Pluvialis squatarola
PM, WV

Common passage migrant and winter visitor to all coasts except N Scotland (where irregular). Generally rare inland, favouring muddy estuaries.

Lapwing
Vanellus vanellus
RB, MB, PM, WV

Very common breeder throughout Britain, though less common in extreme SW England and NW Scotland. Gathers in flocks in winter, mainly inland, and partial to farmland.

Knot
Calidris canutus
PM, WV

Common on passage and in winter on the coasts, but fewer in S and SW England. Typically found in estuaries, often in large flocks. Rare inland.

Sanderling
Calidris alba
PM, WV

Recorded displaying in suitable breeding habitat in Scotland but never proved to have nested. Fairly common on passage but considerably fewer winter. Widely but thinly distributed on sandy shores or the sandier parts of estuaries. Small numbers recorded regularly inland on passage, especially in May.

Little Stint
Calidris minuta
PM, SWV

Regular passage migrant in variable numbers, mainly in autumn from late July to mid-October with a marked peak in September. Occurs inland and on all coasts, with the largest numbers in the E. A few regularly winter, mostly in S England.

Temminck's Stint
Calidris temminckii
SPM, SMB

Has bred regularly in N Scotland since 1969, but only a handful of pairs. On passage, found annually in very small numbers, mainly in E England. The peak periods are May and late August to early September.
Regular sites include 26, 27, 33, 39, 42, 82

Pectoral Sandpiper
Calidris melanotos
SPM

The commonest vagrant American wader with 20–100 per year. Most occur August–October, in SW England and Norfolk, but also found regularly in many other counties. Scarce in Scotland.
Regular sites include 1, 4, 5, 6, 42, 53, 82

Curlew Sandpiper
Calidris ferruginea
PM

Regular passage migrant; scarce in spring, mostly seen mid-July to mid-October. Numbers vary and it may be quite common in some years. Largely at coastal localities, especially on the E and S coasts of England, but also frequent in NW England. Uncommon in Scotland. The main concentrations are on the Humber, Medway, and Wash. Rare in winter.

Purple Sandpiper
Calidris maritima
PM, WV, SMB

Has bred in Scotland since 1978. In winter, widely but locally distributed around the coast, almost exclusively on rocky shores. The bulk of the population is in NE England, E Scotland, and Orkney, with a particularly high concentration on Shetland. Only small numbers winter on the E coast S of Yorkshire and on the S coast, but they are sometimes found there on man-made structures such as piers. Very rare inland.

Fairly common breeder on upland moors and, to a lesser extent, coastal marshes, in Scotland and N England (Pennines). Small numbers breed in Wales and SW England. Very common on passage and in winter throughout Britain, frequenting most coastal localities as well as many inland sites.

Dunlin
Calidris alpina
PM, WV; RB, MB

A transatlantic vagrant, averaging *c* 20 per year, though 67 in 1977. Indeed, it is easier to see this species in Britain than in E North America. Most are in SW England in September, usually on short turf, e.g. airfields and golf courses. Has occurred in small flocks on several occasions.
Sites: 1, 2, 7, 62.4

Buff-breasted Sandpiper
Tryngites subruficollis
SPM

Breeds in variable numbers at a handful of sites, mainly in England, especially the Ouse Washes. Elusive in the breeding season. Common on passage, particularly August–September, occurring widely at coastal sites as well as inland and occupying a variety of habitats. Recently, small numbers have wintered.

Ruff
Philomachus pugnax
PM, WV, SMB

Local winter visitor (September–April), more numerous on passage. Frequents well-vegetated freshwater habitats, always in small numbers and often singly. A hard species to find, but careful scrutiny, preferably from a hide, of the edges of reedbeds in early morning or evening may reveal feeding birds. A more active method is to thoroughly tramp around (in wellingtons) heavily waterlogged grassland or marshes. Jack Snipe sit very tight, and may still be flushed by a patient observer long after all the Snipe have fled.

Jack Snipe
Lymnocryptes minimus
WV, PM

Breeds throughout Britain, though much less common in the S; a recent survey revealed only 2,100 pairs in England and Wales. A bird of wet meadows and marshes but frequently encountered in coastal localities on passage. Widely distributed in winter, though only locally in N Scotland.

Snipe
Gallinago gallinago
RB, WV, PM

Widespread but local breeder over most of Britain but absent in the Outer Hebrides, Orkney, Shetland, and parts of Wales and SW England. Prefers deciduous woodland with damp open areas for feeding. Its crepuscular and secretive habits can make it a difficult species to find. Best located when roding (its display flight) at dusk in early spring. Watch from clearings or woodland rides, and listen for its distinctive calls. Large numbers of continental immigrants arrive from mid-October and may be seen at coastal localities, especially in the E.

Woodcock
Scolopax rusticola
RB, WV, PM

Nests sporadically at a small number of sites in England (occasionally also in Scotland and Wales); the Ouse Washes are the stronghold. Its typical breeding habitat is damp meadows and there are up to 80 pairs in some years. Fairly common on passage, especially July–October, at many coastal localities in England and Wales but less frequent in Scotland. About 5,000 winter, mainly on the S coast. On passage and in winter prefers muddy estuaries.
Sites: Breeding 47
       Winter 10, 16, 18, 19, 69, 70, 72, 91

Black-tailed Godwit
Limosa limosa
PM, WV, SMB

Bar-tailed Godwit
Limosa lapponica
PM, WV

Common on passage and in winter on all coasts, especially in the sandier areas of large estuaries. A substantial passage is usually noted in April on the S coast, especially at Selsey Bill, Beachy Head, and Dungeness.

Whimbrel
Numenius phaeopus
PM, MB

Uncommon moorland breeder of N Scotland. Its stronghold is Shetland, with c 400 pairs. Very small numbers breed on the Outer Hebrides, Orkney, and occasionally the Scottish mainland. Fairly common on passage in both spring and autumn in a variety of habitats though mainly coastal. Usually seen flying over uttering its distinctive seven-note whistle. There are two records of vagrant Hudsonian Whimbrel *H. p. hudsonicus*.

Curlew
Numenius arquata
RB, MB, PM, WV

A common breeding bird of damp moorlands and heaths, both in upland and lowland areas. It occurs throughout Britain, though largely absent from SE England and East Anglia. Widespread on passage and in winter, especially favouring estuaries, when its numbers are swelled by continental immigrants.

Spotted Redshank
Tringa erythropus
PM, WV

Regular passage migrant in small numbers, more frequent in autumn and most numerous on the coasts of East Anglia and SE England. Passage birds also occur widely but sparingly inland. Very small numbers winter at a few sites, mainly on the S coast. Sites: Winter 10, 16, 18, 19, 33, 61.1, 69, 70

Redshank
Tringa totanus
RB, MB, PM, WV

Common breeder over most of Britain, occupying a variety of habitats from inland damp marshes and grassy fields to coastal saltmarshes. Largely absent from SW England and parts of Wales. A recent survey found only 2,400 pairs in the whole of England and Wales but densities in Scotland are generally higher. Common and widespread around the coast on passage and in winter.

Greenshank
Tringa nebularia
PM, MB, WV

Uncommon breeding species restricted to NW Scotland and the Hebrides. Numbers estimated in 1979 at 800–900 pairs. Widespread on passage; the largest numbers are on the coast, but also occurs at many inland sites, with peak numbers August–September. Small numbers regularly winter, largely on the W coast, especially SW England.

Green Sandpiper
Tringa ochropus
PM, WV, SMB

Has bred sporadically in Scotland. Fairly common passage migrant, on estuary creeks and coastal lagoons and at inland sites such as reservoirs, sewage farms, and flooded grassland, most frequently in the S and E. Rarely are large concentrations encountered. A few winter.

Wood Sandpiper
Tringa glareola
PM, SMB

A recent colonist of Scotland, breeding regularly since 1959; usually less than 10 pairs. Uncommon passage migrant, mainly to coastal lagoons on the E and S coasts, but also to the marshy fringes of lakes and reservoirs inland. The majority are seen in autumn.

Common Sandpiper
Actitis hypoleucos
MB, PM, WV

Common breeding summer visitor (April–August) throughout Scotland and most of Wales and N England. Largely absent as a nesting species in central and S England. On passage, it can be seen at any inland water, even small pools, but also occurs at coastal localities. Small numbers winter, favouring the inner parts of estuaries as well as reservoirs, with the majority in SW England.

Summers regularly in N Scotland, especially Shetland, but still no confirmed breeding. Common on passage and in winter on all coasts, with a preference for rocky shores. Small numbers on passage inland, particularly in May.

Turnstone
Arenaria interpres
PM, WV

Breeding restricted to the Outer Hebrides and Shetland, with sporadic nesting on other islands and the mainland of Scotland. Its stronghold is Shetland with c 15 pairs. Otherwise a scarce passage migrant, recorded annually in East Anglia in very small numbers, and occasionally elsewhere. Most passage birds are in August–September.
Sites: Summer 101, 110. Nowhere guaranteed on migration.

Red-necked Phalarope
Phalaropus lobatus
SPM, SMB

Uncommon annual migrant in variable numbers. Most frequent off SW coasts, especially after gales. Much less common and irregular elsewhere. Most records are in late autumn. Very rare in spring or inland. This can be a hard species to catch up with in Britain.
Sites: The more regular sites include 1, 3, 5.1, 8, 15

Grey Phalarope
Phalaropus fulicarius
PM

Uncommon passage migrant in both spring and autumn, mainly off E and S coasts. Most predictable in spring when small flocks regularly pass certain seawatching points on the S coast in the first half of May and large numbers have recently been seen off the Western Isles. An unprecedented influx involving hundreds of birds was noted in autumn 1985 off Shetland and the E coasts of Scotland and England. Exceptional inland.
Sites: Spring 15, 19.1, 22, 23. In autumn, may with luck be seen at any seawatching station, especially on the E coast, 81 being the most regular.

Pomarine Skua
Stercorarius pomarinus
PM

Restricted as a breeding species to moorlands of N Scotland where the population is over 2,500 pairs, the majority on Shetland, Orkney, and the Outer Hebrides. Regular on passage off all coasts, especially in autumn when it is the most familiar of all the skuas in Britain. Rare inland.

Arctic Skua
Stercorarius parasiticus
PM, MB

Scarce but annual migrant, usually 50–100 a year in autumn. Most frequent off the E coast (August–November), especially Norfolk and Yorkshire. A spring passage off the Western Isles sometimes involves large numbers.
Sites: Spring 110. No reliable sites in autumn, but 3 and 81 are probably the best.

Long-tailed Skua
Stercorarius longicaudus
PM

British population is c 6,000 pairs, most on Shetland, but also Orkney, the Outer Hebrides, and a few sites on the Scottish mainland. Regular on passage, usually in small numbers, off all coasts.

Great Skua
Stercorarius skua
MB, PM

Mediterranean Gull
Larus melanocephalus
PM, WV, SMB

First bred 1968 (Hampshire) and slowly becoming established in S England (2–8 pairs at six sites in 1983). Usually nests in colonies of Black-headed Gulls. Otherwise regular in very small numbers, mainly at coastal sites in England and Wales. Should be looked for in any concentration of gulls. Most records are on passage or in winter.
Sites: 3, 4, 13, 14, 22, 23, 24.1, 35, 36, 60, 65, 70, 81 82

Little Gull
Larus minutus
PM, WV, SMB

Sporadic breeder, nesting successfully in 1975 and 1978 in Norfolk and Yorkshire. Summering birds in suitable habitat have been noted on a few other occasions. Regular and widespread passage migrant. Most records July–October, usually in small numbers but large flocks not infrequent. Largest numbers on the Firths of Tay and Forth and in Kent, but also regular at many sites on E, S, and NW coasts of England with small numbers inland.
Sites: 22, 23, 33, 38.3, 39, 72, 80, 81, 88

Sabine's Gull
Larus sabini
SPM

Scarce annual visitor; the peak months are September–October with the majority occurring at St Ives (SW England) and others scattered on S and E coasts. Usually in small numbers but large influxes occur occasionally in appropriate weather conditions.
Sites: 3, 81

Black-headed Gull
Larus ridibundus
WV, PM, RB, MB

Very common and widespread breeder throughout Britain, often in large colonies, especially on coastal marshes but also inland. Scarce in SW England and inland in S England. Very common in winter throughout Britain.

Ring-billed Gull
Larus delawarensis
SWV, SPM

First recorded at Blackpill in 1973, but has since become regular with over 50 per year 1981–4. Most are in Wales or SW England, with a scattering N to Shetland. Recorded all year, with fewest in summer and early autumn, and most in March.
Sites: 13, 60

Common Gull
Larus canus
WV, PM, RB

Common breeder in most of Scotland at both inland and coastal sites; very few breed in England and Wales. Widespread but local throughout Britain in winter, especially inland, but generally commoner in the N.

Lesser Black-backed Gull
Larus fuscus
MB, PM, WV

Breeds widely around the coast through very locally in S and E England. A few breed inland. In spring and autumn, migrants from Scandinavia and Iceland are commonly seen. Increasing numbers winter in Britain, roosting on reservoirs.

Herring Gull
Larus argentatus
RB, WV

Very common resident breeder, mainly in colonies on cliffs and rocky coasts and therefore absent from much of E coast. A widespread and familiar bird of all coasts in winter, also frequenting farmland and rubbish tips inland. A few of the yellow-legged race *cachinnans* have been recorded, especially in SE England.

Iceland Gull
Larus glaucoides
WV

Uncommon visitor, mainly in winter and most frequent in Shetland, N and W Scotland, and NE and SW England. Larger numbers are seen after NW gales in late winter. Regularly recorded elsewhere in very small numbers, chiefly at coastal sites but increasingly in the Midlands and the N at reservoir gull roosts

and rubbish tips. There are 3 records of the North American race, known as Kumlien's Gull *L. g. kumlieni.*
Sites: 3, 13, 52, 52.1, 56, 60, 81, 97.1, 101, 103, 104, 108.1, 110

Mainly an uncommon winter visitor to Scotland, with small numbers regular on the E coast S to Suffolk, SW and NW England, and inland to the Midlands and N; less frequent elsewhere. Most likely to be encountered at large gull roosts, rubbish tips, or fishing ports. A single adult bred with a Herring Gull on Shetland 1975–9.
Sites: England and Wales 3, 4, 5.1, 9, 13, 14, 35, 35.1, 36, 39, 52, 55, 56, 60, 70, 74, 81, 82, 84

Glaucous Gull
Larus hyperboreus
WV

Fairly common coastal breeder, the bulk in Scotland, especially the W coast, Hebrides, Orkney, and Shetland. Also breeds Wales and SW England. Widely distributed in winter on all coasts with small numbers inland.

Great Black-backed Gull
Larus marinus
RB, WV

Breeds colonially, usually on cliffs, at many widely scattered sites. Most numerous in NE Scotland, Orkney, and Shetland. Only a few small isolated sites on E and S coasts of England between Yorkshire and Dorset. Some now nest on buildings (e.g. Lowestoft, Suffolk). More pelagic than other gulls, dispersing to sea in winter, but can be seen off all coasts outside the breeding season.

Kittiwake
Rissa tridactyla
RB, MB, PM, WV

Fairly common but localised breeder in coastal colonies at a number of widely scattered localities, most on the E coast. Migrants are commonly seen on all coasts mid-March to May and July–October, but scarce in NW Scotland and irregular inland.

Sandwich Tern
Sterna sandvicensis
MB, PM

Breeds at a handful of sites, usually islands, mainly Firth of Forth, Northumberland, Anglesey, and Scilly. A single pair has nested at Dungeness for several years. This is Britain's rarest breeding tern; its numbers continue to decline and probably do not exceed 200 pairs. Only infrequently seen on passage, most regularly in SW England.
Sites: 1, 23, 68.1, 83, 88

Roseate Tern
Sterna dougallii
MB, PM

Common breeder, mainly on coasts but also inland on rivers, lakes, and gravel pits. Rather few colonies in NE and SW England and Wales. Widespread on migration and our most familiar tern. May be seen at most coastal sites April–June and July–October; it also occurs widely inland in smaller numbers.

Common Tern
Sterna hirundo
MB, PM

Common breeder, more numerous than Common Tern but with a more northerly distribution. Very few breed S of the Farnes on the E coast or S of Anglesey in the W. May be seen on all coasts during migration and sometimes inland, especially in May, when there may be large movements, though generally less frequent than Common Tern in the S.

Arctic Tern
Sterna paradisaea
MB, PM

Not uncommon, mainly breeding in small coastal colonies at many widely scattered localities. Largely absent in SW England and Wales and most numerous in SE England and East Anglia.

Little Tern
Sterna albifrons
MB, PM

Often nests on beaches where it is particularly vulnerable to disturbance. Population over 1,500 pairs. Regular around the coast on passage but scarce inland.

Black Tern
Chlidonias niger
PM, SMB

Regular on passage, most frequently in SE England and E Anglia, at coastal localities, but also widely inland in S England, especially on larger lakes and reservoirs. Spring passage is usually less prominent and more concentrated than autumn. Has bred sporadically since 1966, mainly on the Ouse Washes.

White-winged Black Tern
Chlidonias leucopterus
SPM

Rare passage migrant, c 20 a year, with more in autumn than spring. August–September are the peak months. Most regular in S and E England.
Sites: 12, 23

Guillemot
Uria aalge
MB, RB, WV

Britain's most numerous seabird, breeding colonially on flat ledges of sheer cliffs, the majority in Scotland. There are also good numbers in Wales and SW England but rather uncommon elsewhere and absent between Yorkshire and Dorset. Disperses to sea in winter when small numbers may be seen off all coasts.

Razorbill
Alca torda
MB, RB, WV

Similar distribution to Guillemot but much less numerous. Colonies tend to be less concentrated with a preference for more sheltered parts of cliffs. Britain and Ireland contain c 70% of the world's population.

Black Guillemot
Cepphus grylle
RB

Fairly common breeder on rocky coasts. Almost restricted to W and N Scotland (including the outlying islands) and largely absent in E Scotland. The only other breeding sites are the Isle of Man, Anglesey, and St Bees Head. Mainly sedentary and occurrences off the coasts of England in winter are rare.
Sites: Away from N and W Scotland 68.2, 68.5, 76, 97.1, 99, 113

Little Auk
Alle alle
WV

Regular off coasts of Shetland, mainly November–February. Annual but irregular off the E coast S to East Anglia. In some years, after northerly gales in late autumn, large wrecks occur. Generally scarce elsewhere.
Sites: More regular localities include 39, 79, 81.3, 101, 103

Puffin
Fratercula arctica
MB, RB, PM, WV

Common breeder, mainly on the N and W coasts, with none between Yorkshire and Dorset (and the small number in Dorset are the only ones on the S coast). Nests colonially in burrows on grassy slopes and usually present March–August. Mainly disperses to sea in winter but a few may be seen offshore at this time, mainly in the E.
Breeding sites in England and Wales: 1, 11, 15, 16.6, 62, 68.3, 76, 81, 83

Rock Dove/Feral Pigeon
Columba livia
RB

Feral Pigeons are common and familiar birds throughout Britain but wild populations of pure Rock Doves are now only found on coastal cliffs in W and N Scotland, the Hebrides, Orkney, and Shetland.

Common resident of parkland and farmland except parts of N and W Scotland. Absent Orkney, Shetland, and the Hebrides. Mainly sedentary, and always less common than Woodpigeon, but often overlooked.

Stock Dove
Columba oenas
RB, PM, WV

Abundant resident, though less common in NW Scotland and scarce on the Outer Hebrides and Shetland.

Woodpigeon
Columba palumbus
RB, WV

First bred in Norfolk in 1955, the beginning of a meteoric colonisation. Now common and widespread, even present on the outlying islands. Strongly associated with man and largely absent from upland areas.

Collared Dove
Streptopelia decaocto
RB

Common summer visitor, April–October, mainly in arable farmland with plenty of trees and hedgerows. Scarce in extreme SW England and W Wales. Only very small numbers N of a line between Lancashire and Durham.

Turtle Dove
Streptopelia turtur
MB, PM

This noisy tropical bird has recently become established as a feral breeder. Mainly found in SE England, especially in the London area, frequenting parks and gardens. Often detected by its loud call as it flies over.
Sites: 19, 21.2

Ring-necked Parakeet
Psittacula krameri
IB

Common and widely distributed, occupying a wide variety of habitats. The call is familiar to everyone but the birds themselves can be elusive and are more likely to be seen in open areas. Adults are present April to July or August; juveniles tend to leave later but are rarely seen after September.

Cuckoo
Cuculus canorus
MB, PM

Resident throughout England, Wales, and S Scotland but declining though still fairly common in SW England, S Wales, S Yorkshire, NW England, and SW Scotland. Chiefly a bird of agricultural areas, breeding in buildings and isolated old trees, but often difficult to locate. Frequently begins hunting before dusk, often along roadside verges, offering the best opportunities of seeing one.

Barn Owl
Tyto alba
RB, SPM

Bred 1967–75 on Fetlar. A few are still resident on Shetland, and birds very occasionally summer elsewhere (e.g. Orkney, Outer Hebrides, Cairngorms). Otherwise a very rare winter visitor, mainly to W Britain, and less than annual.
Sites: 101

Snowy Owl
Nyctea scandiaca
FB, SWV

Introduced in the late 19th century, now fairly common and widespread throughout England and most of Wales. Scarce in Scotland. A bird of agricultural areas with good numbers of old trees and hedges. Although it often perches prominently in the daytime, this is a species which needs to be looked for since it is usually found in habitats which are otherwise ignored by birders.

Little Owl
Athene noctua
IB

A common woodland species often found in towns, parks, and gardens. Occurs widely throughout Britain though absent from the Hebrides, Orkney, and Shetland. Its calls make location easy

Tawny Owl
Strix aluco
RB

347

and it can sometimes be attracted by imitating these. Strictly nocturnal and most frequently seen when driving at night.

Long-eared Owl
Asio otus
RB, WV, PM

An uncommon and elusive species, though widely scattered throughout Britain. Generally much less common in S England and Wales. It occurs chiefly in coniferous woods and plantations, but also deciduous woods and copses. It may be located by call, though still difficult to see. In late spring fledged juveniles give a loud 'squeaky-gate' begging call, especially at dusk, and are more easily tracked down. Small numbers from N Europe winter and are mainly seen on the E coast when they first arrive in October–November (though they are often passed off as Short-eared Owls). Communal winter roosts are often in thick haw-thorns, and are best located by looking for the white-washed branches.
Sites: 38.3, 39.3, 45, 46, 53, 93, 99, 101, 103

Short-eared Owl
Asio flammeus
RB, MB, PM, WV

Fairly common breeder of open country in most of Scotland (absent from Shetland) and N England, with small numbers in Wales and at (mainly) coastal locations on the E coast of England. Occurs more widely in winter when it is a familiar species at many localities on the E and S coasts; some are immigrants from Europe. Best seen at dusk but they readily hunt during the day, especially in winter.

Nightjar
Caprimulgus europaeus
MB, PM

A summer visitor, breeding grounds occupied May to August or September. Population probably only 1,500–2,000 pairs, mainly on dry heathland but also a variety of habitats including moorland and young plantations. Distributed widely over much of England, Wales, and S Scotland, with the main concentrations in Dorset/Hampshire, Breckland, and SE England. Best located when calling or churring at dusk when they can often be seen hunting. Rarely seen on migration.
Sites: 16, 17, 20, 33, 34, 39.3, 45

Swift
Apus apus
MB, PM

Very common and conspicuous summer visitor throughout Britain except NW Scotland, the Hebrides, Orkney, and Shetland. Present late April to August, with small numbers into September.

Kingfisher
Alcedo atthis
RB

Fairly common and widespread resident throughout England and Wales but scarce in Scotland. Found in most freshwater habitats and some dispersal occurs in autumn and winter when Kingfishers are regularly found at coastal localities. Population can be severely affected in hard winters.

Hoopoe
Upupa epops
SPM, SMB

Regular migrant, averaging over 100 birds a year, the majority from late March to mid-May. Hoopoes have been found in most counties but most spring records are from the S coast. Any of the migration watchpoints on the S coast in early spring offer as good a chance as anywhere. Areas of short turf, including large gardens, and dunes are favoured, but Hoopoes can be very elusive despite their conspicuous plumage. Breeds sporadically, mainly in S England.

Formerly a common breeder in most counties in England and Wales, but now extinct there as a breeding species (except for occasional isolated records). However, a limited colonisation of the central Highlands of Scotland has compensated, but numbers remain tiny. Wrynecks are best seen on migration, when small numbers occur regularly on the E coast, and less frequently on the S coast. Most migrants are seen late August to mid-October, usually on the ground near low cover at coastal localities, but also occasionally inland, even in suburban parks and gardens.
Sites: Regular localities include: 1, 15, 23, 31, 33, 35, 39, 40, 43, 49, 79, 81, 84

Wryneck
Jynx torquilla
PM, SMB

Common and widespread throughout England and Wales, less common in S and central Scotland and absent from N Scotland. Favours open woods and parkland as well as heaths and farmland. It often feeds on the ground and is frequently located by its very loud call.

Green Woodpecker
Picus viridis
RB

Common and widespread breeder throughout Britain but scarce in the extreme N and absent from the Hebrides, Orkney, and Shetland. A woodland species, but also occurs in parks and gardens. Its presence is often indicated by its harsh call. Small numbers of migrants from Scandinavia are occasionally noted at coastal localities in the N and E.

Great Spotted Woodpecker
Dendrocopos major
RB, PM, WV

Common resident, widely but thinly distributed over most of England and Wales but virtually absent from Scotland. Not as common as Great Spotted, but not as scarce as many birders believe and frequently overlooked. Occurs in woodlands but is also partial to more open areas, hedgerow trees, and parkland. It is usually found in the tops of large trees, favouring the thin extremities of the limbs. Its presence is often indicated by its distinctive high-pitched call.

Lesser Spotted Woodpecker
Dendrocopos minor
RB

Breeding confined to five areas centred on Devon, New Forest/Dorset, Surrey/Hampshire border, Breckland, and the Suffolk coast. Population varies considerably according to availability of suitable habitat and the severity of winters and was estimated at 210–230 pairs in 1983. Woodlarks occupy a variety of habitats from unimproved agricultural land (e.g. Devon) to cleared forestry plantations, tree nurseries, and heathlands (providing they are not too overgrown). Best looked for in spring when they are singing. Many breeding sites are deserted in winter and some dispersal takes place.
Sites: 17, 20, 45

Woodlark
Lullula arborea
RB

Abundant resident throughout Britain in a wide variety of open habitats. Migrants are seen at many coastal localities outside the breeding season.

Skylark
Alauda arvensis
RB, PM, WV

Summering birds were found in Scotland 1972–7 and breeding proved on several occasions. Regular but very uncommon visitor October–April, mainly to shores and saltmarshes on the E coast. Most frequent in East Anglia and SE England but there are few reliable sites.
Sites: Regular localities include 33, 35, 39, 43, 44, 82

Shore Lark
Eremophila alpestris
WV, SMB

Sand Martin
Riparia riparia
MB, PM

Widespread except in the Northern Isles but has recently suffered a catastrophic crash in numbers. Breeds colonially in burrows excavated in sandy banks and cliffs and is a familiar species over most inland waters and gravel pits, especially in the S on passage.

Swallow
Hirundo rustica
MB, PM

Very common summer visitor throughout Britain but only locally in NW Scotland and the outlying islands.

House Martin
Delichon urbica
MB, PM

Very common summer visitor throughout Britain but only very locally in NW Scotland, the Outer Hebrides, Orkney, and Shetland. Often in close association with habitation.

Richard's Pipit
Anthus novaeseelandiae
SPM

Scarce migrant in variable numbers, mainly September–October. 30–40 per year is usual, but several autumns have produced over 100. Rough coastal grassland is favoured, and birds are often first located by call as they fly over. Records are widely scattered but most frequent in Shetland, the E coast between Yorkshire and Norfolk, and SW England, especially Scilly.
Sites: Regular localities include 1, 39, 79, 101, 102

Tawny Pipit
Anthus campestris
SPM

Scarce annual migrant averaging 25–30 per year. Most are late August to mid-October but small numbers are regular in spring. Most frequent at coastal localities, especially on short turf and dunes, between Norfolk and Scilly; irregular elsewhere.
Sites: Regular localities include 1, 15, 22, 23

Tree Pipit
Anthus trivialis
MB, PM

Common summer visitor throughout most of Britain except extreme SW England, Anglesey, the Outer Hebrides, Orkney, and Shetland. Breeds in a variety of habitats but requires open areas with tall bushes and trees. Widespread on passage when it is most frequently detected by its distinctive flight call.

Meadow Pipit
Anthus pratensis
MB, RB, PM, WV

Abundant throughout Britain but more thinly distributed in parts of central England. Favours rough grasslands, heaths, and moors. Flocks are commonly seen on passage and in winter, some being visitors from Iceland and the continent.

Rock Pipit
Anthus petrosus
RB, PM, WV

Traditionally regarded as a race of Water Pipit. Common resident of rocky coasts, though absent between Kent and S Yorkshire and most of NW England. Some dispersal takes place in winter (e.g. to coasts of E England) and a few occur inland on passage around lakes and reservoirs. The Scandinavian race *littoralis* is regular in small numbers on the E and S coasts, mainly October–November and late March to early April.

Water Pipit
Anthus spinoletta
WV, PM

Regular but local visitor, October–March, mainly to S England. Also occurs in small numbers on passage, especially in early spring. Usually found in freshwater habitats (reservoir and gravel pit margins, watercress beds, wet grassland), but also on brackish marshes. Frequently overlooked because of its rather Meadow Pipit-like call and habit of flying long distances if flushed. There are two records of the American race *rubescens*.
Sites: 5, 12, 13, 25, 33, 39, 70

Fairly common summer visitor to most of England though largely absent in SW England, Wales, and Scotland. Favours damp freshwater habitats (e.g. water meadows, marshy fields) and cereal crops. The breeding race is *flavissima*, but individuals showing characteristics of several other races have been found in Britain, some even breeding. The most frequent is the Blue-headed Wagtail *M. f. flava* which occurs annually in spring and autumn in small numbers, mainly on the E and S coasts.

Yellow Wagtail
Motacilla flava
MB, PM

Common and widespread on inland waterways though largely absent in E England (Essex to Yorkshire), the Outer Hebrides, Orkney, and Shetland. Particularly favours rocky streams and rivers in hilly areas. In winter may also be found around lakes and reservoirs, at coastal sites, and even in town centres.

Grey Wagtail
Motacilla cinerea
RB, PM

Very common breeder throughout Britain (but irregular on Shetland). Some are partial migrants and large roosts may be seen on passage and in winter, especially in reedbeds. The White Wagtail *M. a. alba* from Europe and Iceland is a regular passage migrant in small numbers (late March to May and August–October), and occasionally breeds, especially on Shetland.

Pied Wagtail
Motacilla alba
RB, MB, PM

Annual winter visitor in variable numbers, chiefly on the E coast between Shetland and Norfolk and irregular in the S. Subject to occasional invasions when small flocks are widespread, but generally unpredictable; there are no regular sites. Usually seen feeding on berry-bearing bushes, even in suburban gardens.

Waxwing
Bombycilla garrulus
WV, PM

Fairly common resident of fast-flowing rivers and streams in upland regions. Occurs mainly in Scotland, N England, Wales, and SW England. The Black-bellied race *cinclus* from N Europe occurs annually (October–April) in very small numbers, mainly on the E coast and Shetland.
Sites: 63, 64, 65, 66, 69.1, 93, 95, 109, 111, 112, 114

Dipper
Cinclus cinclus
RB, SPM, SWV

Abundant resident throughout Britain, breeding in almost every type of habitat. One of our commonest birds but numbers can be drastically reduced in severe winters. There are endemic subspecies on Shetland, Fair Isle, St Kilda, and the Outer Hebrides.

Wren
Troglodytes troglodytes
RB, WV, PM

Abundant resident throughout Britain except Shetland. Occurs in a wide variety of habitats but partial to gardens and hedgerows. Migrants from Europe are regular on the E coast, especially Shetland and Fair Isle.

Dunnock
Prunella modularis
RB, PM

Abundant resident throughout Britain except Shetland, in all types of woodland as well as gardens. British birds are mainly sedentary but large influxes of continental migrants are regular on the E and S coasts.

Robin
Erithacus rubecula
RB, MB, PM, WV

Fairly common summer visitor, mainly breeding S of a line between the Humber and Severn estuaries but absent from most of Devon and Cornwall. Most numerous in SE England and East Anglia but numbers have declined in recent years. Favours woodlands and dense scrub but is a skulker, keeping low in the vegetation. Best located by its famous song which can be heard

Nightingale
Luscinia megarhynchos
MB, PM

day or night. A single individual of the E race *hafizi* was seen on Fair Isle in 1971.

Sites: 16, 17, 20, 25, 33, 34, 35, 39, 45

Bluethroat
Luscinia svecica
PM, SMB

Regular passage migrant in very small numbers, mainly on the E and S coasts. Usually smaller numbers in spring (mainly May), with most records from Shetland. The fall in mid-May 1985 was unprecedented; it involved hundreds of birds at many places on the E coast, including 100 on the Isle of May. Generally more numerous late August to October with the largest numbers in East Anglia and Shetland. When racial identity has been determined, red-spotted *svecica* has proved to be much more frequent than the white-spotted *cyanecula*. Favours dense vegetation and reedbeds, generally keeping to the ground. This skulker is usually difficult to see, and is often first located when flushed accidentally. A single breeding record, in Scotland, 1968.

Sites: More regular localities include 1, 40, 79, 89, 101, 102

Black Redstart
Phoenicurus ochruros
PM, WV, SMB

Has bred regularly since 1923, almost exclusively in urban and industrial areas in the SE and locally elsewhere. The population is c 100 pairs, and breeding birds are present late March to September. Regular passage is noted in small numbers at coastal sites, mainly on the E and S coasts. In autumn, most numerous in SW England (especially late October and November) and a few winter. There are three records of birds resembling one of the E races.

Sites: Passage/winter 1, 2, 8, 10, 11, 15, 19, 22, 39.1, 49, 61.3, 79

Breeding 23, 31, 33.1, 35.1, 36

Redstart
Phoenicurus phoenicurus
MB, PM

Common summer visitor, breeding in woodland (especially oak) and sometimes parks and gardens. Widespread, but most numerous in the N and W; generally uncommon in E England and absent from many outlying islands. Fairly common on passage (especially April and late August to early September), mostly on E and S coasts. There are two records of Ehrenberg's Redstart *P. p. samamisicus*, the E race.

Whinchat
Saxicola rubetra
MB, PM

Generally uncommon but widespread summer visitor, mainly to upland areas of N and W Britain (but scarce on outlying islands). Frequents moorland edge, heathlands with gorse, and young forestry plantations. Conspicuous on passage, especially at E and S coast localities.

Stonechat
Saxicola torquata
RB, MB

Common and conspicuous resident, chiefly on the coastal fringe of W Britain but also at many inland sites. Very local in E and central England. Prefers areas of short turf with bracken, heather, or gorse. Some disperse in winter to rough ground and coastal marshes. Distinctive birds known as Siberian Stonechats (mostly *S. t. maura*) are vagrants to Britain, averaging 6–7 a year, mostly September–December on Shetland, the E coast, and Scilly.

Wheatear
Oenanthe oenanthe
MB, PM

Common summer visitor, mainly to uplands of the N and W. Very local breeder in S England but is a widespread and familiar species on passage, being one of the first arrivals in spring.

Ring Ouzel
Turdus torquatus
MB, PM

Uncommon summer visitor, almost restricted to mountain and moorland regions of the N and W (but largely absent on the Outer Hebrides, Orkney, and Shetland). Small numbers breed in SW England. Favours remote gullies and screes up to 4,000 feet. Ring Ouzels are not easy birds to see on their breeding grounds owing to the often inaccessible habitat and thin distribution; they are best located by song. Passage birds are seen regularly in small numbers on the E and S coasts, but may be elusive; the distinctive call is often the first indication of the species.
Sites: Summer 65.1, 66, 69.1, 93, 95, 108, 109

Blackbird
Turdus merula
RB, MB, PM, WV

Abundant resident throughout Britain. The population is augmented in autumn and winter by immigrants from the continent.

Fieldfare
Turdus pilaris
WV, PM, SMB

First bred in 1967 since when very small numbers have nested annually, mainly in Scotland (especially Shetland) but also England. Common and widespread winter visitor September–April, chiefly to fields and rough pasture, but also gardens and parks in hard weather.

Song Thrush
Turdus philomelos
RB, MB, PM, WV

Abundant resident throughout Britain except Shetland, and continental migrants are regular on the E and S coasts. Birds on the Outer Hebrides and Skye belong to an endemic subspecies *hebridensis*.

Redwing
Turdus iliacus
WV, PM, SMB

Formerly a sporadic breeder in Scotland but since 1967 has begun a small-scale colonisation. Numbers vary but could be as high as 300 pairs. Common and widespread winter visitor September–April.

Mistle Thrush
Turdus viscivorus
RB, MB, PM, WV

Common and widespread resident though scarce or absent in extreme NW Scotland, the Hebrides, Orkney, and Shetland. Occupies a wide variety of habitats from moorlands and farmland to parks and gardens.

Cetti's Warbler
Cettia cetti
SRB

First recorded in 1961, and first bred (in Kent) in 1972. Since then has increased steadily to over 300 pairs (1984), though vulnerable to hard winters. The greatest numbers are in SW England, as well as SE England and East Anglia. Resident, usually in reedbeds or overgrown marshes. They keep low in dense, tangled thickets and can be difficult to see, but their presence is indicated by their explosive song. The best chance of a sighting is in the early morning or the early spring before the leaves appear.
Sites: 5, 9, 13, 25, 33, 37, 61.2

Grasshopper Warbler
Locustella naevia
MB, PM

Common summer visitor, more locally in the extreme N. The reeling song is a familiar sound but the birds themselves can be hard to see, keeping low in dense tangled vegetation. They inhabit a wide variety of both damp and dry habitats and are best seen (and heard) at dawn or dusk. Rarely seen on passage.

Savi's Warbler
Locustella luscinioides
SMB, SPM

2–30 pairs breed annually at a number of sites in S England. Occurs almost exclusively in reedbeds and is hard to see. Best located by song, and sings most frequently at dawn and dusk, sometimes near the tops of reeds. Present mid-April to July.
Sites: Regular localities include 25, 33, 38

Aquatic Warbler
Acrocephalus
paludicola
SPM

Scarce migrant averaging c 40 per year, August–September. Most frequent on the S coast with small numbers irregularly on the E coast. Inhabits reedbeds and it requires much luck to see one; early morning is the best time to look. Occasionally in drier habitats such as dense bushes.
Sites: Regular localities include 5, 13, 79, 102

Sedge Warbler
Acrocephalus
schoenobaenus
MB, PM

Common summer visitor, more local in NW Scotland and absent from Shetland. Inhabits a wide variety of habitats from reedbeds (although preferring the drier margins) to any dense low vegetation. Commonly seen on passage at coastal localities.

Marsh Warbler
Acrocephalus
palustris
SMB, SPM

Scarce summer visitor whose range and population have decreased in recent years to only 10–15 pairs, the majority in the Worcestershire stronghold with scattered records of breeding elsewhere. Very similar to Reed Warbler and best identified by song. It prefers meadowsweet, willowherb, and nettle beds, usually near riverside willows. Arrives late May and is most easily seen before mid-June when it stops singing regularly. Rarely recorded on passage, except on the Northern Isles in spring.
Sites: 57, 101, 102

Reed Warbler
Acrocephalus
scirpaceus
MB, PM

Common summer visitor, breeding mainly but not exclusively in reedbeds. Widely distributed in central and S England and East Anglia but local in N England, Wales, and SW England. May be seen in bushes and trees away from water on passage.

Icterine Warbler
Hippolais icterina
SPM, FB

Regular migrant in very small numbers (c 75 a year). Most are on the E coast (from Kent to Shetland) and Scilly, with smaller numbers elsewhere on the S coast and at the Irish Sea observatories. The majority occur mid-August to late September but a few are regular late May to early June, especially on the Northern Isles. Has apparently bred once, in 1907 (Wiltshire).
Sites: Regular localites include 1, 8, 15, 22, 23, 40, 41, 43, 49, 62.2, 67, 79, 81, 82, 89, 101, 102, 103

Melodious Warbler
Hippolais
polyglotta
SPM

Scarce annual migrant (numbers similar to Icterine Warbler) almost exclusively in autumn, mostly August–September. The vast majority are on the S coast and in W Wales; it is decidedly rare on the E coast.
Sites: Regular localities include 1, 2, 8, 11, 15, 22, 23, 62.2, 67, 75

Dartford Warbler
Sylvia undata
RB

Uncommon resident of lowland heaths, ideally mature heather and gorse, in S England. 423 pairs were counted in 1984, almost exclusively in Dorset, the New Forest, and the Surrey/Hampshire border. The population suffers severe losses in cold winters but usually recovers quickly. Individuals occasionally wander away from their breeding areas. Often keeps hidden but song and calls help locate it. Very difficult to find in winter.
Sites: 16, 17, 20

Barred Warbler
Sylvia nisoria
SPM

Regular migrant in small numbers (c 75 a year), almost exclusively August to mid-October, and mostly immatures. Fair Isle and Shetland are the most regular sites, but Scilly and the coastal counties between Fife and Norfolk record small numbers annually. Less frequent on the S coast. Favours thick scrub and

can be skulking.
Sites: Regular localities include 1, 2, 15, 23, 39, 40, 41, 43, 49, 79, 81, 82, 84, 85, 89, 90, 101, 102, 103

Common summer visitor to most of England but local in the N and SW. Occurs sparsely in Wales, mainly the E, and virtually absent from Scotland. Inhabits hedgerows and scrub where it can be elusive, though the distinctive rattle and chatter give away its presence.

Lesser Whitethroat
Sylvia curruca
MB, PM

Common summer visitor to a wide variety of scrubby habitats, though local in NW Scotland and largely absent from the Hebrides, Orkney, and Shetland.

Whitethroat
Sylvia communis
MB, PM

Common summer visitor as far N as S Scotland. Very local further N. Prefers woodland with dense scrub and thick hedgerows but will occupy a variety of habitats. Song is often considered similar to that of Blackcap, but is in fact distinctive.

Garden Warbler
Sylvia borin
MB, PM

Common summer visitor with an almost identical distribution to that of Garden Warbler. Occurs in similar habitats but often damper areas with taller trees. Small but increasing numbers overwinter; the species favours parks and gardens at this season and may be seen on bird tables.

Blackcap
Sylvia atricapilla
MB, PM, WV

Scarce annual migrant, almost exclusively September–November. The commonest Siberian vagrant: numbers vary, but there have been over 100 in several autumns. Mainly recorded on the E and S coasts, as well as the Irish Sea observatories, but rarely inland. The best chance is on Fair Isle (September) or Scilly (October).
Sites: Regular localities include 1, 2, 8, 22, 41, 43, 49, 79, 81, 82, 84, 85, 89, 90, 101, 102, 103

Yellow-browed Warbler
Phylloscopus inornatus
SPM

Fairly common but local summer visitor, distributed over much of Britain. Most numerous in the sessile oakwoods of the N and W but also frequents other mature woodland, especially beech. Very scarce in much of E England and infrequently seen on passage.
Sites: 17, 20, 39.4, 63, 64, 65, 66, 93, 95, 108, 109, 114

Wood Warbler
Phylloscopus sibilatrix
MB, PM

Common from mid-March to October in a variety of wooded habitats, though local in much of Scotland. Passage birds are widespread and conspicuous and small falls in October and November are not uncommon. Continental birds of the race *abietinus* are regular migrants, especially on the E coast in autumn, and Siberian Chiffchaffs *P. c. tristis* are recorded annually in small numbers. Small numbers winter, especially in S England.

Chiffchaff
Phylloscopus collybita
MB, PM, WV

Abundant and widespread throughout Britain except Shetland, but only breeds locally in the Hebrides and Orkney. Passage birds arrive a little later in spring than Chiffchaff and tend to leave earlier.

Willow Warbler
Phylloscopus trochilus
MB, PM

Goldcrest
Regulus regulus
RB, PM, WV

Very common and widely distributed though local or irregular on the Hebrides, Orkney, and Shetland. Mainly a bird of coniferous woodland but occasionally inhabits deciduous woods. Largely sedentary and vulnerable to severe winters. Falls of migrants are quite frequent on the E and S coasts.

Firecrest
Regulus ignicapillus
PM, SMB, SWV

First bred in 1961 in the New Forest, but subsequently found to have a wider distribution, breeding at scattered sites in S England and occasionally Wales with a maximum of 174 pairs (1983). Usually breeds in conifers, especially spruce. Regular passage migrant in small numbers on the S coast and less frequently East Anglia. Spring passage mid-March to April, autumn passage mainly mid-September to early November. A few winter, especially in SW England. Firecrests are elusive in the breeding season and are most easily seen on passage or in winter.
Sites: 1, 2, 8, 9, 11, 14, 15, 17, 22, 23, 24, 31, 41

Spotted Flycatcher
Muscicapa striata
MB, PM

Common and widespread summer visitor though local or absent in the Hebrides, Orkney, and Shetland. May be seen from late April to September in a variety of wooded habitats, often near water and including farmland, parks, and gardens. Migrants are conspicuous on the coast in both spring and autumn.

Red-breasted Flycatcher
Ficedula parva
SPM

Regular migrant in very small numbers (over 100 in some autumns), mainly late August to early November, mostly September–October. Very few show any red on the breast. Most numerous at E coast localities, especially Shetland and between Fife and Norfolk. Smaller numbers on the S coast but very frequent on Scilly. Spring and inland records are rare.
Sites: Regular localities include 1, 2, 8, 15, 23, 40, 41, 43, 49, 67, 79, 81, 82, 84, 85, 89, 101, 102, 103

Pied Flycatcher
Ficedula hypoleuca
MB, PM

Fairly common summer visitor from mid-April to August (but difficult to see after the end of June). Most numerous in Wales and N England, more local in S Scotland, and only small numbers further N and in SW England. Typically found in sessile oakwoods in hill country but also in alder and birchwoods. Passage migrants are widespread on E and S coasts in autumn (especially late August and September).
Sites: Breeding 63, 64, 65, 66, 69.1, 114

Bearded Tit
Panurus biarmicus
RB

Uncommon resident; probably over 600 pairs. Nests at many sites in SE and SW England and N to Yorkshire and Lancashire, but the stronghold is East Anglia. Subject to severe declines after hard winters but rapid breeding allows a quick recovery. Confined to reedbeds and mainly sedentary, but in winter small groups of wandering birds may be seen away from breeding sites, and, when populations are high, dispersal takes place in the form of eruptions. Bearded Tits often keep low in reedbeds, especially in windy conditions, but they are not particularly shy and are easily located by their calls. They are most conspicuous in late summer.
Sites: 13, 25, 33, 34, 35, 37, 38, 39, 42, 43, 61.2, 73, 78

Long-tailed Tit
Aegithalos caudatus
RB

Common resident in woodland and hedgerows, but local in the extreme N and absent from the Northern Isles. Usually seen in small parties and invariably more conspicuous in winter.

Widespread and fairly common over most of England and Wales but only found in the extreme SE of Scotland. Usually in deciduous woodland. Very similar in plumage to Willow Tit and best identified by calls.

Marsh Tit
Parus palustris
RB

Widespread and fairly common throughout most of England and Wales. Its range overlaps with Marsh Tit but it is more widespread in S Scotland and less common in parts of NW England. Occupies a similar habitat to Marsh Tit but shows a preference for damper woodland, thickets, and hedgerows.

Willow Tit
Parus montanus
RB

A very localised and sedentary species which is restricted to mature Scots pine forests in the central Scottish Highlands. Not uncommon within its range (c 900 pairs) and easily located by call, though it can be inconspicuous in winter.
Sites: 93, 98, 99

Crested Tit
Parus cristatus
RB

Very common resident except in Hebrides, Orkney, and Shetland. Associated with conifers, but also occupies deciduous woodland. Largely sedentary but passage migrants are noted occasionally.

Coal Tit
Parus ater
RB, PM

Abundant, occupying a wide variety of habitats but absent from the Northern Isles. Variable numbers of continental migrants winter, especially in S and E England.

Blue Tit
Parus caeruleus
RB, WV

Abundant and widespread except in the Northern Isles. Mainly sedentary but continental migrants occur in variable numbers, mainly in S and E England.

Great Tit
Parus major
RB, WV

Fairly common and noisy resident in mature deciduous woodland throughout most of central and S England and Wales. More locally distributed in N England and largely absent from Scotland.

Nuthatch
Sitta europaea
RB

Common resident in all types of mature woodland though less numerous in NW Scotland and absent from Orkney and Shetland. Commoner than many birdwatchers believe, and often overlooked.

Treecreeper
Certhia familiaris
RB

Rare breeder (up to 30 pairs) at widely scattered sites in S England with the main concentration in East Anglia. Regular spring migrant in variable numbers (averages 20–30 a year) to most counties in S England, especially in the SW and SE, and less commonly further N. Most records are mid-April to early July with a peak in May. Few in autumn. May be seen at any of the coastal migration watchpoints but the most reliable site is Scilly with an average of six per year.

Golden Oriole
Oriolus oriolus
SPM, SMB

Has declined drastically and is now almost extinct as a breeding species in Britain. Only 5–6 pairs nested in 1983 — on dry, bushy heathland in E England. Occasionally breeds in Scotland (c.f. Wryneck). Regular passage migrant in small numbers, chiefly on the E and S coasts in autumn and the Northern Isles in spring.
Sites: Passage, 1, 22, 23, 41, 43, 49, 79, 81, 82, 84, 85, 89, 90, 101, 102, 103

Red-backed Shrike
Lanius collurio
PM, SMB

Great Grey Shrike
Lanius excubitor
WV, PM

Uncommon winter visitor, usually singly, arriving from mid-October onwards. Chiefly found in open country in the E half of England and Scotland. Some birds return to the same wintering area year after year but there are few reliable sites (Spurn Head is perhaps the best), and the species has become much less numerous in the 1980s. *L. e. pallidirostris* (Steppe Shrike) from central Asia has been recorded twice on Fair Isle.

Jay
Garrulus glandarius
RB, WV

Common resident in all types of woodland, but local in S and central Scotland. Occasional influxes of continental birds occur chiefly in October in SE England.

Magpie
Pica pica
RB

Very common and conspicuous resident throughout most of England and Wales but less common in parts of East Anglia. More local in Scotland and largely absent from the NW, the central Highlands, and the border country.

Chough
Pyrrhocorax pyrrhocorax
RB

Uncommon resident, confined to Wales, the Isle of Man, and a few areas in W Scotland. Population over 250 pairs (1982). Occurs chiefly on coastal cliffs but a number breed inland, especially in Wales, in slate quarries.
Sites: 62, 65.2, 65.4, 65.5, 67, 68.3, 112

Jackdaw
Corvus monedula
RB, WV

Very common resident throughout Britain but more local in NW Scotland. Occurs in a variety of habitats including woods, cliffs, and even towns. Some continental birds winter.

Rook
Corvus frugilegus
RB, WV

Abundant resident though local in NW Scotland and the outer islands. Occurs in all types of lightly wooded country. Breeds in colonies in tall trees and remains highly gregarious in winter. Some continental birds regularly winter.

**Carrion Crow/
Hooded Crow**
Corvus corone
RB, WV

The Carrion Crow *C. c. corone* is a very common resident except in NW Scotland where it is replaced by the Hooded Crow *C. c. cornix*. The two races interbreed freely and hybrids are common in the overlap zone, which is gradually shifting N.

Raven
Corvus corax
RB

Fairly common resident, widely distributed in W Scotland and Wales but in England almost confined to the Lake District, Isle of Man, and SW England. Chiefly found in mountains, moorlands, and on sea cliffs. Usually solitary or in pairs.

Starling
Sturnus vulgaris
WV, PM, RB

Abundant resident throughout Britain, and large numbers of continental immigrants winter. The nominate British and European race is replaced in Shetland and the Outer Hebrides by the endemic subspecies *zetlandicus*.

House Sparrow
Passer domesticus
RB

Abundant resident all over Britain. A hard species to miss.

Tree Sparrow
Passer montanus
RB, WV

Common but easily overlooked resident, widely distributed over much of England, Wales, and lowland Scotland. Absent from parts of Wales and most of SW England. Found in a variety of habitats but requires holes (e.g. in trees, buildings, or cliffs) for nesting. Mainly sedentary, but continental immigrants winter on the E and S coasts.

Abundant and widely distributed throughout Britain except Shetland. Occupies any habitat with trees or bushes but the highest densities are in deciduous woodland.

Chaffinch
Fringilla coelebs
RB, WV

Very small numbers (up to ten pairs) breed in Scotland. Chiefly a winter visitor in variable numbers over most of the country (but few in N Scotland). Passage migrants are seen on the E and S coasts mainly from late September to mid-November and March to early May.

Brambling
Fringilla montifringilla
WV, PM, SMB

First bred in Britain in 1967. Since then breeding has occurred with increasing frequency but numbers remain low (up to six pairs), most in English S coast counties. Chiefly a scarce but annual migrant in variable numbers, averaging c 20 a year. Migrants occur in all months, but mostly April–May and October–November, the majority on the S coast with a scattering of E coast records. Very scarce elsewhere and, apart from breeding birds, there are no regular sites.

Serin
Serinus serinus
SPM, SMB

Very common though rather local in NW Scotland and absent from Shetland. Inhabits a variety of habitats from farmland to parks and gardens. Some immigrants regularly winter.

Greenfinch
Carduelis chloris
RB, WV

Common breeder, though sparse in central Scotland and absent in the extreme N. Most of the population migrates to S Europe for the winter and impressive movements can be seen on the E and S coasts in autumn and spring.

Goldfinch
Carduelis carduelis
MB, RB, PM

Fairly common breeder in the Scottish Highlands with scattered pockets in the rest of Britain. Largely dependent on conifers for nesting. Continental immigrants winter widely in variable numbers when they may be found in mixed flocks with Redpolls, feeding on waterside alders and even frequenting gardens.

Siskin
Carduelis spinus
RB, WV, PM

Generally very common, though rather local in NW Scotland and absent from Shetland. Found mainly in open country such as heathland and farmland and particularly partial to feeding in weedy fields. Many of our birds emigrate to S Europe in winter, while others from N Europe winter here.

Linnet
Carduelis cannabina
MB, RB, WV, PM

Common resident in N and W Scotland, mainly in coastal regions but also more locally in the central Highlands; also a completely separate population in the Pennines. Found mainly on heather moors and the short turf of coastal clifftops. In winter, variable numbers winter on the E coast, mainly between Lincolnshire and Sussex; most are probably of British origin.
Sites: Winter 19, 24, 26, 28, 30, 33, 34, 36, 40, 42, 43, 69, 70, 74, 112

Twite
Carduelis flavirostris
MB, RB, WV, PM

Common and widespread except in the Northern Isles, but local in S-central and SW England and Pembrokeshire. Breeds in a wide variety of habitats including forestry plantations, birchwoods, scrub, and carr. Some emigrate to winter in Europe while Mealy (*C. f. flammea*) and Greenland (*C. f. rostrata*) Redpolls are winter visitors and passage migrants in variable numbers.

Redpoll
Carduelis flammea
RB, MB, WV, PM

Crossbill
Loxia curvirostra
RB, PM

Uncommon resident breeding in highly variable numbers in a number of widely scattered pockets throughout Britain. Following influxes of Crossbills from Europe many remain to breed resulting in new areas being colonised on a short-term basis. Such eruptions can be very large with arrivals reaching the E coast from late June onwards. Found almost exclusively in spruces or pines, Crossbills can be elusive but are easily detected in flight by their distinctive call. They also frequently visit puddles and pools to drink.
Sites: 17, 41, 45, 114

Scottish Crossbill
Loxia scotica
RB

Britain's only endemic bird. Confined to the relic Caledonian forest of Scots pines in the Scottish Highlands where the population was estimated at 1,500 adults in the early 1970s, but numbers are variable. Fairly easy to see within its limited range.
Sites: 93, 95, 98, 99, 100, 109

Parrot Crossbill
Loxia pytyopsittacus
SPM, SMB

Very rare migrant subject to occasional influxes, with 76 in 1962–3 and 131 in 1982–3. The latter invasion resulted in the first breeding attempt by two pairs in N England in 1983, probable breeding in Suffolk in 1984, and successful breeding at Wells, Norfolk, in 1984–5.

Scarlet Rosefinch
Carpodacus erythrinus
SPM, SMB

A regular migrant in small but variable numbers, averaging 40 a year. Few in spring, mainly occurring mid-August to October. The majority are on Fair Isle, Shetland, and Orkney, but also regular on the E coast, especially between Fife and Yorkshire, with smaller numbers at other coastal localities around Britain; recently increasingly regular on Scilly. Bred for the first time in 1982 in the Scottish Highlands.
Regular sites include: 1, 89, 101, 102, 103

Bullfinch
Pyrrhula pyrrhula
RB

Very common in a variety of habitats though local in N Scotland and absent from the Outer Hebrides, Orkney, and Shetland. Mainly sedentary. Birds belonging to the N race *pyrrhula* are recorded in small numbers most years, mainly October–December in N Scotland.

Hawfinch
Coccothraustes coccothraustes
RB

Uncommon resident, widely but very locally distributed throughout much of England (except the SW), Wales, and S Scotland. There is a noticeable concentration in the counties around London. Hawfinches favour deciduous woodland, also parkland and orchards, feeding on a variety of fruits and seeds including wild cherry, beech, and especially hornbeam. They are rather shy. The best chance of finding them is in winter when they form small flocks in the tree tops and may descend to feed on the ground in the early morning. Unless care is taken, however, sightings may be confined to glimpses of birds flying off over the canopy, giving the distinctive soft call.
Sites: 21.3, 41, 45, 51, 70.8, 73

Lapland Bunting
Calcarius lapponicus
PM, WV, SMB

Small numbers of passage birds occur late August to early November, mainly in the NW (Hebrides to Shetland) but also on the E and S coasts and in the SW. Small flocks winter on the E coast of England, rarely elsewhere. Irregular in spring. Favours stubble fields, saltmarshes, dunes, short turf, or heath on passage

and in winter; birds are often first located by their distinctive rattling flight call. Bred in Scotland 1977–80, with a maximum of 11–14 pairs.
Sites: 1, 11, 26, 27, 35, 36, 39, 40, 42.1, 44, 81.3, 81.5, 82, 101, 102, 103

Very scarce resident on the tops of the Cairngorms and a few sites in Inverness-shire, only irregularly elsewhere in Scotland. Numbers fluctuate, but there are usually less that 20 pairs (at about a dozen sites) in good years. Small numbers winter on the coast, but few in Wales and the S coast. Most easily seen on the E coast, occasionally in sizeable flocks. Frequents beaches, dunes, and saltmarshes in winter.
Sites: Winter 1, 24, 26, 27, 30, 34, 35, 36, 39, 42, 43, 44, 49, 70, 79, 81, 82, 84, 93, 100, 101, 102, 103

Snow Bunting
Plectrophenax nivalis
WV, PM, SRB

Very common resident, though local in NW Scotland, the Outer Hebrides, and Orkney. Absent from Shetland. Inhabits all types of open country, especially farmland. In winter small numbers of migrants reach the E coast and non-breeding areas such as Shetland and Scilly.

Yellowhammer
Emberiza citrinella
RB, PM, WV

Formerly widespread but it is now almost confined to S Devon (especially the coast between Exeter and Prawle) with very small numbers in Somerset and Cornwall. The population is c 150 pairs. Cirl Buntings are sedentary and inhabit farmland and downs with mature hedges and tall trees for songposts, mainly in coastal areas.
Sites: 8, 9, 10

Cirl Bunting
Emberiza cirlus
SRB

Scarce migrant averaging c 30 birds a year. Most turn up from mid-August to October, with the majority in September. Found on the E and S coasts, most frequently on Fair Isle and in Norfolk and SW England. Spring migrants are scarcer; most are on Fair Isle from late April to June. Very rare inland.
Sites: 1, 11, 15, 22, 23, 40, 79, 81, 101, 102

Ortolan Bunting
Emberiza hortulana
SPM

Very common and widely distributed, more local in upland regions. Formerly confined to reedbeds and wetland habitats (which are still favoured), it has spread to drier areas and is now widespread in farm hedgerows and scrub. Small numbers occur on passage at E and SE coast localities.

Reed Bunting
Emberiza schoeniclus
RB, PM, WV

Widespread and fairly common but patchily distributed. Its distribution is largely governed by a dislike of upland areas and strong dependence on arable land, but its absence from many areas is unexplained. Declines have been noted in many areas for several decades. Small numbers of migrants are recorded on the E coast and in SW England. Easily located in summer by its jangling song. In winter may be found in flocks on saltmarshes, rough grassland, and stubble fields.

Corn Bunting
Miliaria calandra
RB, PM, WV

England

AVON
H. E. Rose, 12 Birbeck Rd, Bristol BS9 1BD

BERKSHIRE
Peter Standley, Siskins, 7 Llanvair Drive, South Ascot, Berkshire SL5 9HS

CAMBRIDGESHIRE
C.A.E. Kirtland, 22 Montgomery Rd, Cambridge CB4 2EQ

CHESHIRE
Ron Harrison, Speyside, 8 St Albans Crescent, West Timperley, Altrincham, Cheshire WA14 5NY

CLEVELAND
John B. Dunnet, 43 Hemlington Rd, Stainton, Middlesborough, TS8 9AG

CORNWALL
S. M. Christophers, 5 Newquay Rd, St Columb Major, Cornwall TR9 6RW

CUMBRIA, SOUTH
Malcolm Hutcheson, Garden Cottage, Sizergh Castle, Kendal, Cumbria LA8 8AE

DEVON
P.W. Ellicott, Wyatts, Trusham, Newton Abbot, Devon TQ13 0LX

DORSET
Dr George P. Green, 104 Foxcroft Drive, Wimborne, Dorset

ESSEX
J. Howard, 6 St Bride Court, Colchester, Essex CO4 4PQ

GLOUCESTERSHIRE
Gordon R. Avery, 12 Hemmingsdale Rd, Hempsted, Gloucester GL2 6HN

GREATER LONDON
Andrew Moon, Chalk Dell House, London Rd, Rickmansworth, Hertfordshire WD3 1JP

HAMPSHIRE
E. J. Wiseman, Normandy Farm, Normandy Lane, Lymington, Hampshire SO4 8AE

HUNTINGDON & PETERBOROUGH
Martin R. Coates, 10 Latham Ave, Orton Longueville, Peterborough PE2 0AD

ISLES OF SCILLY
M. J. Rogers, 4 Pentland Flats, St Mary's, Isles of Scilly TR21 OHY

KENT
I. P. Hodgson and T. N. Hodge, 73 Middle Deal Rd, Deal, Kent CT14 9RG

LANCASHIRE
M. Jones, 31 Laverton Rd, St Annes-on-Sea, Lancashire FY8 1EW

LEICESTERSHIRE
R. Davis, 47 Clovelly Rd, Glenfield, Leicester LE3 8AE

LINCOLNSHIRE
Graham Catley, 13 West Acridge, Barton-on-Humber, South Humberside DN18 5AJ

NORFOLK
P. R. Allard, 13 Dolman Close, Cobholm, Great Yarmouth, Norfolk NR31 OBE

NORTHAMPTONSHIRE
R. W. Bullock, 25 Westcott Way, Favell Green, Northampton NN3 3BF

NORTHUMBERLAND
Mike S. Hodgson, 45 Elmtree Gardens, Whitley Bay, Tyne and Wear NE25 8QX

NOTTINGHAMSHIRE
S. M. Henson, 86 Bedale Rd, Sherwood, Nottingham NG5 3GJ

STAFFORDSHIRE
G. Evans, Flat 5, Kenilworth Court, Mill St, Cannock WS11 3EP

SUFFOLK
R. B. Warren, 37 Dellwood Ave, Felixstowe, Suffolk IP11 9HW

SURREY
J. J. Wheatley, 6 Boxgrove Ave, Guildford, Surrey GU1 1XG

SUSSEX
Paul James, Flat 2, 70 Denmark Villas, Hove, East Sussex.

WALNEY ISLAND
K. Parkes, 176 Harrogate St, Barrow-in-Furness LA14 5NA

WARWICKSHIRE
N. P. Barlow, 1 Yew Tree Cottages, Maxstoke Lane, Great Packington, Meriden, Coventry CV7 7HR

WORCESTERSHIRE
S. M. Whitehouse, 5 Stanway Close, Blackpole, Worcester WR4 9XL

YORKSHIRE
John E. Dale, 158 Lindley Moor Rd, Huddersfield HD3 3UE

Scotland

ABERDEENSHIRE
Michael Innes, 106A Queen's St, Peterhead, Aberdeenshire AB4 6TY

ARGYLLSHIRE
Dr Arthur Jennings, 1 Ferryfield Drive, Connel, Argyll PA37 1SP

BORDERS
R. D. Murray, 143 Eskhill, Penicuik, Midlothian EH26 8DE

CAITHNESS
Sinclair A. M. Manson, 7 Duncan St, Thurso, Caithness KW14 7HZ

DUMFRIESSHIRE
Dr E. C. Fellowes, West Isle, Islesteps, Dumfries DG2 8ES

FAIR ISLE
Nick Riddiford, Bird Observatory, Fair Isle, Shetland ZE2 9JU

FIFE
Douglas Dickson, 133 Duddingston Drive, Kirkcaldy, Fife KY2 6XG

INVERNESS-SHIRE
Roy H. Dennis, Inchdryne, Nethybridge, Inverness-shire PH25 3EF

ISLE OF MAY
Bernard Zonfrillo, 28 Brodie Rd, Balornock East, Glasgow G21 3SB

KIRKCUDBRIGHTSHIRE
A. D. Watson, Barone, 54 Main St, Dalry, Castle Douglas DG9 3UW

EAST LOTHIAN
Alan Brown, 23 Kings Court, Longniddry, East Lothian EH32 0QP

MORAYSHIRE
Martin J. H. Cook, Rowanbrae, Clochan, Buckie AB5 2EQ

ORKNEY
Chris J. Booth, Ronas, 34 High St, Kirkwall, Orkney KW15 1AZ

OUTER HEBRIDES
W. A. J. Cunningham, Aros, 10 Barony Square, Stornoway, Isle of Lewis PA87 2TQ

PERTHSHIRE
Euan D. Cameron, 3 Stormont Place, Scone, Perth PH2 6SR

ROSS-SHIRE
As Inverness-shire

SHETLAND
Dennis Coutts, Da Knowe, Twageos Rd, Lerwick, Shetland ZE1 0BB

SUTHERLAND
A. R. Mainwood, 13 Ben Bhraggie Drive, Golspie, Sutherland KW10 6SX

ANGLESEY   **Wales**
T. Gravett, Tyddyn Llan, Eglwsbach, Colwyn Bay, Gwynedd LL28 5TY

CAERNARVONSHIRE
As Anglesey

CARDIGANSHIRE
P. E. Davis, Felindre, Abcrarth, Aberaeron, Dyfed

CARMARTHENSHIRE
D. H. V. Roberts, 6 Ger-y-Coed, Pontiets, Llanelli, Dyfed SA15 5UN

CLYWD
R. Birch, 8 Thornby Close, Saughall, Cheshire

MID GLAMORGAN
J. R. Smith, 15 Milton Drive, Bridgend, Mid Glamorgan CF31 4QE

WEST GLAMORGAN
Harold E. Grenfell, 14 Bryn Terrace, Mumbles, Swansea SA3 4HD

MERIONETHSHIRE
F. A. Currie, Sandilands House, Sandilands Road, Tywyn, Gwynedd LL36 9AP

MONTGOMERYSHIRE
R. G. Burton, 8 Brynwood Drive, Milford Road, Newtown, Powys SY16 3EG

PEMBROKESHIRE
J. W. Donovan, The Burren, Dingle Lane, Crundale, Haverfordwest, Dyfed

British Birds

This readable monthly journal, available by subscription only, is an essential reference for any serious birdwatcher and publishes a wide variety of material concerning British and Palearctic birds. Main papers range from identification and conservation problems to ecology, behaviour, and breeding biology. Summaries of rarities and rare breeding birds are published annually. 'Recent Reports' appears each month and details all the latest news of interesting records.

Subscriptions: Mrs Erika Sharrock, Fountains, Park Lane, Blunham, Bedford MK44 3NJ

British Trust for Ornithology

Beech Grove, Station Rd, Tring, Hertfordshire HP23 5NR
Tel. 044282-3461

The BTO studies the distribution, numbers, movements, and ecology of British birds. Members can assist in the collection of data by taking part in organised surveys such as the Atlas schemes. The informative *BTO News* is published six times a year and members can subscribe to the journals *Bird Study* and *Ringing and Migration* at a reduced rate.

Nature Conservancy Council

Northminster House, Peterborough PE1 1UA
Tel. 0733-40345

The NCC is a government body set up in 1973 to promote nature conservation in Great Britain. It manages the country's National Nature Reserves, a number of which are featured in the site accounts.

Royal Society for Nature Conservation

The Green, Nettleham, Lincoln LN2 2NR
Tel. 0522-752326

The RSNC is the national association for the 46 county Nature Conservation Trusts with a total membership in excess of 160,000. The Society and the Trusts own or manage about 1,500 nature reserves covering 115,000 acres. *Natural World* is published three times a year and there is a junior section (WATCH).

Royal Society for the Protection of Birds

The Lodge, Sandy, Bedfordshire SG19 2DL
Tel. 0767-80551

The RSPB has almost 400,000 members and is the largest conservation organisation in Europe. Every reader of this book should be a member of the RSPB. It owns and manages over 100 reserves covering some 126,500 acres and many are included in this book. The Society also carries out research, operates special protection schemes for certain species, and is closely involved with the wild bird protection law. There are 13 Regional Offices and a large and growing network of local members' groups throughout the country. A magazine, *Birds*, is published quarterly. The *Young Ornithologists' Club* is the junior section of the RSPB and has a membership of 85,000.

21 Regent Terrace, Edinburgh EH7 5BT
Tel. 031-556 6042

Scottish Ornithologists' Club

The SOC is the foremost society concerned entirely with Scotland's birds. It publishes a quarterly journal, *Scottish Birds*, and an annual *Scottish Bird Report*. Its Bird Bookshop probably has the most comprehensive selection of bird books for sale in the country.

Slimbridge, Gloucester GL2 7BT
Tel. 045389-333

Wildfowl Trust

The Wildfowl Trust carries out research, organises wildfowl counts, and maintains seven collections containing many rare and endangered species. Several of its centres also include wild refuges which provide safe havens for wintering geese, swans, and duck. The Trust publishes *Wildfowl World* twice a year and an annual journal, *Wildfowl*.

Only a small selection of the more important organisations is listed above. There are also many local bird clubs and ringing groups as well as the RSPB members' groups and the Nature Conservation Trusts. We strongly recommend that every bird-watcher with an interest in their local birds joins one or more of these. A full list is published in *The Birdwatcher's Yearbook* (see p. 371).

To protect rare breeding birds, the law forbids intentional disturbance of any species included in Schedule 1 of the Wildlife and Countryside Act 1981 while it is nest-building or on or near a nest containing eggs or unflown young; it is also illegal to intentionally disturb dependent young of Schedule 1 birds. Thus, for example, photographers and scientific researchers cannot lawfully visit such nests unless they obtain approval from the Nature Conservancy Council. Offenders are liable to a fine of up to £2,000.

Schedule 1   Birds which are protected by special penalties.

Avocet	Oriole, Golden
Bee-eater	Osprey
Bittern	Owl, Barn
Bittern, Little	Owl, Snowy
Bluethroat	Peregrine
Brambling	Petrel, Leach's
Bunting, Cirl	Phalarope, Red-necked
Bunting, Lapland	Pintail
Bunting, Snow	Plover, Kentish
Buzzard, Honey	Plover, Little Ringed
Chough	Quail, Common
Corncrake	Redstart, Black
Crake, Spotted	Redwing
Crossbills (all species)	Rosefinch, Scarlet
Curlew, Stone	Ruff
Divers (all species)	Sandpiper, Green
Dotterel	Sandpiper, Purple
Duck, Long-tailed	Sandpiper, Wood
Eagle, Golden	Scaup
Eagle, White-tailed	Scoter, Common
Falcon, Gyr	Scoter, Velvet
Fieldfare	Serin
Firecrest	Shorelark
Garganey	Shrike, Red-backed
Godwit, Black-tailed	Spoonbill
Goldeneye	Stilt, Black-winged
Goose, Greylag (in Outer	Stint, Temminck's
Hebrides, Caithness,	Swan, Bewick's
Sutherland and Wester Ross	Swan, Whooper
only)	Tern, Black
Goshawk	Tern, Little
Grebe, Black-necked	Tern, Roseate
Grebe, Slavonian	Tit, Bearded
Greenshank	Tit, Crested
Gull, Little	Treecreeper, Short-toed
Gull, Mediterranean	Warbler, Cetti's
Harriers (all species)	Warbler, Dartford
Heron, Purple	Warbler, Marsh
Hobby	Warbler, Savi's
Hoopoe	Whimbrel
Kingfisher	Woodlark
Kite, Red	Wryneck
Merlin	

Today's birdwatchers are a powerful force for nature conservation. The number of those of us interested in birds rises continually and it is vital that we take seriously our responsibility to avoid any harm to birds.

We must also present a responsible image to non-birdwatchers who may be affected by our activities and particularly those on whose sympathy and support the future of birds may rest.

There are 10 points to bear in mind:
1. The welfare of birds must come first.
2. Habitat must be protected.
3. Keep disturbance to birds and their habitat to a minimum.
4. When you find a rare bird think carefully about whom you should tell.
5. Do not harass rare migrants.
6. Abide by the bird protection laws at all times.
7. Respect the rights of landowners.
8. Respect the rights of other people in the countryside.
9. Make your records available to the local bird recorder.
10. Behave abroad as you would when birdwatching at home

Welfare of birds must come first

Whether your particular interest is photography, ringing, sound recording, scientific study or just birdwatching, remember that the welfare of the bird must always come first.

Habitat protection

Its habitat is vital to a bird and therefore we must ensure that our activities do not cause damage.

Keep disturbance to a minimum

Birds' tolerance of disturbance varies between species and seasons. Therefore, it is safer to keep all disturbance to a minimum. No birds should be disturbed from the nest in case opportunities for predators to take eggs or young are increased. In very cold weather disturbance to birds may cause them to use vital energy at a time when food is difficult to find. Wildfowlers already impose bans during cold weather: birdwatchers should exercise similar discretion.

Rare breeding birds

If you discover a rare bird breeding and feel that protection is necessary, inform the appropriate RSPB Regional Office, or the Species Protection Department at the Lodge. Otherwise it is best in almost all circumstances to keep the record strictly secret in order to avoid disturbance by other birdwatchers and attacks by egg-collectors. Never visit known sites of rare breeding birds unless they are adequately protected. Even your presence may give away the sites to others and cause so many other visitors that the birds may fail to breed successfully.

Disturbance at or near the nest of species listed on the First Schedule of the Wildlife and Countryside Act 1981 is a criminal offence.

Copies of *Wild Birds and the Law* are obtainable from the RSPB, The Lodge, Sandy, Beds SG19 2DL (send two 2nd class stamps).

Rare migrants

Rare migrants or vagrants must not be harassed. If you discover one, consider the circumstances carefully before telling anyone.

369

Will an influx of birdwatchers disturb the bird or others in the area? Will the habitat be damaged? Will problems be caused with the landowner?

The Law

The bird protection laws (now embodied in the Wildlife and Countryside Act 1981) are the result of hard campaigning by previous generations of birdwatchers. As birdwatchers we must abide by them at all times and not allow them to fall into disrepute.

Respect the rights of landowners

The wishes of landowners and occupiers of land must be respected. Do not enter land without permission. Comply with permit schemes. If you are leading a group, do give advance notice of the visit, even if a formal permit scheme is not in operation. Always obey the Country Code.

Respect the rights of other people

Have proper consideration for other birdwatchers. Try not to disrupt their activities or scare the birds they are watching. There are many other people who also use the countryside. Do not interfere with their activities and, if it seems that what they are doing is causing unnecessary disturbance to birds, do try to take a balanced view. Flushing gulls when walking a dog on a beach may do little harm, while the same dog might be a serious disturbance to a tern colony. When pointing this out to a non-birdwatcher be courteous, but firm. The non-birdwatchers' goodwill towards birds must not be destroyed by the attitudes of birdwatchers.

Keeping records

Much of today's knowledge about birds is the result of meticulous record keeping by our predecessors. Make sure you help to add to tomorrow's knowledge by sending records to your county bird recorder.

Birdwatching abroad

Behave abroad as you would at home. This code should be firmly adhered to when abroad (whatever the local laws). Well-behaved birdwatchers can be important ambassadors for bird protection.

This code has been drafted after consultation between the British Ornithologists' Union, the British Trust for Ornithology, the Royal Society for the Protection of Birds, the Scottish Ornithologists' Club, the Wildfowl Trust and the Editors of British Birds.

Selected Bibliography

British Birds Rare Breeding Birds Panel. Rare Breeding Birds in the United Kingdom 1973–83

British Birds Rarities Committee. Reports on Rare Birds in Great Britain 1958–84

British Ornithologists' Union. 1971. *The Status of Birds in Britain and Ireland.* Blackwell Scientific Publications

Cramp, S., Bourne, W.R.P., Saunders, D. 1974. *The Seabirds of Britain and Ireland.* Collins

Durman, R. (ed) 1976. *Bird Observatories in Britain and Ireland* T. and A.D. Poyser

Elkins, N. 1983. *Weather and Bird Behaviour.* T. and A.D. Poyser

Gantlett, S.J.M. 1985. *Where to Watch Birds in Norfolk*

Gooders, J. 1967. *Where to Watch Birds.* Andre Deutsch

Hammond, N. (ed) 1983. *RSPB Nature Reserves.* RSPB

Hardy, E. 1978. *A Guide to the Birds of Scotland.* Constable

Hywel-Davies, J., and Thom, V. 1984. *The Macmillan Guide to Britain's Nature Reserves.* Macmillan

Lack, P. 1986. *The Atlas of Wintering Birds in Britain and Ireland.* T. and A.D. Poyser

Norman, D. and Tucker, V. 1984. *Where to Watch Birds in Devon and Cornwall.* Croom Helm

Ogilvie, M.A. 1979 *The Birdwatcher's Guide to the Wetlands of Britain.* Batsford

Parslow, J. 1973. *Breeding Birds of Britain and Ireland.* T. and A.D. Poyser

Parslow, J. (ed) 1983. *Birdwatcher's Britain.* Pan Books/Ordnance Survey

Pemberton, J.E. (ed) 1986. *The Birdwatcher's Yearbook and Diary 1986.* Buckingham Press

Prater, A.J. 1981. *Estuary Birds of Britain and Ireland.* T. and A.D. Poyser

Ratcliffe, D.A. (ed) 1977. *A Nature Conservation Review: The Selection of Biological Sites of National Importance to Nature Conservation in Britain.* 2 vols. NCC

Saunders, D. 1974. *A Guide to the Birds of Wales.* Constable

Sharrock, J.T.R. 1974. *Scarce Migrant Birds in Britain and Ireland.* T. and A.D. Poyser

Sharrock, J.T.R. 1976. *The Atlas of Breeding Birds in Britain and Ireland.* BTO/IWC

Sharrock, J.T.R. and E.M. 1976. *Rare Birds in Britain and Ireland* T. and A.D. Poyser

Thom, V.M. 1986. *Birds in Scotland.* T. and A.D. Poyser

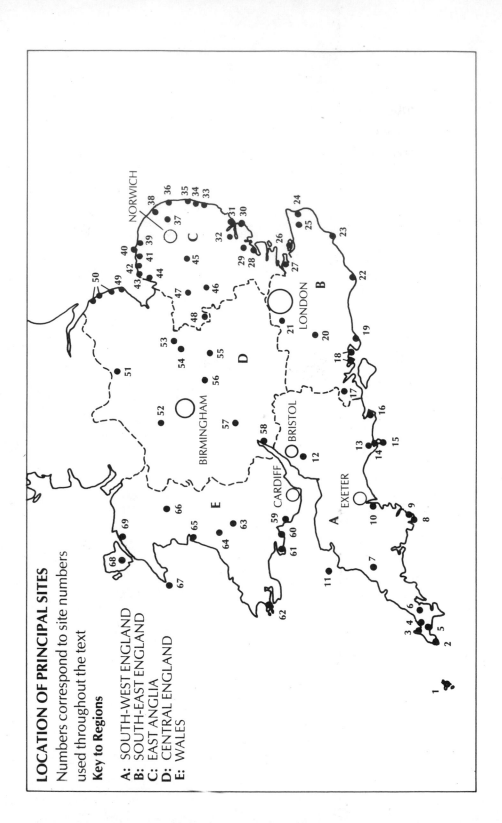

LOCATION OF PRINCIPAL SITES

Numbers correspond to site numbers
used throughout the text

Key to Regions

A: SOUTH-WEST ENGLAND
B: SOUTH-EAST ENGLAND
C: EAST ANGLIA
D: CENTRAL ENGLAND
E: WALES